MW00629233

LOVE AT THE HEART OF THINGS

Douglas Van Steere 1947

LOVE AT THE HEART OF THINGS

A BIOGRAPHY OF DOUGLAS V. STEERE

By

E. Glenn Hinson

Pendle Hill Publications • *Wallingford, Pennsylvania*
The Upper Room Books • *Nashville, Tennessee*

Printed in the United States of America
by Thomson-Shore, Inc., Dexter, Michigan
February 1998: 4,000

Library of Congress Cataloging-in-Publication Data

Hinson, E. Glenn
    Love at the heart of things: a biography of Douglas V.
Steere / by E. Glenn Hinson.
        p.   cm.
    Includes bibliographical references and index.
    ISBN 0-87574-929-1 Pendle Hill
    ISBN 0-8358-0860-2 The Upper Room Books
    (alk. paper)
    1. Steere, Douglas Van, 1901-1995.   2. Quakers--United
States–Biography.   3. Ecumenists–United States–Biography.
I. Title.   BX7795.S74H54   1998
289.6'092–dc21
    [B]   98-5450
                                                                            CIP

To Dorothy M. Steere
in memory of
Douglas V. Steere

CONTENTS

Photographs

Black and White Photographs

Color Photograph Section

Preface

This biography will differ in some ways from most others. For one thing, it will not proceed in a strict chronological sequence. I have relied on chronology for the order in which I introduce events in Douglas Steere's life. But what I have written is closer to a portrait. After telling about his family background and early years, his education, his deep early religious search, and his family, I try then to depict him in his many-sided calling—Quaker global minister, organizer of relief for war-torn Finland, expander of Quaker horizons, ecumenical pioneer, peacemaker, Quaker visionary and guide, teacher of prayer, midwife of saints, consummate letter writer, and existential realist philosopher. Insofar as I could do so, I have also tried to show what an integral part of his life and work Dorothy Steere was. In taking this approach I want to share what I and countless others have learned from Douglas about God, about prayer, about spiritual growth, about caring, about living the Christian life. Not that any of us can *be* a Douglas Steere. We can't. He was unique and we are each unique. As Baron von Hügel would say, "God does not make dittoes." But we can learn from one another, and Douglas and Dorothy Steere have much to teach us by their lives and work. I also have had an interest in helping Quakers see the vision Douglas had for them and how they might make that dream become reality.

The "facts" do not suffice to tell fully who Douglas Steere was and why he touched the lives of others as he did. Who Douglas Steere *really* was is why I will refer to him throughout this biography by his first name. Although he was thirty years my senior and a person whom I regarded with some awe, I felt comfortable calling him "Douglas" from our first meeting. You could tell that he did not feel comfortable being addressed as *Dr.* Steere. The late Henri Nouwen related once his first meeting with Douglas. He had invited him in April 1975 to Yale to speak to a class on spirituality. When he arrived at the train station in New Haven just after the passengers had disembarked, he looked down the platform to see this slightly stooped elderly gentleman in a charcoal suit lugging two heavy suitcases—not his own but those of another passenger who was having trouble carrying them!

Many could enrich this preface with other personal anecdotes. I would like to flesh it out with personal reminiscences, for I am deeply in debt to him as a friend and mentor. I cannot remember when I first met Douglas. I have a vague impression in the back of my mind that I may have arranged one of his trips to the Abbey of Gethsemani to visit Thomas Merton, something I often did for visitors to Southern Seminary, but I have not been able to confirm that from correspondence. I heard him give the Gheens Lectures at The Southern Baptist Theological Seminary in the spring of 1969. On that occasion he asked that the pulpit in Alumni Chapel be moved back so he could sit. He captivated all of us with lectures on the devotional classics delivered in a personal way in that warm and rich baritone of his. Because I taught a course in the classics, I soaked up every word, but something happened beyond words that reinforced what I was doing with those classics. Hearing Douglas speak convincingly about the wisdom he found in them convinced me that what I was doing was both needed and right.

Our paths crossed again in the early seventies when the director of the Vineyard Conference Center in Louisville asked me to do meditations for a retreat Douglas led. Partly because insights gleaned from John Woolman and Thomas Kelly pervaded both of our presentations and partly because Douglas had a remarkable gift for reaching out to another, I immediately sensed the forging of an unusual bond. Before the retreat concluded, Douglas took me aside to say that he would suggest that the Ecumenical Institute of Spirituality invite me as a guest to its next meeting, held at Wainwright House in Rye, New York, in January 1973. The Institute chose to follow his recommendation. Invited into membership, I found in that body, shaped by the spirit of Douglas Steere, companions of the inner way who stretched my mind and heart and gave me rare encouragement. More importantly, participation in this group brought me closer to Douglas Steere himself to benefit from the countless ways he confirmed what was deepest in me and helped me to realize the gift of God in me.

At annual meetings of the Ecumenical Institute of Spirituality, as in retreats, Douglas arranged a personal and private walk or talk with each person, listening beyond words and thoughts, and encouraging and prodding. Until Alzheimer's Disease got the upper hand in his life, I never met with him that I did not go away buoyed up and filled with some of his contagious, well-founded optimism. Like someone gifted with a kind of extra-sensory radar for people needing an encouraging word, he phoned or wrote little notes, not just perfunctory "How are you's" but words that addressed in a profound way the need of the moment. I probably cannot tally the number of times he made personal contact, phoned or wrote as fundamentalists intent on removing me from my teaching position at The Southern Baptist Theological Seminary heightened their attacks.

In some ways this biography is an effort to discover and disclose the secret of Douglas Steere's remarkable gift for affirming and encouraging others. This gift stands out not just in what he did for me, but in a worldwide ministry pursued with boundless yet costly energy so that each could grasp how much his or her own life matters. For me, of course, as for every other beneficiary of it, Douglas's ministry has had a special slant. For one such as I who scarcely knew a real father after my alcoholic natural father left the family when I was about seven years old, Douglas came on the scene as what the ancients often called their bishops, my "father in God." Unpretentiously and unassumingly, he reached out toward me with a life yielded to the besieging love of God. It was a life characterized by steadfast optimism and suffused with love, not of the mushy Hollywood type, but of the costly type God has modeled for us on the Cross. Douglas Steere was experienced in the art of loving with a love that transforms. He knew how to be present where he was.

I have heard it said that when reporters asked Martin Niemoeller, released from prison at the end of the Second World War, how he responded to his Nazi warders when they took him into custody, he replied, "I let love flow out." Douglas Steere let love flow out in abundance all around the world. When he introduced Thomas Merton's *Contemplative Prayer,* he quoted a wonderful line from William Blake which is most fittingly applied to Douglas himself: "We are put on earth for a little space that we may learn to bear the beams of love."[1] He underlined how much we have to do to prepare ourselves to *bear* the beams of love. That love is costly. Those beams suffused his life and work and irradiated all who came near.

How do we account for such a person? Natural gifts? Inspiration? Education? Models? Profound support from his wife Dorothy? Time and culture in which he lived? Life experience? Prayer or other spiritual disciplines? As a historian, I'm inclined always to say, "All of the above." We cannot explain Douglas Steere in any simple way. He was a gifted, precocious person, well educated at Harvard and Oxford whose age and culture and life experiences evoked the highest and noblest. Early on, he learned how to pray and how important prayer was for his own formation. Yet I cannot help but believe that more still is needed to account for Douglas Steere, as Douglas would himself insist—a God of unfathomable love who is at the very heart of all reality, who takes initiative to get in touch with us, and who makes our hearts restless until we find rest in God.

I must say a word of thanks to many persons who have assisted me with this biography. First and foremost is Dorothy Steere, who asked me to write it and who has offered assistance and encouragement throughout. Helen Steere Horn and Anne Steere Nash read the entire manuscript and offered additional information, editorial comments, and numerous other helps. All three Steeres know much about writing. Haverford College gave me lodging for two summers as I went through the vast Steere correspondence and other materials, and the Haverford College Library staff assisted in numerous ways. Library staff of Union Theological Seminary in Richmond helped me access some of the materials I needed. Baptist Theological Seminary at Richmond permitted me much freedom in the use of my schedule. Linda McNally and Carol Smith, our office staff at BTSR, relieved me of many small burdens by Xeroxing and mailing parts of the manuscript as I wrote it. Beth McMahon, Director of Public Relations and Prospective Student Services, helped access some materials. My students gave me a boost by applauding me for sharing some of the insights I came to through the study of Douglas Steere's writings. Two assisted in specific ways. Karen Jeffcoat transcribed some of the tapes of the Stone Lectures which Douglas gave at Princeton Theological Seminary in the spring of 1957. Bob Smith transferred disks from a Macintosh I used in Louisville to an IBM system I use in Richmond. I also thank my son Christopher for help with the index.

I am grateful as well to The Louisville Institute for the Study of Protestantism and American Culture, Louisville, Kentucky, and Dr. James Lewis, its director, for a grant which provided support in the early stages of this project.

Thanks also go to Rebecca Kratz Mays, my editor at Pendle Hill, to Eve Beehler for book design and layout, to Holley Webster and Stuart Mays for proofreading. Appreciation goes also to George Donigian and The Upper Room Books for joining in this publication venture.

I'm glad to see six years of labor come to an end. But my joy there is small by comparison with my thanksgiving to God that Douglas Steere was among us from 1901 until 1995.

Richmond, Virginia
January 29, 1997

Notes

1. Thomas Merton, *Contemplative Prayer* (Garden City, NY: Doubleday & Co., Inc., 1971), 9.

I

Who Was Douglas Steere?

*D*ouglas Steere was a Quaker philosopher and religious leader. He was one of the leading American spiritual writers and guides of the twentieth century. Inspired by a lifelong personal search, he challenged countless others to intensify their quest for "that love which is at the heart of things." "That love which is at the heart of things" fell often from his lips and dripped from his pen, but, even more, it irradiated his life and work. But lest you think I have stumbled into sentimentality, I had better begin with some bare "facts" about Douglas Van Steere.

Born in Harbor Beach, Michigan, on August 31, 1901, Douglas grew up and attended elementary and high school in Detroit, graduating at sixteen by skipping one year of elementary school. He studied agriculture at Michigan Agricultural College, now Michigan State University, receiving his B.S. in 1923 after taking a one-year leave following his junior year to teach biology and coach football in a high school at Onaway, Michigan. During the summers, he inspected potatoes and peddled stock care manuals to farmers.

Pulled ever deeper into a religious search in the last year or so of college, he borrowed money and undertook the study of philosophy at Harvard (1923-25). He earned almost straight A's and an invitation to Phi Beta Kappa despite never having

1

had a course in philosophy before. At the end of two years he qualified for entrance into the Ph.D. program. Meantime, after one dry run, he was awarded the coveted Rhodes Scholarship to study at Oxford (B.A. 1927, M.A. 1953). Thanks to Quaker connections he made at Oxford, he came to the attention of Rufus Jones, Professor of Philosophy at Haverford College, and served thirty-five years (1928-63) first as Jones's colleague and then as his successor as chairman of the Department of Philosophy.

Douglas Steere made a significant scholarly and popular contribution in an area which seized his attention—knowing God. He wrote his dissertation on mystical experience, focusing on "Critical Realism in the Religious Philosophy of Baron Friedrich von Hügel" (Harvard, 1931). In his first published book he focused on *Prayer and Worship* (1938). Numerous subsequent writings, likewise, centered on the spiritual life—sainthood, prayer and work, prayer and leisure, the devotional classics, and a whole row of others. He played a leading role in advancing the retreat movement among Protestants in America. He served on the Editorial Board of *Religion in Life* (1961-80). With Godfrey Diekmann, OSB, he founded the Ecumenical Institute of Spirituality, which held its initial meeting in 1965 just prior to the final session of the Second Vatican Council and continues today as a part of his legacy.

He gained wide recognition as a scholar. He lectured and taught in some of America's most prestigious colleges, universities, and seminaries throughout his career. He played a leading role in the American Theological Society and held membership in the American Philosophical Association. From 1933 on he took part in a group calling themselves the Younger Christian Thinkers which included some of the most significant names in American religious life in mid-century.

Even before joining the Religious Society of Friends in 1932, he and his wife, Dorothy, played an active role in the founding of Pendle Hill, a vital center of Quaker life and thought, and in the reopening of Radnor Meeting. Douglas

2

chaired Pendle Hill's summer program five times and the
Pendle Hill Board from 1954 until 1971, remaining on the
Board until the mid-eighties. He also chaired the Board of the
John Woolman Memorial from 1947 until 1954. The Steeres
helped unite the Arch Street and Race Street Meetings in
Philadelphia, bringing two factions together after more than
a century. Meantime, they rendered steadfast service and
leadership through the American Friends Service Committee and later the Friends World Committee for Consultation.
From 1948 until the early 1970s they logged an incredible
number of miles in a ministry of visitation, usually for six
months every other year, initially in Europe and then from
the fifties on in Africa and in Asia uplifting and encouraging
scattered groups of Friends and others engaged in efforts on
behalf of peace, justice, and humanization of life. Douglas
served two terms as Chairman of the Friends World Committee for Consultation (1964-1970) and helped to frame a
vision and sense of mission for the Religious Society of Friends,
numbering 200,000 members worldwide .

As a leading figure in one of the peace churches, Douglas
played an active role in international peace enterprises.
Establishing European connections in 1933-34 during his
first sabbatical, he made risky visits in 1937 as the threat of
war cast its ugly shadow over the horizon and in 1940 after
hostilities had already begun. During the Second World War,
he guided a Relief and Reconstruction program at Haverford
College (1943-45) in preparation for the task ahead when
the war ended. He played an active role in the International
Fellowship of Reconciliation from an early date, chairing the
American section of it from 1954 until 1966, and served on
national and international commissions addressing the threat
of war in a nuclear age. At the end of World War II he
inspired and rallied Quakers to undertake a relief effort on
behalf of Finland, one of the most devastated countries in
Europe and one that had always promptly paid its debts to
the United States, yet, until then, was the most neglected

after World War II. More than forty years later, the Finnish government remembered, honoring him with its highest honor, knighthood in the Order of the White Rose.

Among Protestants Douglas was an ecumenical pioneer. The Roman Catholic Church held a lot of attraction for him because it took the quest for God so seriously. At the beginning of his first sabbatical in 1933 he took a one month retreat at Maria Laach, the Benedictine monastery which fostered the Catholic Liturgical Renewal movement. Early in his retreat leading he drew heavily from the Benedictine tradition. Later he developed his own style in which there were more exchanges between himself and those who attended, along with periods of silence and personal half-hour visits with retreatants. Retiring early from Haverford College as the T. Wistar Brown Professor of Philosophy (1950-64), he represented the Religious Society of Friends as an official Observer-Delegate in three of the four sessions of the Second Vatican Council (1963-65) and as an Observer at the Lambeth Quadrilateral of the Church of England (1968).

Douglas continued a very active life after he completed his term as Chair of the Friends World Committee for Consultation until Alzheimer's disease diminished his faculties. Douglas and Dorothy conducted retreats together at Pendle Hill and Douglas in many other places. At the same time he served on numerous other boards and committees and advised various religious bodies in the development of creative ways to foster the life of the Spirit in today's world. Programs such as the Academy for Spiritual Formation of the Upper Room and the journal *Weavings* owe much to his counsel. Through his mid-eighties, he still traveled widely and maintained a schedule which would have worn out persons who were years younger than he. He and Dorothy continued to live in Haverford, a suburb of Philadelphia, Pennsylvania, first at the college and then in a nearby retirement center until he plunged into the vast and endless sea of love which he believed to be "at the heart of things."

4

II

Fallowing Ground

*D*ouglas Steere sank his roots deep in soil which could nurture his remarkable life. On his mother's side those roots went back to a New York family of Dutch immigrants, the Van Buskirks. His great-grandfather, Joseph Van Buskirk, emigrated to Pine Run, Michigan, near Flint, where he pursued a career as a blacksmith and carriage builder. During the Civil War, he served in the northern army from which he was mustered out at the rank of Captain. Subsequently he moved north 150 miles to start a lumber business near what became Harrisville. Douglas' great-grandmother, Mary L. Van Buskirk was descended from an old Quaker Wilbur family. His mother's mother, Mary Frances Van Buskirk, married George Monroe, one of her father's employees, at age sixteen. Monroe was of French descent. They settled in Harbor Beach, Michigan, and had four children—Wilbur, Stewart, Edith Ruby, and Inez. Douglas' mother, Edith Ruby, was born May 8, 1876.

Douglas' father had English Methodist roots. His grandmother, Helen Morris, was the daughter of Sarah Lincoln Burlingham and Frank C. Morris. Trained in law, Frank Morris was a devout Wesleyan who came to Canada to do religious work. Douglas' grandfather, Edward Steer (then spelled without a final -e), graduated from the University of

5

Toronto and came to Michigan as pastor of a Free Methodist Church. He met and married Helen Morris in Pontiac, Michigan in the early 1870s. Edward Morris Steer, Douglas' father, and his three brothers added -e to the family name.

The Steer children did not get a favorable impression of religion. Their father's salary, like that of many another rural pastor, was often paid only in food and his pastorate moved from town to town, making them feel rootless. Edward Morris Steer and his three brothers—Collis, Frank, and George—and one sister—Bess—were all born in different places. Their mother died at age forty after contracting typhoid through drinking water at an evangelistic camp meeting. Steer practiced severe discipline. He whipped Edward for the vanity of wearing a necktie like other boys and pushed him out of the nest at age fourteen to serve as an apprentice to a baker in Alpena. The boy sent most of his wages home. Fortunately, a University of Michigan trained lawyer named Douglas Hitchcock befriended him and took him into his home, a kindness Edward remembered by naming his first son Douglas after Hitchcock.

At eighteen Douglas' father returned to Pontiac. He worked in the bakery of his mother's brother, Robert Morris, for a time and then entered Railway Mail Service, initially assigned to a small line running between Port Huron and Palms. In this job he met Edith Ruby Monroe. They married December 12, 1899, and took up residence in Harbor Beach, Michigan. Douglas was born there August 31, 1901. In early years the family called him Van after his great-grandfather Joseph Van Buskirk.

In 1902 the family moved to Detroit when Edward took a run from Detroit to Mackinaw City under the employ of the Michigan Central Railway. He remained with that company until his retirement thirty-seven years later, first as a helper and then as Senior-Clerk-in-Charge on the night run. He worked six days and had six days off. Sensitive to his own father's neglect and abuse, he spent time with his family,

6

DOUGLAS (ABOUT AGE 9), HELEN, RUBY (DOUGLAS' MOTHER),
AND BRUCE STEERE

sharing the housework and doing nearly all of the baking. He forged a close bond with Douglas which remained vital throughout Edward's life.[1]

In 1913 the Steere family experienced one of those tragedies which cut a deep furrow in Douglas' young life. In April Douglas came down with scarlet fever and was sent to Detroit's Kiefer Municipal Hospital. He evidently recovered quickly and the hospital sent him home, but perhaps too soon. His seven-year-old sister, Helen, was infected and died on March 26 of complications of diphtheria and streptococci infection. Douglas had adored the gentle and loving Helen and always bore a profound sense of responsibility for her death. The impact of it on his father and mother, both of whom he loved dearly, was especially telling. In his UNPUBLISHED JOURNAL

7

Douglas wrote: "I have never gotten over the sight of my father sobbing his heart out and my mother broken by the loss of this, their only daughter. I had a feeling that I was to blame, for I had been eager to get out of this grim contagious disease hospital and felt that if I had been more patient, Helen might have been spared the germ."[2] To render the situation still more tragic, Stewart Van Buskirk, his mother's uncle whom he held in awe, died of Bright's disease a day later at age fifty-one. Stewart had given Douglas money to attend stock company plays in Harrisville, Michigan, hired him to chop weeds on his farm, let him ride his high-spirited horse, and took him for rides in his new McIntyre auto.

Just after these deaths, Douglas himself had another close call. He spent the summers at Springport, near Harrisville, on the shore of Lake Huron with his grandmother Van Buskirk. The Van Buskirk lumber business had prospered in the last three decades of the nineteenth century, and Mary Frances Monroe lived comfortably after the death of her husband George in 1905. Douglas learned how to fish for trout, a lifelong passion, near the dam set up for the Van Buskirk sawmill. Although he did not know how to swim, he thought he could dance across the deep part to the shallows. But he got in too deep. Years later, he reported his experience:

> I had all the kaleidoscopic experience of Helen's death and of other vivid experiences of my life rushing through my mind as I went down twice and took in a lot of water. My friends, seeing my plight, managed to get a plank pushed out to me and I grabbed for it, but my hands slipped off the first time. I had just strength enough to make one more [grab] and somehow I was able to hang on and be pulled in to where I could stagger ashore. I lay there for a while and finally pulled myself together to dress and go home, but it had been the closest brush with death that I had ever had up to that time.[3]

8

Grandmother Van Buskirk exerted a positive religious influence. She took the family to the Methodist Church in Harrisville in a horse-drawn surrey and specialized in "There's a Church in the Valley by the Wildwood" on her "Jew's Harp." She also instilled the work ethic. If Douglas complained about food served at mealtime, she asked if he would like to go and live with the local ne'er-do-wells with too many children. She may accidentally have honed his humor, too. When the family went berrying in a wagon drawn by her old horse, Cap, she was always concerned that Cap not be overstrained. As the wagon rolled uphill on the way back, with their buckets full of huckleberries, she asked Douglas and Edward, his father, to hold the pails over the side so "Cap," her horse, would not have so much weight to pull!

Douglas' namesake, Colonel Hitchcock, also entered prominently into his development in these years. The Colonel twice invited Douglas to come to Alpena to visit. He took Douglas to visit Niagara Falls and sent money so that Douglas could see Maeterlinck's "The Blue Bird" and Barrie's "Peter Pan." Hitchcock brought delicacies when he visited Detroit, sent Douglas a gold watch when he graduated from the eighth grade at the top of his class, and left him a legacy of $400 toward college along with a beautiful set of nature books.

Douglas felt very close, too, to several other family members. One favorite was his aunt Bess Steere, his father's sister. She lived with the Edward Steeres for a while. When he was a seventh grader, Douglas served as an usher at her wedding to Reuben Crandall. He was crushed when Crandall took her to Spokane, Washington, where he pursued a law career. Douglas dedicated *Dimensions of Prayer* to Bess Crandall. Another of whom he was fond was his mother's younger sister Inez, "a great letter writer,"[4] who accompanied her husband, Glenn Cragg, to teach in a U.S. government school in the Philippines. Because her departure came at the same time as Bess's, and on the heels of Helen's death, it struck a heavy blow.

Not all family members stood so high in Douglas' estimation. He disliked his cousin May, one of Robert Morris' daughters. One day, when he came to deliver something for her, he threw burrs in her hair and raced off home in his wagon. This act produced enough guilt to make him confess immediately to his father. Edward, who was less than fond of May himself, granted a quick absolution.

The Steeres were a close-knit family who liked being together. In 1913 they started spending summers in Mackinaw City so they could have more time with Edward. There Douglas discovered the brook trout in Mill Creek and got a further boost for his lifelong love of trout fishing. "As I grew up," he commented in late years, "if anyone had ever asked me where I would rather be than any other place on earth, I would have had no hesitation to answer: a mile or so up from the road on Mill Creek!"[5] In 1916 Edward Steere bought a little cottage facing the Straits of Mackinaw which the family named Laff-a-lot. Skilled in crafts and practical things, Edward invented a pulley system for lowering milk and butter down on a platform into the well to stay cool. He raised a big garden. The family picked raspberries, blackberries, and huckleberries. Douglas took advantage of the time with his father to expand his knowledge of "the birds and the bees."[6]

The two persons who figured most prominently in Douglas' life and did most to shape his outlook were his parents. He always enjoyed a healthy relationship with both his mother and his father. He understood his mother's frustration.

> My mother was an intelligent, quick, well-organized person with lots of temperament and an intense loyalty to those she cared for, but she was not especially demonstrative in her expressions of her affection. . . . She was a proud person with tastes for the best whether it was in a rug for the livingroom or furniture for the house or a dress or a hat for herself. She had married

10

a man who was devoted to her but who simply did not have the means to make her able to have many of the things she would have loved to have.[7]

Even as a youth, Douglas took some pride in helping her to have a few of the things she desired. One was lunch on the Pere Marquette train to Bay City, Michigan. He remarked, "My own relations with my mother are really too deep for me to throw much light upon."[8] He worried that he was never the tidy person his mother hoped he would be. His younger brother, Bruce, was the neat one. When Douglas married Dorothy, Ruby adopted her as the daughter she had lost years before. Douglas wrote of Dorothy: "Mother adored her and her hunger for a daughter was filled by Dorothy in such a wonderful way."[9] Reading Anders Nygren's *Agape and Eros* in the fall of 1933 evoked a new vision of his mother's love. He sat down to write and express his realization and asked for her forgiveness that he had never "sufficiently expressed it to her before." She was overwhelmed and replied warmly in a letter. Ruby died at age sixty-five in 1941.

Douglas felt even closer to his father and knew well his debt to him. Edward Steere taught Douglas to do many things such as carpentry and gardening.

> But his legacy did not stop there. He had an integrity and a sense of doing whatever you do well and in such a way that no matter how it is scrutinized it is seen to be all of one piece—a gift that hangs like a plumb line and so often shows the flaws in my own performance of my tasks.[10]

In his UNPUBLISHED JOURNAL Douglas paid moving tribute to Edward, who lived with Douglas and Dorothy during his last year or so:

> As for my father, I doted on him and enjoyed him all the way up, and in his later years, for he outlived my

mother by almost fifteen years, there were some occasions where I could express that to him. In the very last year of his life when he was so weak that I had to wash his feet and to help him bathe and to cut his toenails and do small things of this kind, I felt it was a privilege to be able to share this kind of sacrament together.[11]

Edward loved to tell stories. "He was a great story-teller and his friends enjoyed his capacity to have a suitable story for most occasions and situations, and his chuckle was always contagious."[12] He liked to joke and rib people. "My father was a very humble man and being himself content with little and able to live on it and to enjoy it, his life was saved from many tensions that the fiercely ambitious are subject to."[13] He was good company. He had only an eighth-grade education, but he read. Those who know Douglas Steere well will discern in his eulogizing of his father the qualities which Douglas himself not only cherished but also displayed: gifted story telling, humor, humility, wisdom, sensitivity.

Edward Steere suffered from being a preacher's kid, but he was recovering. When Douglas was about ten, Edward returned to religion after shunning it for many years. The family walked over a mile to the Methodist Church on the corner of Boulevard and Gratiot Streets in Detroit. Several years later, they started attending a Presbyterian Church nearer their home. Edward often talked to Douglas about religion, but he placed right living above right doctrine. "While he was eventually an elder and a trustee of the Congregational Church, theology, as such, played little role in his estimation of religion. What mattered to him was day-to-day performance in our relations to our neighbors, and in this area few could match him."[14]

Between 1913 and 1915 Edward wrestled with a decision as to whether he should run the Van Buskirk farm in Harrisville or stay with the railroad. Although very interested in scientific farming, he saw the risk in the deteriorating condition of the farm and finally declined to take the job. His decision proved wise, for Wilbur Monroe, one of Ruby Steere's older brothers, took the job and eventually had to sell out. Edward Steere nearly died of smallpox at this time, evidently contracted from a letter. However, he got a new ointment from Charles Morris, a doctor cousin in Hamtramack, which cured his pox and left him with almost no scars.

EDWARD STEERE 1938

During Douglas' first year at Michigan Agricultural College, the family left Detroit and, after a two-year stay in Pontiac, moved to Oxford, Michigan, where they remained until Ruby Steere died in 1941. Edward then moved to Seattle, near his son Bruce, where he bought a house and raised a garden which provided some food for his neighbors as well. He told Douglas that he was on his knees in the garden one time when he was overwhelmed with thankfulness to be right where he was. After Ruby died, he married her younger sister, Inez, divorced from her husband some years before. She was unwell and needed Edward's care. Bruce and his wife, Dawn, who also lived in Seattle, helped, but Bruce died at age forty-three, three years before Edward. So Edward spent his last year at Haverford with Douglas and Dorothy. Douglas delighted in that time together. "My father was a man *sans* guile and he lived in me as a delight."[15] After his father's death in mid-August 1954 Douglas continued to wear Edward's old work shirt when he fished, feeling

13

DOROTHY AND DOUGLAS STEERE WITH DOUGLAS' FATHER, EDWARD,
AND NEPHEW, DOUG/TEX

"as though I take him with me on these trips and strongly suspect that he enjoys them."[16] Douglas summed up what he cherished most about his father.

> As a father, his humility, his humor, his thoughtful-
> ness and his utter trust in me through all the years,
> even though we lived in different worlds, are all things
> I never cease to be thankful for. His love of Dorothy
> and his deep affection for Helen and Anne made his
> moving on into the next dimension a deep loss to
> us, but with it all we were so deeply thankful that we
> had had the gift of his presence with us in that last
> precious year of his life.[17]

In a very touching way elsewhere in his JOURNAL, Douglas pays the ultimate tribute: "Perhaps most of all, I can say that throughout my life I have known that my father loved me

14

and the love was returned."[18] One hardly need look farther to discern a source of Douglas' faith in "that love which is at the heart of things."

The Steere family encouraged industry and Douglas required little encouragement. He was always looking for ways to earn money. During elementary school years, he peddled manure, obtained from one neighbor with horses, to other neighbors in his little wagon, even printing up his first business card, D.V. STEERE, MANURIST. He secured a paper route which required him to get out at 4:00 a.m. He repaired door bells. He sold from door-to-door knitted ties and handsome little ribbon rosette pins his mother made. He tried but sold only a few cuspidors for which his uncle Collis Steere had become an agent.

During the summers from 1914 to 1918, Douglas found remunerative jobs around the railway station in Detroit carrying bags, selling papers, and, for two summers, running the Union News Company's stand in the station selling various wares and periodicals. He also checked cars for the Michigan Central Railroad and served as baggage master. After graduating from high school at age sixteen, he joined the Boy's Working Reserve and worked for a farmer named Dan Lake in southeastern Michigan . This job, for which he earned a dollar a day, kept him in the field from 4 a.m. until 9 p.m. Not surprisingly, he contracted yellow jaundice near the end of the summer.

For a summer job following his first year at Michigan Agricultural College (MAC)Douglas sold *The Practical Stock Doctor* in southwestern New York state near Olean. He found this work lonely and depressing. Fortunately he had two student colleagues with whom he could rendezvous on weekends. "How we treasured each other and what a camaraderie in pain we experienced together," he mused later.[19] When funds ran low in late summer, the three of them hopped freight trains to an agreed-upon meeting place. In New York City they stayed in "a fifty-cent-a-night flophouse with its usual bed-bugs."[20] Inconveniences notwithstanding, Douglas sold well over three hundred copies of *The Practical Stock Doctor* and netted $650 for his fall study. The next spring he sent letters to a number of farmers to whom he had sold books and got favorable testimonies from many about the value of the book. A second venture at selling *The Practical Stock Doctor*, however, did not turn out well. He failed to make sales in rural eastern Iowa and quit. He got a letter blistering him as a "quitter" and predicting a life of failure. That letter taught him the value of accentuating the positive in dealing with youth. Years later, he still felt the pain of it. It sandpapered his own sensitivities.

> This letter from an older man confirmed my own feeling of having been a "deserter" and having involved two other students in a crushing disappointment and it burned away in my inward thoughts for years. I hope it has taught me how *not* to deal with someone who has failed and is already all too conscious of the gap between what he meant to do and what he did![21]

Douglas' gentleness would be the opposite pole from this man's unthinking harshness. On returning to East Lansing he took a job as a "grunt" for the Lansing electric utility on a repair and installation crew, digging post holes, hoisting poles, and assisting the linemen. Worn down by earning his own way, he decided to take a teaching post for a year in Onaway, Michigan, a small town fifty miles southeast of Mackinaw City, before completing his final year of college.

At Onaway Douglas taught agriculture and chemistry and public speaking, and coached the football team. An older, gifted football fan wisely counseled the novice at the game never to touch the ball or go out on the field! He also guided a section of manual training, coached the Onaway debating team, and helped students prepare the *Onaweea*, a yearbook. To prepare for his teaching, he worked for Michigan Agricultural College in the plant-breeding field plots of Professor

Spragg, an internationally known geneticist. To get ready for football coaching, he went to late afternoon briefing sessions and a four-week summer football coaching school. The football team at Onaway did well, thanks to its outstanding athletes. Douglas turned twenty just before school began.

Douglas almost had his contract canceled for lack of credentials by the "ancient commissioner of education," Martha Caldwell. He remained more or less mute during her scrutiny of his resumé, and she gave him the necessary certificate. Onaway had no lab for chemistry, so he had to set one up. At the end of the year Dr. Waggoner, Secretary of the School Board, who had hired him, wrote a glowing letter of recommendation.

Douglas took part in civic affairs too. He played in the city band and Baptist Sunday School orchestra. He became Onaway's milk inspector for a stipend which enabled him to buy his first car, a second-hand Ford pickup truck, for $175. Farmers, however, balked over new requirements, and the Town Council caved in to their pressures. He also got his first taste of the work of agricultural agents at Onaway. During the summer of 1922, he served as county 4-H Club leader, edited and published the Presque Isle County Fair handbook, and took a student potato-disease demonstration unit to perform at the state fair in Detroit. The more exposure he had to agricultural work, however, the more he realized it was not his vocation.

Nonetheless, on graduation from MAC in 1923 Douglas was hired as a potato inspector, a role he filled again in 1924 and 1925 after his school years at Harvard, and in 1927 after taking his honor exams at Oxford for the B.A. He made significant friendships among the farmers. Farmers labeled him "galloping Doug." Not surprisingly, Douglas Steere sprinkles agricultural metaphors liberally in his writings.

In these early experiences we can see the foundation laid. A loving father and mother and experiences of loss were deepening his tenderness and raising his awareness as a per-

17

son. Other people and happenings added encouragement. And this remarkable youth responded confidently and intelligently to openings. Combined with his formal education, his early upbringing established for him an outlook on life which prepared him to be a seeker and a leader.

Notes

1. See the exchange of letters in Chapter XVI.
2. Douglas V. Steere, UNPUBLISHED JOURNAL, 11. This work, which supplied much information for this biography, is an extended journal recorded chronologically with no chapter divisions .
3. Steere, JOURNAL, 15.
4. In Chapter XVI, I will explore Douglas' own gifts as a letter writer. This comment may give some clue as to how he developed his skills in early years.
5. Steere, JOURNAL, 32.
6. In a letter to his father dated February 27, 1925, Douglas wrote: " . . . I thank providence that I have had a Dad who first told me the secrets of life—who took me berrying with him—who came out and played catch with me occasionally and to whom I didn't feel hesitant about taking anything that was on my chest to get his opinion on."
7. Steere, JOURNAL, 42.
8. Steere, JOURNAL, 44.
9. Steere, JOURNAL, 45.
10. Steere, JOURNAL, 46.
11. Steere, JOURNAL, 46.
12. Steere, JOURNAL, 47.
13. Steere, JOURNAL, 47.
14. Steere, JOURNAL, 47.
15. Steere, JOURNAL, 48.
16. Steere, JOURNAL, 48.
17. Steere, JOURNAL, 49.
18. Steere, JOURNAL, 49.
19. Steere, JOURNAL, 55.
20. Steere, JOURNAL, 56.
21. Steere, JOURNAL, 59.

III

Equipping for a Calling

*A*s a child, Douglas took to school as a bear to honey. Bright and mature for his age, he completed elementary school in seven years. He went to kindergarten at Van Dyke School in Detroit. He attended Berry School for the first and second grades. Some altercations in the third grade caused him to shift to the Myra Jones School, where he continued from the fourth through the eighth grades, graduating as valedictorian.

He remembered the Myra Jones School as one which had some excellent teachers. He especially appreciated a sixth grade teacher who suggested him when Frances Curtis, head-librarian, asked her for the name of a boy in her class who might like to join the newly formed Alexander Macomb Club. The club, meeting every week or two in the library or her home, was evidently a project of the Daughters of the American Revolution designed "to inculcate a deep sense of citizenship and patriotic feeling for the country in these growing boys."[1] Fortunately, Frances Curtis did not go by the book. She, of course, wanted "to civilize us and teach us some of the amenities of polite society, but she was basically out to broaden our horizons and to teach us to think and to discuss public issues."[2] She drilled the boys thoroughly in *Roberts Rules of Order* and, before long, got them involved in

DOUGLAS STEERE, TWELVE YEARS OLD

debating before the public in the basement of the library. "I think that almost nothing that I participated in during the years between eleven and fifteen," Douglas commented years later, "meant more to me than the stimulation that I got from this club."[3]

The Alexander Macomb Club opened the way for other means of growth. Douglas formed friendships with some members such as Robert Wieneke, his closest friend in high school. He and Douglas Hemming published a newspaper during the early part of his association with the club. They typed it on a small disc typewriter. Experience in debate in the Macomb Club equipped Douglas to represent his high school on the debate team almost from the beginning. Later on, some club members formed an orchestra in which Douglas played his slide trombone. Occasionally this group received invitations to entertain at events such as the German men's *Sing-Verein* (Singing Union), in which beer flowed freely and the hall reeked of cigar smoke. Douglas had to make amends to his father by bringing him a cigar. His mother insisted that he get his smoke-and-beer-smelling clothes out on the clothes-line almost at daybreak. Douglas continued his friendship with Frances Curtis until the very end of her life. He considered her patience and interest in the members of this club "a gift that can never be measured."[4]

Douglas got an excellent foundation for college at Detroit Eastern High School. A large and strong school, it gave him "first rate" instruction in mathematics, Latin, English, physics, and chemistry. Douglas found lab work "rather dull," but he "enjoyed the intellectual problems that were set for us."[5] Students "venerated" the principal, a classicist and Greek scholar. Not athletically inclined, Douglas was not up to expectations of athletes in such a large school, but he felt at home in debating and dramatics. The school principal, a Mr. Sooey, took a real interest in Douglas and his future, en-couraging him to study law at the University of Michigan so as to become a United States senator, an exalted expectation which Douglas recalled with amusement through the years.

Although election as senator seemed remote, study of law did not. Had he not experienced strong family influences in the direction of agriculture, Douglas remarked later, "there is little doubt that this is the direction that I would

DOUGLAS STEERE,
TWENTY-ONE YEARS OLD

have taken."[6] Edward Steere's interest in agriculture quickened again under the influence of another mail clerk the year before Douglas graduated from high school. Moreover, his father's brother, Frank Steere, at the height of his career as an engineer, "was always eager to talk agriculture" when he and Edward got together. He felt that manufacturing had drawn too much of the brains of the country and agriculture had been neglected. Farm machinery even remained "kid's stuff."

Seeing agriculture as the "sleeper" in the country's development and needing the best talent available, he strongly recommended Michigan Agricultural College (MAC), then second only to Cornell in the field. "My early days at Harrisville and my father's keenness for the prospects of extension work and Frank Steere's broader vision of the awakening field finally carried the day with me and I applied to Michigan Agricultural College for admission and was accepted."[7]

World War I still raged as Douglas entered MAC in September 1918. The Student Army Training Corps enlisted all except forty-five of the males entering as freshmen. Douglas had not yet heard of the witness for peace at that time. He recalled his great grandfather Captain Joseph Van Buskirk's

Civil War sword. He admired his namesake, Colonel Douglas Hitchcock, who had served in the Spanish-American War. But he did not join S.A.T.C., and it was disbanded when the war ended in November. Since MAC required two years of Reserve Officers Training Corps of all male students, however, he could not escape military service entirely. He entered R.O.T.C. and attained the rank of sergeant before leaving to play his slide trombone in the military band, in which he remained during his entire four years at MAC.

Michigan Agricultural College was a small school in 1918, enrolling about 1,800, very modest by comparison with what it has become today as Michigan State University. Women took home economics; men studied agriculture, engineering, forestry, horticulture, and veterinary science. Teaching in sciences was "first class." He gained immensely from a Professor French in two courses in rural education. French "took a personal interest in me as a human being."[8] In his second and third years at MAC Douglas did well, but he did not like lab work in chemistry and botany and had trouble staying awake in physics. He enjoyed oral communication and joined the debate team in his sophomore year. The team came off well, losing only once in ten debates with schools such as Iowa State, Marquette, Purdue, Massachusetts Aggies, and the University of Maine.[9] Douglas captained the MAC debate team during his final year. He also liked dramatics, playing "Ingomar" in a play of that name in his junior year and "Hamlet" in his senior year. But the role of barbarian chief Ingomar resulted in his being thrown from a horse. He played in the Michigan Aggie Band for four years, holding the first trombone chair the last two. As a junior, he was elected to edit *The Wolverine*, MAC's annual. He was the first in his class chosen to Alpha Zeta, a national agricultural honorary society, "as near as the agriculturists ever got to Phi Beta Kappa."[10] He was one of six chosen for membership in Excalibur, the highest fraternity honor MAC could confer upon any student for service.[11]

In his final year at MAC, following his teaching stint at Onaway, Douglas gained a new friend of immense importance for the rest of his career in Ray Bennett Weaver, whom he had come to know just slightly during his second year. Weaver taught English and was associated with the Community Church which served the college Protestants. Douglas did not yet understand the poet in himself. "But I knew somehow that he loved me and that he believed in me and that it needed implementing. I talked over my path with him."[12] This exchange broadened Douglas' horizons. He turned to more general courses and made new friends, but "Buck" Weaver was the most important.

> While his vision and reach as a poet and as a lover of literature and art and philosophy so far surpassed mine, I caught increasingly a deeper glimpse of his vision than I had in our earlier years, and he kindled me. But more than anything else, he believed in me and as Martin Buber once said at Haverford College in speaking of the greatest thing any man [or woman] can do for another, he "confirmed the deepest thing that was within me."[13]

Weaver helped Douglas organize a Men's Student Forum, which drew 200 to 400 students together twice a week to discuss topics of vital interest to students: "What Are We in College For?" "What Has the World a Right to Expect of the College Man?" "Is Our Curriculum Over-Crowded?" "Why Crib?" "How Much Do I Owe This College?" "Inventory Nite." In his *Rhodes Scholarship Application* Douglas credited work with the forum, especially reading for it, with stimulating an interest in philosophy.

Weaver and his colleague, W.W. Johnston, head of the English department, pointed Douglas toward Harvard for a year or two of philosophy. Though Douglas had never had a course in philosophy, Johnston's recommendation to Dean Briggs of Harvard gained him admission. The secretary of Michigan Agricultural College secured a loan of $1,000 for him at five percent interest.

Harvard's philosophy department when Douglas entered in 1923 included a distinguished lineup: William Ernest Hocking, Ralph Barton Perry, James Haughton Woods, Clarence I. Lewis, and junior professors Raphael Demos, Scott Buchanan, and Ralph Eaton. Alfred North Whitehead came in 1924. Never having had a course in philosophy, Douglas had a mountain to climb. In his first semester he took the massive survey of philosophy taught by the whole staff, "Problems of Philosophy" with Demos, "Ethics" with Perry, and a graduate seminar on Kant's *Critique of Pure Reason* with Lewis. With only two years of Latin in high school, he had also to do French. He audited a course in church history at Boston University School of Theology three days a week.

The stress of this endeavor produced a sense of isolation which he found "a searching experience." He questioned the meaning of his own life and even contemplated "the worth of going on living" in the spring of 1924. He visited Harvard Square Church, but found that "they had little that spoke to my condition."[14] The Graduate Society sponsored by Phillips Brooks' House came closest to furnishing fellowship and encouragement. Douglas made friends and heard significant lectures by Wilfred Grenfell of Laborador, Kirsopp Lake, and George Herbert Palmer. Nevertheless, by the spring of 1924 he found that his concentrated reading in philosophy, "far from helping me to sketch a map within which I might find a place for religion, had steadily eroded away what faith I had and left me largely stripped of any certainties." He felt "overwhelmed by my aloneness, my inadequacies, and my sense of hopelessness about myself."[15] He began to attend an Oxford Group Movement Meeting where he practiced quiet time and attentiveness to God. With all of its faults, he remarked later, the Oxford Group meeting "marked a turning point in my life, a turning inward for strength, and things that happened later grew out of this turning."[16] Thoughts of suicide faded. He made all A's except for one B+ in the second semester.

Charles Foster Kent, a Professor at Yale, offered Douglas a Kent Fellowship for his second year at Harvard, but he declined because he was not sure he could bind himself to an academic career as the fellowship stipulated. Instead, he accepted a post assigned to him by the philosophy department as assistant to Clarence I. Lewis, whom he greatly admired, and then a fellowship paying twice as much. Still needing money, he took a secretarial job for Charles Townsend Copeland, a "character" on the Harvard faculty. In subsequent years Douglas tried always to visit Copeland on trips to Cambridge, knowing that he had only student friends left. He also assisted Palfrey Perkins with a Sunday School class at First Unitarian Church in Weston, Massachusetts.

Douglas took no courses with A.N. Whitehead when Whitehead came from Kings College, Cambridge, in the fall of 1924, but Whitehead invited him to open houses in his home. He also put him in touch with his son North when Douglas went to Oxford as a Rhodes Scholar the next year. Douglas learned most from Clarence I. Lewis, who argued for a version of realism although he has been classified as a pragmatic empiricist.[17] Although he was "drawn personally" to W.E. Hocking, he took only one of Hocking's classes, an introduction to metaphysics. At the time Hocking was moving from Roycean idealism to mystical realism, just as Rufus Jones did.

In the spring of 1925 Douglas prepared to take the comprehensive examinations for admission to the Ph.D. in philosophy. Doubts assailed him and he contemplated postponement, but a mystical experience the night before he took the exams enabled him to proceed. He slept well, wrote the next four days "in composure and steadiness," and passed.[18] He still had to pass the German and French examinations in order to pursue the Ph.D., but he did not return to Harvard until he took his oral examination. His three years at Oxford as a Rhodes Scholar (1925-28) diverted him, but it also gave him time to launch a dissertation. In 1931 the Harvard faculty awarded him the Ph.D. for his study of *Critical Realism in the Religious Philosophy of Baron Friedrich von Hügel.*

The winning of a coveted Rhodes Scholarship to study at Oxford crowned an already distinguished academic career. A fellow teacher at Onaway and member of the Methodist Church Douglas attended had given him a prospectus for the Rhodes Scholarship, planting a dream. He applied first in 1923. That time he did not get the scholarship, but he learned that he had been a runner up and was encouraged to apply again. The second application proved successful. W.W. Johnston, W.H. French, Bennett Weaver, C.I. Lewis, Ralph Barton Perry, and others wrote strong and forceful letters of support, calling attention not only to Douglas' academic achievements but also to his personal qualities and promise as a leader.[19] In the late autumn of 1924 he appeared before the Rhodes Scholarship committee and was awarded a three-year scholarship. Oriel College at Oxford accepted him for admission in the fall of 1925. After spending the summer inspecting potatoes, he sailed for Southampton in the company of the other thirty-one Rhodes Scholars, whose numbers included James Fulbright, later U.S. senator from Arkansas and architect of the American Fulbright Exchange Program.

The Rhodes Scholarship introduced Douglas to a different and grander culture than the modest one he had grown up in. At Oriel College he roomed with Chet D'Arms, a Princeton classics major who had come to read classical "Greats," in spacious quarters looked after by a "scout" who cleaned and tidied up the rooms, made the beds, brought hot water to wash and shave with, carried breakfast to them, and later in the day brought tea, and discharged any errands they might have. Their "scout" was particularly deferential, always addressing them as "sir." Douglas was not used to such attentions or the rule that a gentleman never carried his own

DOUGLAS STEERE ON A VISIT HOME FROM OXFORD, ENGLAND

bag. When he went to visit an English family for a few days, he was shocked to find his bag had been unpacked and his belongings placed in their proper drawers with his shirts each separated from one another by a silver sachet. He soon learned, however, that such coddling had limits in Oriel College. He had to walk the full length of one quadrangle to reach the toilets and baths.

The Rhodes Scholarship program offered more than access to Oxford tutorials, libraries, and academics. Frank Wylie, Resident Secretary of the Rhodes Trust, and his American wife did their best to help scholars make the most of their years in Oxford, bringing speakers and writers like Salvador Madariago, a Spanish literateur who later served as Spanish Ambassador to the United States.

Douglas Steere chose to take a new Oxford sequence introduced after World War I. Instead of intensive study of Greek and Roman civilization which characterized the "Greats" program, this one centered around the civilization of Britain from 1760 to the present and included a study of philosophy, politics, and economics. It was as near as Douglas could come to studying philosophy if he were to take the honour's course without selecting classical "Greats," for which he felt "totally unprepared."[20] Students were encouraged to accent one of the three disciplines, so Douglas naturally chose philosophy. Tutors and lecturers included W.D. Ross, then the leading translator and interpreter of Aristotle in Britain; F.C.S. Schiller, a pragmatist who represented the Jamesian tradition in Britain and was almost shunned by orthodox Oxford philosophy dons; Harold Arthur Prichard, an expert on Immanuel Kant; John Macmurray, a young Scottish personalist philosopher at Balliol College who moved later to London and Edinburgh; A.D. Lindsay, Master of Balliol, who lectured on moral and political philosophy; G.N. Clark, historian and Douglas' tutor at Oriel in the political aspects of "Modern Greats."

Of these scholars Macmurray made a deep mark on Douglas with his lectures on various aspects of "a kind of personalism that probed the self to its ground of mystery."[21] In time they became good friends and maintained contact through the years. In 1930 Douglas called on Macmurray in London, where he had taken a post at London University. Macmurray introduced him to the Berlin psychotherapist Fritz Kunkel, who later became one of Douglas' most intimate friends. Following a long career at the University of Edinburgh, Macmurray moved back to England and settled near Old Jordan's Friends Meeting in Buckinghamshire. After attending the Meeting for a time, he joined the Religious Society of Friends. Douglas credited Macmurray with helping to shape many of his own basic life commitments. "His passion for community, for human solidarity, his insights into friendship and into fresh dimensions of the nature of human freedom have all enriched me."[22]

G.N. Clark also impressed Douglas by his penchant for looking at the 17th century through Dutch binoculars and chasing fresh angles on the British political path in the two middle quarters of the 19th century. Years later, Douglas learned that Clark had been educated in the Yorkshire Quaker's preparatory school at Bootham and that he and his

Roman Catholic wife took a keen interest in the Quaker service bodies in which Douglas himself played such a major role. Clark followed W.D. Ross as Provost of Oriel College.

In his first year at Oxford Douglas began speaking in the Oxford Union, a favorite of many students who gathered for weekly evening meetings to listen to or take part in a debate on a political or social topic. Usually the presiding officer called on speakers known to be witty and able and left the unknown and untried speakers for later. Sometimes distinguished visitors, British cabinet members, and even the prime minister accepted invitations to open the debate. Three or four times Douglas was invited to be among the opening quartet. As his "schools" (honors examinations) approached in 1927, however, he withdrew "because of the time involved and with a sense that this chapter was over for me."[23] It had helped him come to know some interesting students he would not have met in another way, some of whom became leading political figures in Britain.

The serious religious search Douglas' study at Harvard had launched continued in Oxford, as a philosophical and a spiritual quest blended into one another. Douglas soaked himself in the writings of the Christian mystics as he prepared for his honors exams, and felt drawn both toward Quakerism and Roman Catholicism, Quakerism eventually coming out on top by virtue of important personal and professional contacts. However, he began reading the writings of Friedrich von Hügel, a Roman Catholic philosopher and spiritual director who had died in London in January, 1925, and decided to do his Harvard dissertation on the religious philosophy of von Hügel. Since he had finished his honors course in two years, he had the third year free to work on his dissertation. In the summer of 1927 he took his ten three-hour examinations in five days and returned to the United States. Before he left Oxford, he visited Henry Gillett, a Quaker medical doctor whom Douglas had gone to see when he pulled a muscle rowing the second Oriel boat. Gillett asked if he could

DOUGLAS STEERE, NEW PROFESSOR AT HAVERFORD

suggest to Rufus Jones at Haverford College that he and Douglas have a visit to discuss job possibilities. Douglas had already received two job offers, but he chose to visit Haverford. Rufus Jones and William Comfort, President of Haverford College, asked him to send references for his work at Harvard and at Oxford. Six weeks later, he received word of his appointment as Assistant Professor of Philosophy on a three-

31

year contract beginning in 1928. He returned to Oxford and launched research for his dissertation. He finished writing it during his first two years of teaching at Haverford.

At Oxford, C.C.J. Webb, Oriel Professor of Christian Philosophy, guided Douglas in his research on von Hügel. In an effort to gain more personal insight into his subject, he had tea with Evelyn Underhill (Mrs. Stuart Moore), an Anglican and recognized authority on Christian mysticism, for whom von Hügel served as spiritual director. In the spring of 1928 Douglas gave a paper on Baron von Hügel to the Oxford Quaker meeting. In von Hügel's *Eternal Life* he came across the name of Søren Kierkegaard and read Harold Hoffding's *Søren Kierkegaard* on his next vacation. What struck Douglas Steere about Kierkegaard was his concern for transcendence. During his sabbatical in 1933–34, he began to translate Kierkegaard's *Purity of Heart,* but it was not published until 1938.

In his years at Oxford Douglas initiated the pattern of seeking "wisdom in human hide" which came to characterize his approach to life. Among visitors to Oxford with whom he first became acquainted were Burns Chalmers and Donald Stevenson, both of whom were on a year's leave from Yale Divinity School studying in Edinburgh and Oxford. They became lifelong friends. Together they heard C.H. Dodd, one of Great Britain's leading New Testament scholars, lecture at Mansfield College. Douglas also visited Rendel Harris, living in retirement at Birmingham. Harris, a Quaker New Testament scholar, had taught for a while at Haverford College, Johns Hopkins University, and Cambridge University before being chosen as Director of Studies at Woodbrooke, a Quaker center, in 1903. In the summer of 1928, on a visit to Germany, Douglas got to know Frederick Heiler, author of a classic on *Prayer*, and Martin Heidegger, leading existentialist. He heard Rudolf Bultmann, existentialist New Testament scholar, lecture at Marburg. His most vivid memory, however, was a visit with Rudolf Otto, to whom Rufus Jones had given him a letter of introduction. Otto was author of a classic study of *Das Heilige*, published in German in 1917 and years later in English as *The Idea of the Holy.*[24] Douglas was impressed by the fact that Otto was "much taken with Quaker corporate worship and the use of silence."[25] Otto and Heiler took turns leading worship in the Elizabeth Chapel of the *Elizabethkirche.*

Douglas returned to the United States in the fall of 1928 and went directly to Haverford College to begin his professional career as an associate of Rufus Jones. His spiritual quest through the study of philosophy finally anchored itself in the Quaker tradition which that college represented. The religious search merits closer examination.

Notes

1. Douglas V. Steere, UNPUBLISHED JOURNAL, 27.
2. Steere, JOURNAL, 27.
3. Steere, JOURNAL, 27.
4. Steere, JOURNAL, 28.
5. Steere, JOURNAL, 38.
6. Steere, JOURNAL, 38.
7. Steere, JOURNAL, 39.
8. Steere, JOURNAL, 58.
9. Douglas V. Steere, *Rhodes Scholarship Application,* Part One.
10. Steere, JOURNAL, 51.
11. Douglas V. Steere, *Rhodes Scholarship Application,* Part One.
12. Steere, JOURNAL, 71.
13. Steere, JOURNAL, 72.
14. Steere, JOURNAL, 80.
15. Steere, JOURNAL, 82.
16. Steere, JOURNAL, 83.
17. E.M. Adams, "Lewis, Clarence Irving (1883-1964)," *Encyclopedia of Ethics,* edited by Lawrence C. Becker (New York and London: Garland, 1992), 697.

18. Steere, JOURNAL, 91.
19. Bennett Weaver, *Letter to Mr. James K. Watkins,* November 19, 1923, characterized Douglas as "the most powerful and able college man I have known in nine years close association with college men, both as teacher and pastor." J. Frank Morford, President of the Onaway State Savings Bank, Onaway, MI, *Letter to Mr. James K. Watkins,* December 1, 1923, described him, among other things, as "a man of great promise in the scholastic field," "a hustler of the first order," and "an upright man of sterling moral character and superior integrity." N.A. McCune, Pastor of The People's Church in East Lansing, *Letter to Jas. K. Watkins,* November 21, 1923, noted that Douglas was regarded as "one of the strongest men who has gone out from this college in recent years" and that "Without pushing himself forward, he was accorded leadership by common consent." C.I. Lewis, *Letter to the Committee for the Selection of Rhodes Scholars from Michigan,* October 27, 1924, labeled him "a natural leader, not from any conceit—which he utterly lacks—but because his whole personality bespeaks sanity, honesty, temperance, and good-will." James H. Woods, Chairman of the Department of Philosophy and Psychology at Harvard, *Letter to J.K. Watkins, Esq.,* October 28, 1924, described him as "a man of exceptional vigor without any trace of bumptiousness," "a natural leader," and a "hard worker" who "never loses his cheerfulness."
20. Steere, JOURNAL, 96.
21. Steere, JOURNAL, 97.
22. Steere, JOURNAL, 88.
23. Steere, JOURNAL, 101.
24. Rudolf Otto, *The Idea of the Holy,* translated by John W. Harvey (New York: Oxford University Press, 1958).
25. Steere, JOURNAL, 115. Otto devoted an Appendix of *The Idea of the Holy* to "Silent Worship" of Quakers.

IV

Seeker

*D*ouglas Steere had a diverse religious experience. Although he could claim some Quaker roots by way of Mary L. Van Buskirk, he traveled a long road before he and Dorothy joined the Religious Society of Friends in 1932. Methodism figured much larger in his religious background and upbringing, and it continued to hold a prominent place in his career activities. He spent considerable time in early years in Presbyterian or Reformed churches. Despite early negative impressions, Roman Catholicism, with its grand edifices and its mystics, exerted a profound attraction before Douglas and Dorothy cast their lot with the Quakers. Douglas had one stint among Baptists, playing in the Sunday School orchestra at Onaway.

Douglas' mother, Ruby, served as the family's anchor in Methodism until Douglas was about ten years of age, for his father, Edward, took a vacation from it until that time. Grandmother Van Buskirk perhaps strengthened the Methodist ties, but Edward's experience as son of a Free Methodist minister had left a bad taste for religion. The summer of 1913, following his sister Helen's death and his own brush with it, Douglas was fascinated with both the Catholic and the Protestant cemeteries in Springport, Michigan. In these years, however, the Steere family did not leave Douglas with a favorable impression of Roman Catholicism. In fact, anti-Roman Catholic sentiment entered in a major way into a conflict between Ruby and Edward. Ruby favored but Edward opposed Douglas' taking dancing lessons at the Roman Catholic Knights of Columbus Hall in Detroit. His mother prevailed, but Douglas picked up some anti-Roman Catholic feeling from reading a fiercely anti-Roman Catholic publication entitled *The Menace* sent to his father by the husband of his Aunt Sybil Birlingham. When he went to the hall for classes, he tried all the doors to see if he could get in "to see the rifles and ammunition that were supposed to be hidden in all Knights of Columbus buildings that would be handed out to Roman Catholics when they were ready to take the rest of us over!"[1]

Edward M. Steere's return to religion entailed a reconnection with Methodism through the church at the corner of Boulevard and Gratiot in Detroit. Douglas was deeply touched when at about age fourteen he heard a boy evangelist at the church. He went to talk to the minister, a Reverend Chapman, and asked him to help him prepare himself for membership. He was baptized into the Methodist Church. Within a year or so, however, the family was attending a Presbyterian Church nearer its home. Another year later, Douglas transferred his membership to an Evangelical and Reformed Church "because they needed me badly to play my slide trombone in the Sunday School orchestra."[2] During the summers from 1913 on, the Steeres attended the Presbyterian Church in Mackinaw City. Ruby played the piano and loved to sing in the church choir. Edward later served as an elder and trustee of the Congregational Church in Oxford, Michigan, and liked to talk to Douglas about religion.

However variable the formal religious connections, Edward and Ruby Steere obviously modeled and inculcated deeply spiritual and human values in their children: love, kindness, goodness, humility, discipline, hope, faithfulness, trust. Such qualities surfaced when Douglas found himself on his own during college years and his year of teaching at Onaway. For the rest of his life he embodied them. As has happened so often, however, Douglas' educational pilgrimage, which carried him far beyond what either parent had experienced, stretched the thin threads of his early religious experience and commitment to the breaking point. In his study of philosophy at Harvard he reached a point of crisis in his religious search that his years at Oxford and his study of the religious philosophy of Baron Friedrich von Hügel as well as other lifelong efforts had to help him transcend. Philosophy could not satisfy a deep personal hunger to know God. His own intense struggle doubtless had much to do with shaping Douglas Steere as an open and inquiring seeker who could guide others in their search into the mysteries at the heart of human existence and the world.

Thanks to "Buck" Weaver and W.W. Johnston, Douglas' vocation became routed in the direction of the study of philosophy at Harvard during his final year at Michigan Agricultural College. Douglas described his religious life at this point as "mainly that of a seeker."[3] He had passed beyond the evangelical fervor of his first encounter in his early teens, but he attended the local community church serving Protestants and "was being steadily fed by the solid preaching of Newell McCune."[4] McCune asked Douglas to speak, and he chose "Life's Goals" as his subject.

Douglas loved the woods and streams "where I felt closest to the heart of things." Yet he also felt touches of what he later found Quakers calling the "Inward Guide," and the decision to study philosophy bore religious undertones for one willing to explore the deep issues of existence.

At the beginning, Harvard intensified those "deep existential problems," as one might expect in the case of a student undertaking an M.A. program in philosophy without ever having had a course in the subject. Kenneth Brown invited him to an Oxford Group Movement meeting. He found some help in "the sincerity and the obvious sense of concern and zeal that I felt in this gathering," but he "was repulsed to the core by almost a contest in the gory detailing of their whopping physical sins."[5] He heard lots of carnal confessions, but none about pride and its shadow side of "deep self-doubt, a sense of inadequacy and brooding." Douglas "sensed these to be far more self-destroying than the sins of the body and to call for a far deeper remedy than their public display."[6]

Yet he did find in the Oxford Group Movement meetings something of immense value from then on, the use of quiet time and emphasis upon attentiveness. He found the urge to pray "as a way to see what my life was meant for and to get me to come back into touch experientially with what I had given up."[6] He followed up by continuing to join in prayer with two students of Episcopal Theological Seminary in Cambridge, Massachusetts. The discovery of prayer in this setting marked a new stage in his life. From this point on, prayer would hold a central place in Douglas Steere's personal life, teaching, and ministry, and he would become one of the most significant contributors to the understanding and practice of prayer in the twentieth century.

A profound experience, as he prepared to take the comprehensive examinations for admission to the Ph.D. in philosophy at Harvard, confirmed his conviction about prayer's importance. On the verge of postponement as a consequence of feeling unprepared, he wrote years afterwards,

> I had an occasion then when my drawing to a season of prayer was strong and after half an hour on my knees, I rose perfectly sure that it was right to go on with the examinations, to take them in quietness, and to write what I could and let the consequences, whatever they might be, take care of themselves.[8]

The successful outcome was noted in the last chapter.

In his last year at Harvard, as noted earlier, Douglas also came under the tutelage of Palfrey Perkins, Pastor of First Unitarian Church in Weston, Massachusetts. Perkins put him in charge of the Sunday School. Douglas gave a short talk and taught a class each Sunday. Teaching helped to consolidate his thinking and confirmed that he had something worth sharing.

> This was a most wonderful experience, for my new hold on the inner center much needed consolidation and needed the shaking down in a setting where I would not be pushed into having to profess more than my intellectual monitor could accept. It had a second gift for me in that it compelled me to share each week what was real to me in the limited religious experience that I had, and to discover that others responded to this and found it valid.[9]

The friendship of Perkins, "a Unitarian minister with an honest hunger for God and a sensitive concern for the men and women of his congregation,"[10] was also a gift. Perkins accepted Douglas as a colleague, loaned him books, and, above all, shared with him "the sense that the answers were less important than the questions and that he accepted me as a companion on the road, on 'the way'."[11] He also helped him to see where Jesus could be fitted into the larger framework of things. "I learned from Palfrey Perkins that one could start by taking Jesus for the greatest man I knew about and then go on with him until he became even more, and for this freedom I have always been deeply grateful."[12] As a testimony to this connection, the Steeres invited Perkins to perform their marriage vows in the home of Dorothy's parents in Hudsonville, Michigan, in 1929.

By the time he left Harvard, Douglas had hurdled the existential crisis in religion which had loomed so large in the spring of 1924. Study under the Rhodes Scholarship at Oxford opened the way for him not only to shape further his own philosophical outlook, but also to clarify his religious perceptions, which blended imperceptibly into his philosophical quest. Douglas characterized himself at this time as "an unattached seeker sometimes referred to in a less pleasant way as an irresponsible religious tramp."[13] The Student Christian Movement appealed to him. Douglas also found spiritual resources in the sermons of William B. Selbie, a distinguished Congregationalist theologian, at Mansfield College. He heard Maude Royden preach in London, an experience which made him conclude that "if I ever had any doubts about a woman's role in the Christian ministry, they were swept away by the power of this great woman and her messages."[14] He got to know L.P. Jacks, Principal of Manchester College, whose views paralleled those of Rufus Jones, and attended St. Mary's, where J.H. Newman had fired the Oxford Movement with his *Plain and Parochial Sermons.* He heard W.R. Inge, Dean of St. Paul's in London, noted for defense of the rationality of *Christian Mysticism;* G.A. Studdert Kennedy, the popular but slightly unorthodox Anglican theologian; and Ronald Knox, then chaplain to Roman Catholic undergraduates at Oxford University, at St. Aldate's. He became an intimate friend of William Sheers, a minister in the London slums, who took him trout fishing. Douglas depicted Sheers as a model of ministry.

> This man was a parson for whom God was real and Christ and his redeeming power was a constant reality. Yet here was an immensely practical man who padded the streets of his parish day after day and knew the needs of his people and was always there and expendable to help them in the face of their crises.[15]

Douglas made his first significant contact with Quakers in the spring of 1926, when he had to seek medical help after pulling a muscle rowing in the second Oriel boat. His physician turned out to be a Quaker, Henry Gillett, who "radiated his faith" and "felt it was too good a thing to confine to those already enjoying it."[16] After Douglas shared with Gillett his reservations about the Oxford Movement for himself, Gillett invited him to his home, where he met Neave Brayshaw

40

and other distinguished Quakers. He started attending the Quaker Meeting in Oxford but "found it stuffy and dull" and went only a few times. What salvaged this connection was an invitation of B.H. Streeter, a distinguished New Testament scholar and church historian, to join the reading parties at the Quaker Old Jordan's Hostel in Buckinghamshire. Douglas had brought a paper on mystical experience that "got a good hearing." On Sundays about twenty attended the Quaker Meeting next to the hostel, where Isaac and Mary Penington and Mary's daughter Guilelma, William Penn's first wife, are buried. "Here for the first time," Douglas recorded, "I experienced a deep and moving corporate Quaker silence."[16]

Quakerism, however, did not hold out the only attraction for Douglas Steere at this time. Douglas also felt drawn to Roman Catholicism. It, too, looked like a promising source of help in his ardent and earnest quest to know God. While preparing for his honors examinations in 1926-27, he "had been soaking [him]self in the writings of the mystics."[18] During vacations, he took trips to the Continent and "found the Roman Catholic Church, with all of its inviting buildings open for prayer throughout the day, very moving places to visit." In the summer of 1926, while living with a German family and taking a language course, the cathedral "became very precious to me, and the lure of the Roman Church was kindled in my heart as the seed-bed of the great mystics and as a church that cared about the inner life and made facilities for its cultivation readily available."[19]

In 1927-28, then, Douglas was drawn toward Quakerism and Roman Catholicism, both of which offered more satisfaction for his search than conventional Protestantism. In retrospect he said:

> Conventional Protestantism with its forensic accent on preaching, as I experienced it in Britain and in Germany, had less and less attraction for me in the later Oxford years and for those that followed, as I

continued to search for some religious community with which I might identify myself.[20]

This perception may have added some weight to Douglas' decision to choose a position at Haverford College over two other offers—one from Kenyon Butterfield, President of what was by then Michigan State College, to set up a philosophy department; and the other from Lynn Harold Hough asking him to be a colleague at Central Methodist Church of Detroit. The invitation to teach at a quality Quaker college as a colleague of Rufus Jones doubtless tilted the scales on the Quaker side, but not at once.

Douglas did not chart a path toward the Friends alone. During his years at Oxford, he had felt drawn closer and closer to Dorothy MacEachron, whom he had first met at Michigan Agricultural College in May 1925 as he prepared to set out for England as a Rhodes Scholar. Soon after the second term began in Oxford, he wrote to express his love for her, and their affection grew. The next thing Douglas did after checking in at Haverford College in the fall of 1928 was to make a beeline for Michigan and a reunion with Dorothy. Dorothy belonged to the Congregational Church in Hudsonville, Michigan, and Douglas did not know what her response might be to the Quaker experience he was just beginning to know for himself. At the invitation of Alfred and Mary Scattergood they attended the Coulter Street Friends Meeting in Germantown, Pennsylvania. It was Dorothy's first experience of a Quaker Meeting. To Douglas' "delight," "she was touched to the quick by its solemnity and depth" and she "felt completely at home in the silence."[21] She could respond with this sense of appreciation, Douglas judged, because "her inward life was without walls and she felt the integrity of the utterly simple waiting on God."[22] Following their marriage June 12, 1929, Douglas and Dorothy proceeded step by step toward their affiliation with the Religious Society of Friends in the spring of 1932.

Douglas planted his feet in the Quaker stream, but that by no means signaled the end of his own serious religious search. He continued on a quest to know God, not just *about* God, for the rest of his life. He engaged in that search not by way of religious or philosophical a priori's and abstractions, the way of scholars, but by way of deep personal engagement with other seekers, the way of saints. Douglas was the kind of person who basked in the light which others radiated, soaking up in a highly personal way the richest insights life had given them. He displayed an obvious partiality toward contemplatives, mystics, existentialists, social activists, and others who shared his person-centered orientation toward life.

Central in the shaping of Douglas' outlook and even the shape of his vocation was Baron von Hügel, whose researches focused on knowing God, exactly the issue which burned so brightly in Douglas' mind and heart.[23] Von Hügel was also extraordinarily skilled in helping others to know God. Having completed much of his research during his third year at Oxford, Douglas began writing during his second year at Haverford and sought to complete his dissertation in the summer of 1930 during the Steeres' visit to Europe. That trip enabled Douglas to get a feeling for the setting of *The Imitation of Christ* and to visit the home of Nicholas of Cusa, where he saw Eckhart's *Commentary on John* annotated by Cusa. He submitted his dissertation on his return to the United States in the fall. Although he chose not to publish *Critical Realism in the Religious Philosophy of Baron von Hügel,* despite strong encouragement by Henry P. Van Dusen to do so, he did try "to repay in a small way my incalculable debt to von Hügel" through the publication of *Spiritual Counsel and Letters of Friedrich von Hügel*[24] before his retirement from Haverford College.

In the early phases of Douglas' career, his colleague at Haverford College, Rufus Jones, assisted him immeasurably. Another significant model was Henry T. Hodgkin, M.D., the first Director of Pendle Hill. "Here was a man who was a window to God, lovable, wise, generous and yet beset in this completely uncharted adventure in adult education by every kind of human and physical problem."[25] Hodgkin's wife challenged the view of those who thought her husband just "naturally" good. She pointed out that "he was up early in the morning and spending the first hour of the day 'leaning on the windowsill of heaven' with a portion of it in silent prayer, a portion in spiritual reading, and a portion in writing in his day book that no one ever saw, the leadings that had come to him."[25] Douglas Steere recalled that Hodgkin often used the phrase *"to be tendered, to be made tender* as another authentic sign of the action of the presence."[26] Hodgkin died in 1933, and Douglas was touched by an invitation to succeed him as Director of Pendle Hill.

A complete roll call of all the persons from whom Douglas Steere drew incarnate wisdom would make this a very lengthy chapter, but we can scarcely understand how he became who he was without noting, in its early stages, the *modus operandi* of his spiritual search. In late June 1931 he met Ernest Freemont Tittle, pastor in Evanston, Illinois, and John Mackay, later President of Princeton Theological Seminary, at a huge world Methodist meeting. Tittle "preached a daring social message that spoke truth to power" in his church, and Douglas used the occasion of their first meeting to question him in depth about his way of communing with God. Tittle explained that he "just opened himself up utterly to God's scrutiny";[28] otherwise, within a month he would be just play acting. Douglas soon brought him to Haverford College to lecture. With Mackay, then writing a dissertation on Miguel de Unamuno, the famed Spanish existentialist, Douglas shared a deep common interest in existentialism. In 1957 Mackay invited Steere to give the Stone Lectures at Princeton Theological Seminary.

Early in 1931, he met Maria Schlüter-Hermkes, a Roman Catholic and the first woman invited by the Carl Schurz Foundation to lecture in the United States. She gave lectures

44

in Philadelphia on Hildegard of Bingen, Teresa of Avilá, Catherine of Genoa, and Catherine of Siena. Douglas shocked Maria Schlüter-Hermkes by proposing that she add John Woolman to the list of saints "in order to quicken us to the radical transformation of values that our time required."[29] She pointed out in reply that the United States was far too young to produce saints, for "real sanctity could only appear when there were centuries of tradition to furnish the protecting pot in which a saint would have to grow!"[30] The exchange proved fruitful, nonetheless, for she suggested that he study Roman Catholic spirituality in Germany and had her husband Johannes arrange for Douglas to do a retreat at Maria Laach during his first sabbatical in 1933.

This visit to Maria Laach carried Douglas a step deeper into the Catholic stream he had waded into through his study of Baron von Hügel and launched an important lifelong friendship. He had never been to a monastery before. A day or two after his arrival, he met Abbot Herwegen. The abbot turned down his request for a spiritual guide, explaining that Benedictines do not practice private but rather communal spirituality. The Jesuits do private retreats, he said. To Douglas' benefit, however, the abbot assigned a young monk named Damasus Winzen to guide him. They read and discussed Anders Nygren's *Agape and Eros.* Of that first en-counter, Douglas observed, "I began through him to see what real Christian charity is like and I have experienced ever so much of it within the Roman Catholic Church."[31] During the day, Douglas attended the liturgical hours, read, meditated, and walked in the fields. He had to leave Maria Laach abruptly in the midst of his stay to minister to the family of Richard Cary, the American Friends Service Com-mittee representative in Germany, who died of a stroke at age forty-seven. On his return to Maria Laach, however, he resumed fruitful visits with Damasus Winzen. He was able to continue this friendship with Winzen a year later, for the lat-ter came to the United States in 1935, founded Mount Savior

Monastery near Elmira, New York in 1951, and never returned to Germany, dying in the United States in 1973. Later, in 1934, Douglas went with two Scottish friends to the Benedictine monastery at Beuron in Germany, the pioneer of the Catholic liturgical renewal movement. In subsequent years he drew heavily from the Benedictine tradition to shape retreats and to develop his approach to spiritual growth and development.

In addition, while still at Maria Laach in the fall of 1933, he visited Karl Barth. They had a good talk about Maria Laach, but Barth was "very critical of prayer's excessive subjectivity." Only Jesus' crucifixion could save one from Hell. Prayer would not matter. When Douglas asked why Barth continued to visit the monks at Maria Laach, he replied, to "refute them." The encounter helped to confirm Douglas in his newly adopted Quakerism, which did not hold such reservations about the cultivation of the inner life. "I felt so released and freed," he wrote in his JOURNAL, "that I almost broke into whistling on my way to the train."[32]

Douglas Steere sought out numerous other scholars and persons of insight during this sabbatical. He went to Copenhagen to obtain the counsel of Eduard Geismar, an expert on Kierkegaard, concerning translation of Kierkegaard's *Purity of Heart*. Later he contacted Henni Forchammer, author of the grammar he used to learn Danish, to sharpen his grasp of the language. At Tübingen he had weekly visits with Karl Heim, a staunch Lutheran, from whose views Douglas found relief by reading George Fox's *Journal* at night. He discovered that Karl Adam in the Catholic Theological Faculty gave a view of humanity much more amenable to his own than Heim's. On visits to Stuttgart he sought out the principal translator of Kierkegaard's works into German and visited the famous Waldorf School, founded by Rudolph Steiner, which emphasized interiorization and drew the wrath of the Nazis.

Especially revealing of the way in which Douglas went about expanding his store of insight are contacts he made in Berlin with Nicholai Hartmann, Fritz Kunkel, and Romano Guardini. He sought out Nicholai Hartmann at the University of Berlin. Having already read Hartmann's *Ethics,* he came away with a still deeper impression. Hartmann's personalism, he commented in later years, "influenced deeply my approach to the subject in the years that were to follow."[33]

Douglas had both a personal and a professional interest in Fritz Kunkel, to whom John Macmurray had introduced him in 1930. On a personal level, the view of the self which Kunkel had set forth in a book entitled *Let's Be Normal* came very close to one of Kant's. This Kantian view set Douglas to formulating. He wrote, "His insights into the layers of egocentricity that freeze up the deep healing and creative springs of the mysterious and unfathomable self came so close to my own life that I wanted to see if he could help me to bring the process of at least their partial dissolution."[34] On the professional level, he needed better to equip himself to teach abnormal psychology and felt that this time in Berlin offered his best chance for advancing his own self-understanding. Kunkel welcomed him warmly and accepted him both as a patient and as a learner. Twice-a-week visits brought Douglas close to both Kunkel and his second wife, Elizabeth. Within a week or so, Kunkel asked Douglas to take on several nonpaying persons who needed help. Although they discussed a possible visit Kunkel might make to the United States, they could not foresee how often their paths would cross in the future. Kunkel taught several times at Pendle Hill and Douglas visited Elizabeth during the Second World War, since she elected to stay in Germany.

Of like consequence were Douglas' meetings with Romano Guardini. Guardini, a Roman Catholic Guest Professor at the University of Berlin, "was in a way the spiritual guide of that second quarter-century period of Roman Catholic life in Germany."[35] He had led a Roman Catholic youth group called the Quickborn in a religious revival movement. During the term Douglas was in Berlin in the spring of 1934,

Guardini lectured on Dostoyevsky, not only to students but also to a wide range of other people of all ages. Douglas judged, after hearing Guardini one semester, that he had "never heard his equal."

> He had a genius for interpreting these figures in such a way that the deeper dimensions of their message were laid bare and before he had finished with a course of lectures the congruity of what underlay this message and that which the Christian message was feeling after were made ever so clear.[36]

They met often that winter and frequently talked late at night about the very ground of faith. Douglas found Guardini "eager to share and to compare experiences and to know as much as I, in my callow beginnings in the Quaker way, could tell him about the root and the testimonies of the Quaker faith and life."[37] Douglas visited Guardini again in 1940, when authorities had already forbidden him to preach but allowed him to say mass. During those repressive days, Guardini wrote books on prayer, the use of the rosary, and other simple religious practices. "He was expendable for the needs of the faith in whatever corridor life's most urgent needs drew him," Douglas observed admiringly. Douglas saw him after the war in Tübingen and then several times in Münich.[38] Douglas tried to visit Guardini in the hospital a few weeks before he died, but he was not allowed visitors. "His friendship and the measured wisdom of his advice and his example in writing on the spiritual life is one of the richest gifts I have to remember," Douglas said years later.

The circle of persons from whom Douglas Steere sought incarnate wisdom constantly widened throughout his life. Through repeated visits he sought to deepen contacts with persons who had already made a mark on his life. He constantly reached out to others, inviting them to lecture at Haverford College or visiting them to engage them in conversation about urgent issues of life and faith. His contacts included some of the most eminent persons in the field of philosophy, religion, or literature such as Martin Buber, D.T. Suzuki, Albert Schweitzer, Martin Heidegger, Alan Paton. He sought out political leaders who could assist in such projects as relief for wartorn Finland. At the same time he reveled in meetings with ordinary seekers who were to him as important as world luminaries in his search for the Other at the heart of things.

Notes

1. Douglas V. Steere, UNPUBLISHED JOURNAL, 29.
2. Steere, JOURNAL, 31.
3. Steere, JOURNAL, 73.
4. Steere, JOURNAL, 73.
5. Steere, JOURNAL, 73.
6. Steere, JOURNAL, 73.
7. Steere, JOURNAL, 83.
8. Steere, JOURNAL, 91.
9. Steere, JOURNAL, 87.
10. Steere, JOURNAL, 87.
11. Steere, JOURNAL, 87.
12. Steere, JOURNAL, 88.
13. Steere, JOURNAL, 102.
14. Steere, JOURNAL, 102.
15. Steere, JOURNAL, 103.
16. Steere, JOURNAL, 104.
17. Steere, JOURNAL, 105.
18. Steere, JOURNAL, 105.
19. Steere, JOURNAL, 105.
20. Steere, JOURNAL, 106.
21. Steere, JOURNAL, 122.
22. Steere, JOURNAL, 122f.

23. Von Hügel's name will appear often in this biography. What especially drew Douglas to him will be presented in Chapter 18, in which Douglas'philosophy is summarized.

24. *Spiritual Counsel and Letters of Friedrich von Hügel* (London: Darton, Longman & Todd, 1964).

25. Steere, JOURNAL, 138.

26. Steere, JOURNAL, 138.

27. Steere, JOURNAL, 139.

28. Steere, JOURNAL, 139.

29. Steere, JOURNAL, 142.

30. Steere, JOURNAL, 142.

31. In Douglas' memorial account of their friendship in a *Festschrift* published in *Monastic Studies,* 15, following Fr. Winzen's death.

32. Steere, JOURNAL, 158.

33. Steere, JOURNAL, 163.

34. Steere, JOURNAL, 165.

35. Steere, JOURNAL, 163.

36. Steere, JOURNAL, 164.

37. Steere, JOURNAL, 164f.

38. Following the 1947 visit, Douglas next saw Guardini in later 1950 after his move to München. See *General Newsletter from Douglas Steere,* #6, Berlin, 8 November, 1950, 7.

$\mathcal{V}$

Dorothy

*T*he person-centered approach to life brought Douglas Steere into contact with many people from whom he gathered insight, but none touched his life and ministry as deeply as his wife, Dorothy. They were spiritual seekers together, quickening each other's understanding. Dorothy's listening, her thoughtful questioning, and her warmth nurtured Douglas as he coped with his many challenges. After joint encounters with people, she would often identify their yearnings and help Douglas weigh the implications. They threshed out decisions together on how to move in delicate situations. As keeper of the home, Dorothy managed the practicalities of their lives with grace. She sheltered and fed their guests from all over the world. As parent, she raised their two daughters with loving attentiveness during Douglas' frequent absences. As editor and typist of Douglas' manuscripts, she brought to the work a fine sense of language and meaning and a patient devotion to accuracy. As co-retreat leader, her genuine interest in how individual participants were struggling to grow in the Light affirmed their efforts. As traveling companion, she shared adventures, making Douglas at home away from home, and helped him articulate the significance of their rich encounters.

Douglas first met Dorothy MacEachron on a blind date in 1925 as she was finishing her first year at Michigan Agricultural College. She was just seventeen and valedictorian of her high school graduating class. She confessed in retrospect that she had never met anyone like Douglas Steere, or had a date quite like her first one with him. They left the alumni dance and talked about what communion with God meant to them.[1]

Douglas met her again twice in the fall before departing for Oxford. They then carried on their friendship by correspondence. Both superb letter writers, their friendship deepened quickly. On a skiing trip to Switzerland not long after his second term, Douglas wrote to tell her that he had found, in Quaker parlance, "clarity" to tell her of his "deep caring for her."[2] After taking his honors exams at Oxford in the summer of 1927, he returned to the United States to see Dorothy and to seal their engagement, although he did not give her a ring until her birthday a year later. Dorothy spent some of the summer in northern Michigan, where Douglas had resumed his role as potato inspector. They had evenings together.

Dorothy finished her last two years of college at the University of Michigan in Ann Arbor. She dated Milton Staub, a pre-med student, knowing that Douglas was seeing other women. She had resigned from her sorority, Kappa Alpha Theta, her sophomore year because of its elitist policies, but was accepted her junior year into an honors dorm where she found many kindred spirits. She was active with international students, in the Women's League and the YWCA, and had a successful semester of practice teaching at University High School. She warmed to courses on literature, the biblical prophets, and reformation history, and wrote her senior thesis on *The Imitation of Christ*.

Dorothy was six and a half years younger than Douglas. Although intelligent and mature, she did not have the advantages his education provided. She explained in her *Reminiscences and Reflections:*

I had strong premonitions that the reason he had been drawn to me was because of some inward light—not my own—which seemed to be alive in me and prompted his own longing for that light. It was me, and yet not me, that he wanted. I sensed that I was not adequate either as the bearer of the light he thought I was, or even as his companion. I felt this in various ways when I was with his Oxford or Harvard friends. This brought about a rather rough period in our relationship during his last Oxford year.[3]

Dorothy graduated at age twenty, having prepared herself to teach English. She had had a job offered to her to teach drama and English in the Upper Peninsula of Michigan. She sensed that she should test her skill in that vocation. However, Douglas and her parents thought it would be better for her, their only child, to have a year with her family to prepare for homemaking while Douglas had his first terms of teaching at Haverford College. She had a searching year, asking herself who she really was and whether she was failing to answer her calling. She had almost died at birth and felt that she might have been brought back for some special purpose. Would she fulfill it being a helpmate to Douglas?

When Dorothy visited him in Haverford before the Christmas holiday, Douglas sensed her inner confusion. He expressed concern that her faith did not seem strong enough to keep up her spirits. He admitted that he had counted on her spiritual resources to anchor both of them and wondered if they were really meant for each other after all. He later wrote in his *Autobiography:* "It brought great pain to Dorothy who had her own moments of self-doubt which were only confirmed by my unsettlement . . . Our love for each other was deep enough to absorb this pain, but both of us knew when she left to return to Hudsonville that we had passed through a dark night and found even in the darkness that something sustained us."[4]

They were married in the MacEachron home in Hudson-ville June 12, 1929. Palfrey Perkins came to marry them. Ray Bennett Weaver served as best man. The newlyweds spent their honeymoon in Mackinaw, driving a new Roosevelt car given them as a wedding present by Dorothy's father. They spent the summer in a house owned by John Lester, a Haverford alumnus, in Wedgeport, Nova Scotia. Douglas worked on his dissertation. Dorothy read and struggled to cook on a woodstove.

When they came back to Haverford in the fall of 1929 Dorothy was immediately caught up in her husband's busy life. Shortly after returning, the Steeres spent a week at Wells College on Lake Cayuga as guests of the National Council of Religion in Higher Education. When college opened, students often met in their living room for seminars. The Steeres combined Sunday night suppers and play readings, bringing together Haverford and Bryn Mawr College students to share the meal preparation, dishes, and fellowship. Dorothy joined a campus Madrigal Group; she had a strong alto voice. In late autumn she and Douglas were invited to take part in the planning of what became known as Pendle Hill.

Dorothy continued to question whether she should be proving herself in her teaching profession. It bothered her that she had never earned a cent on her own. Amy Watson, a faculty member at Haverford, chided her for letting woman-kind down by hiding her light under a bushel. In the summer of 1930, however, she accompanied Douglas to Europe and helped him edit and type his dissertation on Friedrich von Hügel. She was thrilled to visit Deventer in Holland, where the Brethren of the Common Life had lived and Gerrit de Groote was said to have written the *Imitation of Christ*. Here she could pursue her study of this great classic which had been the subject of her senior thesis with Albert Hyma at the University of Michigan. Since Douglas also loved this book, this stay in Deventer was a meaningful experience for them to share.

54

DOROTHY MacEACHRON STEERE

The following year she was invited to teach literature in the winter session of a Bryn Mawr College Summer School Program for Philadelphia factory workers and immigrants. Although a volunteer job, this opportunity was a godsend. She enjoyed contact with the competent and caring women running the program and with the students eager to read poetry that took them into nature and ideas beyond the drabness of their urban lives. She especially warmed to the foreign students and invited some of them to visit the Steere home.

Douglas and Dorothy proceeded cautiously in their formal affiliation with the Religious Society of Friends. Both were intrigued with it and quite regularly attended Haverford (Buck Lane) Meeting. They decided, however, that they did not want to join right away. They wanted to be sure they were not doing it because that is what the community expected. One of the greatest influences in nudging them in the direction of membership was reading the *Journal* of John Woolman, who combined so well the active and the contemplative life.

In 1930 they helped reopen Radnor Meeting, four miles from the Haverford campus. Built in 1718, it had been closed for fifty years. Dorothy rang doorbells to invite seekers to join them and, at age twenty-three, served as the first clerk. Douglas, already recognized as possessing ministerial capacities, planned Sunday evening forums. Dorothy took a leading part in beginning a First Day School at Radnor Meeting and served on its Religious Education Committee for about ten years.

Radnor Meeting was the second Meeting in Philadelphia to unite Orthodox and Hicksite Quakers. Dorothy was a spirited advocate for united meeting status, attending a series of gatherings to work through resistance and iron out the details. She later served on a committee which accomplished a merger of the two Philadelphia Yearly Meetings at Race Street and Arch Street in 1935. The effort led to some good-natured ribbing between the Steeres. Dorothy leaned toward Hicksite Race Street because of its social concern, Douglas toward Arch Street because of its spiritual emphasis. He called her "Hicksie Pixie." She called him "Starchie Archie."[5]

DOUGLAS AT RADNOR MEETING

Despite their involvements and the joy of anticipating their first child, Dorothy continued to feel inadequate. Two books by Fritz Kunkel, *Let's Be Normal and God Helps Those Who Help Themselves,* strengthened her confidence. Growing up, she had been affirmed as a superior student and leader in her school and community, but now her life was hitched to another rising star. She later wrote:

> I had to recognize that I had value too, that I was a person with my own being and capacities. That was hard to learn. It was partly the structure of society at that time that put me down as a woman. . . . I had to learn that it was a form of pride to *have* to be like Douglas, that I had to be like *Dorothy* was supposed to be.[6]

A "golden text" of scripture she had memorized as a child came back to her and had impact at that time: "I can do all things in Him who strengtheneth me" (Phil. 4:13). She realized that she need not worry whether she was doing precisely what she wanted intellectually. She could let go and trust herself to a Power beyond herself.

The advent of a child shifted the focus of Dorothy's attention. On April 11, 1932, Dorothy gave birth in a Grand Rapids, Michigan, hospital to a daughter. She was named Helen after Douglas' sister and paternal grandmother and Weaver after Ray Bennett Weaver, who was then Professor of

English Literature at the University of Michigan. Dorothy experienced a difficult delivery, as her mother had in her own birth. Douglas, although not intending to visit until the end of the semester, dismissed classes and hurried to Grand Rapids. A second daughter, Anne, was born March 24, 1935, this time in a somewhat easier delivery. Dorothy had had a curvature of the spine from birth which complicated her pregnancies and caused her back pain all her life.

Like many another mother, Dorothy placed care of her daughters ahead of public activities for a time. She stayed with her parents during the first half of Douglas' first sabbatical in 1933-34, for instance, but joined him in Berlin for the second half. She and the two girls stayed with the MacEachron family again during Douglas' trip to Germany and Scandinavia in the summer of 1937. She, Helen, and Anne remained behind also when Douglas undertook his risky journey over the same route in 1940-41 on behalf of the American Friends Service Committee.

Having children, however, did not close the damper on Dorothy's involvement locally. She almost always accompanied Douglas to Pendle Hill Board meetings. During one summer, she served with Anna Brinton as Co-Head Resident. Anna encouraged Dorothy to take on more responsibilities and to speak more.

The Steeres had some household help when the children were small. Helen Wilson, a capable and intelligent woman of middle age, relieved Dorothy of kitchen duties and gave her more freedom to be with the children and take part in outside activities. Anna Margareta Olden, daughter of a new Norwegian Quaker, loved Helen and Anne and shared herself and her Norwegian culture in a rich way. These and others made it possible for Dorothy to chair the Yearly Meeting's Religious Education Committee for three years. She served on the local NAACP Board and helped to initiate the Main Line Community League, an interracial group, to promote racial harmony and reduce discrimination. Dorothy

58

herself worked to secure the employment of capable African Americans as sales persons at Strawbridge and Clothier, a department store in Ardmore. She challenged the excuse that it would hurt business, and within a year the store began employing African Americans in sales. The League also made it possible for African Americans to sit anywhere in the movie theaters and not to be discriminated against in rooms at Bryn Mawr Hospital. Dorothy took part in the opening of the Ardmore YMCA to African Americans.

Her early local experience expanded in 1955 when the Philadelphia Yearly Meeting sent Dorothy, George Harden, and Clarence Pickett to Montgomery, Alabama, during the bus boycott. They talked with Martin Luther King, Jr., his wife Coretta, and some white sympathizers. They attended a moving mass meeting where King and Ralph Abernathy spoke to African-Americans about ways to conduct themselves and live through the crisis they were facing. On Sunday Dorothy and another member of the Yearly Meeting delegation spoke to white church groups. Dorothy, having recently visited South Africa with Douglas, described the negative effect of apartheid on South African society, leaving the congregation to draw its own parallels.

The Main Line Co-op Store was born in the Steere living room. The store functioned well for about six or seven years as a model of economic justice. Ultimately, the ACME chain started a supermarket across the street, slashing prices until it put the Mainline Co-op Store out of business. During the summer of 1945, while Douglas opened up relief work in Finland, Dorothy lead an American Friends Service Committee work camp providing recreation for children in the isolated fishing village of Stonington, Maine. She took Helen and Anne with her. Although she was intimidated by the prospect of coping with all the tasks that running even a small camp required, including the accounts and menu-planning in the face of war-time food shortages, she met the challenge. At first the community stood aloof from the work campers as outsiders, but when local people realized that they were there as unpaid volunteers full of good will, they flocked to the program. Dorothy knew she had engaged in something truly significant. Most summers the Steere family managed to spend two months together at Mackinaw.

By the time Douglas' third sabbatical rolled around in 1947, both Helen and Anne were old enough to accompany their parents abroad. In August 1947 the Steere family headed for Sweden aboard the Swedish American Line's "Drottning-holm." Dorothy enrolled Helen and Anne in the Quaker boarding school just outside Stockholm called Viggbyholm, then crossed to Helsinki to join Douglas. There Finnish government officials formally expressed appreciation for the Quaker relief effort. Dorothy accompanied Douglas on visits commissioned by the AFSC throughout Germany, renewing ties Douglas had made on earlier trips, meeting scholars and government officials, and speaking to a variety of groups. Before Christmas they crossed to Denmark and Sweden. They gathered as a family to spend Christmas and New Year's day at Are, 250 miles north of Stockholm. When the girls returned to Viggbyholm, Douglas and Dorothy settled in at the Sigtuna Foundation, where he worked on writing projects.

During this year, Dorothy often felt like "a fifth wheel." Since their daughters were away at boarding school, she was cut off from much of the parenting that had been a major focus. (She was unaware that, at age twelve, Anne was dealing with considerable sexual harassment and could have used her guidance.) She tried to concentrate on learning German, but she felt uprooted from the many activities she cherished in the Philadelphia area. In May, 1948, while Douglas and Helen were traveling in Germany and she was visiting among Danish friends, she received news of her father's death. Elise Thompson, with whom she was staying, made arrangements for her to fly back to Michigan. Dorothy lived with her mother until the family returned from Sweden. She helped her mother work through her grief and adjust to life without her husband. Jennie MacEachron lived for three years after her husband's death.

Anne accompanied Douglas and Dorothy on their 1953 trip to Europe and studied in Germany. While there, she and Dorothy traveled back to Scandinavia and revisited Viggbyholm School, where Anne had gone through such a confusing time. Anne took Dorothy to some of the places in the woods which she had sought out when she felt the most miserable. Both broke down and cried, experiencing a new level of understanding and release.

From the 1950s on, Dorothy regularly accompanied Douglas on his travels in Africa and throughout the world on behalf of the American Friends Service Committee, and shared some in the writing of travel letters. Although she did not always want to go because of her own local involvements, because of Helen and Anne, and because of the increasing pain in her back, she thought it was important for them to be together. She admits, in her *Reminiscences and Reflections,* to some anxiety dreams about losing track of Douglas in strange cities where she could not speak the language, or being suddenly alone without a passport of her own as a plane was about to leave. Nevertheless, the rich experiences of the travel and the cultivation of friendships ultimately caused her to do so gladly.

The 1960s were years when Dorothy was still feeling her way toward a full sense of herself as a person "with a passport of her own," apart from her traditional roles as helpmate, parent, and community volunteer. She recorded in her journal one painful encounter with Helen, who, at twenty-nine, was struggling with her own identity. Dorothy had expressed to Helen her longing for Helen to do more poetry writing and be less burdened with the social conscience that was driving her to teach world history. Dorothy had poured her own considerable talent as a writer into editing Douglas' manuscripts and corresponding with friends. Helen felt

61

pressured and told Dorothy to stop feeding on others' lives, to be somebody herself, so as to free Helen to find her own way. She challenged her to stop being pushed around by others. Musing on this fiery blast, Dorothy linked it in her journal with a description from *The Inner World of Choice*, by Frances Wickes, of some who let their lives drift by and feel self-pity. She yearned to be clearer with her daughters about the Light she had glimpsed and followed. Such private journaling and soul searching out of her encounters, her reading, or her dreams have characterized Dorothy's inner growth process throughout her life.

Dorothy joked about being the chicken that went along to keep Douglas, the elephant, company on his travels, but she really felt her role was more important than that. She had become a member of the Personnel Committee of the AFSC and was gaining a surer sense that she had "a capacity to move out from a solid center." The AFSC wanted both Steeres to be their international representatives, thinking four eyes were better than two. Dorothy observed in retrospect: "One of the wonderful things about my time abroad was having chances to talk with people individually or with small groups of women."[7] After ten years of this partnership with the American Friends Service Committee, the Steeres continued their itinerant ministry from 1964 to 1970 while Douglas served as chairperson of the Friends World Committee for Consultation. Meeting with Quaker groups all over the world, they sought to discover what was going on in Quaker life, to discern differences in interpretation of Quaker principles and testimonies, and to nurture the shared seeking for continuing revelation that lies at the core of all Quaker experience. Representation of Quakers in an official way at three sessions of the Second Vatican Council (1962-65) was another important experience Dorothy shared with Douglas. She was with him in Rome for two of the three sessions, during which they enjoyed staying with the Dutch Ladies of Bethany on the Piazza Navone.

By the 1960s Dorothy was finding her own direction. She conducted retreats at Pendle Hill for mothers and a retreat for the wives of overseas afsc workers, women who were experiencing much the same struggle she had had for so many years. She gave them strong words of encouragement.

DOROTHY STEERE WITH SALLY PALMER,
PENDLE HILL CRAFTS TEACHER 1986

Once they saw their children reach maturity, they would be free and still have energy to share in their husbands' travels as she shared in Douglas'. From the 1970s on, she enlarged the role she played in retreats Douglas led, meeting with half of the retreatants individually while Douglas met with the other half.

About 1972 Dorothy led in the formation of a worship-sharing group called Women Among Friends. After experiencing such a group among Quakers on a trip to Earlham College in Richmond, Indiana, she had tried to introduce the idea to a Radnor spiritual study group in the 1960s, but they were not yet ready to be as personal as such a group challenges participants to be. Women Among Friends encouraged spiritual growth through monthly worship-sharing around mutually chosen topics such as Changes, Leadings, Loss, Masks We Wear, Joys and Sorrows. Following an early gathering of this group where they had committed themselves to relying more fully on their own intuitions despite society's honoring of rational thought, Dorothy had a pair of telling dreams:

> I dreamed I was looking out the window of our cottage at the Straits of Mackinac and I noticed birds swimming in the water. At first I thought they were ducks or sea gulls, . . . But as I looked more closely, I was astounded to see that they were chickens— chickens of all colors and sizes, beautiful chickens, swimming along together as happily as could be— completely at home in this new element![8]

In a second dream, a chicken was picking at a tough but perfectly-shaped piece of excrement. It tried to eat it, then tossed it away. Dorothy wrote in her journal, "I was glad it did. It knew what it wanted and what was not worth bothering with."[9] This spirited group has continued meeting in Dorothy's living room monthly and reinforces Dorothy's own sense of meaning and purpose.

In the 1970s Dorothy was invited to become a member of the Ecumenical Institute of Spirituality which Douglas and Godfrey Diekmann had founded in 1965 to share insights concerning prayer and the inner life. Although she is one of the few people in the group not a monk, nun, minister, or professor, her presence and contributions are treasured by all other members. When she first began to attend, however, she felt uncertain about this welcome. About that time, Douglas brought home a quotation from Fr. Damasus Winzen that deepened Dorothy's trust in God's loving acceptance. Someone, knowing Fr. Damasus had lived through heart-breaking times, asked him, as he lay dying, what kept him so full of joy, thanksgiving, and confidence. With scarcely a moment's hesitation, he replied, "I am certain that I am infinitely loved by God." Dorothy wrote:

That certitude and the infinity that he spoke of made something drop away from my feeling of despair. I was released from "oughts" in my own life to the "givenness" of God's love. Though I had heard about the love and grace of God over and over all my life, and I knew it was there, it was that certitude and the infinitude of the love that suddenly struck me and made me feel, "All right! It really doesn't matter how many weaknesses I have. It doesn't matter how inadequate I am. I am *loved!* And if I am loved in that way, then everybody else in the world is loved in the same way. One just has to lean back on that love, know it's there, know it's infinite, and know that every other soul is surrounded by that love." It was my recognition of what St. Paul talked about—the height and depth and breadth of the love of God—that I had never quite been able to sense in terms of my own life before. And it was just as if, once again, a burden had been lifted from my shoulders and my heart.[10]

Dorothy Steere considers this a "turning point" in her life. "It makes me feel there must be a continuum," she affirms. "On earth we may feel only moments of this love, but the God of Love must want us, all of us, to be loving. There must be an infinitude of time when we can learn to grow in love, no matter what our present earthly state."[11] This sense reminded Dorothy of Browning's line, "On earth the broken arcs, in heaven the perfect round."

Out of experiences such as these Dorothy developed an awareness that she may have been pursuing her true vocation all along, as a listener and encourager and affirmer of what is deepest in others. While the children were growing up, she had not thought of herself as a counselor and listener. She simply cared deeply for people. Serving on the Personnel Committee of the AFSC for many years, beginning in the 1970s, she loved meeting and drawing out prospective workers. She began to realize in this that her vocation was closer to personnel work than to teaching. Traveling with Douglas, she sensed her gift for one-on-one relationships. When she spoke to Douglas about this, he commented,

> Well, Dorothy, I know you wish you had had training in counseling . . . but, after all, it seems to be a natural gift. This is something that you have come into from your psychological reading and from your deep personal spiritual experience. I don't feel you need worry because you're not a professional.[12]

Douglas' book *On Listening to Another* is an attempt to define this gift as what others most need from us and what God offers to us most intimately. It is an indication of how much he came to honor that capacity in his wife.

As people came to Douglas, so too did they come to her. Both "tried to be releasers of the dreams in other people."[13] Dorothy reflected on this vocation:

> We destroy when we fail others' need, when we fail to release others from certain preconceptions we have had of them, when we hold them tightly to ourselves, when we fail to listen and comprehend what goes on beneath the surface of their lives. By our own concern for the value of life, its ongoingness, we can be a link in the loving redemptive process. This is our chance to fulfill the purpose for which we were placed on earth.[14]

In recent years Dorothy followed her vocation through ministry to Douglas as Alzheimer's disease reduced his capacity to make decisions for himself. She sustains close contact with her circle of friends in Haverford, especially in the Women Among Friends group. She corresponds extensively. Whereas earlier Dorothy had depended on Douglas considerably, at the end of his life he depended on her to guide him in the most elemental things and to carry on the listening that goes beyond words. Physically frail and in pain herself, she manifested the strength born of a deep inner life. Close ties with Helen and Anne and a web of friendships helped to sustain her during this trying period. Dorothy had to witness not only the diminishment of her brilliant husband's mental and physical faculties but also the death of Anne's husband, Paul Nash; the Parkinson's disease of David Horn, Helen's husband; and Helen's battle with cancer. Yet she has continued to find time and ways to minister. Relieved of some chores such as cooking and cleaning by their move to the life care community of Quadrangle in Haverford, she sees many people for intimate talks each week. Her conversation, her empathetic letters, and her *Reminiscences and Reflections* all give evidence of the vitality of her mind and of the quest that still goes on. She has said YES to the One who loves all unconditionally. Her own words provide a fitting end to this chapter as her life story is still being written:

> I have both a deep sense of that tenderness and also that inner urging that beckons you ever beyond where you are. Something that says, "All right, you have come this far, but you must go further." It is both frightening and intriguing, this sensing in you that you can never stop. You can't "stay put" in the life of the Spirit. Thankfully, there has been that golden thread, that sense of wonder and mystery which I wouldn't have called a sense of the Presence when I was a child, and yet it has been that very thing that I have held on to through the ups and downs of my journey.[15]

Notes

1. Dorothy M. Steere, unpublished *Reminiscences and Reflections* (1992), 6.
2. Douglas V. Steere, UNPUBLISHED JOURNAL, 103.
3. Dorothy Steere, *Reminiscences*, 10f.
4. Steere, JOURNAL, 123.
5. Dorothy Steere, *Reminiscences, 16.*
6. Dorothy Steere, *Reminiscences,* 20f.
7. Dorothy Steere, *Reminiscences,* 40.
8. Dorothy Steere, *Reminiscences,* 44-45.
9. Dorothy Steere, *Reminiscences,* 45.
10. Dorothy Steere, *Reminiscences,* 47.
11. Dorothy Steere, *Reminiscences,* 48f.
12. Dorothy Steere, *Reminiscences,* 52.
13. Dorothy Steere, *Reminiscences,* 53.
14. Dorothy Steere, *Reminiscences,* 54.
15. Dorothy Steere, *Reminiscences,* 59.

$\mathcal{VI}$

The Steere Family

*I*n the midst of his busy public life, Douglas Steere's role as father of two energetic daughters put him to the test. You may wonder how this continent-hopping figure could find time for children. Wouldn't all the attention he showered on his global family preclude serious attention to his own? Wouldn't his frequent travels during his daughters' early years throw the burden of child raising onto Dorothy's shoulders and make the girls resent him for missing important moments in their lives? Could anyone involved in so many large, important matters—teaching, speaking, writing, traveling, corresponding, organizing—keep the matter of his children in mind and be genuinely present to his family?

There are ample indications in letters that Douglas experienced moments of serious self-scrutiny about his absenteeism from his family. He tried to make up for frequent and lengthy periods away from home through almost daily correspondence with Dorothy. He also sent frequent letters or cards to Helen and Anne, describing his adventures and often mentioning pets or wild animals he had encountered.

Although he usually went on his travels alone when they were young, occasionally he could take them with him.

DOUGLAS, ANNE, AND DOROTHY WITH KITTEN

Once, for instance, when Anne was ten, he took her on a speaking tour of women's colleges, including Vassar and Holyoke. Helen accompanied him on a part of his European tour in 1948. And when he came home from trips, Dorothy recalls, he adhered to his own principle of being present where he was. He took time to play and share his abundant humor in stories. The Steere family had a wonderful summer home in northern Michigan, which provided maximum opportunity for togetherness on vacations.

The Steere household, however, stretched all of its members. Even in Michigan, visitors brought concerns and engaged the family in searching conversation. The need for new vision and social change on many fronts was made clear. Douglas' lauding of the leaders he admired laid heavy expectations on his daughters' minds.

The "Shadow Side"

Although Douglas had a strong, positive influence on Helen and Anne, his absences, his involvement with what he termed "key people," and his tendency to "call the tune" caused some negative reactions as the girls groped toward their own identities. When Anne did some training in family therapy in her thirties and thought about her relationship to Douglas, she depicted him in a family sculpture striding ahead with Dorothy and Helen running along behind him trying to minister to his needs. She, in the meantime, stood at some distance but would dart in from time to time in front of him "to sort of trip him up or try to get his attention for a second or two."[1]

Both Helen and Anne agree that he was "way too busy," too "driven." Where did his "drivenness" come from? Did it go back to a feeling that he had to justify his existence because he was to blame for the death of his seven-year-old sister Helen? Did he have to prove himself because he had started his academic pilgrimage at an agricultural college? Did he get caught up in public life with such success that he could not easily abandon it? (Although he belittled worldly ambition, he admired achievement and "people of stature.") Was it simply a powerful sense of calling in a terribly needy time? Or was it a little of all of these and many other factors as well? Douglas liked to work, whether physically or mentally. He had tremendous reserves of energy. He idealized good workmanship. Work was often his play.

As the older child who was more exposed to Douglas in his early teaching years, Helen saw him as often intellectually impatient. He thought so fast that he put words in people's mouths when they articulated too slowly for him. His mind was alive with quotations from other thinkers and he often seized center stage. Helen remembers, however, that he once rose and sang fervently in Radnor Meeting the spiritual, "Temper my spirit, O Lord. Keep me long in the fire." His spirituality helped tender these traits over the years.

71

Like many fathers of his generation, Douglas could be a patriarch who demanded compliance with his directives. Anne remembers Douglas as a "benign despot" on their trips to northern Michigan. "He would drive the car, set the pace, decide when we would stop, and ask loudly to our embarrassment if we didn't need to go 'toidy'."[2] He expected his daughters to do "stints" in the evenings, on weekends, and in the summer time to pull their weight and build their character. He defined and scheduled most of these chores. He spent mornings at Mackinaw in his study shed. After lunch, a look at the mail, and a short rest the projects would begin. Besides cutting wood and piling it up for the Norwegian fireplace, they cut birch switches for use in the Steere's Finnish-style sauna and collected rocks for retaining walls. At other times the work was more extensive, such as building the sauna or pouring a slab of concrete for a patio outside the kitchen.

One morning, Douglas roused Helen and Anne from their beds well before breakfast to help him in the cellar, which had a dirt floor. Sticking up in one corner was a huge rock. Douglas had decided that the three of them could dig a large hole, push the rock in and bury it so that, when the cement truck arrived at 9:00 a.m., the rock would be gone and the new concrete floor unbroken. They dug and dug. Dorothy stood at the top of the cellar stairs wringing her hands and crying, "Doug, Doug, they'll strain themselves, and they haven't had any breakfast." Douglas was unmoved. They kept digging until he felt the hole was deep enough. Then they pushed the rock and it fell into the hole. The underside was deeper than he imagined, however, and, as Anne describes it, "a rock alligator remains floating in the sea of concrete in the basement of Watersmeet to this day."

Helen usually obeyed Douglas' directives, but not always. She recalls that once he asked her to stack logs while she was in the midst of reading Jean Stratton Porter's *Girl of the Limberlost*. She said that she would do it herself when she finished the book, but that apparently seemed insubordinate

DOUGLAS AND DOROTHY STEERE WITH DAUGHTERS, HELEN AND ANNE

or undisciplined to Douglas. He called up more than once to the bedroom where she was avidly reading. He then corralled Anne and lit into Helen's chore with Anne "as though," Helen said, "I were a deadbeat who could not be counted on." Helen came down, anxious and with the book unfinished, to find her sister virtuously doing *her* job. Furious at Douglas for forcing the issue, she shoved Anne aside and slammed logs into place. On some level, she thinks he knew such controlling was outrageous. He liked to quote an old Finnish general who regimented his family so like an army that, when anyone was leaving on a journey, he would command, "Time for hugging!" Douglas announced that in jest many times as a departure neared.[3]

Anne remembers asking Douglas questions in connection with her school work and having him send her to "look it up" in the formidable *Encyclopedia Britannica* with its fine onion skin paper. She was always annoyed because she knew he could easily have told her the answer. She did not feel comfortable with Douglas' unrelenting questioning of her as a teenager about her thoughts and experiences, though she recognizes in retrospect that it grew out of his own deep interest and curiosity. Sometimes, over the dishes, he would ask her about her "spiritual life." "I think Daddy had something special in mind," she says, "something where I felt I would surely fall short, and I didn't want him asking me about it."[4] She has avoided such interrogations of others in her own life.

Anne recalls being on a train with Douglas in Germany in 1953 when he did his usual questioning of fellow passengers. He especially queried one young man about the price of bread and butter and the political and religious climate. When Douglas got up to stretch his legs outside the compartment, the young man said to other passengers in the compartment, "Whew! Stats Exam!" (Like a final examination!) Anne is amused that when she told Douglas and Dorothy that she wanted to marry Paul Nash, an Englishman ten years or so her senior, Douglas seemed concerned lest her mind not be free to develop and she be dominated intellectually by this very articulate and intelligent fellow.

Honeymoon accommodations he made for them, however, did lead to one of the few occasions she ever saw Douglas truly contrite. Douglas arranged for them to stay at an inn in Washington's Crossing the first night after their wedding at Radnor Meeting, before going on to Mackinaw. Dorothy and Douglas were off to Africa the next day. When the newlyweds arrived at the inn, they found that their room had twin beds and, since the hotel was full, there were no other options. When Douglas had made a trip to the inn, he looked at a room with a double bed but forgot to mention that it was a wedding night. He assumed Anne and Paul would have the room he had looked at. He was embarrassed when they called and asked what he might have had in mind!

Anne realized as an adult how many souls of all ages Douglas held in his heart. It was her grandfather MacEachron who made her feel especially cherished as a child. When her grandmother sent Anne to her room as a punishment, "Grampie Mac" would sneak up with comic books and bubble gum for her. Anne admits that she sometimes felt like only one of Douglas' many, many children. She consoled herself, however, by reflecting that she and Douglas had only shared a roof for fifteen of his ninety-plus years and that, notwithstanding, she was special to him. Not until she herself had a daughter did she accept fully that it had been okay for her to be a girl. "I grew up thinking I really should have been a boy because Douglas already had a girl," she confesses. But "his delight in his granddaughter matched or even surpassed his delight in his grandson. She was a familiar species."[5]

In reaction to their parents' intense involvement, Helen and Anne both shied away from taking major leadership roles in the Religious Society of Friends. As a teenager Helen said at one point, "I've had enough Quakerism. I'm full of Quakerism." She was also uncomfortable with Douglas' tendency to refer to certain leaders he admired and worked with as the "key people." In her forties, she became an active feminist, perceiving many unsung women to be the ones who held life together. She did serve in executive roles in two local Friends Meetings, teach religious education, and share frequently in vocal ministry. She was plenary speaker at one Yearly Meeting and led a workshop at a Friends General Conference. Anne has participated in Radnor, Montreal, and Wellesley Meetings, but she has never gone to a Yearly Meeting. She has a sense of being in community through her work and friendships and does not value institutional Quakerism to the extent that Douglas and Dorothy did.

Both daughters have observed that their upbringing gave them little grounding in dealing with anger and conflict. Douglas and Dorothy, as newly convinced Friends, were embracing pacifism as a way of life and still evolving in their acceptance of conflict as a healthy part of a relationship. The girls did not often see their parents get angry or show strong differences of opinion in front of them. For all their insight, Douglas and Dorothy were both products of the patriarchal tradition. It took years for this to run its course. In their early marriage, Dorothy did not speak up. She had feared there would be a divorce when her own mother and father got into an argument. She had breathed sighs of relief when her father apologized. Helen started out imitating Dorothy in this. Anne was more feisty. As a teen, she would say, "Don't touch me!" when she did not want Dorothy to scotch her anger. Both girls, however, experienced considerable freedom to work out problems on their own.

Family Funmaker

Helen and Anne, understandably, credit Dorothy and her helpers more than Douglas for their early upbringing. Dorothy was the one who listened. She tended their cuts and bruises. "I don't remember a lot of times alone with Daddy in Haverford," Anne has recounted. "Mother and her sometimes helpers were more memorable. They were the ones who were there when I came home from school."[6] Dorothy was the one who read and said prayers and sang with the girls before bedtime.[7] Because both parents "had so many irons in the fire, so many people to keep track of and so many places to go," Anne adds, "Helen and I often were thrown together to make our own fun."[8]

They do remember, however, that when Douglas came home, he was a good story teller. In Haverford dinner hour was often a time for tales about his day's encounters with interesting people. He enjoyed using different accents or dramatizing their mannerisms. In the summer he would share juicy bits from his reading. Many things tickled his funny bone and livened up the family circle. One time he discovered a how-to book on Zen meditation which gave Westerners directions on how to use thick phone books under their tailbones to help them assume the lotus position. He got the girls down on the floor, propped them up, folded their legs, and then hastened to try, amid much merriment, to achieve this feat for himself.

Douglas was also a high-spirited playmate with whom Helen and Anne could roughhouse and blow

FAMILY FUN
DOROTHY, DOUGLAS AND ANNE

off steam. One of his favorite German expressions was *Spass* ("fun"). He invented "barging," for example. He stood in the middle of the room with its furniture pushed back and let the girls come at him sideways from two directions at once until they banged into him just as hard as they could. He would make loud groans and explosive noises to increase their delight. They would run back to their respective sides and barge into him repeatedly.

"Newspaper whomping" was another of his antidotes for cabin fever or frustration. Lamps and other breakables were pushed back and sections of the *New York Times* were rolled into cudgels by the two girls. All three were blindfolded and then advanced from opposite ends of the room, hitting whatever they bumped into. The girls' goal was to whomp Douglas, who was again in the middle of the floor. Tall and solid and with a rollicking laugh, he seemed impervious to attack, but once more there were cries of anguish and mortal injury. The blind advances and retreats were repeated until the rolled newspapers were in tatters and the room was covered with scraps. The girls claimed, however, that just as they were warming up, Douglas would say, "Stop! Stop! That's enough!"

There were other favorites games such as "Duck on the Rock" near the cottage at Mackinaw and croquet on the front lawn in Haverford. Douglas loved to crack the girls' balls off into the bushes when he managed to target them right. In the winter there was always some skiing together on the Merion Golf Course. Douglas had gotten a taste for that during his vacations from Oxford when he went up into the Alps. He took the girls as teenagers cross-country skiing in northern Sweden and in Canada. Due to her bad back, Dorothy was unable to participate in these outings although she stayed with the family in ski lodges and read or wrote letters. In the spring and the fall, while Dorothy prepared dinner, there were Sunday tramps after Meeting with Douglas on the Woolman Walk which circled the Haverford College campus. Evening walks with the whole family were a tradition in Mackinaw.

When Douglas was teaching psychology, he tried out some of his motivational theories on his daughters. Like many children, they resisted eating certain healthy foods such as spinach and prunes. On the other hand, they enjoyed eating asparagus if they could be uncouth and pick up the stalks with their fingers the way Douglas had learned to eat it in Britain. He, therefore, invented "The Asparagus Gulpers' Club" to which he and the girls would belong. He imaged them as the gusto eaters, but Dorothy as the Club Enemy since she always cut up her asparagus spears and ate them in ladylike bits. Whenever asparagus, or other club foods like spinach or prunes, were served, the three members would sing a club song to the tune of "Columbia, the Gem of the Ocean" and eat the foods with gusto. (" . . . *Oh, cold black prunes forever! Oh, we love cold black prunes!*") They also sang, "*Mama's in the highchair! Who put her up there? Pa, pa, sis boom ba! Asparagus gulpers, rah, rah, rah!*" The highchair was a place of scorn and derision, and the spinach and prunes were gulped down with a blind sense of solidarity that must have filled both Douglas and Dorothy with glee.

To balance this taste for the uncouth, Douglas picked up a cue from Munro Leaf in his humorous 1930s book of admonitions called *Manners Can Be Fun* and created drawings of *Watchbirds* watching his daughters talk with their mouths full, leave dirty socks on the floors of their closets, and other uncivilized behaviors. He was openly delighted when they retaliated with drawings of *Watchbirds* watching *him* leave whiskers in the bathroom sink or bring in company the back way past the smelly cat box which he had failed to empty!

Douglas loved cats, and the Steeres almost always had one. The cats had mostly biblical names: Noah, Nebuchanezzar, Boaz, Sampson, and Delilah. There was also Rufus (because he sat on the roof) and Sextus (because he had six toes on each of his front feet). One summer their cat had kittens enroute to Mackinaw at the MacEachron house in Hudsonville. Douglas had the painful task of disposing of them. He told the girls that he had taken them to the Great Farmer.

Mackinaw

Helen's and Anne's fondest memories of Douglas involve summers spent in Mackinaw in northern Michigan, a favorite family get-away from the late thirties on. As early as 1914, Edward and Ruby Steere had had a summer home in Mackinaw which they called Laffalot. Given Douglas' love for trout fishing in Mill Creek, it is not surprising that, in 1938, he and Dorothy would seek out a site to build their own summer home. Because it was located on the shore at the narrowest point on the Straits of Mackinaw between Lake Michigan and Lake Huron, they called it Watersmeet. Douglas himself enlisted a construction team. An Italian architect friend worked out a plan with all the specifications. A skilled German mason built the all-weather walls out of beautifully colored granite stones found along the shore or on the edges of farmers' fields. From time to time Douglas himself wheeled cement and carried rocks for the mason. He

EDWARD STEERE 1950

learned from this experience how to lay stone and finish cement. Edward Steere, whose cottage was only two miles away, also pitched in to help on his off days from the railway line. The living room featured a corner fireplace with a Norwegian-style hood reaching halfway to the ceiling. The cottage was completed in 1939. It had an outdoor privy, kerosene stove and lamps, and a hand pump in the kitchen for over a decade and, until the 1980s, no telephone. This haven enabled the Steere family to withdraw from the pressures of their extraordinarily active lives and concentrate more on one another. Douglas and Dorothy went there every summer until 1990. They sold the cottage in 1991, when Douglas' Alzheimer's reached an advanced stage.

Family walks were a summer evening tradition in Mackinaw. The Steeres would stroll up the sidewalk which had been built along the rocky shore of the Straits to McGulpin's Point to watch the sunset. Dorothy would often point out wild flowers and identify birds—Indian paintbrush, yellow ladyslippers, sandpipers, cedar waxwings. There was a huge boulder at the point which Douglas dubbed "Paul Bunyan's Shoe Pebble." There were also many flat limestone shards which made good "skipping stones." Douglas and the girls would vie to see who could skip a stone the most times out across the water.

One summer, Douglas borrowed a tent and had an overnight campout at McGulpin's Point with his daughters and their girl friend who lived in a nearby lighthouse. As the girls were finally drifting off to sleep, he crept out of the tent and

DOUGLAS FISHING WITH GRANDCHILDREN

pretended to be a bear crackling in the brush and growling hungrily. They shrieked with delighted terror. Another summer, when Helen was seventeen and Anne fourteen, the whole family went camping to the West coast. Douglas caught a huge mess of fish at Glacier National Park one day. Dorothy remembers trying to fry them on her camp stove with the mosquitoes eating her alive while the rest of the family sat in the car munching trout. She ended up stuffing about half of the fish down gopher holes. On this same trip they encountered real bears at night as they tented near a garbage dump in Yellowstone National Park. Wide awake, Helen clung to Douglas as bears huffed and puffed, scavenging in the dump. Douglas consoled Helen, saying, "They'll be gone tomorrow when we wake up." Helen responded, "If those bears get in our tent, there won't *be* any tomorrow!" Anne slept through it all and was angry at Dorothy for not waking her up.

Occasionally Douglas would take the girls to his favorite Mackinaw fishing stream, Mill Creek, to see a beaver dam or try to sight a fox. There were splendid wildflowers there—tall

MACKINAW COTTAGE 1970

scarlet spikes of cardinal flower, white boneset, rosy Joe Pyeweed. The three of them picked blackberries in the overgrown fields of an abandoned farm nearby, then cut through bracken and birches to the car. The whole family would go blueberrying in the sand dunes above Lake Michigan, often driving the sandy back roads in Douglas' high-slung Model-T Ford, which he had to crank up in the front to start. Douglas taught the girls to belt their lard cans to their stomachs so they could "milk in" the blueberries with both hands just as his father had taught him.

Swimming was another favorite summer activity, although the girls never took to Douglas' urging that they institute a daily morning dip. The Straits were icy, and the times they proved themselves by doing it, they raced back, stripped off their wet suits, rubbed dry, and jumped into Dorothy's big warm bed with her. Dorothy's modesty was shocked by Douglas' habit of taking off his swimming trunks on the back stoop in full view of the public road and toweling off in leisurely fashion before coming indoors. Douglas taught the girls the breast stroke, side stroke, and crawl. He took them biking around Mackinaw Island once each summer. The bike ride included a splendid windy boat ride across the four-mile Strait, a harbor full of expensive yachts to ogle at, carriage horses to pat, a picnic at Arch Rock or Sugar Loaf Rock, and exploration of the old fort or the swank Grand Hotel.

Douglas loved to sing, had a strong melodious bass voice, could harmonize well, and managed to enjoy music even when he could no longer hold a conversation near the end of his life. The two-day trips from Haverford up to northern Michigan and back were occasions for much family singing. Dorothy and Douglas led hymns and University of Michigan songs, and the whole family learned the African-American "spirituals" Douglas picked up at conferences, such as "I've Got Shoes," "We Are Climbing Jacob's Ladder," and "Standing in the Need of Prayer." During the summer, the family often attended a Presbyterian or Methodist church in Mackinaw City since there was no Friends Meeting there. Organists dragging their accompaniment irritated Douglas. His daughters accused him of often belting out hymns to speed them up to a pace he liked. To the mixed delight and embarrassment of the girls, Douglas also led them in singing aboard ship on the way to Europe in 1947. They circled the promenade deck in the wind, singing innumerable verses of a sea chantey honoring "The Cape Cod Boys," who used each part of the cod for some special humorous thing. *Oh, the Cape Cod boys, they have no sleds. Heave-a-ho, heave-a-way! They slide down hill on codfish heads. Oh, we're bound for Australia!*

On Douglas' seventy-fifth birthday, Helen and Anne returned with their husbands for a party at Mackinaw to stage memorable scenes like this from his life, to bake a fish-shaped cake, and to honor his achievements, Helen and David went for a walk in an abandoned orchard the afternoon before the festivities and found a branch laden with rosy summer apples. They broke it off to bring back to the cottage as a symbol of his abundant years. Anne and Paul also went out hiking and, serendipitously, saw a spruce branch heavy with cones which they broke off with the same sense of symbolism. The girls set their branches on windowsills at either end of the cottage living room in joyful celebration. Despite its challenges to them, their overall sense of their father's life was deeply positive.

High Expectations

By his very being, Douglas set high goals for Helen and Anne. Achieving as much as he did and circulating in the company of other achievers, he did not need to make direct suggestions. Those came with the environment. Douglas regularly had philosophy students to the Steere home for seminars. (He admitted that the fellows might have remembered Dorothy's homemade cookies more than the content of their discourse!) The Steere family frequently hosted eminent guests of Haverford College, friends made during world travels, conscientious objectors to the military, spiritual seekers, and local friends engaged in common concerns. People came for afternoon tea, supper, Sunday dinner. Conversation was spirited and leisurely. In the evenings there was often demitasse by the fire. Helen and Anne learned early to set and clear the table for company. Anne remembers moving out of her bed in the middle of the night more than once to accommodate an unexpected guest. "When Helen and I stopped sharing a room and I was given the little back room looking out to the baseball diamond and the oriental dogwood, mine was the preferred guest room. When I awoke in the other twin bed in mother's room, I would vaguely recall going down and up the two little steps on either side of the landing during the night."[9]

Douglas regularly sang the praises of persons he met in his travels, admired, or featured in his classes, persons who gave their lives in selfless service—Albert Schweitzer, Florence Nightingale, Jane Addams, Matilda Wrede. His lauding made its mark on sensitive young minds. At seventeen Helen threw herself into Quaker volunteer "workcamping," plastering and painting the homes of inner city elderly. She was shocked into awareness of her previous insulation from risk and the realities of poverty. Of course, there are many forms of poverty and suffering. Numbers of burdened people found their way to the Steere's home, seeking support and direction. Anne noted wryly that both she and Helen developed a certain attachment to suffering, conscious of how their parents gave special attention to people with problems.

The girls were frequently exposed to Douglas' ministry in Radnor Friends Meeting. In the summer, when they were more often alone as a family, the Steeres made a point of having Bible readings after breakfast with different members taking turns. Douglas also read aloud to the family from such writings as *The Little Plays of St. Francis* by A. E. Houseman and *What Men Live By* by Tolstoy. On board ship enroute to Sweden in 1947 he pulled out a copy of Dorothy Sayers' BBC plays on the life of Jesus, *The Man Born to Be King*. He invited a Broadway actor whom they met to join the family around a table in a small lounge to read the plays aloud in the evenings. Helen wrote that such experiences transmitted "a feeling for invisible dimensions, for leadings, for compassionate encounters and prophetic fire."[10]

As the first child, Helen felt pushed to fulfill some of the ideals the Steere family held dear. She has had an active life of teaching, writing, counseling, and ministry herself. After graduating from Oberlin College, she assisted the director of the American Friends Service Committee's Overseas Workcamp Program in Paris for two years. She then took a master's degree at Radcliffe in teaching English and taught English and history for eight years to college prep students at Germantown Friends School and Francis W. Parker School, among others. She did creative dramatics with ghetto children in Roxbury, Massachusetts, helping in the civil rights movement while teaching in the night school at Boston University. She organized engagements for anti-Vietnam War speakers through the AFSC and accompanied husband David, an engineer and amateur naturalist, to Senegal, where he helped villagers build a rice irrigation system through the Agency for International Development. Helen and David adopted a daughter, Becky, now a registered nurse. Back in Ohio, where they have lived on a working farm since 1971, Helen obtained a Jennings Foundation grant to fund a Community Learning Resources Project to enliven the schools in their underfunded Appalachian county. She taught English for two and a half years in a rural high school, coordinated a program for a local senior center, co-organized the Appalachian Peace and Justice Network, and collected oral histories of women from area mining towns. In her sixties, she has worked as a community counselor after earning a master's degree in this field from Ohio University. A frequent participant in workshops at Pendle Hill, in the last decade she has served as a workshop leader and visiting teacher of autobiographical writing there. Pendle Hill published her own spiritual autobiography as a pamphlet in 1997 under the title, *There Is a Fountain: A Quaker Life in Process.* Helen's poems, stories, and essays appear in *Friends Journal* and *Friendly Woman.*

As the second child, Anne was spared some of the pressure to meet expectations that Helen absorbed. However, being the Steeres' daughter did make her feel under obligation to do well at Westtown Friends School. The hidebound restrictions angered her. Douglas agreed that the strict demands were overbearing. She especially appreciated, therefore, his flouting the deadlines and taking his time to return her to the boarding school after a weekend at home.

Anne, too, has had a fruitful life and career which shows the Steere stamp. Graduating in 1956 from Oberlin College with a major in German, she obtained a master's degree in elementary education from Harvard in 1957. She taught in public schools and as a private tutor. She went on to get an

86

Ed.D. in counseling and school psychology from Boston University in 1974. Since then, she has had a small private practice of psychology, done human relations training, and served as a school psychologist and consultant. Since 1982 she has been the school psychologist at Shady Hill School in Cambridge, Massachusetts. In addition, she has conducted numerous workshops on education and psychology, facilitated trustee retreats for several independent schools, and written articles. A recent one is about "Putting Children First: Why It Is So Difficult These Days."[11] It sounds themes one may find in her father's writings but also calls attention to things his busyness may have caused him to overlook when it came to his own daughters.

Anne took time out of her challenging career to rear two children, Christopher and Jennifer. They are now married with children of their own. Christopher works in real estate development and architecture. Jennifer is a science teacher. In the midst of her own schooling and work, Anne did much to encourage Paul Nash in his career on the faculty of Boston University and at The Rhode Island School of Design and collaborated with him in leading numerous workshops.

Like Helen, Anne has helped look after Douglas and Dorothy during their trials. She has had to cope with and move on from the unexpected death of her husband in 1993. At Douglas' memorial service at Radnor Meeting March 4, 1995 she spoke of her father's "relentless optimism" which "got him places most people would never have even thought of. Things happened for him that wouldn't happen for others because he believed they could." In sum, she said, Douglas "gave me that legacy of energy, optimism, engagement with the world that I cherish."[12] He gave the same to vast numbers of people all over the world.

Notes

1. Anne Steere Nash, Unpublished paper "Life with Father: A Brief Memoir of Being the Younger Daughter of Douglas V. Steere." Except where specifically noted, information in this chapter will have come from this source, Helen Steere Horn's "Memories about Living with Douglas Steere," and personal conversations with Dorothy, Helen, and Anne at various times between 1991 and the present, especially an extended conversation December 21, 1996.
2. Nash, "Life with Father."
3. Helen Steere Horn, "Final Fire," unpublished letter to Douglas.
4. Nash, "Life with Father."
5. Nash, "Life with Father."
6. Nash, "Life with Father."
7. Helen Steere Horn, Unpublished paper "Memories about Living with Douglas Steere."
8. Nash, "Life with Father."
9. Nash, "Life with Father."
10. Helen Steere Horn, "Memories about Living with Douglas Steere."
11. Anne Steere Nash, "Putting Children First," *Children's Lives*, Fall 1993, 39-41.
12. Nash, "Life with Father."

VII

Haverford College

*T*he most fertile imagination could hardly conceive
of finer soil into which Douglas Steere could sink
his roots to nourish a ministry of world scope than
Haverford College, one of the small, rigorous Quaker
schools in the Philadelphia area. He taught there for thirty-
five years, from 1928 until 1963, first as a colleague of Rufus
Jones and then as his successor as chair of the Philosophy
Department.

During his years there Douglas enhanced the reputation
of the school, but Haverford also provided an environment
within which he found affirmation and stimulation of his
remarkable gifts. From the start Douglas felt a strong sense
of commitment to the school and, predictably, turned down
a number of invitations to teach in other schools or to
play other leading roles. In 1929 Vassar and in 1930 the
University of Rochester invited him to join their philosophy
departments. Before the 1935-36 academic year ended
Wilhelm Pauck, a fellow member of the Younger Christian
Thinkers, invited Douglas to join the faculty of the Chicago
Theological Seminary. Nestled in this comfortable and challenging context, however, he did not find it hard to turn down
such invitations. The last, as a matter of fact, convinced him
that he "belonged in a college and not in a permanent

professional post of training people for the pastoral ministry" and the offer "did not search me as the invitation to Pendle Hill had done."[1] He sensed early on that this was where he belonged, and administration and faculty all seemed to have had the same perception. Haverford gave him freedom to fly and he soared.

Douglas' first contacts with Haverford College came through Dr. Henry T. Gillett, the Oxford physician who had commended him to Rufus Jones. Though familiar with the writings of Rufus Jones, Douglas knew nothing of Quakers in the United States or Haverford College. His visit, however, led to an invitation to join the faculty and he quickly consented.

When he returned to the United States in the fall of 1928, he took two weeks in Michigan to get reacquainted with Dorothy and then settled in at Haverford. He found there a college which, he observed, often increased "reverence for truth, a sense of awe and wonder, humanness, and responsibility for others." It was small. There were just 275 male students. In the years ahead it would struggle as first the depression and then World War II hit hard at its resources.[2] Yet Douglas found much to embrace and cherish about it.

Douglas Steere and Rufus Jones

Of first importance was his colleague and mentor in the Philosophy Department and the most distinguished member of the faculty, Rufus Jones. Rufus and Elizabeth Jones and their daughter, Mary Hoxie, having just returned from their summer residence in South China, Maine, gave him a warm welcome. Rufus launched his young colleague's career in a grand way. He introduced Douglas to members of the board and patrons of the college and to the Fullerton Club, a monthly gathering of philosophers in the Philadelphia area. He proposed membership for him in the American Theological Society. More importantly, he arranged visits to a tea room in Bryn Mawr, where they could discuss books and ideas.

90

Although Douglas did not quote Rufus often in his published writings and occasionally took care to distinguish his views from the latter's,[3] the life and thought of Rufus Jones saturated his own. His reaction to news of Rufus's death on June 20, 1948, went beyond mere grief.

> For me it was as if a great piece of the island that had been my life at Haverford had suddenly crumbled into the sea. I could only think of Claude Montefiore's words at the time of von Hügel's death: "Souls like that, one has to have God to account for them." Losing both Dorothy's dear father and Rufus Jones within less than two months, searched me deeply and weighed me down, leaving me aware as I had never been before of just how much I counted on and cared for both men.[4]

Douglas' philosophy and outlook on life germinated in the depths of his own search and were fertilized by his never-ceasing engagement with persons everywhere who shared that search; in Rufus Jones, Douglas found a scholar and saint who embodied and articulated with consummate skill the verities which informed his own life and work. Both held a profoundly personalist philosophy. "The true path [to God]," according to Rufus Jones, "is through personality."[5] Sounding like Dietrich Bonhoeffer a generation later, he urged attention to "a Beyond within ourselves."[6] Both emphasized that God takes initiative in the divine-human relationship. "The reason we can hope to find God is that [God] is here, engaged all the time in finding us," Rufus insisted.[7] In mystical experience God breaks through "like a thrust from beyond . . . like the tides from the Ocean beyond the ocean where we bathe."[8] Both held a high view of human nature and potential. Nothing is truer than that human beings are, by nature, finite-infinite beings and that "some persons at some moments in their lives are carried beyond the usual level of their range of thought and reasoning, and arrive at flashes of truth and insights into the meaning of life and the nature of God, which seem to the recipient like spontaneous gifts of wisdom from above."[9] Both resisted a Kierkegaardian overemphasis on "that solitary individual." "Personality at every stage involves interrelation," Rufus insisted.[10] "There is then no self-realization for any individual who is only a bare individual. [One] can advance toward personality only by being an organic member of a whole."[11] Both insisted on the centrality of Jesus in the Quaker tradition. That the universe is "fundamentally spiritual" has become evident in and through Jesus Christ, history's highest and best revelation of personal life, Rufus said.[12] Divine love is "at the heart of things" and constantly revealed in personal lives and supremely in the life of Jesus, "a concrete person who is divine enough to show love and grace in consummate degree, and human enough to be identified with us, that we can be assured of love at the heart of things."[13] Christ and not Adam is the *head* of the human race.

Rufus and Douglas emphasized experiential, mystical religion which is as available to us through prayer as to the apostles. "The new age cannot *live* on naturalism or on secularism," the former contended. "Life becomes sterile and futile without the depth and power which come from participation in eternal realities."[14] Like Teilhard de Chardin, he located the key to life in improvement of human potential to "see" the Eternal in the midst of time.[15] Science, by itself, is not enough, great though its contributions may be. "Science has not closed, and will never close the soul's east window of divine surprise. We are built for two kinds of worlds—one a space-time world and one a world of spiritual values—and we can be denizens of either world."[16] The heart of the modern tragedy lies in absolutist claims for scientific method. Yet religion must not seal itself off from the discoveries of science; if it is to be vital, it must accept whatever is true. Neither religion nor science must assume that it holds the only acceptable method of knowing. Something is to be gained both by the spectator method of the scientist and the method of vital experience of the mystic. More persons have mystical experiences than many suppose, for most religious persons possess an "undeveloped and uncultivated form of mystical consciousness."[17] Both Douglas and Rufus found in John Woolman the practical justification for their contemplative activism, citing the same passage in Woolman's *Journal:* "To turn all we possess into the channel of universal love becomes the business of our lives."[18] Both considered prayer the central thing in religion, and believed that it could reach beyond the person who prayed and, reaching out by divine telepathy, could "work extraordinary effects in the lives of others."[19] Prayer is natural to human beings. "The human heart is sensitive to God as the retina is to light waves," Rufus wrote. "The soul possesses a native yearning for intercourse and companionship which takes it to God as naturally as the homing instinct of the pigeon takes it to the place of its birth."[20] Both believed that prayer has power extending even to nature. Rufus wrote:

> Prayer releases energy as certainly as the closing of an electric circuit does. It heightens all human capacities. It refreshes and quickens life. It unlocks reservoirs of power. It opens invisible doors into new storehouses of spiritual force for the person to live by, and, as I believe, for others to live by as well. It is effective and operative as surely as are the forces of steam or gravitation.[21]

Both emphasized the importance of corporate prayer or worship and remained steadfast in their appreciation for the silent Meeting.

On a more personal level these two men shared a gift for inspiring others and challenging them to give an account of the hope that was in them. Rufus reminded his readers that we today have an advantage over the first apostles in "the luminous trail of saints whom Christ has made" and centuries of Christian victories over the world.[22] He urged people to fuse the contemplative and the active lives. "There are deeps in us all far below our ideas," he insisted. Sometimes the walls between visible and invisible "grow thin and almost vanish away" and we feel we are in contact with more than ourselves.[23] We must not conform ourselves to the environment, as Herbert Spencer urged, but conform the environment to what it ought to be.

Caring and Creative Teacher

Students and colleagues of Douglas Steere testify to his gifts as a teacher. Students and alumni often turned to Douglas for personal as well as academic counsel.[24] As the years passed and Douglas rose to international stature, students stood in some awe of him. Richard Norris, later a Rhodes Scholar himself and Professor of Church History at Union Theological Seminary in New York, who took several classes with him, found Douglas "larger than life." Arthur C. Kelsey, a student at General Theological Seminary in New York, taking a course in Classics of Christian Devotion with Douglas at Union Theological Seminary, wrote "that the privilege of considering with you the records (as Miles Yates says) of 'what great souls have been like' and 'what they have disclosed about our relation with God', has been a walking with one who walks with them, which is more than merely an academic matter."[25] Douglas obviously influenced some students deeply. Charles Thorne, responding to an announcement of Douglas' retirement, remembered both personal and academic dimensions of his teaching. "The courses I had with you, and the teas in your home are most vivid in my mind," he wrote. "What is more, the example of your personal life, as a scholar, teacher, and man of God has been such an inspiration to me."[26] Alice Marsh expressed dismay when she learned that Douglas' Haverford days were over. He had, she judged, "most faithfully and loyally, carried on the traditions which Rufus Jones started, adding the strength of your own personality to his."[27]

Douglas himself, however, did not try to keep students floating always on an ethereal plane. His daughter Helen recalls that he developed a custom of taking his senior philosophy majors out to dinner at Bookbinders Restaurant shortly before graduation. Bookbinders was a famous old seafood place on the Philadelphia riverfront. As a sort of rite of passage, he expected everyone to eat a lobster, smoke a black cigar, talk philosophical theory, and not throw up. Since he never smoked except on these occasions, this must have been a challenge for his stomach as well, but he always seemed to survive it. He would report to the family with devilish glee afterwards about who had "looked a little green around the gills."[28]

Douglas taught a wide variety of courses, taking advantage of Haverford's encouragement to plough new ground, but one can see throughout a preference for the personal. In his first semester he scheduled a philosophy seminar around Meister Eckhart with Rufus Jones interpreting texts. He taught a course on Kant and another on modern philosophy from Cusa to Kant. In addition, Rufus Jones asked him to lift from him the burden of teaching psychology. Douglas enjoyed this subject. He offered a small course in abnormal psychology in which students read Freud, Jung, Adler, and Kunkel. He continued to teach all of the psychology courses offered at Haverford until 1934, when he succeeded Rufus Jones as head of the philosophy department. He then turned elementary psychology over to Elton Trueblood, who had joined the Haverford faculty in 1933. Ten years later, Haverford established a department of psychology.

Following his sabbatical in 1933-34 and now chairman of the department of philosophy, Douglas split the teaching load with Elton Trueblood. Douglas' share included the history of modern philosophy, ethics, nineteenth-century thinkers, abnormal psychology, plus a senior philosophy seminar one semester each year (Kant in 1933, Aquinas in 1934, and Dante in 1935). In addition, strongly inclined toward cultivation of the inner life, he replaced Rufus Jones's "History of Christian Thought" with "Classics in Christian Literature," a course inspired by one Dean Willard Sperry had offered seniors at Harvard Divinity School. Douglas varied the selections each year, but those which appeared frequently were Augustine's *Confessions,* the *Rule* of Benedict, Bernard of Clairvaux's *On Consideration, The Little Flowers of St. Francis, The Imitation of Christ,* Francis de Sales' *Introduction to the Devout Life,* Pascal's *Pensées,* John Woolman's *Journal,* Newman's *Apologia,* Tolstoy's *Twenty-three Tales,* Evelyn Underhill's *Letters,* Bernanos's *Diary of a Country Priest,* and Charles Williams's *Descent into Hell.* A decade later, Douglas described the course in a volume entitled *The Vitality of the Christian Tradition* edited by his friend George F. Thomas.[29] This essay encouraged others to follow in Douglas' footsteps. In 1953 the enrollment in this course swelled to such an extent that Douglas had to break it into two sections for discussion.

By 1939-40 Douglas' teaching focused principally on modern philosophy from Nicholas of Cusa to Henri Bergson. He took the second half of the basic history of philosophy course and carried it through Kant, who always received a lion's share of attention. He followed this with a semester elective on the nineteenth century, spending a month each on Schopenhauer's *World as Will and Idea,* Nietzsche's *Beyond Good and Evil* and *Thus Spake Zarathustra,* Bergson's *Introduction to Metaphysics* and *Two Sources of Morality,* and Tolstoi's *What I Believe, Twenty-Three Tales,* and *Resurrection.* He continued to teach abnormal psychology. He and Thomas Kelly, who had joined the department in 1936 following the departure of Elton Trueblood, alternated in leading the senior seminar, Kelly conducting it the first semester and Steere the second but with both in attendance. Offerings varied from year to year, featuring the ancients such as Plato,

Aristotle, and Plotinus or modern greats such as White-head, Berdyaev, Von Hügel, Kierkegaard, Buber, Dewey, or William James.

In the fall of 1943, President Felix Morley asked Douglas to direct Haverford College's Relief and Reconstruction Training program, preparing graduate students to help oversees after World War II. When Haverford launched a Social and Technical Assistance program in the fall of 1951, Douglas declined to direct it, but he served on the administrative committee and offered his course on social reformers. Following a trip to Lambarene to visit Albert Schweitzer in 1953, he relinquished courses in abnormal psychology and political philosophy to newly-appointed colleagues in order to give attention to motivational courses for the Social and Technical Assistance graduate program as well as teach courses in modern philosophy. He also conducted a seminar session for the Crown Prince of Japan in cooperation with the latter's Quaker tutor, Elizabeth Grey Vining.

Douglas Steere never let himself get caught in a rut with his teaching. As he read, wrote, and engaged dozens of scholars and religious leaders, the horizon of his ministry expanded. He fed his experiences into courses which could challenge students. Obviously, in line with his own philosophy, the personal always held the spotlight. In 1949-50 he prepared a new course on "Some Aspects of Religious Life and Literature since the Reformation" to alternate with his Classics course. Topics included: Luther and German Protestantism, Thomas More and the Erasmian Tradition in England, Teresa of Avilà and Spanish Mysticism, Lancelot Andrewes and Seventeenth Century Anglican Piety, Isaac Penington and the Corporate Mysticism of the Quakers, John Wesley and the Evangelical Revival, John Frederick Oberlin and the Rural Apostolate, John Henry Newman and the Oxford Movement, Albert Schweitzer as a Critic of Contemporary Civilization, William Temple and the Ecumenical Movement, Evelyn Underhill and the Life of the Spirit and the Life of Today, and Rufus Jones and the Religious Situation of Our Time. Douglas taught two new courses in the fall of 1958 and spring of 1959, one in philosophy and the other in African studies.

Mutual Benefactors

Douglas' long cherished friend from Oxford days, A. Burns Chalmers, commented perceptively on the occasion of Douglas' retirement in 1963: "You (Douglas and Dorothy) have both given so *very* much to Haverford through the years. Haverford is known to countless people mainly through you. It is astounding what you have done and I hope Haverford has told you so in deep and reflective accents, even though your province has been so much wider."[30] None did more than Douglas Steere to bring this small school to the attention of people around the world, and the college did indeed respond.

Douglas' gift for reaching out and making contact with religious leaders and scholars proved immensely beneficial to the college. Like Rufus Jones before him, Douglas attracted to his department and to the college, as well as to Pendle Hill, persons of national and international reputation who could inspire and instruct a whole generation of eager students. During his absence from Haverford in the fall of 1950-51, Douglas got William E. Hocking, recently retired from Harvard, as a substitute who would share his presence with the community. To help him in his motivational course for the Technical Assistance program, Douglas brought Charles Malik, Lebanese Ambassador to the United Nations; Sir Zafrilla Kahn, a distinguished Muslim from Pakistan; and Daisetz Suzuki, a professor at Columbia University and a leading authority on Buddhism, to speak to the class. Thanks to Douglas, Haverford's lecturers in 1951-52 included Paul Tillich, Martin Buber, and Mark Van Doren. In 1953-54 Daisetz Suzuki and Dorothy Day, creator and leader of the Catholic Worker also lectured.

Douglas also played a major role in securing financial help for a small school which often dreamed big dreams but had limited resources. He played a key role in securing a Ford Foundation Grant for Haverford's Social and Technical Assistance Program which sent Haverford students to Gold Coast, where they assisted in the Department of Social Welfare.[31] Although many persons rallied to other projects and programs Douglas worked with, some, both in the United States and elsewhere, specifically focused on Haverford College.[32] In December 1954, for instance, William H. Danforth, a long time friend and, through Purina Mills, a major supporter of the relief effort in Finland, sent Douglas a $5,000 check made out to Haverford College "definitely to be earmarked for the personal distribution by you for worthy campus needs."[33] Danforth paid Douglas' salary for five semesters between 1950 and 1960, enabling the college to employ someone to fill in as he pursued his global ministry.[34]

Presidents of Haverford College quickly recognized Douglas' immense value to the school. Just two years after he joined the faculty he was promoted to Associate Professor and given a five-year contract, as he declined invitations from Vassar and the University of Rochester. Anticipating the retirement of Rufus Jones at age seventy in 1934, the college arranged an early sabbatical for Douglas so that he could succeed Rufus as chair of the department of philosophy and added Elton Trueblood to the faculty. In 1940 he was promoted to full professor. January 20, 1950, he received word of his appointment as T. Wistar Brown Professor of Philosophy.

The immense breadth of his involvement in lecturing, teaching, writing, ministering to Quakers around the world notwithstanding, Douglas Steere played a role in steering Haverford College through the challenging years of his tenure there. Douglas was among faculty members interviewed regarding a successor for William Comfort when he announced his retirement in 1939. A year before, Douglas had recommended to Comfort that Haverford ask Felix Morley, an alumnus and Rhodes scholar, then editor of the *Washington Post,* to deliver Haverford's commencement address. The address evidently raised the profile of Morley, for the trustees chose him as the next president. When Morley resigned in June of 1945 after shepherding the school through the difficult war years with their drain on enrollment, Archibald MacIntosh served as Acting President for one year (1945-46) until the election of Gilbert White, a geographer who had served in Harold Ickes's Department of the Interior during the war, then as Associate Secretary of the AFSC. During his nine years as President of Haverford College, White turned often to Douglas for counsel,[35] and supported Douglas in his world ministry on behalf of the American Friends Service Committee. As White's departure from Haverford to return to teach at the University of Chicago in 1956 came as a hard blow to Douglas, so too did the prospect of Douglas' retirement from Haverford strike Gilbert White. In January 1963 he confessed that he was unable to adjust to the prospect of Douglas' retirement and hoped he would keep a Haverford base. Fittingly, on the fifteenth anniversary of his retirement, Haverford asked Douglas to deliver the commencement address.[36]

Sabbaticant and Quaker Minister

Worthy of special mention is the encouragement Haverford gave Douglas to hone his academic tools by granting frequent leaves to broaden his contacts with thinkers around the world. In the summer of 1930 he completed his Ph.D. thesis during a visit to Europe and submitted it for the degree in the fall. The first sabbatical signaled the direction in which his career would head and at the same time plunged him more and more deeply into Quaker ministry around the world. Later sabbaticals blended increasingly into Douglas' burgeoning world leadership in the Religious Society of Friends.

Many of Douglas' activities during his first sabbatical—his retreat at Maria Laach, his ministering to the family of Richard Cary, his visit with Karl Barth, contacts to assist in his translation of Kierkegaard, meetings with Karl Heim and Karl Adam at Tübingen, visits to the Waldorf School at Stuttgart, and more extended encounters with Nicholai Hartmann, Fritz Kunkel, and Romano Guardini in Berlin—have already been noted in Chapter 4. Concern for Quakers, however, also prompted him to travel about. Following Dorothy's arrival in Berlin in February 1934, the Steeres responded to a plea from Emma Cadbury to hasten to Vienna. Forfeiting plans for a trip to Italy and Greece, they spent six days, March 23-29. They advised the American Friends Service Committee in its work of distributing relief funds to the families of 8,000 outlawed Socialist workers in Vienna and other industrial centers in Austria whom the government had oppressed. In the midst of this effort, they experienced a baptism of fire, for they were arrested and had their passports confiscated. Both, however, welcomed it. "Dorothy and I were new to Quaker field work abroad and this experience in Vienna was a baptism that we have always been thankful for," Douglas remarked years later.[37]

Leaving Vienna, they visited the Neuhof Bruderhof, an intentional community near Fulda, and conversed with Eberhard Arnold, the founder. From thence they went to Copenhagen for a six-week stay with Quakers Rejnar and Deborah Halfdan-Nielsen, where Douglas enlisted Henni Forchammer, author of the grammar he had used to learn Danish, to further sharpen his Danish. By the time they returned to Haverford in mid-September Douglas had "nearly finished" his translation of Kierkegaard's *Purity of Heart*.[38] Surprisingly, he had trouble finding a publisher, having to circulate it for three years despite strong support from Reinhold Niebuhr. Eugene Exman at Harpers finally took a risk with it when Harpers learned that a British publisher had issued a translation by two British scholars under the title

Purify Your Hearts. The translation has remained in print almost sixty years.

Subsequent sabbaticals fed much more directly into the stream of service among Quakers around the world. His second sabbatical, planned for 1940-41, was cut in half by the unexpected death of his colleague Thomas Kelly on January 17, 1941. Douglas managed to carry out only the first part, a risky visit to Germany and the Scandinavian countries on behalf of the American Friends Service Committee, as war already darkened the European horizon.

The next sabbatical followed an exhausting two years at the helm of the Finnish Relief project at the end of World War II. This time, Douglas directly forged a link with the American Friends Service Committee. As his sabbatical for 1947-48 approached, he worked out an agreement with the AFSC to give a half year to visits in Scandinavia and Germany and then repeat this plan in 1950, the AFSC picking up his salary and benefits during the semester he would be away from Haverford. Gilbert White gave Haverford's approval. As it turned out, this set a pattern throughout the 1950s.

Following a stint at Union Theological Seminary in New York in the summer of 1947, the Steeres set out in August for Sweden and from Sweden to Finland to examine again the results of the Quaker relief effort. Dorothy got Helen and Anne settled in at the Viggbyholm School in Sweden and then joined Douglas at Helsinki. Thence they proceeded to Germany, where Douglas renewed acquaintances with Friends he had known in earlier visits. Typically, Douglas sought out significant people on the way: in Berlin Emil Fuchs, a Quaker with strong socialist leanings; in Heidelberg Hans von Campenhausen, a Lutheran church historian, and Karl Jaspers, one of the architects of modern existentialism; in Bad Boll Eberhard Müller at the Evangelical Academy; in Tübingen Romano Guardini, Karl Heim, Helmut Thielicke, popular Reformed theologian, Heinz Horst Schrey, Lutheran ethicist, and several Catholic scholars: Philip Dessauer, an

Oratorian; Arnold Schoeningh, editor of *Hochland,* "the most distinguished Roman Catholic publication in Germany"; Max Pribilla, a Jesuit and editor of *Stimmen der Zeit;* Willfred Braunmueller, a Benedictine; August Rösch, also a Jesuit and head of the Roman Catholic Caritas; Manfred Hohhammer, a Capuchin and leader in Pax Christi; Joseph Bernhardt, a scholar of mysticism; Ernst Wiechert, a novelist; Joachim Jaenicke, a former student of Douglas; and Karl von Müller, a historian.

By terms of the agreement regarding their stay, Douglas had to return to Berlin every thirty days to share insights with the Religious Affairs branch of the High Commission on Germany while Dorothy remained in Frankfurt. Besides meeting Berlin Friends, many of whom came from the eastern zone under difficult conditions, he lectured to a large group of professors and students at a full-dress dinner at Harnack House. He and Professor Holborn of Yale toured German universities in the western zone and made proposals to revive them. From Berlin he and Dorothy united in Kassel to visit groups of Friends; in Marburg they met Carl and Eva Hermann. Ernst Benz, a distinguished church historian, invited Douglas to lecture to about 150 to 200 students and faculty on Quakerism. Douglas also visited with Friedrich Heiler, author of the classic study of *Prayer* and an active member of Una Sancta. In Frankfurt Douglas carried on a conversation about the renewal of society, perhaps along lines of Third Order Franciscans, and exchanged books with Walter Dirks, a liberal Catholic political thinker who had offered active opposition to National Socialism during the Weimar Republic. In Freiburg he lectured to some 300 members of the university community on the spiritual situation in Europe and the need to return to "responsible inwardly-guided decisions," person-to-person contacts, and "from this to a new kind of personally-charged community."[39] He also contacted Lutheran church historian Gerhard Ritter. At Hintergarten he visited Georg Picht, head of Birkelhof

School, and drove to Todtnauberg to meet Martin Heidegger. Although Henry Cadbury asked Douglas and Dorothy to join him in representing the American and British Quaker service organizations as they received the Nobel prize, they had to decline.

The whirlwind of visits continued. At times both Douglas and Dorothy must have wondered whether they could keep up such a pace. Each time, however, they found a rationale that kept them going. As Douglas commented in his personal journal: "This is a strenuous life we are leading, but this interpretation work is so badly needed in order that our Quaker work can be seen in its true perspective and not as just another social agency, another *Winter-Hilfe* as in the Nazi time."[40]

While Dorothy stopped to catch her breath in Frankfurt, Douglas went to Coblenz and Maria Laach and visited the Pallatine Monastery. Back in Berlin together, Douglas reported to the High Commission on Germany, whose director asked him to join the staff; had long visits with Berlin Friends; and took part in a Fellowship of Reconciliation gathering which assembled there at that time, meeting peacemakers with whom they would work in years to come—Pastor Mensching, Asta Brügelman, Siegmund Schulze, Margarethe Lachmund, and Percy Bartlett, Vice-Chairman of the British Friends Service Council. From Berlin the Steeres journeyed to Braunschweig and Hannover. In the latter they met Katherine Petersen, head of the Quaker School at Ommen in the Netherlands, who was in charge of all elementary schools in lower Saxony, and Hans Lilje, Bishop of Hannover. After spending a few days in the Quaker center at Bad Pyrmont they returned to Freiburg to visit again with Martin Heidegger and Reinhold Schneider, with whom they conversed about prayer and what it meant at that time. Meantime, Ruth Oechslin, a Quaker jurist, asked Douglas to speak to Nazis interned near Bad Boll awaiting trial. The five hundred who attended heard him reiterate the Quaker conviction of the dignity of each human being. The next day, the Steeres called on Ida Görres, who came to lecture to the same group on Charles Peguy.

Throughout their service to the AFSC the Steeres mixed Quaker and other visits. They dropped in on Otto and Hanna Frick, Friends trying to live and act according to the model offered by John Woolman, in Karlsruhe; spent a day in Frankfurt with the AFSC staff; then visited Maria Schlüter-Hermkes in Rhonsdorf. They spent some time with Father Welty at the Dominican convent at Wallbersberg, near Cologne, then met a Quaker group at Wuppertal, including Nicholas Ehlen, who had helped workers build houses during the depression. In the Luneberger Heide they stopped to see Bertha Scharf, a Quaker nurse and saint, who at almost eighty set up a children's home. In Hamburg they met Brother Douglas, an Anglican Franciscan who cared for badly wounded veterans in a bombed-out shell of an apartment house. After a brief reportorial trip to Berlin, his fourth and last, Douglas returned to Hamburg to witness the arrival of "a Quaker miracle," sixteen truck loads of food for the people of Hamburg assembled by Quakers in Norway, which had been occupied by Germany during World War II.

Just before Christmas Douglas and Dorothy returned to Copenhagen. There Douglas spoke at the new Folk High School patterned after Pendle Hill and agonized with Swedish Quakers about whether to continue plans of the late Per Sundberg to bring twenty Germans for a month of rest and visits with westerners.

Sabbatical time finally came in the second half of the year. The Steeres moved to the Sigtuna Foundation to spend the next four months. Douglas settled in to write two books he hoped to complete: *Doors into Life,* an introduction to five devotional classics, and *Time to Spare,* an introduction to the method Douglas used for weekend retreats he had conducted for business and professional persons.[41] Nevertheless, the Quaker connection was always close at hand. Both Douglas and Dorothy worked with the Per Sundberg project, which took place at Viggbyholm the week before Easter. Douglas was convinced that this gathering had a major impact on what the Steeres did in subsequent visits to Europe, "for many of the things we were able to do in the years of almost annual visitation to Germany for the following decade were immeasurably assisted by the good offices of friends we made in that moving week we spent together."[42]

In May 1948, on receiving word of her father's death, Dorothy had to return to the United States. At this time sixteen-year-old Helen was with Douglas. They journeyed down the western corridor of Germany through Switzerland and France to England. The AFSC had granted maximum freedom for them to travel as they chose. En route Douglas and Helen visited again many of those with whom Douglas had established ties on his earlier journeys. The pattern of stops reveals Douglas' interlocking concerns—Quakers, spirituality, philosophy, and peacemaking. Notable especially were visits to André Trocmé's Protestant Lycee at Le Chambon; Taizé, the Reformed monastery; Glasgow, where George Macleod led them in a tour of workers projects sponsored by the Iona Community Movement; and Cambridge, where they had lunch with Canon Charles Raven, a pacifist, who was then Vice-Chancellor of the University and Master of Christ's College. They also contacted Herbert Farmer, who had taught at Pendle Hill in the summer of 1932. At York they sought the site where John Woolman was buried in the old Meetinghouse Burial grounds. In retrospect, Douglas commented, "Helen and I stayed a long time at this spot and felt the life and the spirit of J.W. calling on the Society to raise up a company of men and women who would live in his spirit and dedication."[43] He returned to New York with Helen and Anne on the Swedish-built oceanliner "Stockholm" and rejoined Dorothy in Hudsonville, Michigan, at the MacEachron's.

Many institutions would consider Douglas' bi-annual leaves to tramp all over the world on behalf of the AFSC as adequate substitutes for sabbaticals. Haverford College did not. It

granted Douglas a full sabbatical in 1954-55, during
which he again devoted
most of his energies to AFSC
concerns, this time in South
Africa. A crushing travel
schedule notwithstanding,
he managed to prepare the
Swarthmore Lecture under
the title "Where Words
Come From," which be-
came in the United States
the classic *On Listening to
Another.* He commented
years afterwards: "I doubt
if any book I have written
has been more useful

DOUGLAS AT CAMP MINNEWANCA

both within and outside the Society of Friends than *On
Listening to Another.* "[44] The Steeres returned to Haverford just
in time for commencement on June 3 and to speak on Quaker
Projects in Africa at Pendle Hill on June 5, 1955. During a
summer's "hibernation" at Mackinaw, Douglas read widely,
prepared an anthology of Thomas Kelly's writings for a pamphlet published by the Upper Room, wrote five lectures for
the Danforth Fellows meeting at Camp Minnewanca in mid-
September, and rewrote the Rauschenbusch lectures he had
given in 1952 on *Work and Contemplation.*[45]

In 1961-62, during what would have been his final
sabbatical at Haverford, Douglas taught at Union Theological Seminary in New York

.

Complications in Vocations

This extraordinarily gifted person discharged more than one
vocation. He was by choice, abilities, and deep sense of
calling a teacher committed to a college which cherished him

107

and valued him for his scholarship and teaching while freeing him for other roles. Soon after he came to the Haverford philosophy department, however, he found himself thrust into a role of leadership in the Religious Society of Friends even before he and Dorothy joined the Society in the spring of 1932. And that role grew and grew: Pendle Hill, the John Woolman Memorial, visits among Friends in Germany and the Scandinavian countries in 1937 and 1940-41, preparation for relief and rehabilitation after World War II, organization of a relief effort for war-torn Finland in 1945-46, visitations on behalf of the American Friends Service Committee every other year from 1950-60, attendance as an official Observer Delegate at three of the four sessions of the Second Vatican Council (1963-65), and President of the Friends World Committee for Consultation (1964-70). At the same time Douglas Steere kept an incredibly heavy schedule of lectures, retreats, teaching assignments, and other roles of leadership around the world.

Douglas felt often the strong pull toward leadership in the Religious Society of Friends independent of Haverford College. As Dorothy joined him in Berlin in February 1934, he found himself "searched" by an invitation to become the Director of Pendle Hill, a matter on which he did not reach a final decision until he and Dorothy returned to the United States in the fall. He loved Pendle Hill and "felt that it had a very special role to play in deepening the life of the Society of Friends at just this point in Quaker history."[46] Nevertheless, he also felt that teaching was his vocation and declined the invitation to be director. He was attached to Haverford, had not yet published anything, and had agreed to shoulder the load laid down by Rufus Jones. At the same time he did not want to keep this fledgling Pendle Hill experiment from flying. He and Dorothy put themselves at Dean Joseph Platt's disposal.

Douglas himself became increasingly sensitive to the position in which his frequent absences placed Haverford College. He wondered out loud in a letter to Robert Yarnall,

108

Director of the AFSC, in 1953 whether he should take the AFSC job which required traveling six months out of every twenty-four. He chaired the John Woolman Memorial and the American section of the International Fellowship of Reconciliation, was heavily committed to Pendle Hill, and needed to write more.[47] During his extended ongoing missions for the AFSC, he secured funding for his salary and adequate stand-ins—William Ernest Hocking in the fall of 1950, André Trocmé in the spring of 1953, Paul Ricoeur in the fall of 1954. He left the reins in the hands of department colleagues but kept in as close touch as his travels permitted. Teaching at Union Theological Seminary in New York as Harry Emerson Fosdick Visiting Professor for 1960-61, he persuaded Frank Parker to stay at Haverford rather than take a similar position at Washington and Lee, offering to relinquish the chair of the department to him. Parker, however, declined, assuring him that he had no desire to chair the department as long as Douglas would remain at Haverford.[48] As acting chairman in this period, Parker consulted Douglas about promotion from assistant to associate professor and tenure for Paul Desjardins,[49] and Douglas wrote a letter in support of both. Indicative of Douglas' pastoral ministry to colleagues, Desjardins wrote him about personal matters.[50] Parker also sought Douglas' counsel regarding the appointment of a fourth professor,[51] whom Douglas welcomed into the department in a subsequent letter,[52] and about a substitute for Desjardins during a leave.[53] Douglas later sent a list of comprehensive exam questions and asked to see the papers May 23-24, 1962.[54] Douglas also wrote letters in support of Parker's application for a Guggenheim and other fellowships. In the academic year 1962-63, he kept Parker informed about departmental matters during Parker's sabbatical in Athens.[55]

Douglas Steere remained attentive to detail until he retired from Haverford College in 1963. The call of the larger Quaker fellowship and of the church universal, however, sounded ever more urgently as one of the most momentous happenings in the history of Christianity exploded on the world scene, the election of Angelo Roncalli as Pope John XXIII and his decision to convene a council which has changed forever not only the Catholic Church but the very face of Christendom. It did not take long for Douglas Steere, and other Quakers who looked to him for leadership, to realize that the Council was a happening in which he needed to speak for his tradition. None was better equipped than he, either by gifts or wisdom or experience, to do exactly that. Haverford College had helped to prepare him for such a time.

Notes

1. Douglas V. Steere, UNPUBLISHED JOURNAL, 185.
2. May 24, 1946 Douglas reported in a letter to Nancy Cunningham that Haverford had almost 300 undergraduates and prospects of 400 to 450 by fall. During World War II, however, Felix Morley had struggled to maintain faculty and staff as enrollment dropped steeply with drafting of all males eighteen or older. In spite of the college's dire financial straits Morley refused to take on ordinary military units, but he did finally agree to set up units for instruction in the weather sciences and in post-war government of captured territories. Steere, JOURNAL, 367.
3. See Chapter XIII, n. 51. Jones leaned more toward idealism than toward the realism which Douglas adopted.
4. Steere, JOURNAL, 509f.
5. Rufus Jones, *Social Law in the Spiritual World. Studies in Human and Divine Inter-Relationship* (Philadelphia: J.C. Winston Co., 1904), 44.
6. Rufus Jones, *Pathways to the Reality of God* (New York: Macmillan Co., 1931), 199.
7. Jones, *Pathways*, xi.
8. Rufus Jones, *Spirit in Man* (Stanford, CA: Stanford University Press, 1941), 58.

9. Jones, *Pathways*, 149.
10. Jones, *Social Law*, 58.
11. Jones, *Social Law*, 76-77.
12. Rufus Jones, *The Inner Life* (New York: Macmillan Co., 1916), 178.
13. Jones, *Pathways*, 144.
14. Rufus Jones, *A Preface to Christian Faith in a New Age* (New York: Macmillan Co., 1932), 42.
15. Rufus Jones, *New Eyes for Invisibles* (New York: Macmillan Co., 1943), 12-14.
16. Jones, *A Preface*, 55-56.
17. Jones, *The Inner Life*, 178.
18. Jones, *New Eyes*, 183.
19. Rufus Jones, *A Call to What Is Vital* (New York: Macmillan Co., 1948), 138.
20. Jones, *A Call*, 139.
21. Rufus Jones, *The World Within* (New York: Macmillan Co., 1918), 102.
22. Rufus Jones, *The Luminous Trail* (New York: Macmillan Co., 1947), vi.
23. Jones, *New Eyes*, 59, 61.
24. Howard L. Schambelam, for instance, in a letter dated December 12, 1961, reported to Douglas the shock of transition from Haverford to Harvard Law School and confessed uncertainty whether law was his calling. Arthur C. Kelsey consulted Douglas several times regarding his dissertation at General Theological Seminary in New York.
25. Arthur C. Kelsey, *Letter to Douglas V. Steere*, January 21, 1962.
26. Charles Thorne, *Letter to Douglas V. Steere*, March 12, 1963.
27. Alice R. Marsh, *Letter to Douglas V. Steere*, May 11, 1963.
28. Helen Steere Horn, "Memories about Living with Douglas Steere." I have incorporated her written account with only minor modifications.
29. Douglas V. Steere, "The Devotional Literature of Christianity," in *The Vitality of the Christian Tradition*, ed. George F. Thomas (New York & London: Harper & Bros., Publishers, 1945), 185-203.
30. A. Burns Chalmers, *Letter to Douglas V. Steere*, June 24, 1963.
31. Douglas V. Steere, *Letter to Robert Gardiner, Director, Department of Social Welfare, Gold Coast*, June 15, 1954.
32. Douglas, for example, in a letter dated June 7, 1954, thanked Marlis Gildemeister, a Swiss Quaker, for her generous gift to Haverford.
33. William H. Danforth, *Letter to Douglas V. Steere*, December 9, 1954.
34. Steere, JOURNAL, 736.
35. During Douglas' absences, White tried to keep him informed about the college. He corresponded regarding an invitation to Lewis Mumford and Gabriel Marcel to lecture at Haverford

111

(March 20, 1952; May 18, 1952). He reported on salary increases for 1953-54 (May 22, 1953) and the general state of the school (June 20, 1953). He informed Douglas of an anticipated visit by the Crown Prince of Japan (June 23, 1953) and thanked him for changing his schedule to return and teach a seminar for the Crown Prince (July 10, 1953).

36. Published as a pamphlet entitled *Reflections* (Philadelphia: Wider Quaker Fellowship, 1978).
37. Steere, JOURNAL, 171.
38. Steere, JOURNAL, 177.
39. Steere, JOURNAL, 441.
40. Steere, JOURNAL, 441.
41. Douglas V. Steere, *Doors into Life through Five Devotional Classics* (New York: Harper & Bros., 1948); *Time to Spare* (New York: Harper & Bros., 1948). Douglas' approach to retreats will be discussed in Chapter 15.
42. Steere, JOURNAL, 477.
43. Steere, JOURNAL, 494.
44. Steere, JOURNAL, 724.
45. Douglas V. Steere, *Work and Contemplation* (New York: Harper & Bros., 1947).
46. Steere, JOURNAL, 168.
47. Douglas V. Steere, *Letter to Robert Yarnall,* November 4, 1953.
48. Frank Parker, *Letter to Douglas V. Steere,* May 10, 1961.
49. Frank Parker, *Letter to Douglas V. Steere,* May 10, December 9, 1961.
50. Paul Desjardins, *Letter to Douglas V. Steere,* July 15, 1962.
51. Frank Parker, *Letter to Douglas V. Steere,* February 18, February 20, 1962.
52. Douglas V. Steere, *Letter to Aryeh Kosman,* April 26, 1962.
53. Frank Parker, *Letter to Douglas V. Steere,* March 26, April 10, 1962.
54. Douglas V. Steere, *Letter to Frank Parker,* April 25, 1962.
55. Douglas V. Steere, *Letter to Frank Parker,* January 19, 1963, reporting on the department and how well graduates have done obtaining fellowships for graduate studies; April 19, 1963.

VIII

Pendle Hill

*T*he Steere imprint is stamped all over Pendle Hill, the Quaker center for study and contemplation in Wallingford, Pennsylvania. This center has exerted an influence on American religious life far beyond what its modest size would lead anyone to expect. Even before joining the Society of Friends, Douglas and Dorothy Steere helped conceive Pendle Hill and bring it to birth. Douglas directed its summer school five times, gave public lectures there, and clerked the board for twenty-two years. He and Dorothy led a number of its retreats. Pendle Hill published eight pamphlets authored by Douglas and made two of Dorothy's talks available on tape. Their daughter Helen taught, co-led workshops, and published her spiritual autobiography there. The whole family were enthusiastic advocates for an enterprise which generated Quaker leaders and sparked similar centers in other countries.

In the late autumn of 1929 Douglas and Dorothy were invited to meet with a group of concerned Friends of both Arch Street and Race Street Meetings in Philadelphia to found what became known as Pendle Hill. The Woolman School had moved from Swarthmore to Wyncote, Pennsylvania, and then closed. The day was devoted, according to Douglas Steere's recording of it, to discovering how, under new and inspiring

113

leadership and a new board, might be established an informal Quaker Center for religious and social studies. It was hoped that such a Center might explore afresh the depths of Quaker experience of silent worship, of personal minding of the Light, and of the social testimonies that have sprung from these centuries of Quaker practice.

The new center would be "Not a monastery, not an ashram, not a commune, not a graduate school or a theological seminary, but a spiritually-centered learning community where something of the Benedictine rhythm of work, worship and study interpenetrate each other . . ."[1] The Steeres "felt deeply involved in this challenge." They were appointed to a small committee to secure a site in the Media-Wallingford area.

The steering committee purchased property and started refurbishing buildings in the spring of 1930. They struggled to agree on a name but finally transcended the reservations of one board member based on painful experience at the hands of a person named Pendle and called it Pendle Hill, The name comes from the site in Lancashire where George Fox had his vision of the gathering of a great people and of his life work taking on new proportions. As recounted in his *Journal,* Fox had encountered much misunderstanding and heavy opposition in Derbyshire and proceeded into Lancashire.

> As we went I spied a great high hill called Pendle Hill, and I went to the top of it with much ado, it was so steep; but I was moved of the Lord to go atop of it; and when I came atop of it I saw Lancashire sea; and there atop of the hill I was moved to sound the day of the Lord; and the Lord let me see a-top of the hill in what places he had a great people to be gathered. As I went down, on the hill side I found a spring of water and refreshed myself, for I had eaten little and drunk little for several days.[2]

114

EARLY PENDLE HILL LEADERS
AGNES TIERNEY, HENRY HODGKIN, MARY LIPPENCOTT (FIRST ROW FROM LEFT),
DOUGLAS STEERE (FOURTH FROM LEFT ON LAST ROW), OTHERS INCLUDE:
JAMES WALKER, HAROLD EVANCE, VINCENT NICHOLSON, HENRY CADBURY,
HOMER MORRIS, BERNARD WALTON, CLARENCE PICKETT, D. ROBERT AND
ELIZABETH YARNALL, GRACE RHOADS, HORNER HART, EDNA MORRIS,
EDITH PLATT, PAUL AND BETTY FURNAS

The committee hoped Pendle Hill might retain its connection with this incident.[3]

Pendle Hill got off to a good start in its first year, thanks to the able leadership of Henry T. Hodgkin, a medical doctor and the first secretary of the National Christian Council in China, and his wife, Joy. Joseph Platt, another China hand, assumed the role of Dean and Business Manager. Henry B. Sharman, formerly a professor of New Testament at the Divinity School of the University of Chicago, served as the one full-time member of the teaching staff. Both Rufus Jones and Henry Cadbury, then a professor at Bryn Mawr and later at Harvard, offered courses during the first year. Douglas Steere and George Thomas, a professor of philosophy at

115

Swarthmore and later at Princeton, jointly taught a year-long seminar on "Religious Humanism." Henry Hodgkin offered a seminar entitled *Seeing Ourselves through Russia*, in which students examined the American social and economic system under the searchlight of Russian criticism and experience. Hodgkin edited the students' papers and published them as a book in 1931. Pendle Hill under Hodgkin's leadership "was built around a morning half-hour of silent meeting."[4]

When Henry Hodgkin's health began to fail in the summer of 1932, he called on Douglas Steere to pinch hit for him. Staff included W.O. Mendenhall, President of Whittier College, and Herbert Farmer, a British Presbyterian theologian teaching at Hartford Theological Seminary. Douglas taught a course on Spiritual Classics, laying the groundwork for his innovative teaching at Haverford College. The illness and death of Henry Hodgkin early in 1933 put Pendle Hill through a severe test. Joseph Platt and his wife, Edith, "helped hold the place together."[5] Notable faculty such as Rufus Jones, Henry Cadbury, and James Moffatt, Washburn Professor of Church History at Union Theological Seminary in New York, gave distinction to the program and enrollment increased markedly the second year.

Once again in 1933, before setting out on his sabbatical, Douglas Steere served as director of the summer school and gave a lecture on John Henry Newman and the Oxford Movement in which he suggested that the time had come for Pendle Hill to publish something like Newman's "Tracts for the Times." Anna Petit Bromell picked up on that to form a publication committee of the Pendle Hill Board. Publication, especially of pamphlets, became one of the major functions of Pendle Hill.

Douglas Steere's importance to Pendle Hill rang loudly and clearly when, in 1934, in the Pendle Hill Board extended him an invitation to succeed Henry Hodgkin as director. His teaching vocation won out, but he did not find it easy to say no. As he explained in retrospect, he loved Pendle Hill "and felt that it had a very special role to play in deepening the life of the Society of Friends." Teaching was his vocation, however, and Haverford College had already called on him to pick up the load laid down by Rufus Jones. By the time he and Dorothy returned to the United States in the summer, he felt the Board should seek elsewhere for a director. The Steeres put themselves at the disposal of Dean Joseph Platt, however, and they directed much of their energies toward Pendle Hill throughout their active careers from that time on.

In 1935 Douglas delivered a brief address on "The Function of Pendle Hill" outlining the vision which has guided it from the start. The founders, he explained,

> meant it to be a place where men and women could come apart for a time in order to perfect needed inner adjustments and to be renewed, enlarged and strengthened in their religious mission in life.

Not content with the study of the Christian religion as a social phenomenon or as an intellectual exercise, Pendle Hill has, in the gentle way which has characterized Quaker teaching, sought to expose those who have come to the personal claims of a God-centered life. Through the classroom, the seminars, the private visits and the meeting for worship it has been a "school of the heart" with a concern for the inner growth of its members. In fun it has often been called a "Quaker monastery," and it has always been glad that its devotional emphasis merited the best sense of that term. But just as Fox left Pendle Hill energized and prepared for this greatly enlarged life task, Pendle Hill has always been acutely aware that in its midst men and women were preparing not for life's balcony but for the road.[6]

Pendle Hill would deepen and broaden the outlook and experience of the leadership and ministry of the Religious Society of Friends; provide a laboratory in which some could

DOROTHY STEERE IN THE KITCHEN WITH DOUG GWYN,
QUAKER WRITER AND HISTORIAN

give attention to the changing spiritual, intellectual, and social frontiers; be a center uniting the invisible community scattered everywhere in all walks of life; and maintain an extension service.

AS A PLACE WHERE THE QUAKER LIFE MIGHT BE EXPERIENCED, Pendle Hill included also some elements Douglas gleaned from the Benedictine tradition he had come to know firsthand in 1933 during his retreat at Maria Laach. Pendle Hill had fall, winter, and spring terms and a one-month summer session. The daily regimen combined time for private meditation; the silent meeting for worship with the entire community; intellectual work in the library and seminars or in research projects; one hour each day of household or garden chores; crafts such as hand-printing, book-binding, and weaving; outdoor sports such as tennis, ping pong, and volley-ball; and arts such as plays, poetry, and music. Field trips involved students in social problems and creative efforts

118

to solve them. The American Friends Service Committee sent prospective staff to Pendle Hill to get a feeling for Quaker worship and approaches to relief, rehabilitation, and social education.

As a LABORATORY, Pendle Hill would provide a place for people who could "give their continuous attention to the changing spiritual, intellectual and social frontiers to which we must present definite answers."[7] It would seek solutions to problems of the devotional life, the articulation of Quakers' belief in obedience to the Inner Light, and alternatives to violence. After reviewing seminars and publications which had addressed specific problems, Douglas Steere added:

> Valuable as the work at these specific practical problems is conceived to be, it is not enough. For each problem throws us back upon what our Quaker interpretation of life really is. Pendle Hill believes it to be a primary function to go behind specific practical problems and to lead students through the rigorous intellectual discipline of formulating a philosophy which will seek to be adequate alike to the spiritual insights of their tradition and to the physical and social world in which they find themselves.[8]

Pendle Hill would also provide a place in which Quakers could seek solutions to problems of the ministry, the meeting for worship, and the secular and religious education of children.

As a CENTRAL COMMUNITY, Pendle Hill would like all of its members, resident and non-resident, and alumni/ae to consider themselves members of the home community. Persons representing many vocations who have come to Pendle Hill could continue to have close connections with the center.

As an EXTENSION SERVICE, Pendle Hill would send competent leaders out to Quaker colleges and preparatory schools; conferences; yearly, quarterly, and local meetings who could interpret the spiritual, intellectual, and social problems of the day in light of the Quaker tradition. It would prepare

DOUGLAS STEERE 1935
SUMMER SCHOOL AT PENDLE HILL

suitable literature. The summer school as well as the regular program would extend the Pendle Hill findings to people from many other religious communities.

Douglas clerked the Curriculum Committee of Pendle Hill for many years. In 1947, when a new era opened after the war, the committee decided, with the Board's encouragement, to assess current offerings and take a new look at what Pendle Hill should offer in the future. The curriculum had been largely in the hands of Howard and Anna Brinton during the preceding decade. A panel of visitors was asked to review it. The panel consisted of Henry P. Van Dusen, President of Union Theological Seminary in New York; Clarence Shedd, Professor at Yale Divinity School and a consultant on the structure of curricula in theological institutions; Paul Braisted, a Quaker and President of the Hazen Foundation and one of the two who accompanied Douglas on his trip to Germany and the Scandinavian countries in 1937; and Alexander Purdy, a noted New Testament scholar and member of the Pendle Hill Board. Van Dusen made the startling observation that Pendle Hill was not teaching enough of the main Quaker witness to the interior or mystical dimension of religion, insisting that, if done as the main accent with power and incisiveness, Pendle Hill would not be able to handle all those who would want to come. It was this dimension for which

Protestantism was starving. All four panelists thought Pendle Hill offered too many subjects and tried to cover too much ground. Douglas considered the visit a "creative" and "searching" one for Pendle Hill.[9]

When Douglas returned with his family from his sabbatical leave in Europe in 1948, he included Pendle Hill among the projects he needed to work on through 1950, along with his teaching. The others were guiding the work of the AFSC; taking an active role in the Younger Christian Thinkers which met twice a year; and supporting Viittakivi, an international folk-high school in Finland directed by Esko Saari, whose vision for it had been inspired by a stay at Pendle Hill. As his schedule unfolded, the AFSC claimed the lion's share of his time, but he put much energy into the others as well. In 1949 the Board of Managers at Pendle Hill agreed to sponsor a fund-drive for Viittakivi and to receive money for its establishment under its tax-free privileges.

Douglas served on the Board of Pendle Hill from its inception until 1982, and it would not be inaccurate to say that, in that capacity, he played a major role in shaping the character of this center of Quaker life. Heavily committed not only to Haverford College but also to the AFSC and engaged in numerous other responsibilities, Douglas agonized over taking the chairmanship of the Board of Pendle Hill at the beginning of 1954. D. Robert Yarnall had held the post since Pendle Hill opened in 1930. To take the job, Douglas had to give up his chairmanship of the John Woolman Memorial Center in Mount Holly, which he had held for more than a decade. He finally decided he could do so only with the assistance of Mary Hoxie Jones as Vice-Chairperson. Possessed of unusual pastoral sensitivities, he helped to guide the Board through the kinds of difficult situations that occur in all institutions.

One issue was the working relationship between the Board, the Executive Director, and the staff. Communication was crucial. Another was the division of staff responsibilities. Who, for example, should take leadership in student recruitment?

121

Who should be the major fund raiser? Other issues arose. How should succession be handled when a director became ill, and what financial provisions should be made for a transition period? What should be the balance between courses on spirituality and courses on social issues?

Personal attacks sometimes divided staff and Board, or staff and students. There were resignations. Douglas must often have wondered whether he had made the right decision in accepting the role of clerk. He was carrying a load few other people would even contemplate undertaking, as well as traveling frequently on other continents. Nonetheless, when they could, he and Dorothy met face-to-face with those enmeshed in such problems, and he carried on a voluminous correspondence with them when overseas.

In May 1971 he wrote members of the Pendle Hill Board to say that, at age seventy, he felt it was time for them to look for a new clerk. He paid special tribute to the service of Mary Hoxie Jones as Assistant Clerk.[10] The Board, however, recognized that Douglas Steere, even at his busiest, brought something to the chair few others could bring. Tom and Betty Jones, for instance, could not see how enthusiasm for Pendle Hill could be revived "unless *you* continue! . . . You and Dorothy are the most constant and radiant examples of what Pendle Hill stands for—and we simply cannot do without you!"[11] He did remain in the post one more year and on the Board another decade.

Douglas repeatedly served as director of the Pendle Hill summer school (1933, 1936, 1943, 1950) and offered a variety of courses despite his unbelievably heavy schedule. Besides those already mentioned, he taught "Eight Explorers of the Inner Life" (1936) and "Quaker Faith and Practice" (1950). Dorothy assumed the role of Co-Head Resident with Anna Brinton in 1943 and again in 1950. After Douglas concluded his chairmanship of the Friends World Committee for Consultation in 1970, he and Dorothy together conducted almost annual retreats at Pendle Hill.

STAFF OF 1935 SUMMER SCHOOL
G. RHOADS WITH "LITTLE BUM," M. BAILEY,
D. STEERE, AND R. GREGG

Pendle Hill published many of Douglas Steere's addresses in its pamphlet series, the first *Community and Worship* in 1940. Others included *Bethlehem Revisited* (1965), *Prayer in the Contemporary World* (1966), *On Being Present Where You Are* (1967), *The Hardest Journey* (1969), *Mutual Irradiation* (1971), *On Speaking Out of the Silence* (1972), *Contemplation and Leisure* (1975), and *Traveling In* (1995).

Pendle Hill benefited from Douglas and Dorothy Steere's worldwide visitations. On their excursions they spread the word about this center, in which they took such a keen interest and drew both faculty and students to it. Fritz Kunkel, for instance, a psychotherapist whom Douglas sought out in Germany during his first sabbatical and who later moved to the United States, taught there beginning in the summer of 1936 and returned in 1939, 1943, and 1950. Students touched by contact with Douglas and Dorothy Steere came from all over the world. Olaf Rikberg, who with his mother Selma played a leading role in establishing a permanent Quaker Meeting in Finland, came in the winter of 1936-1937. Helen Campbell came from Ireland in 1960 and again in 1972. Kachiko Yokogawa, a young Japanese Zen Buddhist woman, spent 1967-1968 at Pendle Hill following conversations

123

between Christians and Buddhists in Japan arranged by the Steeres under sponsorship of the Society of Friends.[12]

In 1974 Douglas helped find a replacement for Robert Scholz as Executive Director of Pendle Hill. In 1975 he arranged for Elaine Prevallet, a nun in the Order of Sisters of Loretto who had just returned from two years in Japan, to spend two years on the staff at Pendle Hill. In 1976 he played a major role in enlisting Sally and Parker Palmer to come to Pendle Hill as a a teacher of crafts and as dean, respectively. They remained until 1984, when they became staff members at a Benedictine ecumenical community in Madison, Wisconsin.

Pendle Hill remained at the heart of Douglas Steere's ministry until Alzheimer's limited his public involvement. He played a major role in a Pendle Hill fund drive in 1967-1968, as clerk of the Board offering encouragement and assistance to Development Director, Lloyd Lewis. Many gave to Pendle Hill because of the Steere ministry there. After the Steeres led a retreat at Pendle Hill in 1973, Brett White wrote that the solution to the center's financial problems was to have more Steere retreats.[13] In the 1980's the Steeres and Polly Starr of Boston led off a new fund drive to expand the Extension Program's overcrowded facility for weekend programs.

In 1969, the state had condemned a corner of Pendle Hill's campus for the construction of a highway. With the funds

received as compensation for the property, Pendle Hill purchased a spacious home on a 5-acre lot across the street from the main campus and named it Brinton House. The Board had approved the purchase of Brinton House on the condition that it be possible to add a wing with single rooms for improved retreat space. Douglas and Dorothy Steere, with their affection for monastic life, were particularly keen on the expansion. Moving with caution characteristic of Quakers and concerned about the feasibility of raising the money for such a big undertaking, Pendle Hill postponed building the new wing. When the Board conceptualized a capital campaign called *Open the Way* with fund-raiser Paul Jolly in 1989, they gave top priority to the fulfillment of the Steeres' dream.

Douglas and Dorothy offered a generous gift to get the project started. They modestly consented to allow their

DOROTHY AND DOUGLAS AT THE
OPENING OF THE STEERE WING
AT BRINTON HOUSE 1991

name to be attached to the project, after being assured that the building would continue to be known as Brinton House. They wrote letters inviting others to join them in giving. As before, many of the donors who provided support did so out of their love for Douglas and Dorothy and their care for the dream of expanded retreat space. The support was diverse and widespread. From one church in Michigan came contributions from eighteen individual members as well as from the board and women's committee. Another single donor matched Dorothy and Douglas' gift. One supporter pledged $120 in 1991 and has unfailingly sent $10 every month ever since. The opening of the Steere wing, in October of 1991, was a joyous occasion, celebrating Douglas and Dorothy, their commitment to contemplation and study, and all else they had done for Pendle Hill over the course of its sixty years.

Many who participated in Pendle Hill rightly wrote to Douglas Steere to express appreciation, for it represented so directly his vision and inspiration. From Belfast, Ireland, Helen Campbell wrote:

> I spent only nine months among you—at Pendle Hill and with Friends,—but the nine months was more packed with rich experience than any other nine months of my life.

126

The question is how can we get far more Friends into touch with the living center of Pendle Hill? —So that other "Pendle Hills" may be created.[14]

Mildred Zylstra, Grand Rapids, Michigan, who was not a Quaker, spoke of the profound impact a period at Pendle Hill had on her:

Pendle Hill was a wonderful experience. When I look back on it I see it like an island rising green and still from the midst of a rough sea. There is a spring of spiritual refreshment in the center of the island. I was moved by the silent meetings. I had never attended any before. I could feel the stillness gather into a "speaking" stillness. Not always, of course. But sometimes when you felt that everyone was thinking about God you could feel God come very close. It was an experience I am most grateful to have had. I felt I could pray again. I realized that it was I myself who had shut God out because I keep rebelling against the situation I am in. I don't like the situation I am in. But that isn't the important thing, I see more clearly now. I have a new notion of "holy obedience" and I hope it will enable me to face the demands of the days with more courage and a more positive attitude.

She wrote again a month later after further reflection to reinforce what she had said :

The more I think about Pendle Hill, the more I value the experience. You know how it takes a little time for an experience to crystallize and to take shape. There is a vital spiritual life manifested there. I saw people there whose lives were transformed by the love of God, whose faces glowed with it, who were selflessly dedicated to a purpose other than themselves. It was a thing I particularly needed to see because it is the love of God which I have doubted these last years. . . . I learned something at Pendle Hill about childlike simplicity (not childish simplicity) and holy obedience.[15]

These observations came very close to Douglas Steere's own perception of what made Pendle Hill of value to many. In an exchange of letters with Esko Saari, the director of Vittakiivi, in 1953 he said, "People need time to catch up with their own souls, and an educational approach which isn't too strenuous seems to do something for them that nothing else can. We have so much to learn about the rhythms at which people can be inwardly healed and released."[16]

Notes

1. Douglas V. Steere, UNPUBLISHED JOURNAL, 132.
2. *Journal of George Fox,* edited by John L. Nickalls (London: Religious Society of Friends, 1975), 103-4.
3. Douglas V. Steere, Unpublished paper on "The Function of Pendle Hill," dated 1935.
4. Steere, JOURNAL, 139.
5. Steere, JOURNAL, 152.
6. Steere, "The Function of Pendle Hill," 1.
7. Steere, "The Function of Pendle Hill," 3.
8. Steere, "The Function of Pendle Hill," 4.
9. Steere, JOURNAL, 394.
10. Douglas V. Steere, *Letter to the Pendle Hill Board of Managers,* May 13, 1971.
11. Tom and Betty Jones, *Letter to Douglas and Dorothy Steere,* July 19, 1971.
12. See Kachiko Yokogawa, *Letter to Douglas V. Steere,* April 24, 1967; Douglas Steere, *Letter to Maseo Abe,* Kyoto, Japan, December 22, 1967.
13. Brett White, *Letter to Douglas V. Steere,* April 30, 1973. In a May 11 letter White reported an increase in giving as a result of Douglas' efforts.
14. Helen Campbell, *Letter to Douglas V. Steere,* September 27, 1961.
15. Mildred Zylstra, *Letter to Douglas V. Steere,* July 31, 1962; August 25, 1962.
16. Douglas V. Steere, *Letter to Esko Saari,* December 23, 1953.

IX

Global Quaker Minister

*A*lthough Douglas and Dorothy Steere did not join the Religious Society of Friends until 1932, they found themselves drawn deeply into its heart and life as they took part in the founding of Pendle Hill, the reopening of Radnor Friends Meeting, and the ministry of the American Friends Service Committee. Even before they joined, the deep need of this tiny fellowship scattered around the world cried out for the visionary leadership which Douglas could offer, and he gave himself unstintingly. In much the same way John Woolman devoted himself to the cause of justice two centuries earlier, Douglas Steere served as a minister to the worldwide Quaker community.

Forming a Pattern of Visitation

Douglas' involvement in AFSC projects antedated his and Dorothy's decision to join the Quakers. In the fall of 1931, persuading a Haverford student and two Germantown high school students to go with him, he got his first taste of AFSC work in the form of a relief program for striking miners in West Virginia. He had never seen real hunger and poverty before. As we have seen earlier, the Steeres' service through the AFSC expanded during Douglas' sabbatical in 1933-34 with

129

ministry to the family of Richard Cary and assistance to Emma Cadbury in Vienna. In the fall of 1936, however, the pattern of ministry took a more definite form. A "concern unfolded" to Douglas about taking a Quaker companion or two, moving around Scandinavia during the summer of 1937, and making a visit to German Friends he had come to know in 1934, to see how they fared in the Hitler climate. He spoke and then wrote to Clarence Pickett, Secretary of the AFSC, mentioning Alfred Garrett, Paul Braisted, and Henry Gillett as possible companions. When the embassy committee of the AFSC turned down the proposal, he and Dorothy funded his own travel; others sought funding for Paul Braisted. On March 2, 1937, he wrote Henry Gillett that he was "clearer than ever that I should go, even at my own expense."[1] Pickett put the matter before the embassy committee again, and it reversed its earlier decision on March 16. Douglas and Paul Braisted departed June 5 on the Norwegian American *Bergenfjord*. Greta Sumpf, a German Quaker who had been a family helper and companion of Quaker Mary Cary in Baltimore between 1934 and 1937, accompanied them on the trip over and during the Norwegian stage, then went home to Germany. In the second week of July Paul Braisted stayed with his family in Veldre for three weeks as Douglas went to Germany. Henry Gillett joined Douglas in Berlin and then again in August for the remainder of their traavels in Denmark, Sweden, and Finland. Alfred Garrett shared their last two days in Oslo. On a card to Clarence Pickett dated August 31, 1937 Douglas stated that he thought it would have been helpful to have had Dorothy along, too. On this trip Douglas wrote his first travel letters.[2]

The trip set the pattern for a Steere style of ministry to and through communities of Friends. Douglas took advantage of AFSC or other offices to make contacts. He also built on connections with both individuals and groups which he had established during his sabbatical in 1933-34. Contacts centered on Friends, but, given Douglas' academic interests, the circle widened to embrace many others. Fluent in German, he engaged people in a deeply personal manner. The extent of the visits required constant travel by every available means. On all these visits Douglas sought especially to encourage and uplift others.

Douglas, Corder Catchpool, representative of the British Friends Service Council in Berlin, and Henry Gillett, meeting in Berlin on July 11, quickly had to assist Quaker families considering emigrating on account of the growing threat from National Socialism. They worked through the American Ambassador, Professor William Dodds, intimate German friends Maria Schlueter-Hermkes and her husband Johannes and Fritz and Elizabeth Kunkel. From Berlin they retraced the steps of Douglas' 1934 journey. They proceeded to Breslau in Silesia, meeting with Quakers as they traveled. In Freiburg Douglas spent an afternoon with Romano Guardini and struck up a friendship of lifelong significance with Edmund Stinnes, a German industrialist who opposed Hitler and later emigrated to the United States, and his wife Margianna. They met a group in the home of Professor Schultze von Gävernitz, father of Margianna Stinnes, a political economist and member of the Reichstag before Hitler. The gathering consisted of a half-Jew, a Protestant ex-pastor, a Roman Catholic priest, and several confessional and Roman Catholic church members. Douglas gave an ecumenical challenge about Protestant-Catholic rapprochement to meet the present threat. He remarked, "Our German friends feel especially the need for talk with those outside their increasingly sealed enclosure."[3]

In those years when the Nazi hand lay heavy, meetings with Quakers in Germany often caused tensions to surface. At Bad Teinach Douglas and his companions encountered Elizabeth Krukenberg-Conze, a Quaker who had become a Hitler devotee and justified it by claiming the Inner Light and citing Jesus' expulsion of the money changers from the Temple. Quakers who gathered at Bad Pyrmont for their

Yearly Meeting rebuked them for having truck with Nazi sympathizers. In an executive committee meeting a heated dispute arose regarding how to counsel Quaker youth about military service. Such tense engagements, however, deepened Douglas' appreciation of the power of silence in the Quaker meeting. "When that meeting was over, I saw those two earlier adversaries embrace each other and, with tears running down their cheeks, walk out of the meeting with their arms around each other."[4]

The Scandinavian portion of the mission was less stressful. In Copenhagen Douglas and Henry Gillett were met at the Halfdan-Nielsen's by Paul Braisted, Albert O. Linton, and Jonathan Steere, Jr. They gave lectures at the Grundtvighus in Copenhagen on the Inward Light (Gillett), non-violent aspects of Quaker thought (Braisted), and silent worship (Steere). Jonathan had to return to the United States in August because of illness. Greta Stendahl, Clerk of the Swedish Yearly Meeting, and her sister Ingrid turned up at the close of the visit to Denmark to accompany them on the first leg of their trip to Sweden.

Douglas and Henry departed on August 9 to get a look at "the small but vital little cell of Quaker life that was there."[5] At Hasselholme, Greta Stendahl took them to meet Elin Wägner, one of Sweden's leading women writers who had joined the Religious Society of Friends a year before, and they spent two days at the annual meeting of the Swedish Fellowship of Reconciliation. In Stockholm they met the heads of the YMCA and YWCA, Hugo and Elsa Cedegren. Elsa was the niece of King Gustaf V, the reigning Swedish monarch. They spent a weekend at Viggbyholm School, a co-ed boarding school directed by Quaker Per Sundberg, which used the Pestalozzi method. Helen and Anne would spend the year at Viggbyholm School during Douglas' sabbatical in 1947-48. They met Emelia Fogelklou Norlind, the first woman honored with a D.D. by the University of Uppsala, whom Douglas described as "the Swedish Quakers' special jewel."[6] They were warmly received by the Archbishop of Uppsala and paid a visit to Sigtuna, the old thirteenth-century spiritual capital in which Manfred Bjorkquist had established the Sigtuna Foundation. The Foundation sponsored German Lay Evangelical Academies, centers focused on the renewal of church life after World War II. On the day preceding their departure Quakers assembled from all over Sweden to hear them speak at Viggbyholm in "a truly 'covered' meeting."[7]

A trip to Finland, made in response to the request of Selma Rikberg, mother of Olaf, who had visited Pendle Hill in the winter of 1936-37, concluded the mission. Although entered into somewhat reluctantly by the tired troop, it represented a first step toward Douglas Steere's post-war ministry to Finland, viz., his "Finnish concern." In retrospect, he remarked of this visit, "When the five days that we were there were over, we counted these days as perhaps the most important of the journey. I have come in my later years to regard reluctance as almost a sure sign that I will end up doing a thing and as almost a sign of its rightness."[8] The visitants met several leaders of the Finnish Christian Settlement Movement who would help so admirably in the post-war Quaker relief program. They spoke to a large peace meeting assembled in their honor and had to defend their views against those of theology students and against a Pastor Pakkala, who favored conscription. Douglas scheduled two visits with the American Ambassador to Finland and an hour with Miss Fogelberg, a companion and friend of Elizabeth Fry and the late Matilde Wrede, both prison reformers. On their last night in Helsingfors they held a Quaker meeting in the living room of Selma Rikberg, which led to a regular Quaker meeting for worship in Finland.

Returning to Stockholm, Douglas and Albert Linton visited a conscientious objectors' camp. They also visited Swedish author Selma Lagerlof at Merbäcke and Erling Kjekstad at Oslo. Anna Margareta Olden accompanied them back to the United States, where she lived in Haverford with the Steeres for the next two years. Douglas hoped to increase contact with the Scandinavian people and learn their languages.

A Risky Return

During the first half of his sabbatical in 1940-41, Douglas reiterated this pattern of ministry begun in 1937, undertaking a risky trip to Germany and to the Scandinavian countries on behalf of the AFSC. Entering Europe by way of Lisbon, Portugal, he traveled by bus to Geneva. As he awaited a visa, he visited with Margianna Stinnes. From Switzerland he proceeded directly to Berlin to meet Leonard Kenworthy, representative of the British Friends Service Council. He and Kenworthy got a strong taste of anti-American as well as anti-British sentiment during his days in Berlin, and both had to spend quite a bit of time in air raid shelters as R.A.F. bombers dropped their loads on the city. By citing Quaker assistance to German prisoners of war, however, Douglas managed to secure permission to visit British troops captured at Dunkirk. He made scattered visits here and there: with Elizabeth Kunkel, who had elected to remain in Germany during the war while Fritz emigrated to the United States; the Quaker Legatis family in Breslau; Annemarie Cohen in Muenich; Greta Sumpf in Vienna; and Rudolf Schlosser and Alfons Paquet in Frankfurt (both of whom died in the war). In Berlin he met others who resisted Hitler.

In a report on "Quaker Life in Germany in the Autumn of 1940," dated February 1, 1941, circulated by the AFSC, Douglas drew the attention of American Friends to the tense situation in which their German counterparts lived. Older Quakers who had lived through World War I faced their situation calmly but with a sense of shame and responsibility for what Germans were doing in Poland. Younger Friends longed for a lighter and more positive word. Young men risked being shot or beheaded for resisting the draft. None had yet openly resisted. What appealed to many was work for British,

French, and Polish prisoners of war. Many Quaker families and groups maintained their fellowship with Jews. Margarete Lachmund, whose husband was a judge and not a member of the Religious Society of Friends, organized a clothing drive for German Jews deported to Poland. Annamarie Cohen, whose husband was a Jew, made their apartment a receiving station for clothing, shoes, and other items. Groups of friends throughout Germany kept meeting, the regardless of the risk. Douglas ended this report with a list of eminent Quaker leaders, many of whom he sought out in subsequent visits: Emil Fuchs, a socialist removed from his professorship in Berlin; Martha and Fritz Legatis, Douglas' hosts in Breslau in 1937; Schultze von Gävernitz, professor at the University of Freiburg now living in a mountain village in Silesia; Greta Sumpf, director of the Quaker Center in Vienna who had earlier enlisted the Steere's help; Carl and Eva Hermann, Quaker leaders at Mannheim; Alfons Paquet, authority on the geography of the Rhine valley and editor of the *Frankfurter Zeitung;* Otto Buchinger, director of a sanitarium at Bad Pyrmont and pillar of the Quaker community there; Theresa Herzog, author and spiritual director of the Quaker community at Bad Pyrmont; Wilhelm Mensching, pastor of the village parish in Petzen and luminous Quaker leader; and Bertha Scharff, a nurse and friend of peasants near Hamburg.[9]

Thanks to the intercession of Leonard Kenworthy, Douglas also managed to arrange a return visit to Finland after a long wait and despite an earlier denial. It was this second visit that "in many ways led on to the Quaker Finnish relief project that was undertaken four and a half years later."[10] He stayed in the home of Selma Rikberg for a week.

Although the entire mission would have tried stout hearts, the return to Lisbon proved the most harrowing experience. On his re-entry into Switzerland at Schaffhausen on the way to Basel on New Year's eve an official stamped his visa "no longer valid." He was taken off the train. After some pleading, officials sent him back to Schaffhausen at midnight.

Unable to go on to Basel, he headed to Zürich, where he got better acquainted with Schwester Anny Pflüeger, a Quaker nurse who assisted Jewish refugees. The next morning, he discovered the probable reason authorities at the border had checked his whereabouts so closely. The *Züricher Zeitung* reported that on the night of December 30 the Anhalter Bahnhof in Berlin had been severely damaged by a bomb planted by some enemy hand and that the German frontiers were placed under special alert! From Zürich he crossed to Lausanne, where he met the Swiss Quaker peace activist Helene Monastier and Pierre Ceresole, founder of the International Voluntary Service Corps in Switzerland. He proceeded via Geneva, Marseilles, and Perpignan to Lisbon, where he boarded the *Liboney* on January 17, 1941, bound for New York. In Marseilles he touched base with Burns Chalmers and a staff assisting refugees, in Perpignan with Don Stevenson, both friends of Oxford days. Margianna Stinnes and her daughters took the same ship.

Ambassadors of the AFSC

These early ventures undertaken under sponsorship of the American Friends Service Committee disclosed Douglas Steere's extraordinary gifts as a global minister. His leadership in the Quaker relief effort for war-torn Finland immediately following World War II, reinforced this perception many times over. Not surprisingly, therefore, the AFSC enlisted him and Dorothy on a more regular basis as its ambassadors. Cornelius Kruse explained in a letter what such visits would mean in encouraging not only Quakers but others as well. When these visits confirmed Kruse's assessment, the AFSC extended the arrangement into the sixties, gradually shifting the focus from Europe to Africa.

Douglas and Dorothy repeated their European sojourn in the fall of 1950, offering again their remarkable ministry of encouragement and commenting on the changing spiritual situation of Germany and the Scandinavian countries in a series of newsletters. In Germany, debate raged over the re-arming of Germany. Douglas took advantage of the situation to offer a Quaker peace witness. He carried out part of the visit with André Trocmé, Secretary of the European Fellowship for Reconciliation. Douglas took a keen interest in evangelical academies, retreat and study centers seeking the renewal of Europe, as "one of the most important post-war spiritual mutations in Germany"[11] and reported on several. Following visits to both West and East Berlin, he lamented the lack of attention to inward growth. In Finland, the Steeres counseled Friends who had been working since 1948 to develop Viittakivi, a center of social and religious studies similar to Pendle Hill. Douglas hoped to solicit small American donations and locate an American couple to volunteer for the staff. He thought the Finns had coped with the aftermath of the war better than the Germans because *all* had shared the pain of the war in Finland. The German people needed more spiritual and moral leadership.[12]

In 1952 Douglas and Dorothy Steere and the AFSC turned their attention from a rapidly rebuilding Europe to Africa. American Friends had manifested an interest in Africa for many decades—first in Liberia, then in Kenya, where the Five Years Meeting Mission Board had experienced considerable success. Thomas Jones, President of Earlham College; Burns and Elizabeth Chalmers; and Rufus and Elizabeth Jones had visited before World War II; James and Ruth Vail had made a lengthy visit just after the War. For the Steeres the door to Africa may have been opened by Douglas' admiration for Albert Schweitzer. Early in 1952, Gilbert White, President of Haverford College, asked Douglas if he would like to visit Schweitzer in Lambaréné to invite him to be a presence at Haverford College without specific duties. Eugene Exman, an editor at Harpers who had just returned from Lambaréné, and Emory Ross, head of the Albert Schweitzer Society in America, urged Douglas to go. Columbia University, Union Theological Seminary in New York, and Colby College added invitations. Departing on April 29, Douglas visited friends en route and stayed eleven days at the hospital in Lambaréné. Although Schweitzer wanted "very much to come"[13] to the United States, he could not fit it into his hectic schedule at Lambaréné, a second visit by Douglas and Dorothy nine months later notwithstanding.

The Steere's African mission for the AFSC began in January 1953. Having "some deep questions about [their] suitability" to leap into uncharted and unfamiliar territory,[14] the Steeres stopped in England to secure information on Africa, especially South Africa. By way of Paris, Strasbourg, Münich, and Rome, they proceeded to Nigeria and the Gold Coast, where they contacted public officials about sending Haverford Social and Technical Assistance students. Hopping from Lagos, Nigeria, to Accra, in what became Ghana, Douglas met with the Acting Director of Social Welfare and his deputy, Prime Minister Nkrumah, and two cabinet ministers. At the request of the Prime Minister, he secured the help of Arthur Morgan, a Quaker engineer who had played a leading role in the Tennessee Valley Authority, for a dam project. From Accra, the Steeres crossed by way of Leopoldville and Brazzaville to Lambarene and then to Johannesburg for a two-and-a-half-month'`s visit to South Africa. Some thought the Steeres came to South Africa with money to spend, and Douglas had to clarify that they wanted "to know South African Friends, to visit them in their different communities, to share in their spiritual life, and in the concerns that it laid upon them." In an aside he explained:

> We hoped at the same time to grasp something of the racial, social and political scene and especially to come close enough to a few of the far-sighted South African leaders to see something of their vision of South Africa's future apart from the "stay as you are" apartheid program of the Nationalist Party which was just being voted into a second term of office.[15]

138

Douglas and Dorothy wrote eight journal letters describing their experiences.

In Africa, as in Europe, Douglas favored "wisdom in human hide." On their second evening in Johannesburg, the Steeres attended a meeting at St. Benedict's, a retreat house of the Community of the Resurrection, where Trevor Huddleston, the prior, had gained a reputation for espousing African rights. They also sought out Arthur Blaxall, an English clergyman, and his wife Florence who were engaged in training African blind persons and developing Wilgespruit farm, a South African version of Iona and Kirkridge retreat centers, located at Roodespoort, fifteen miles by train from Johannesburg's city center. Blaxall introduced Douglas to Nelson Mandela, then a young African National Congress leader. They visited the South African Institute of Race Relations guided by Quinton Whyte. They met, too, with about twenty or twenty-five Quakers, a fraction of the two hundred Friends then in South Africa, who turned up for two Sunday Meetings.

In Cape Town, where Quakers owned the only meeting-house in South Africa, the Steeres arranged to meet Douglas Buchanan, a lawyer who fought for political and economic rights for all; dined with Sheila Van der Horst, Professor of Economics at Cape Town University and chair of a branch of the Race Relations Institute, and with the President of the University; visited Stellenbosch University, the Harvard of South Africa; and met several leaders of the "colored" people to learn about their situation. In Durban they met Albert Luthuli, then head of the African National Congress trying hard to inculcate non-violent resistance. In retrospect, Douglas remarked, "Dorothy and I came away from two and one-half hours of visit with Chief Luthuli with a sense that the journey to South Africa would have been justified if we had done nothing else."[16] They also got acquainted with Manilil Gandhi, the oldest son of Mahatma Gandhi, who was free on appeal of a sentence for taking part in the Defiance of the Unjust Laws Campaign; Edgar Brookes, one time

Principal of Adams College, a boarding school for Africans; and Alan Paton, author of *Cry the Beloved Country* and leader in opposition to apartheid.

Many would doubtless have thrown up their hands in despair when asked what two hundred Friends could do about the crisis precipitated by the policy of apartheid in South Africa. According to newsletters reporting on their visit, Douglas Steere did not. He stated what many others doubtless felt, "an increasing conviction that something is drying up in the soul of South Africa. With its glorious climate, its magnificent scenery, its prodigal resources, and its great prospects for the future, it is still a country whose soul is withering."[17] At the same time he pointed to signs of hope in "Some Great South African Servants of Their People"—Edgar Brookes, Albert Luthuli, Malilil Gandhi, and Alan Paton. And he outlined some specific things this small band of Friends could do: (1) deepen their spiritual resources and their inner commitment, (2) visit in the ministry to strengthen these, (3) "emigrate to South Africa and throw in their lives with the local Friends groups and bring them new force and vision by strengthening their ranks!"[18]

South African Friends longed to deepen their spiritual lives and felt "much under the weight of the racial situation in the country" and wanted "to be a significant force in altering the will of the people for changes in the right direction, . . ."[19] They had engaged in small projects such as school feeding in a very poor non-European school and conducting a Sunday school at the slum African village at Moroka. They shared, too, in the work of the Race Relations Institute, but non-Europeans were losing confidence in it. They wanted to do more. Noting some other specific projects such as meeting-houses, Douglas commented:

> There is no short cut to this business of dissolving the tough, gristly, arthritic growths of race prejudice and misunderstanding and the deep hidden fear of the

loss of privileged status. There are no social miracle drugs that with any flash of cortisone can roll away the stone. But there is the slow and sure action of deep concern and proven caring that may or may not be able to avert catastrophe, but that is the thing a person would be thankful to be doing whatever comes, for they are sound and it is only out of such a mood that the final solution can come. In the course of this kind of work, unexpected, or should I say "expected" openings come in unexpected moments, and having earned the right to speak or act, unbelievably important things are accomplished. It is good to know that we do not work alone in these matters and that all over the place things are happening that are good and sound in any vernacular.[20]

The Steeres devoted the bulk of the African journey to South Africa, but they touched down also in Southern (now Zimbabwe) and Northern (now Zambia) Rhodesia and Kenya. In Salisbury, their Quaker hosts, John and Virginia Hoover, the U.S. Ambassador and his wife, held a dinner party at which the Steeres met Anglican Archbishop Paget and Sir Robert Tredgold, Chief Justice of the Supreme Court of the new Central African Federation, who became, during the next twenty years, Douglas' "dearest friend in Rhodesia."[21] Douglas felt more optimistic about African participation in their government in Southern Rhodesia than in South Africa. He had an opportunity to make a case for a multi-racial university, changing his travel plans long enough to speak to the issue.

In Kenya, Douglas and Dorothy intended to spend a week finding out what lay behind the Mau Mau rebellion then in progress. They had been commissioned to write publishable letters on black-white relations and make suggestions Quakers could use to "assist in a non-violent and just resolution of acute racial tensions that existed there."[22] Even before he and Dorothy reached Nairobi, however, he knew that they must visit Kaimosi, site of extraordinarily successful Quaker mission work begun in 1902. Where Quakers numbered only 200 in all of South Africa, in the Kaimosi area alone they tallied 20,000. The revision of their itinerary confirmed for them what they learned on numerous other occasions, that is, that life's interruptions often turn out to be God's opportunities. Leaders in the African Quaker community met with the Steeres for hours to get help in persuading the Richmond Mission Board to reverse its decision against the secondary school system the government had asked them to develop. They drove the Steeres the 180 miles over rugged roads to Lugulu, where the government wanted to locate the school. Douglas spent three hours with the Secretary of the Christian Council of Churches of Kenya and received invaluable advice and agreement on information he needed to present to the Mission Board in Richmond. Before departing for Zürich, he worked well into the night drawing together his report on the situation in Kaimosi. After meeting with Douglas on August 20, the Mission Board responded favorably to his recommendation that they reconsider their negative decision regarding the school. In his JOURNAL he footnoted his own learning experience:

> How often I have been compelled to learn all over again that while a rough itinerary in advance is a necessity in the world that we live in, most of the things that in the end seemed really to matter on these trips of ours for the AFSC had a way of appearing as utterly unpredictable interruptions, openings, demands, that often badly upset what I meant to do! These intrusions, I had finally to admit, often contained hidden within them the carefully concealed purpose of our whole journey.[23]

The side trip to Kaimosi turned out to be "perhaps the most important service of our entire journey."[24] In addition to Douglas' assistance on the school issue, he helped Horst Rothe, a surgeon he had befriended in the U.S. and Germany, obtain funding for a small surgery and TB center in Kaimosi.

Ending the first African sojourn with revisits to Germany, England, and the Scandinavian countries, cementing anew the strong ties with Quakers and other friends, Douglas and Dorothy Steere were extending the pattern of visitation they had initially directed toward Europe. For another two decades they continued their correspondence and visits to both Africa and Europe, even as they turned their attention to Asia during Douglas' sabbatical in 1954-55. There they prepared the ground for a series of colloquies between Christians and Buddhists in Japan, as well as Christians and Hindus in India, sponsored by the Friends World Committee for Consultation. They revisited Africa in the spring of 1955, in the fall of 1957, in the fall of 1959 (Egypt), in the fall of 1961, and then, after an interruption to attend sessions of Vatican Council II, in the fall of 1966, and in the spring of 1971.

In the interim Douglas used his widening influence to implement ideas for solving problems he had discerned during their first visit. Early in the fall of 1953, for instance, he successfully entreated heads of Princeton Theological Seminary, Union in New York, Yale Divinity School, and Andover-Newton to offer one scholarship apiece to help bring a half-dozen of the top theological graduates of the principal Dutch Reformed seminaries in South Africa to the United States for a year of study to broaden their outlook. Frank Loescher later obtained Ford Foundation funding to bring Afrikaaners and, subsequently, black leaders to the United States and took Americans to South Africa. Douglas and Dorothy composed a booklet for the Friends World Committee for Consultation and Pendle Hill on *Friends Work in Africa.* Douglas helped secure Haverford students to work in the Haverford-Ford Foundation project with the Department of Social Welfare of the Gold Coast (now Ghana). Behind these often exhausting and ever risky ventures lay a carefully considered rationale which Douglas articulated years later in his UNPUBLISHED JOURNAL:

> As I look back upon the kind of steps that Frank Loescher (who with his wife Mildred began their trips to South Africa soon after our own) and Dorothy and I took in order to try in practical ways to strengthen the forces for change that already existed in South Africa, they appear frail indeed. But they were a beginning. Perhaps the most important thing about them was the fact that as American Quakers we were concerned enough not only to come at all but to keep coming back year after year. Out of these successive visits, we formed friendships of varying depth with perhaps a hundred persons, among whom were many of the most self-giving people I have encountered in any society in the world. Pained to the core by their deep awareness of the wrongness of the existing pattern of white domination in which they existed, they lived inwardly in the long loneliness and reached out for the smallest encouragement. While our ties were especially with the white community, friendships with Chief Luthuli, Bishop Zulu, Professor Z. K. Matthews of Fort Hare and with Manilil Gandhi were deep ones, and through my brotherly ties with Arthur Blaxall way was always open to the African leaders.[25]

These words embody an outlook and method by which Douglas Steere sought to work for social change and to acquaint American Quakers with opportunities to offer support around the world.

Notes

1. Douglas V. Steere, UNPUBLISHED JOURNAL, 199.
2. Steere, JOURNAL, 200.
3. Steere, JOURNAL, 210.
4. Steere, JOURNAL, 214.
5. Steere, JOURNAL, 216.
6. Steere, JOURNAL, 221.
7. Steere, JOURNAL, 224.
8. Steere, JOURNAL, 224.
9. Douglas V. Steere, "Quaker Life in Germany in the Autumn of 1940," unpublished.
10. Steere, JOURNAL, 259.
11. Douglas V. Steere, *General Newsletter 6 from Douglas Steere,* Berlin, 8 Nov. 1950, 33.
12. Douglas V. Steere, *General Newsletter 8 from Douglas Steere,* Aboard S.S. America, 27 Dec., 1950, 61.
13. Steere, JOURNAL, 566.
14. Douglas v. Steere, *Newsletter #1 from Dorothy and Douglas Steere,* Rome, Italy - Kano, Nigeria, February 22-23, 1953, 2.
15. Steere, JOURNAL, 588.
16. Steere, JOURNAL, 603.
17. Douglas V. Steere, *Newsletter #5 from Dorothy and Douglas Steere,* Salisbury, Southern Rhodesia, June 12, 1953, 9.
18. Douglas V. Steere, *Newsletter #6,* Nairobi, Kenya, June 20, 1953, 8.
19. Douglas V. Steere, *Newsletter #3,* Capetown, South Africa, April 6, 1953, 7.
20. Douglas V. Steere, *Newsletter #6,* 10-11.
21. Steere, JOURNAL, 616.
22. Steere, JOURNAL, 623.
23. Steere, JOURNAL, 622.
24. Steere, JOURNAL, 623.
25. Steere, JOURNAL, 642.

X

---◆•◆---

"The Finnish Concern"

*D*ouglas Steere's "Finnish Concern" might not have unfolded as it did at the end of World War II had it not been for the plea of Selma Rikberg, mother of Olaf, who had stayed at Pendle Hill during the winter of 1936-37. His side trip to Finland, as Douglas himself viewed it in retrospect, was "perhaps the most important"[1] of his 1937 journey to Germany and Scandinavia. He and the others who accompanied him met, on that occasion, several leaders of the Finnish Christian Settlement Movement who would assist so notably in the post-war Quaker relief program. The trip established personal bonds which drew him back for a one-week visit in 1940, leading to the Quaker Finnish Relief project in 1945.

When War Shall Be No More

Douglas Steere had ample preparation for his leadership in the Finnish Relief program of the AFSC. In 1941- 42 he chaired a committee of the AFSC Work Camp Program and visited the camps early in the summer of 1942. In the fall he turned his attention to the Quaker Civilian Public Service camps for conscientious objectors to military service and arranged a leave for five academic weeks plus the Christmas holidays to visit them. On his return to Haverford, Felix Morley asked him to become the director of the Relief and Reconstruction Training program (R & R) at Haverford College, which Douglas had envisioned, beginning in the fall of 1943. R & R graduates served, among other places, in Finland.

In preparation for directing the R & R program, Douglas visited New England Civilian Public Service camps, consulted with leaders of a Columbia University course in International Administration, and looked in on a Catholic Worker CPS camp near Warner, Vermont, and a Quaker CPS camp in West Compton, New Hampshire. Douglas and others spent the months from February to June 1943 working out "a modest course" on "an advanced undergraduate level" for ten Haverford and ten other college students.

Clarence Pickett used the auspices of Eleanor Roosevelt to get President Roosevelt's approval for the release of conscientious objectors to do medical and health work in China.[2] Applications poured in, and the first trainees were brought to Haverford in the summer. Douglas persuaded Don and Lois Stevenson to head this unit, while he recruited women for the R & R master's degree course. Nineteen students, only six of whom were men, entered in the fall. Divided into four periods of eleven weeks each, the course began on September 27, 1943.

Douglas and his associates designed the R & R program with the end of the war in view. "The aim of the course," he explained in a backward look, "was to fit graduates not only for emergency feeding and sanitation services, but for the longer term operations of handling displaced peoples; administering and doing personnel work in transit camps, rest homes and rehabilitation centers; and administering or sharing in work camps and labor services."[3] The curriculum revolved around four centers: (1) an area study of Germany under the direction of Edmund Stinnes, a former German industrialist; (2) social work and international relief administration headed by Herta Kraus, a professor on the graduate faculty of Bryn

148

Mawr; (3) applied work taught by various members of the Haverford College faculty; and (4) the motivation of the relief worker led by Douglas himself.

In the last, Douglas sought to help students understand the importance of making contemplation the spring from which their action would flow and featured "the lives of persons whose caring for their fellows sprang from inner resources."[4] He considered such persons to be uncanonized saints. He launched the course with a lecture on "The Saint and Society," in which he argued that the saint could change society's vulnerable center by helping it to recover its dream, its vision, and purpose.[5]

Douglas' models for the R & R's included Francis of Assisi and the Third Order Franciscans, Vincent de Paul and the pattern of Roman Catholic charity, John Woolman and the Quaker approach to social reform, John Frederick Oberlin and the rural revolution, Florence Nightingale and emergency nursing, Henri Dunant and the International Red Cross, Jane Addams and the use of the settlement, Albert Schweitzer and the ministry of healing, Matilda Wrede and Finnish prisons, and Fridtjof Nansen, ambassador to the refugees.[6] Following his inauguration of the Finnish Relief program in 1945, Douglas taught a course on "Mental Hygiene of the Relief Worker." He recommended a few indispensable books, some small musical instrument, and a modest journal as a relief worker's *vade mecum.*

Staff of the Finnish Relief program included Mary Barclay, a member of the first Haverford R & R class. Barclay coordinated the work camps in Northern and Middle Finland, where about 150 workers helped war victims to rebuild their houses or, in the case of the Karelians, build houses on land newly granted to them by the government.[7] Douglas maintained contact with her by letter and visited her when he returned to Finland,[8] as he did R & R graduates in other countries, encouraging them with letters and sending books. The second R & R group left in January 1946.

Finnish Relief

Following his visit in 1940, Douglas had continued excursions to the Finnish Legation in Washington, D.C. until it was closed in 1943, despite FBI surveillance on account of Finland's connections with the Soviet Union.[9] When Finland concluded an armistice with the Soviet Union in 1944, his hopes for helping the Finns heightened. He spoke to three prominent Finnish Americans about the AFSC concern and found the Finnish American community ready to offer help. The President's Committee on Relief responded favorably to AFSC inquiries. On June 21, 1945 the AFSC sent Douglas to inquire into the situation via Stockholm.

In Stockholm Elsa Cedegren, head of the Swedish AFSC, put him in touch with her brother, Count Bernadotte, director of the Swedish Red Cross. Enlisting the assistance of Per Sundberg, Quaker founder and head of Viggbyholm School, and others, he sought first to see what Sweden had done and was doing to meet Finland's food, clothing, and medical needs and to determine whether the AFSC needed to do more. His report to the AFSC showed "both Finland's urgent need and the ready openness of access to Finland that Sweden provided."[10] He arrived in Finland July 9 and remained until August 4, spending ten days in Lapland accompanied by Heikki Waris, General Secretary of Suomen Huolto, the official Finnish relief agency.

The AFSC, already heavily committed to relief projects elsewhere, had to be convinced to undertake another, and Douglas Steere presented a strong case. On withdrawing from Lapland in the summer of 1944, the German forces had adopted a scorched earth policy, burning every house, barn, and hospital on the main path of their retreat as well as destroying bridges and culverts, chopping down every second or third telephone pole, and mining roads or other places and objects. Rovaniemi, the administrative center of Lapland, was "a shambles." People were pouring back into the area

150

and trying to survive in the ruins, cellars, packing cases, or anything they could find. The primary need was clothing, shoes, and food. The food ration was 1187 calories a day, less than half the amount required by cold climates. Dire as their situation was, the people could not expect much help from their nearest neighbor, Sweden, because of (1) higher taxes, (2) harder days ahead for Swedish industry, (3) lessening of private charity due to expectations that the state was helping, and (4) Swedish weariness with helping the same people for so long. Nor could they count on assistance from other countries and were not on UNRRA's list of countries.

Aware that the AFSC could not sponsor a major effort, Douglas recommended concentration on Lapland, where needs were most acute. He proposed that Quakers implement a supplementary school feeding program in the provisional schools of Rovaniemi, Kemijarvi, and other villages in the area during the 1945-46 school year. The Finnish government would supply staples such as oatmeal and potatoes; the AFSC, powdered milk, cod-liver oil, sugar for porridge, fats for soup, as well as the facilities for cooking. He recommended also that the AFSC supply 150 tons of clothing collected by the Finnish-American community and 10,000 pairs of new shoes for school children to be distributed through Suomen Huolto and its affiliate organizations. The AFSC could post a small staff to check on the distribution. He suggested that Quakers set up two service centers, one at Rovaniemi and the other at Kemijarvi, which would provide bases for inspection of clothing, distribution of shoes, and the feeding program. The centers would also supply living quarters for staff and serve as community centers where people could gather for recreation, entertainment, classes, etc. Although Douglas thought it was logical to employ Finnish personnel, he noted that they suffered from such fatigue that a half-dozen "fresh, strong, able workers possessing a variety of skills and with bold resourcefulness" would inject needed vitality, hope, and courage to go on. He urged also supplying a wood-burning car and a wood-burning truck as emergency equipment for the center in case regular transport broke down. Finally, he proposed that a small American staff come to assist the Finns in organizing at least one voluntary work camp in Rovaniemi to assist in rebuilding. He suggested a budget of $250,000.[11]

Attentive to the importance of working with and through the Finnish people, Douglas discerned the need for a gifted agent and found one in Heikki Waris who met Douglas in Stockholm and opened doors for him.[12]

Douglas directed his attention especially to the Karelians, the neediest of the needy. In Rouvaniemi, Finnish Lapland, he reported "ruins by systematic destruction."[13] After ten days there he sent the AFSC a letter detailing the need for shoes (with sizes), clothing, and other help. He favored direct help from the Save the Children's Fund.[14] In Helsinki he had a moving visit with Elvo Kilpi, Cabinet Minister of Social Affairs, and contacted other cabinet ministers to get a briefing on the political situation. Anna Margareta Olden, the Steere's Norwegian young friend and helper a couple of years before, met him in Oslo to lend assistance. Douglas also contacted Erling Kjekstad, a Norwegian Quaker who had done relief work among the Poles from 1921-28, and visited Quakers in Stavanger.

Returning to Stockholm, he had a profoundly uplifting and confirming experience during a Quaker meeting at Elsa Cedegren's home. He reported in a letter to Dorothy:

> About 8:50 I gave a brief prayer that came of itself and then Fred [Tritten, an English Friend] prayed, and in a flash I was melted down and the glorious release of the life of God was mine for an instant. My face was wet with tears and I felt that nothing in the world mattered that could disturb this certainty, and I felt ever so close to each one there and as we closed I saw two others who seemed to be having the same moving experience.[15]

In August he received word that the AFSC Relief Committee backed the Finnish Relief project. In September the AFSC gave the go-ahead to buy food and powdered milk for school feeding and sent clothing and shoes. Quaker representatives began to come. Douglas also established connections with the American Red Cross, UNRRA, the Save the Children's Fund, Swedish Relief Committee, and other groups.

Although the AFSC showed less interest in Douglas' proposal for a trip to Poland, Douglas and Fred Tritten scheduled a trip there as well. Flying to Warsaw, they spent ten days traveling 1400 kilometers in a jeep with no side curtains in drenching rain over pock-marked roads. Since they did not have AFSC permission, they could not promise leaders assistance for work camps, but their visit may have opened the way for a work camp in Poland led by Dave Richie after World War II.

On their return to Stockholm Douglas, joined by James Andrews, an American Friend, hurried to Rovaniemi for eight days before his return to the United States scheduled for October 21. Heikki Waris made arrangements for them to meet government officials and relief agency representatives. Andrews remained in Stockholm most of the time after Douglas departed to arrange for the purchase and movement of supplies and taking care of finances. Thomas Harvey, a member of the AFSC Board, was appointed leader of the mission.

A Costly Continuance

Although Douglas returned to the United States and resumed his role as director of the R & R program and chair of the Department of Philosophy at Haverford College, he did not cease in his energetic efforts to aid the Finnish people. He interceded with former president Herbert Hoover, living in the Waldorf-Astoria in New York City, to persuade officials in the capital to press UNRRA for aid to Finland. Hoover, a Quaker, took careful notes, and Douglas, attentive to details in an issue so vital, sent a memo. Hoover turned over to the AFSC funds held over from his 1939-40 Finnish Relief Fund, Inc. In less than two months UNRRA dispatched a Russian

American in their employ to Finland to make a general survey. Eventually UNRRAA gave Finland $2,750,000 worth of materials. In January 1946 the AFSC reported that $277,044 had been contributed to the Finnish Relief Project.[16]

Thanks to Douglas Steere's energetic efforts through letters and personals contacts, other generous gifts poured in. William Danforth saw to it that Ralston Purina Company would give huge quantities of cereals to feed children. The Church of the Brethren gave 120,000 pounds of Quaker Oats. Clothing and shoes came from several sources. An American drug company supplied seven million vitamin tablets. Although the AFSC was not obligated to assist two Finnish-American organizations in fund raising, Douglas kept in close contact with them in December 1945 and January 1946. He spoke to Finnish American audiences, making trips to New England, Northern Michigan, and the far West. Douglas also worked to strengthen the Finnish Work Camp movement in the summer of 1946 and maintained constant communication with the AFSC about Finnish affairs as the Steere family rested in their summer home at Mackinaw City, Michigan.

The AFSC Finnish Relief program grew steadily. Many Finns who started with UNRRA shifted to the more personal AFSC. Although both efforts were needed, Douglas noted in retrospect, the UNRRA program was faceless and "left few traces of real inward connection with the Finnish people." In the Quaker program. "What they remembered was not the materials that were transferred to them but the people who came and lived with them and helped to restore their hope."[17] Douglas persuaded Arthur Morgan, the first director of the TVA, to go to Finland for four months.

Douglas Steere's virtual non-stop drive to aid the Finnish people exacted a price. Early in 1947 he came down with a low-grade fever and general weakness diagnosed later as mononucleosis. He was put to bed for nearly six weeks, long enough to permit him to read much of Arnold Toynbee's multi-volume *A Study of History*.

However, his efforts also brought much-deserved recognition as well as personal satisfaction. Beyond the deep friendships which the Steeres cherished so much, the Finnish people remembered. In May 1946 Heikki Waris came to Haverford to present Douglas a painting by Lennart Segerstrole on behalf of Suomen Huolto and Finnish authorities in recognition of his work in Finnish relief.[18] On September 12, 1947, the Finnish Social Ministry held an official reception in Helsinki to express appreciation for the Quaker effort not only to supply food and clothing but also competent and caring people.[19] In a response Douglas made modest claims for Quakers as "only" "the channel through which these friends of Finland have worked" and emphasized Finnish facilitation.[20] He went on to explain the Quaker rationale for their social ministries.

> People often ask me if the Quakers do not get discouraged helping people after troubles and then seeing troubles come again and the same people have to be helped again. I can only answer that we believe that the troubles of wars must cease, but that they will only stop when men and women have felt a common friendship that is deeper than the differences, a common liability for each other that is deeper than their conflicting interests. And we believe so deeply that beneath even the present conflicts there is to be discovered this common liability for each other.[21]

Official acknowledgements would not have pleased the Steeres as much as their deep friendship with Heikki and Emmi Waris, Selma and Olaf Rikberg, and others, but the Finnish people and government did not forget Douglas' extraordinary efforts. In 1987, more than forty years after he had persuaded the AFSC to undertake a relief effort there, the Finnish Consul General in the United States, Antti Lassila, noting that Douglas had "never received proper recognition for his work," awarded him the Decoration of Knight First Class of the Order of the White Rose of Finland "in recognition of his services on behalf of Finland." Douglas Steere accepted the honor with characteristic modesty. "I think it's awfully decent of them. . . . I'm an old man, and this took place a long time ago."[22]

Notes

1. Douglas V. Steere, UNPUBLISHED JOURNAL, 224.
2. Memo dated February 13, 1943 cited in Steere, JOURNAL.
3. Steere, JOURNAL, 307.
4. Steere, JOURNAL, 309.
5. Douglas indicated in his JOURNAL that the first lecture was published as the first chapter of *On Beginning from Within* (New York and London: Harper & Bros. Publishers, 1943). This will be summarized in Chapter 16.
6. Steere, JOURNAL, 309.
7. Douglas V. Steere, *Letter to R. and R. Company*, August 23, 1947, 1.
8. Douglas V. Steere, *Letter to Mary Barclay Howarth, AFSC, Rovaniemi*, June 7, 1946; July 11, 1947. In an undated letter, evidently 1946, he commended her "maturity in handling the situations."
9. Finland resisted the Soviet Union, then allied with Germany, from October 1939 until March 1940. Defeated by the Soviets, Finland signed a treaty on March 12, 1940.
10. Steere, JOURNAL, 327.
11. AFSC, "Statement Concerning Finland for the Information of the Board of Directors," 1-4.
12. Douglas V. Steere, *Letter to Dorothy M. Steere,* July 8, 1945.
13. Douglas V. Steere, *Letter to Dorothy M. Steere,* July 23, 1945.
14. Douglas V. Steere, *Letter to James Andrews, AFSC Letter 4, from Helsinki,* July 27, 1945.
15. Citing a letter to Dorothy in Steere, JOURNAL, 344.
16. AFSC, "Current Developments on Finnish Relief Project," 2/13/96.
17. Steere, JOURNAL, 387.
18. Steere, JOURNAL, 376.
19. Steere, JOURNAL, 400.
20. Steere, JOURNAL, 400.
21. Steere, JOURNAL, 400-401.
22. Michael D. Schaffer, "Finland Says Thanks, 40 Years Later," *Philadelphia Inquirer,* 1987, 4B.

XI

Expander of Horizons

<big>T</big>he longer and farther the Steeres pursued their remarkable ministry, the more Quakers looked to Douglas for guidance and the wider he expanded Quaker vision. In the thirties and forties, as an ambassador of the American Friends Service Committee, he and Dorothy forged strong bonds with Friends in Europe. After World War II they made bi-annual journeys to Germany and Scandinavia to raise hope in an age of pessimism and despair. In the fifties they turned their gaze toward southern Africa. Once again, they risked life and limb on rickety airplanes and primitive roads to bring hope to scattered bands of Friends and others who lived and worked to create more just, fair, and humane societies. Just below the surface in all of the Steere ministries lay the question of the mission of the Religious Society of Friends in relationship not only to Christianity but also to the other religions of humankind. The expanding of the Steere journeys to include Asia, especially to give the Nitobe Lecture in Japan, focused the issue more clearly and made it more urgent than ever. As a consequence not only of his wide travels but also his own deep immersion into a mystical dimension shared by eastern religions, none was better equipped than Douglas Steere to speak to the question.

157

Looking Eastward

After repeated visits to Europe and Africa, Asia was a logical choice for the ministry of Douglas and Dorothy Steere to scattered communities of Friends. An AFSC request to go to Africa delayed their visit to India from 1952-53 to 1954-55. Since the latter was Douglas' sabbatical year, the Steeres offered an additional six weeks to permit them to travel the western route to India via Hawaii, Japan, Hong Kong, and Bangkok. After visiting with Douglas' family in Seattle for three days, they flew on October 23 to Honolulu to spend nine days meeting with Friends and speaking on three occasions. One of these, at the University of Hawaii, evoked memories of Douglas' late colleague, Thomas Kelly, who had gone to Hawaii to teach in 1935. Kelly had hoped to study the religions and philosophies of India, China, and Japan and to find a place where the cultures of Asia and the West could interpenetrate.[1] From there the Steeres proceeded to Tokyo to attend the Japan Yearly Meeting, at which Douglas delivered the Nitobe Lecture.

In this lecture, "The Quaker Message: Unique or Universal?" he pictured Quakers standing "before a major crisis and a major opportunity." The great world religions are no longer separated by "the Chinese wall" of distance, language, and cultural isolation that once made them feel secure. Buddhism, Hinduism, and even Islam are asking Quakerism whether it is universal and inclusive, so as to respect their worship and practice, or unique and exclusive, so as to negate them. Citing Arnold Toynbee, he contended that the really vital question of this age is not in East/West military confrontations but in what happened to Buddhism and Christianity when they really interpenetrated one another for the first time in history. For Quakers the key issue is whether they can trust the Universal Christ enough to be open to people and ideas of other faiths in the way the Fourth Gospel, Justin Martyr, Clement of Alexandria, or Origen were in earlier centuries.

Too often have Protestants tried to throw "a screen of unique-ness" around Christ to protect him from humankind, reveal-ing thereby their lack of faith. Christians need to acknowledge their vulnerability just as persons of other faiths have con-fessed theirs, for instance, admitting the horrors of their crusades and wars and whites' oppression of blacks. The more vulnerable way would be the way of Francis of Assisi, Raymond Lull,[2] Nicholas of Cusa,[3] and John Woolman.

The mystical Christianity of Friends has before it the task of internalizing the encounter with the Universal Christ to such an extent that it will not erect fences but repel impulses of fear. It will renounce war and bear the consequences of a radical peace witness. It will welcome encounters with persons of other faiths and seek to learn from them. It will not fear discoveries of science. It will find common ground with others in the conviction that the Universal Christ en-compasses all of life. Such a sharing of Christ, they must recognize, will be costly and Quakers cannot undertake it with-out deepening their meetings, simplifying their lives more, serving others more intensely. The goal is to irradiate the world with the universal reconciling love of Christ.[4]

Douglas' address inaugurated a process of reflection on the Quaker mission which reached maturity in his Richard Cary Lecture entitled "Mutual Irradiation," delivered at the German Yearly Meeting in Bad Pyrmont in 1968. The visit, moreover, enabled Douglas to begin laying out initial plans for a Buddhist/Christian colloquy launched in 1967. Con-tacting Daisetz Suzuki, a professor at Columbia University living until January 1955 in Kamamura, he secured introduc-tions to persons in the Japanese Zen Buddhist world, chiefly in Kyoto, who could help him "feel something of the vitality of its life in Japan today."[5] He also hoped to learn as much as he could about Zen meditation. Once again, the personalist approach prevailed, as Douglas elected to meet with a Roshi (Zen priest), a distinguished philosopher of Zen named Hisamatsu, the founder of a Franciscan-type community called

Ito-En, and others such as Mumon Yamada in Kyoto. Back in Tokyo, he also visited the newly established International Christian University, where he discussed with Emil Brunner, eminent Reformed theologian, the shape of Christian mission. While Douglas visited Kyoto, Dorothy flew to Seoul to make contact with Quakers in Korea.[6]

In Hong Kong Douglas, obviously set to glean all the insight he could for interpreting the Quaker mission, focused his attention on the new concept of Christian outreach experimented with by Karl Reichelt, a Norwegian pastor he and Paul Braisted had met on their visit to Norway in 1937. Having spent his life in China, Reichelt set up a hostel where Buddhists could stop and study the Christian way in a well-stocked library, use the facilities of a chapel, or counsel with him. Thus, he hoped, they might discover Christianity for themselves and then bring to it "a meditative depth, a tradition of deep sympathy for the suffering of all sentient beings, and many fresh aspects of the problem of meeting pain and evil that would immeasurably enrich the Christian tradition."[7] Scandinavian friends of Reichelt funded the *Tao Fong Shan* Institute built about fifteen miles outside the city of Hong Kong between 1931 and 1938. Although the current directors were diminishing the liberality Reichelt had built in, Douglas and Dorothy thought the Institute still had "the look of the future about it" as a place where Christianity, Taoism, and Buddhism "might really interpenetrate each other and that a response to the living Christ that would be unfrocked of Western dress might really emerge."[8] Stops in Thailand and Burma (now Myanmar) exposed the Steeres to the struggle of Buddhism to impact effectively the lives of the masses.

In India the Steeres directed their attention to the spiritual climate and to spiritual centers and people who shone rays of hope on the starkly depressing background of the vastly-overpopulated country. They visited Santiniketan, a four-hour train ride northwest of Calcutta, where Rabindrinath Tagore had set up a college in which East and West could meet and learn about one another; the Ramakrishna Mission at Belur; the Aurobindo ashram at Pondicherry, India's largest with over a thousand residents; the Ramana Maharshi ashram at Tiruvanamali; the training center for Hindu priests where Sankara, an Eckhartian type Indian mystic and philosopher, lived; K.K. Chandy's Christian ashram near Kottyam in Travancore; and The Friends of Truth at Wardha, led by S.K. George, a community which sought to bring Hindus, Christians, Muslims, and Parsees together for worship and deeper understanding. Douglas thought the Christian ashram projected the most vital Christian thrust in India. In Chandy's ashram people lived on the simplest level and used their gifts in teaching, village improvement, leading religious retreats, looking after homeless boys, and living out a Christian witness in the community.[9]

The most impressive person the Steeres met in India was Vinoba Bhave, a Gandhi disciple whom Gandhi thought surpassed himself in spiritual maturity. In his Bhoodan Yagna, land sacrifice program, Bhave sought to implement a plan by which land owners would voluntarily share plots of land with the landless. The Steeres traveled 350 miles to contact Vinoba and his team. Douglas joined him and about twenty-five others for worship at 3:30 a.m. and for a twelve-mile walk at 4:00! In their newsletter Douglas commented: "It would be hard to exaggerate how deeply we were impressed by this man, or to exaggerate what his life, if it is spared for a few years, may mean to India."[10] Next to him perhaps was Radhikrishnan, Vice-President of India and its most distinguished philosopher, with whom Douglas discussed such political matters as India and Communism, the future of Kashmir, and Indian minorities along the east coast of Africa.[11] The Steeres also looked in on Quaker projects in India: a medical center at Barpali in Orissa province, a British Quaker medical and agricultural center in Rasulia near Hoshangabad, and the Quaker International Center in Delhi. At Sevagram they "caught a glimpse" of Gurdial Malik, a Quaker Sadhu who would figure prominently in Douglas' hopes for a Quaker ashram which could bring Christians and persons of other faiths together.

Ongoing Reflection on the Quaker Task

The task of Quakers in the modern world kept churning in Douglas' mind as he and Dorothy continued their visits. In an address to the Friends General Conference at Cape May, New Jersey, June 23, 1956, he sounded the alarm again about the urgency of the times. Quakers have an attic full of postponed actions and unfinished business, "one of the most stubbornly resistant" of which is "the Quaker attitude toward the missionary outreach of Christianity, the approach of Christianity to other world religions such as Buddhism, Hinduism, and Islam."[12] It did not surprise him that Quakers did not have clarity about missionary activity, but the common situation in which Christians and people of other faiths confront each other pressed Quakers to face the issue of the approach they would take to other religions. The visits to Japan and India in 1954 had left him with the feeling that representatives of Buddhism and Hinduism knew Christians better than Christians knew them. Christians, he felt, had much to learn from them, above all, about the inner life and willingness to confess their vulnerabilities with openness and candor. What are the alternative approaches Christians may take to other world religions? There are four: (1) extermination, (2) syncretism, (3) coexistence, and (4) the one for which Douglas would make a case, mutual irradiation. The presuppositions on which he based his conviction were these: (1) that Jesus Christ is the fulfillment of the great world religions; (2) "that God has been playing on the hearts of [people] from the very beginning, and that [God] has never [been] without a witness in any age or region of the world";[13] (3) that religion is human response to God's initiative so that the great religions are all marked by similar features; (4) and

162

that, if these assumptions are true, then extermination of one religion by another is excluded and the Christian task is to understand, learn from, and speak to persons of other faiths. None of this implies, however, that all human responses to God are equally adequate and can thus be "patched together into some form of nervous universalism as syncretism or blending suggests."[14] "Nor does it imply that we must or can ever accept a hygienic coexistence as the final goal."[15] Coexistence is better than a war of extermination, but it cannot bring real peace; that can come only from vital interaction, for which we have models in the Anglican missionary work of C.F. Andrews among Hindus in India, Karl Reichelt among Buddhists and Confucianists in Hong Kong, John Van Ess among Muslims in Iraq, and some small centers such as Charles Malik proposed for Lebanon or K.K. Chandy's ashram provided in South India. What, then, should Quakers do? Douglas hoped that they would establish in India, Japan, the Middle East, and Southern Africa "at least one center not unlike a small Pendle Hill where this process of mutual irradiation is being fearlessly carried on."[16]

Middle-East Mission

Douglas had a "growing sense of the importance of deepening the understanding of the great world religions for each other and of [his] increasing feeling that perhaps the Quakers, with their mystical core of an inward experience of the Christian religion, possessed an openness that might lay on [them] a special responsibility for this task."[17] Recognizing this in 1959, the AFSC asked the Steeres to spend some time in Cairo among spiritually-centered Muslims and try to interpret Muslim spiritual insight in letters. Although the Steeres had "fought shy" of the Middle East up to this time, thinking entrance into the Islamic and Jewish worlds required more expertise than they possessed, they yielded to the Committee's argument that a brief visit by amateurs might discover "whether there was any hint, on the religious level, of a reconciliation of the deep clefts that divide this part of the world."[18] In addition, Douglas thought the visit offered an opportunity to experience a creative encounter of the world's religions in what he called "mutual irradiation." As preparation, he held long talks with Charles Malik, Lebanese delegate to the United Nations, who proposed some kind of spiritual center to bring Christians and Muslims together in Lebanon. He also solicited advice from a number of others having firsthand knowledge of the Middle East, Islam, and Judaism, including his long time friend Abraham Joshua Heschel, professor of ethics and mysticism at the Jewish Theological Seminary of America in New York City. In their newsletter the Steeres noted a number of things about Islam which had always "fascinated" Quakers: its lay character with no group properly called priests, its iconoclasm, its insistence on living the devout life "in the thick of things," and its emphasis on universal brotherhood without distinction by race or class. In the Sufis they "felt a certain kinship with their witness to the accessibility of God and to [God's] compassionate longing to kindle and transform the human heart."[19]

In Cairo, with the help of President McLain and Professor Charles Geddes of the American University, Douglas met a number of leading Muslims whom he got to know well enough to speak about issues with great frankness.[20] He presented in writing to the Rector of Al-Azhar, the Egyptian Oxford, a set of twelve questions, translated into Arabic, which searched for connections between Quakers and Islam. They included: the past and present vitality of Sufism in the renewal of Islam; whether Islam faced a problem of secularism and how it was responding to it; whether there was any basis in Islam for non-violent approaches to conflict; whether lay leadership continued in Islamic missions; whether Islam's respect for Jesus prompted closer relations with Christians as both faced a secular world today; whether there was value in a small

164

center in the Middle East where Muslim and Christian scholars could meet to explore differences and commonalities; and whether exchanges of students at the doctoral level would be of value. Dorothy visited an Egyptian farm and sought information on the role of women in Islamic society. Before leaving Egypt, Douglas also visited leading authorities in the Coptic Church, notably Father Makary, the spiritual secretary to the Patriarch or Pope of the Coptic Church, and the Patriarch himself, and made trips to three monasteries. He later sent books to the Al Suriary monastery, where Abu Shenuda, a professor turned monk, helped him to understand the monastic regimen, and to Father Makary.[21]

In Beirut, Lebanon, the Steeres gave their time principally to the International Quaker Center and Brumanna, the old Quaker preparatory school near Beirut, but they also conferred with the Druze leader Kamel Jungblatt, and Douglas spoke to faculties of American University and of the Near East School of Theology. In Jordanian-controlled Jerusalem they were met by Quaker directors of Near East Relief work and visited the principal Arab refugee camp to hear the Palestinian case. They talked with the Anglican Archbishop of Jerusalem about the Christian study center for modern Islam set up by Kenneth Craig. In Israeli-controlled Jerusalem they made contact with numerous Jewish scholars, including Martin Buber, who could help them gain insight into the Jewish world, and shared in a Jerusalem sabbath, which they found "not only novel but profoundly moving."[22] After nine days in Jerusalem, they visited different types of kibbutzim and other land settlements, a Hebrew language school, the Weizmann Institute, and community development work among Arabs sponsored by Quakers.

As they moved about, they kept asking whether the ice between Arabs and Jews could be melted. Buber insisted that, in the present situation, no dialogue was possible. The Steeres saw in this an urgent task for Quakers, "feeling that Friends must search themselves to the core to ask whether or not we have any direct responsibility to help in some way in creating the conditions where such a genuine conversation might again be fashioned."[23] In 1969 the American Friends Service Committee and the Friends World Committee for Consultation followed up on this concern with a peace initiative in the Middle East.[24]

Once Again the Far East

Following their Middle East tour, the Steeres made a second exploratory trip into India and Japan in the beginning of 1960 with a view to preparing the ground further for dialogues between representatives of the world's great religions. A four-hour layover in Teheran on the way to India permitted them to visit a Protestant mission staff carrying on "a fierce discussion on the state of Islam in Iran today."[25] In India they focused their attention on Gandhi's continuing impact and on the prospect of Hindu/Christian interpenetration. Although they were disappointed to find that Bhave's land-sharing plan had not worked well and that Bhave was withdrawing, in the typical pattern of the Indian saint, they learned that the Ghandian Memorial Foundation had registered greater success, administering more than $25,000,000 collected for the poor since Gandhi's death in 1948. They conferred with the Director, G. Ramchandran, and with Gandhi's physician and secretary. In addition to visiting several Quakers who would play a role in the first dialogue between Christians and Hindus in 1967, they spent two days at Pachmari to check with an architect about remodeling the Quaker house for a center and made visits to other centers where the engagement of Christianity with Hinduism was projected—the new Christian Institute for Society and Religion at Bangalore, a small abbey near Peermade in Kerala where Bede Griffiths and another Cistercian hoped to build a conference center for retreats, and K.K. Chandy's ashram at Kottayam. Before leaving, they spent twenty hours traveling by train to see again the Quaker

Village Development program at Barpali and twenty-two hours to return to Calcutta (only 450 miles)! On the way to Japan they touched down in Hong Kong to visit again *Tao Fong Shan,* the center founded by Karl Reichelt and now under direction of his son, which focused at the time on the study of Buddhism and Confucianism. Noting the financial struggle of the institute, Douglas expressed the hope that the site might be used

> to develop this study of these two world religions and to associate with them young scholars from Asia, Europe, and USA who might come out there on fellowships for such study, as well as to serve the Hong Kong, Taiwan, and South Asian Christian churches and seminaries through courses and institutes that would bear on this central issue of the creative encounter with these world faiths.[26]

A short time later, the World Council of Churches assumed sponsorship and turned *Tao Fong Shan* into a study center for the Chinese religions.[27] In Japan, taking one more step toward the colloquy between Christians and Buddhists, the Steeres conferred with Professor Hisamatsu in Kyoto, plumbing "the core of the issue that divides Zen from Western thought,"[28] and again visited the International Christian University in Tokyo.

Ecumenical Interlude

The exchange between eastern and western cultures and religions assumed an increasingly prominent place among Douglas Steere's concerns as he and Dorothy concluded their journey to the Orient in the fall of 1959 and beginning of 1960. An event of immense universal import, notably the Second Vatican Council, however, intervened to interrupt and postpone until 1967 his dream of colloquia between Christians and people of other faiths and cultures. The Council itself sharpened rather than diminished his vision, for it raised to a new level reflection upon Christian attitudes toward the Jewish people against the background of the Holocaust and Christian relationships with people of other faiths. At the third session of the Council Douglas and another Quaker leader, Dean Freiday, questioned Father Neuner, a Jesuit theologian who taught in India, about the plans of the Secretariat for the Non-Christian Religion, and exulted at a forty-page memorandum Jacques Cuttat, Swiss Ambassador to India, had addressed to the Secretariat calling for dialogue with Hindus. "The night I read it," Douglas remarked in a newsletter from the Council, "I could hardly sleep for excitement."[29] He raised with Neuner and Archbishop de Souza of Bhopal whether Quakers might host dialogues such as Cuttat suggested and received an enthusiastic yes. His mind immediately shifted into a planning mode and he blueprinted a plan amazingly close to the one Quakers later used in Japan and India.[30] At a meeting of Observers with the Secretariat for Promoting Christian Unity to discuss the schema on Missions, Douglas queried "how the schema could almost completely neglect the whole change of outlook which would come over the mission operation if a serious approach was being made to the Non-Christian Religions and how they could present a strategy of missions for the future with no consideration of this." The Catholic scholar preparing the schema listened sympathetically.[31] During the fourth and final session of the Council, Douglas offered his opinion that the schema on the Non-Christian Religions with its declaration on the Jews, passed by a large majority on November 20, 1964,

> contains the essential points that should be made, but that it also contains more preaching of Roman Catholic doctrine than was necessary or even suitable to make a humble confession of past wrong and determination for future amendment as well as to express the immeasurable debt of the Christian religion

to its Jewish heritage and the peculiar bond of tenderness that must always exist if we were to be in a right relationship with our Jewish brethren.

It also left much to be desired regarding the background of relationships to the other world religions. Yet it did offer hope that the churches would be encouraged to move in the right direction, which is one where "Christian theology is going to have to rethink its position most drastically in the remaining years of this century if it is not to fail in its universal mission to our contracting world where these interpenetrations of the world religions are so much a reality in our day."[32]

Colloquia in Japan and India

The 1966 journey to Japan and India wound through Europe, Africa, Australia, New Zealand, and Korea. In late October and early November, the Steeres stopped in Geneva to confer with Victor Hayward, Director of the World Council of Churches' Center for the Study of the World Religions, and in Rome to share plans for the colloquia with Bishop Willebrands, Thomas Stransky, and Louis Dupré at the Secretariat for Promoting Christian Unity. They proceeded then to make brief visits in Cairo, Kenya, Zambia (northern Rhodesia), Southern Rhodesia (Zimbabwe), South Africa, Australia, New Zealand, and Hong Kong. In Australia Douglas delivered the James Backhouse Lecture "On Being Present Where You Are" at the Friends Yearly Meeting and received much encouragement regarding the upcoming colloquia. In Wellington, New Zealand, he spoke to Roman Catholics and Protestants on "Creative Encounter of the World Religions." In Hong Kong the Steeres visited *Tao Fong Shan* once more. In the Steere travel letters Douglas disclosed again his fervent hopes that it would be a place of genuine encounter in an era when the war in Vietnam laid bare the weaknesses of cultures based on the Christian faith.

The real issue is whether this Center is to become a kind of sophisticated "public relations" post for enabling Christian leaders to learn and to "deal with" the world religions, or whether it is to be a place for the far deeper task of helping the Christian religion to open itself to the message which the Holy Spirit has to speak to it through Buddhism, Taoism and Confucianism. If it did only the former, it would leave China to continue to identify Christianity through the heavily institutionally-weighted Western versions of it; would not give the Chinese people the opportunity, with its help, to come to terms with their own Buddhist past, as Reichelt in his reverent way longed to do; and would not prepare the ground for what may be Christian theology's greatest task in the balance of this century; namely, the exploration in the light of the challenge of the great world religions like Buddhism, of the universal element in Christianity. It seems to me that only in this way can this Center help in the great self-searching that Christianity must go through.[33]

In Korea the Steeres met Ham Sok Hon, "a kind of Gandhi of the Korea of today," who had visited Pendle Hill in 1962-63. They dialogued with a small group of Koreans who asked "searching questions" about the Religious Society of Friends and its relevance for their society. Meantime, they visited with Friends day and night and with various others, and Douglas spoke several times.

The long and eagerly awaited colloquies finally took place in the spring of 1967. Douglas and Dorothy Steere carefully looked after every detail, even making a stop at the Quaker Center in Tokyo before going on to Korea. Flying from Seoul to Osaka and traveling by bus to Kyoto to make final preparations for the Colloquium, they talked over plans with Eshin Nishimura, a Pendle Hill resident in 1960-61, and Kachiko Yokogawa, who came to Pendle Hill a year later. Douglas

170

also contacted President Tetsutaro Ariga of Kobe College, Rev. Norbert Klein, Professor Masao Abe, and several other participants about the colloquium. They proceeded then to Tokyo to go over plans again with the Quaker team and Professor Heinrich Dumoulin, S.J., a professor at Sophia University and author of *A History of Zen Buddhism*. After worshipping in the Quaker Meeting on Easter Sunday, they drove to Oiso, where

HAM SOK HON

they were to have the exclusive use of a beautiful Japanese villa.

True to the Steere outlook and philosophy of life, the colloquy assumed a strongly personalistic character which would allow for maximum sharing of experience. Composed of an impressive group of scholars representing both religions,[34] it combined more formal presentations with intimate biographicals and leisure time. Afternoons were kept free allowing time for personal exchanges. For the more formal presentations Buddhists and Christians met separately and decided on the persons and the order in which they would speak on the two topics—"The Inward Journey" and "Social Responsibility for Ordering Our World"—so that each person in the group would address one or the other of the topics. Speeches were not to be prepared far in advance and were to be limited to fifteen minutes, although the chair did not enforce the rule very strictly. The morning was divided into two periods—9:00-10:30 and 10:50-12:20. In each a Zen Buddhist

171

and a Christian made a presentation not of an academic paper but of a topic followed by discussion. The meetings were carried on entirely in Japanese. Evening sessions ran from 7:00 to 8:45 followed by a snack and a Japanese bath. Douglas was impressed with the degree to which Christianity and Buddhism intersected in their discussion of the inward journey.

This topic seemed extremely timely, bringing together members of both the Christian and the Zen groups, as they spoke of how they had come through the crises and into the religious life, into a realization of their common need and of the ways that need had so often been met. It was intensely interesting to see how nearly every Japanese Christian in the group, whether he was a birthright Christian or had come directly from Buddhism, had a deep Buddhist layer in his interior life, a layer that had often been carefully insulated away from his Christian life in order to keep it from threatening it, and yet that had gone on working in him. And in the same way almost every Buddhist who told his story had, at some time or another in his life, had an encounter with Christ or with Christianity. This meant that, for both Christian and Buddhist, the problem of the inward journey and of expressing it to the group was a bringing out into the open what was in reality a continuous dialogue in the unconscious life of each man., and thus these sessions were anything but academic affairs; rather, they were intensely existential and personal.[35]

On the topic of social responsibility Christians had a ready theology, but Buddhists admitted they did not, clearly placing their accent on the inward journey, *satori*. Both groups found the exchange enlightening.[36] Spontaneously at the close of the colloquium, participants chose a committee of six to arrange a three-day session the following year and the Buddhist/Christian Colloquium continued for a decade. It prepared the way for other dialogues as well.[37]

The morning after the Buddhist/Christian Colloquium concluded, the Steeres flew by way of Hong Kong to Delhi, meeting that evening with forty persons in Quaker House. Two days later, they made their way to Bangalore and, after visits to United Theological College and the Center for the Study of Religion and Society and with various persons, they proceeded to Ootacamund to prepare for the Hindu/Christian Colloquium with the help of Ranjit Chetsingh, one of the Vice-Chairmen of the Friends World Committee for Consultation, and his wife Doris. Despite some late withdrawals, the colloquium drew seven Hindus and nine Christians, a "miracle" considering the difficulty of traveling in India.[38]

The Hindu/Christian Colloquium used essentially the same pattern as the Buddhist/Christian save that it used only one topic, "The Inward Journey." All participants introduced themselves and explained what drew them to the meeting. In his introduction Douglas articulated his own vision as it was in process of formation:

> The very fact of our being here together this afternoon is, for me, the realization of a dream that has been going on for many years. I have long felt that the time has come when the isolation and misunderstanding and chasms between the great World Religions must in some way be overcome, and that perhaps in such a small gathering as this there could be a genuine experience of mutual irradiation if we could freely share the treasures of our respective traditions with each other. This will only be possible if we can lay aside our preaching fronts and not try either to defend ourselves or to polemicize each other. This opportunity for Christian and Hindu scholars and men [and women] of the spirit to share with each other may even give us an experience of how this is to be done so that we can share it with others.[39]

This colloquy did not go as deep as the one at Oiso and lacked the radical Sankara position of Hinduism, but Douglas described it in his report as "open and searching." Participants were impressed with the sensitivity they showed to one another and decided to meet again the following year, perhaps holding two colloquies, one in the north and one in the south. The future of this colloquium, however, was much less certain than that of the Buddhist/Christian Colloquium because of the difficulties of travel in India. One more was held in North India but none in the South.[40]

From India the Steeres flew to Rome. On April 24 Douglas presented a report on the colloquia to the Secretariat for Christian Unity. The Secretariat arranged an audience for him with Pope Paul VI. The Pope said he wanted to thank the Quakers for the meetings and believed they were very important. Douglas thanked him for his efforts to negotiate an end to the war in Vietnam. Predictably, on the way home, the Steeres stopped to visit friends in Switzerland, Finland (5 days), Sweden (6 days), and England (12 days). They returned to Haverford June 1 in time to attend the Friends World Conference held at Guilford College in North Carolina.

From Nitobe to Cary

From a purely physical point of view the Steere globetrotting was extraordinary. They were exerting incredible energy to help Quakers grasp a global vision and purpose in an age when the changing world situation mandated such breadth. Douglas Steere stood in the *avant garde* of persons such as metahistorian Arnold Toynbee who could foresee the urgency of genuine East/West understanding and interaction as modern technology welded their economies and cultures and, yes, survival as never before. From the Nitobe Lecture in Japan in 1954 to the Richard Cary Lecture in Germany in 1968, goaded forward by Vatican II, he sounded with increasing urgency and clarity his summons to the Quaker world fellowship to undertake a mission for which they were uniquely equipped as a part of the mystical body of Christ.

Notes

1. *Douglas and Dorothy Steere's Travel Letter, #1,* Hong Kong, November 30, 1954.
2. Lull (c. 1233 - c. 1315) was a Franciscan missionary who, in the age of Crusades, tried to win Muslims by love and persuasion rather than by the use of force. On three occasions he went on missions to North Africa.
3. Nicholas of Cusa (1401-1464) followed in the tradition of Augustine, Pseudo-Dionysius, and other Neoplatonists. He was a forerunner of the Renaissance in Northern Europe. Douglas esteemed especially his mystical theology.
4. Douglas V. Steere, "The Quaker Message: Unique or Universal?" *The Friends' Quarterly,* 9 (April 1955), 49-56. A slightly revised form appeared in *Christian Century,* August 3, 1955, 893-5.
5. *Steeres' Travel Letter, #2,* Delhi, India, December 28, 1954, 1.
6. *Steeres' Travel Letter, #3,* Delhi, India, January 26, 1955, 1.
7. *Steeres' Travel Letter, #3,* 3.
8. *Steeres' Travel Letter, #3,,* 3-4.
9. *Steeres' Travel Letter, #4,* Salisbury, Southern Rhodesia, 22 March 1955, 8.
10. *Steeres' Travel Letter, #4,* 12.
11. *Steeres' Travel Letter, #5,* Johannesburg, South Africa, 31 March, 1955, 1-3.
12. Douglas V. Steere, "The Christian Approach to the World Religions," *Friends Journal,* August 4, 1956, 1.
13. Steere, "The Christian Approach," 4.
14. Steere, "The Christian Approach," 4.
15. Steere, "The Christian Approach," 4.
16. Steere, "The Christian Approach," 6.
17. Douglas V. Steere, UNPUBLISHED JOURNAL, 782.
18. *Steeres' Travel Letter, #4,* Delhi, India, 8 January, 1960, 1.
19. *Steeres' Travel Letter, #4,* 4.
20. *Steeres' Travel Letter, #4,* 3.
21. Douglas V. Steere, *Letters to Abu Shenuda, Al Suriary, Coptic Monastery, Wadi Natrun, Egypt* and *Father Makary, Coptic Institute, Cairo,* April 5, 1960; Rev. Shenouda El Souriary, Blessed Virgin Monastery, Wadi el Natrun, Egypt, *Letter to Douglas V. Steere,* November 1, 1961.
22. *Steeres' Travel Letter, #5,* Tokyo Japan, January 24, 1960, 7.
23. *Steeres' Travel Letter, #5,* 15.
24. See Chapter 14, p. 253.
25. *Steeres' Travel Letter, #6,* Haverford College, February 14, 1960, 1.

26. *Steeres' Travel Letter, #6*, 14.
27. *Steeres' Travel Letters, #5 (Korea and the Colloquia in Japan and India)*, 1-2. The entirely new staff consulted Douglas on this visit about its future direction.
28. *Steeres' Travel Letter, #6*, 14.
29. Douglas V. Steere, *Session 3: Journal from Rome, V*, 2.
30. His statement merits citation. "The Clarens sort of meeting if there were some financial means available to back it, with carefully selected guests and a light program, and opportunity for men and women from the different religions in India to become acquainted and to leave way open for the program to shape up if there were one or two resource persons of real substance present, may have the seed of something in it worth further exploration. It has already begun in different ways in India and might happen in the Middle East or in Japan." (Steere, *Journal from Rome, V*, 2.)
31. Steere, *Journal from Rome, V*, 6.
32. Douglas V. Steere, *Session 4: Journal from Rome, III*, 14.
33. *Steeres' Travel Letter, #5 (Korea and the Colloquia in Japan and India)*, 1f.
34. To avoid encumbering the text, I will list these here. The list reveals how much the cultivation of personal friendships year after year through repeated visits was worth to the Steeres. The **eleven Christians** were: Tetsutaro Ariga, President of Kobe College and founder of the WCC Institute for the Study of Japanese Religions; Jun-Ichi Asano, Professor of New Testament at Kobe College; Heinrich Dumoulin, S.J., identified above; Yukio Irie, a Quaker professor of literature in Tokyo and chair of the meetings; Kazo Kitamori, Protestant Barthian theologian; Enomiya Lassalle, S.J., author of a book on the nature of Zen "Enlightenment" residing in Hiroshima; Ichiro Okamura, Carmelite student of Zen in its relation to the Carmelite tradition of meditation; Shigeto Oshida, a Dominican who had established a rural retreat center; Masa Sekine, teacher of Hebrew and Old Testament; Sei-ichi Yagi, a noted young Protestant theologian; and Norbert Klein. The **ten Buddhists** were: Masao Abe, Professor at Nara University who had written much on Zen Buddhism and comparative religions; Shikin Furuta, a professor and disciple of Daisetz Suzuki; Yasuaki Nara, a young Zen teacher and member of the Soto Zen sect; Reirin Yamada, President of Komazawa University and noted theologian of the Soto Zen sect; Eshin Nishimura, a young Zen Buddhist scholar in doctoral work at Kyoto University; Zenkei Shibayama, Zen master and abbot of Nanzenji Temple and Monastery in Kyoto; Torataro Shimomura, distinguished Japanese philosopher

176

and Zen scholar; Takashi Hirata, Professor at Hanazoni Zen College in Kyoto; Mumon Yamada, President of Hanazoni Zen College and Zen master of a temple in Kobe; Kachiko Yokagawa, young Zen woman scholar helping to edit a volume in honor of Suzuki. Professor Hisamatsu would have been the eleventh Buddhist scholar, but illness prevented his attendance. *Steeres' Travel Letter,* #5, 6.

35. *Steeres' Travel Letter,* #5, 10.

36. Douglas V. Steere, *Letter to Professor Hisamatsu, Kyoto, Japan,* May 27, 1968, thanking him for the message he sent to the colloquium at Oiso and expressing his joy that another would take place; *Letter to Professor Heinrich Dumolin, S.J., Tokyo,* May 27, expressing appreciation for the fine paper he wrote about the first colloquy. "There is nothing more important at this time than our working at the very difficult formulation of the concept of the universal in Christianity. We have worked for so long at its uniqueness that we have lost our capacity to explore its universality. No one has a really adequate formula for it, but somewhere in the theology thinking there must be a way of putting this which will give us a freer ground to move on as we approach the other great world religions." Douglas wrote a similar letter to Father LaSalle, Hiroshima, dated May 28, 1968, rejoicing that LaSalle would take part in the second colloquy. Yoshio Watanabe, Tokyo, *Letter to Douglas and Dorothy Steere,* June 10, 1968, reported that participants of the second colloquy would be mostly the same and the themes would be "My Religious Experience" and "Peacemaking as a Superreligious Movement." Watanabe, *Letter to Douglas V. Steere,* August 10, gave more specifics and commended the idea of a study group on Zen. "It may prove a way for getting Quakerism indigenized in Japan where Quakerism has not yet taken root firm and safe to my thinking."

37. See Douglas V. Steere, *Letter to Professor Maseo Abe, Kyoto, Japan,* December 22, 1967, inquiring about plans for the second colloquy in Kyoto in March, 1968; Tetsutaro Ariga, Kobe College, *Letter to Douglas V. Steere,* December 22, 1967; Masao Abe, Kyoto, *Letter to Douglas V. Steere,* January 24, 1968, reporting a postponement of the second colloquy until the summer; Douglas V. Steere, *Letter to President Tetsutaro Ariga,* March 21, 1968, thanking him for letter detailing plans for the second colloquy on August 26-30; Douglas V. Steere, *Letter to Masao Abe, Kyoto,* April 22, 1968. The length of the exchanges is documented by Yukio Irie, et al., *A Zen-Christian Pilgrimage: The Fruits of Ten Annual Colloquia in Japan, 1967-1976* (Tokyo: Takuro Isomura, 1981). In an article entitled "New

Horizons for Buddhist-Christian Encounter," *Bulletin of the Council of Societies for the Study of Religion*, 22 (September 1993), 67-68, David W. Chappell, Vice-President, Society for Buddhist-Christian Studies, University of Hawaii, cited the 1967 colloquy as one of the embrryonic meetings in Buddhist-Christian encounter. Most who had engaged in this meeting continued in other colloquia.

38. **Hindu scholars** were: Swami Chidananda, a disciple of Swami Sivananda educated in Christian schools; R.S. Misra, a professor of Indian philosophy and religion at the Hindu University at Banaras; S. Krishnaswamy, a professor of modern Indian history at Madras Christian College with a Ph.D. from the University of Chicago; V. A. Devasenapathy, a professor at Madras University; M. Yamunacharya, a former professor of philosophy at Mysore University working for the Gandhi Peace Foundation; K. Sivaraman, educated in philosophy at Banaras and Harvard; and R.G. Chabria, a medical doctor in Bombay. Besides Douglas and Dorothy Steere and Ranjit and Doris Chetsingh, **Christians** were: V. C. Samuel, Professor at United Theological College, Bangalore; John Carman, an assistant professor in the School of World Religions at Harvard; Chrysostom, Bishop of the Mar Thoma Church in Kerala; Paramananda Divarkar, S.J., a professor of philosophy of religion in Bombay and Rector of Xavier College; Bede Griffiths, a Benedictine monk who established an ashram at Peermade; Herbert Jai Singh; K. Klostermaier, a priest of the Society of the Divine Word and participant in the colloquies gathered by Swiss Ambassador Cuttat between 1962 and 1965; Laurie Baker, a Quaker architect for Mission for Lepers with an ashram near Bede Griffiths'; Nette Bossert, Dutch Quaker working in Delhi and Santineketan; Marjorie Sykes, once a teacher at the college founded by Tagore in Santineketan and at Sevagram since 1959 at Kotagiri. *Steeres' Travel Letter, #5,* 14-21.

39. *Steeres' Travel Letter, #5,* 14.

40. Ranjit Chetsingh, Rajpur, India, *Letter to Douglas V. Steere,* January 12, 1968, reported correspondence with Sivaraman about a second colloquy but had not received replies to two letters. He and Chludananda had agreed to convene a group at Rajpur Study Centre on March 22-24. Ranjit Chetsingh, *Letter to Douglas V. Steere,* May 10, 1968, related his inability to convene more than a very short "family-like gathering." Douglas V. Steere, *Letter to Bede Griffiths, O.S.B. Kerala, South India,* May 27, 1968, expressed disappointment that no second colloquy had taken place in South India but pleasure that one had been held in North India.

XII

———◆◆◆———

Ecumenical Pioneer

$\mathcal{D}$ ouglas Steere was a catholic Christian, catholic with a little c, meaning one who belonged to the church universal. Though he concentrated most of his energies on the Religious Society of Friends, he shared his ministry far beyond that small body of believers, and the breadth of his openness and the depth of his insight spoke to the condition of Protestants, Catholics, and other believers.

Douglas Steere was an ecumenical pioneer, one of those who led the way in the outward rippling of the ecumenical movement from its Protestant beginnings to its embrace of Orthodox and Roman Catholics and persons of other faiths as more and more came to discover that their individual experiences were mere waves in a vast ocean of humankind's reaching out toward God. What is remarkable is *how early* he waded down the Protestant stream in which he had grown up toward the Catholic mainstream and then to that vast ocean from which emerges the faith of all humankind. What prepared him for such a role?

Ecumenical Conditioning

One clue is that the Steere family did not have strong anchorage in any single denomination. Although they had Methodist

179

roots on both sides and Douglas was baptized at age fourteen into a Methodist church, the family transferred their membership a year or so later to a Presbyterian church nearer their home. A year after that, Douglas joined an Evangelical and Reformed church whose pastor wanted him to play his trombone for their Sunday school orchestra.[1] The year he taught at Onaway, Michigan, Douglas also played in the Baptist Sunday school orchestra. Of that he remarked years later, "Ecumenism apparently started early."[2]

Although Douglas was not exposed favorably to Roman Catholicism in his early years,[3] he had experiences which encouraged greater openness in his years at Michigan Agricultural College and at Harvard. When he attended Harvard, his critical religious search drew him to audit a course in Church history at Boston University, attend an Oxford Group Movement meeting, and join in prayer with two students at Episcopal Theological Seminary. More crucial, however, for enlarging his ecumenical universe was the friendship and encouragement of Palfrey Perkins, minister of the First Unitarian Church in Weston, Massachusetts. Perkins helped him discover a principle which would free him to range far and wide. From Perkins he learned not to judge by denomination.

During his three years at Oxford, a panoply of opportunities expanded Douglas' awareness, for Oxford overflowed with ecumenical currents. Still an "unattached seeker" and perhaps "irresponsible religious tramp,"[4] he felt drawn to the Student Christian Movement; found spiritual nourishment in the sermons of William B. Selbie at Mansfield College; visited St. Mary's, where J.H. Newman had preached the sermons that fueled the Oxford Movement; heard Dean W.R. Inge, G.H. Studdert-Kennedy, and Ronald Knox at St. Aldate's; and marveled at the preaching of Maude Royden in London. Then, more by accident than by design, he discovered the Quakers through Henry T. Gillett and Quakerism through Canon B. H. Streeter.

More positive impressions of the Roman Catholic Church also took shape in Oxford days. During vacations on the continent, he felt attracted to the Roman Catholic Church's "inviting buildings open for prayer throughout the day." He looked upon Catholicism as "the seed-bed of the great mystics" and encourager of the inner life.[5] Although Douglas Steere chose to become a Quaker, he did not relinquish his appreciation and love for the church that expended the most energy in conserving and fostering the contemplative or mystical tradition on which the Quakers also fed. He resorted early, often, and deeply to this tradition to quench his own thirst for living waters and that of others who turned to him for companionship and counsel in the same search.

From Maria Laach to Vatican II

Douglas Steere's study of Baron von Hügel's religious philosophy put him in debt not only to the Baron but to the whole Catholic contemplative tradition, as it did much to shape his own philosophy of life and sense of vocation.[6] Von Hügel's own expansive Catholicism, lived out in the context of the repressive anti-Modernist era,[7] enabled Douglas to affirm and appropriate what was good in the Catholic tradition rather than to dismiss it wholesale. Appropriately, in 1964, as he participated in the Second Vatican Council as an official Observer-Delegate, he sought in part to repay his debt to von Hügel with the publication of *Spiritual Counsel and Letters of Friedrich von Hügel.*[8]

Early in 1931, just after completing his dissertation on von Hügel, Douglas saw another door open toward the ecumenical future when he met Maria Schlüter-Hermkes. She urged Douglas to spend a sabbatical in Germany where she would open the world of Catholic spirituality to him. The month he spent at Maria Laach in September and early October of 1933 introduced him to the rich spirituality of the Benedictine tradition, which he drew on the rest of his life[9] and secured a life long friendship with Damasus Winzen. In addition, Douglas developed friendships with Roman Catholic scholars such as Romano Guardini. In matters relating to the spiritual life, Douglas usually found himself more comfortable in company with Roman Catholics than with Protestants and developed many other deep friendships with Catholic scholars after World War II. He returned repeatedly to Freiburg, Germany, for instance, to engage Reinhold Schneider in conversation about prayer.[10] Following World War II, he took a keen interest in the Una Sancta movement which had united Catholics and Protestants during the war, and he made it a regular practice to visit Catholic monasteries.[11]

Observer-Delegate at Vatican II

Given these long years of encounter with Roman Catholics, Douglas Steere was a logical choice to represent the Religious Society of Friends at the Second Vatican Council, the most remarkable and unexpected ecumenical event since the Reformation of the sixteenth century. Although the Friends World Committee for Consultation asked Douglas to represent them at the Council, he was unable to do this until Session 2 because of his teaching responsibilities.[12] He taught at Union Theological Seminary in New York as the Harry Emerson Fosdick Visiting Professor in 1961-62 and was heavily involved in the organizing of an East-West Colloquy held near Prague in January 1962 to promote understanding and ease tensions between the two blocs. He planned to retire from Haverford College at the end of the 1962-63 academic year, thus freeing him and Dorothy to devote much more time to the other sessions.

His delay in getting to the Council notwithstanding, Douglas' presence during the remaining sessions assured a good hearing for major concerns of the Religious Society of Friends and other groups which shared them. By virtue of their personalities, sensitivities, experience in relating to persons of other cultures, and world awareness, he and Dorothy came to the Council unusually well equipped for the Steere-style of personal diplomacy which could get a hearing in a cumbersome system of soliciting Protestant opinion.

The Second Vatican Council involved such vast numbers (64,000 crowded into St. Peter's for the opening of Session 4 on September 14, 1965!) that even the 2,300 bishops, those who voted, needed strong communication skills to have an impact. To their credit, Roman Catholic officials did make an effort to see that official Observer-Delegates knew each day's schedule, could hear discussion in their own language (though Latin was the official language of the Council), and would receive a sympathetic hearing about their concerns as the commissions prepared different schemata for approval of the bishops. At the request of Bishop J.G.M. Willebrands, associate to Cardinal Augustin Bea in the Secretariat for Promoting Christian Unity, Douglas prepared a statement on the laity. He also made a formal "Intervention" in the fourth session regarding Chapter V of Schema XIII concerning a statement on peace. Like many other observers, he worked diligently behind the scenes in his trademark style. He frequently contacted staff of the Secretariat for Christian Unity, which was hosting the official observers, especially Bishop Willebrands, and made one official visit with Cardinal Bea regarding Pope Paul VI's proposal that the Curia set up a Secretariat for the Non-Christian Religions and possibly invite representatives of these faiths to the third session of the Council. He talked with many participants in the coffee bar when the tedium of the Council caused them to retreat. He and Dorothy, in Sessions 2 and 4 which she attended, hosted numerous meals for observers, for *periti* (experts) working on different commissions, and even for bishops. Douglas and Dorothy published a *Journal from Rome,* a newsletter on the Council, for all three sessions.

Conscientious Objection and Nuclear Deterrence

The issues before the Council which claimed his attention as a Quaker leader included: conscientious objection and nuclear deterrence, the laity, Christianity and the non-Christian religions, the Jewish people, and spirituality. When Bishop Willebrands greeted them at the Secretariat for Promoting Christian Unity and briefed them on session 2, assuring them that their comments would have a hearing and impact, Douglas asked what had happened to Richard Ullmann's statement on conscientious objection.[13] The Cardinal assured him that it would be used and that he was personally sympathetic with it.[14] Obviously an issue of highest priority to the peace churches, Douglas kept it at the forefront of his attention until the Council finally approved Schema XIII, The Church and the Modern World, which dealt with war and peace. He broached the subject to Karl Alter, Archbishop of Cincinnati, in November 1963 during the second session. When the bishops took up discussion of the section on Peace and War, he found the statement "very bold," especially vis-à-vis nuclear weaponry, but noted that Quakers would have a few lines they would want to see in the appendix making room for conscientious objection. The problem was that the statement came in the appendix, not in the text itself, and Douglas spent considerable time with leading bishops—Cardinal Koenig, Cardinal Alfrink, Bishop McGrath, Bishop Joyce of Vermont, and others—and Professor Bernard Häring lobbying for a change.[15]

At the beginning of Session 4, on September 27, 1965, the Steeres traveled across Rome to meet with a little group of Roman Catholic peace activists—including Hildegard and Jean Goss-Meyer, Dorothy Day, Gordon Zahn, and James Douglas—nine of whom were undertaking a ten-day period of fasting and prayer. The next day Douglas addressed Observers meeting with the Commission on Schema XIII, The Church and the Modern World. In his "Intervention" he noted that, while the schema favored conscientious objection, it left a loophole for governments to enforce military service.[16] He objected to a statement allowing the use of nuclear weapons as a deterrent. Not *possession* but *preparation for use* is what poses a danger, he argued.[17] This carefully crafted statement had an effect on the commission preparing the schema, for, backed by strong statements of Cardinal Alfrink, Bishop Cuthbert Butler, and others, the two sentences he objected to were removed from the final document.[18]

The role of the laity in the Church

On the Steeres' arrival Bishop J.G.M. Willebrands asked Douglas to submit a statement on the role of the laity in the Church, "stating briefly some of the Quaker experience in this area, . . ."[19] On October 22 Douglas told a meeting of Observer-Delegates with the Commission for Promoting Christian Unity that he thought few actions would be more welcomed in the free churches than the one on the laity, for few things have made them doubt the apostolic character of the Roman Catholic Church more than the role accorded to the laity. Rather than playing up lay persons, "this section of the schema is quite rightly bent on abolishing the laity and accounting instead the priestly responsibility of every [person] whom the Holy Spirit has baptized."[20] He found God working through quite a few non-clerical figures: Benedict, Francis of Assisi, Gerard Groote, Hildegard of Bingen, Bridget of Sweden, and Catherine of Siena. He would agree with Bishop Dubois' connecting of the laity with the total apostolate of the church.

> In this extension of the role of the priesthood to the laity, to the priests in the world, the Church may be taking a step of renewal that will involve her in a whole new epoch of life. In steps of this kind when they are genuinely implemented, the common ground with non-Roman Catholics is more than evident.[21]

He found it "fascinating" that the schema on the Apostolate of the Laity went through almost unanimously "while schema 13, that deals with the dialogue with the world which these laity are in such large measure going to have to carry out, is being scathingly torn apart in the discussions."[22]

The relation of Christianity to the religions of humankind

The relation of Christianity to the religions of humankind stood at the center of Douglas Steere's attention at this time, and it is not surprising to see how much energy he gave to promote some sort of progress. In November 1963 he offered a frank critique of a draft of the schema on ecumenism— insufficient recognition of ecumenical dialogue going on, inadequate attempt to understand non-Catholic positions, exaggerated distinction between Church and Communities that seemed to lead to preferential treatment of Eastern Churches, and failure to raise the schema to the level of the Pope's statement opening the Council that left more room for diversity in unity. He did express appreciation in a letter to the Council that it made reference to persons outside the church. "Ecumenical" should not refer only to reconciliation of Christians. "To carry on the real Ecumenical task means that those beyond the 'manifest' churches must be always in consideration." Douglas would keep the Jewish chapter where it was and "express somewhere in the document the still wider context that all of this Ecumenical endeavor is set in."[23] In a circular to Friends in April 1964, he was encouraged that Pope Paul VI had appointed Cardinal Marella and Father Humbert-Claude to begin forming a Secretariat for the Non-Christian Religions and had spoken to Cardinals Koenig and Bea about steps needed to do that and the importance of choosing the right person to head the Secretariat. In a "Memorandum for Appointment with Cardinal Bea" he showed the great care he took to present his case.[24] He suggested inviting two or three representatives of

186

the major (non-Christian) religions to come to the Council as "guests," an issue he had raised with several outstanding Muslims and two Copts. Although Koenig and Bea were sceptical at first, they realized on reflection

> that we are living in a period of great openness when the Holy Spirit has indicated the worth of doing many impossible things and that this is no less impossible than many other things that have actually been accomplished in these last two remarkable years and that to delay because of the obstacles which the worldly mind may muster is not worthy of this open moment God has given us.[25]

Although the schema on Non-Christian Religions moved forward and Douglas found many who shared his enthusiasm for dialogue with the other religions, he was distressed to learn in October 1965 that the Secretariat for the Non-Christian Religions had stagnated under Cardinal Marella's direction. His initial visit to Marella depressed him, for he saw that Marella had no "central interest" in the matter and it would be "hopeless . . . to press him farther."[26] At the urging of the White Father who was preparing this schema, he wrote Cardinal Marella suggesting that he, Lukas Vischer, Director of the Faith and Order Commission of the World Council of Churches, and Professor Van Holk, International Congress of Liberal Religion, represent Observers in a meeting with the Secretariat. The conference, which took place November 24, 1965, left Douglas "deeply depressed about the result of the meeting, . . ." However, consultants whom he saw later rallied him and "insisted that this had been the first sign of life in a year, and that they would now have a meeting to talk out some of the things that had been raised in this gathering."[27] Douglas saw more hope in consultants such as Henri de Lubac, Jean Daniélou, and others and in gatherings such as he assembled in Japan and India two years later.

The Jewish people

How the Council would modify the Church's long-standing attitudes toward the Jewish people also claimed a large share of Douglas' attention. This was encouraged by close friends such as Abraham Heschel.[28] On October 23, 1963, during the second session, Douglas tried to acquaint himself with the course of development of a statement on the Jews which Cardinal Bea had pushed through. It was being held in secret[29] in the hands of the Secretariat for Promoting Christian Unity and about to be distributed to the Council.[30] Two days later, he ignored a heavy cold to entreat Bishop Willebrands about the importance of getting out a statement on the Jews.[31] On November 8 Willebrands informed him at the coffee bar that the schema on the Jews was being passed out that morning. In his newsletter from Rome Douglas noted his joy:

> I had been working and hoping for this for a fortnight and was thankful to know that at last this was to be put into our hands labelled as a fourth chapter of the schema on Ecumenism. This, I knew, would bring rejoicing not only to Jews around the world, as a further step in religious openness among Catholic Christians, but to fairminded men and women everywhere who could see how a schema that dissociated the whole Jewish community from the charge of guilt for the killing of Jesus took away this particular seed of anti-semitism once and for all in this great Christian community. Even Arabs, who have never been racists, might be glad that this act of religious restitution was being proposed.[32]

Spirituality

In a very real way, spirituality stood at the center of everything Douglas Steere did at the Second Vatican Council.

Spirituality drew him toward the Roman Catholic Church. The rich stream of devotion flowing into the Quaker tradition and into Douglas' own life of prayer informed and transformed what he said and did at the Council. He reveled in the company of soul friends like Bernard Häring, Godfrey Diekmann, Jean Leclercq and other heirs of Benedict of Nursia, Bernard of Clairvaux, and hundreds of other saints. As he wound his way down the many paths he had to tread at the Council, he added to his own rich lode of spiritual wisdom, and he observed with approval the emphasis the Council placed on reform of moral and spiritual life. All factors considered, it is not surprising to see that the most enduring gift of the Council to Douglas Steere was the Ecumenical Institute of Spirituality, which held its first meeting at St. John's Abbey in Collegeville, Minnesota, August 31-September 7, 1965, just before the final session of the Council began.

The Ecumenical Institute of Spirituality

The idea of a little ecumenical institute of Protestants and Catholics to explore the issue of prayer originated October 10, 1963, during the second session, in a coffee bar discussion with Godfrey Diekmann, OSB, a monk of St. John's Abbey and a professor of liturgical studies at St. John's University in Collegeville. Douglas' friend, John Coburn, Dean of the Episcopal Theological Seminary in Cambridge, Massachusetts, had just proposed a journey to see what British Anglican scholars were doing in this field. Douglas remarked how helpful it would be if John Coburn "could have the privilege of a real exchange in a spiritual institute with Roman Catholics who have made such unusually fine contributions to this whole field of the nurture of the inward life." Fr. Diekmann replied, "Why don't we do it? I will write to my Abbot at Collegeville at once and see if he would encourage us to work out such a spiritual institute."[33] On receiving an enthusiastic response

189

from the abbot, Diekmann and Steere laid plans carefully for what they initially called the Ecumenical Working Party on Contemporary Spirituality.

The meeting drew an illustrious group representative of diverse traditions in spirituality. Roman Catholics present were: Bernard Haering, a Redemptorist; Jean Leclercq, a Benedictine; Barnabas Ahern, a Passionist; Thomas Kilduff, a Carmelite; Elmer O'Brien, a Jesuit; Robert Lechner, professor at DePaul University in Chicago and editor of the journal *Philosophy Today;* D.H. Salman, a Dominican; John Caulfield, a Roman Catholic layman; Michael Marx, a Benedictine; and Godfrey Diekmann. Thomas Merton was invited, but Father Abbot James Fox refused to give him permission to attend.[34] Non-Catholics were: John Coburn; John Oliver Nelson, a Presbyterian and founder and director of Kirkridge; Gordon Cosby, pastor of Church of the Savior in Washington, DC; Horton Davies, a Presbyterian professor at Princeton University; Richard Luecke, a Lutheran; Keith Watkins, a Disciple of Christ; Thomas Hopko, a Russian Orthodox; Arthur Kelsey, Chaplain of General Theological Seminary in New York, who died two months before the meeting; and Douglas Steere.

Four topics were treated in papers from each side, but as they walked and talked, participants found no division along confessional lines. Excited about this encounter, they voted to meet the following year at Pendle Hill and scheduled just four papers on prayer. In Rome for the opening of Session 4 of the Council, Douglas wrote:

> My own feeling about the ecumenical movement and about the ecumenical significance of these great gatherings such as we have been having at the Vatican Council, is that they must be tested and weighed out ultimately in the scales of these grass roots projects of common work that they give rise to. And when they enter common work on the living center out of which

the inward life of all religious groups must come, then they are dealing with the ultimate ground that underlies all our differences.[35]

The Ecumenical Institute of Spirituality continues as a legacy of Douglas Steere and the Second Vatican Council.[36]

Lambeth

By the time the Second Vatican Council concluded Douglas had been elected Chairman of the Friends World Committee for Consultation. In that capacity the Meeting for Sufferings of the London Yearly Meeting invited him to attend the Lambeth Conference of the Church of England convened July 25-August 25, 1968. He was "more than willing to accept this invitation," because of his high regard for the Episcopal Church and its worship. Quakers, he thought, had much to learn from such persons as Lancelot Andrewes, John Donne, Jeremy Taylor, George Herbert, Thomas Traherne, William Law, Evelyn Underhill, Dorothy Sayre, Dean W.R. Inge, William Temple, Charles Brent, Charles Williams, T.S. Eliot, and C.S. Lewis.

> In the crisis in spirituality in which we stand, the Anglicans are among the few bulwarks of the great contemplative tradition of the West and are, as we have seen in men like Kenneth Cragg, not closed to the great traditions of other religions that may keep this inward dimension in [humankind] alive and awake and in living touch with the moral problems of the time.

Douglas felt deeply in touch with radical Anglicans such as Arthur Shearly Cripps, whose biography he was writing, and Arthur Blaxall, an apostle to the blind in South Africa.[37]

Although he could tease about all the purple worn by bishops as contrasted with his "sack suit" and criticize bishops

191

"wearing their war decorations and even campaign ribbons on their cassocks with the pectoral cross that hung round their necks rubbing against them as it swung" as symbolic of "what an 'established Church' may come to mean,"[38] he sounded mostly positive notes. At Lambeth, Anglicans made Observers a full part of the process and encouraged them to speak during the sessions until the last week. Douglas found the small working committees most important and joined one on "Dialogue with the World Religions," chaired by George Appleton, Archbishop of Perth, Australia, and attended parts of a committee on "Faith and the Spiritual Life." The Archbishop of Canterbury followed the morning devotionals with fifteen minutes of silence, and the assembly passed a resolution encouraging silent prayer. Douglas thought Quakers could learn from Ian Ramsey, Bishop of Durham, who argued that loosening up in faith would not erode but stretch it.

Douglas discerned in the measured response at Lambeth to *Humanae Vitae*, the highly controversial encyclical prohibiting the use of the "pill" as a contraceptive, a sign of hope for ecumenism. The experience of pain which all in attendance felt for Roman Catholics conveyed "that it was almost as though it had happened to us." The reaction "made very clear that even such a difficult problem as this poses, cannot in the end shake the ecumenical connections even though it greatly complicates and harasses them."[39]

Mutual Irradiation

Two decades of ministry among Friends all over the world, engagement with world class scholars, cultivation of friendships and conversations with persons of other faiths, significant participation in the Second Vatican Council, conducting colloquies between Christians and Buddhists and Christians and Hindus, and attendance at the Lambeth Conference brought Douglas Steere's ecumenical perceptions to maturity. The Richard Cary Lecture at the German Yearly

192

Meeting on October 11, 1968 at Bad Pyrmont provided the occasion for him to refine and articulate again the theme he had expounded since the mid-fifties in the captivating phrase "Mutual Irradiation." One hears echoed in this remarkable address the wisdom of one who embraced all humankind.

The "ecumenical surge" which demanded Christian attention, he argued, came not just from traditional Protestant ecumenism or the Catholic ecumenism of the Second Vatican Council but from "the new relations that are beginning to emerge between Christians and people from the other great religions of the world: Buddhists, Hindus, and Muslims, whose members by far outnumber Christians in the share of the world's population which they include."[40] Interpenetration of the world religions will be painful for Christians "who suffer from hardening of the categories," but it will have far greater consequences for human-kind than the struggle between communist and free-enterprise societies. Genuine ecumenism means "world-embracing" and will entail moving fences outward to "embrace but not erase the unique and very special spiritual witness of the different religious groups, . . ."[41]

Rejecting elimination, syncretism, and mere coexistence as adequate approaches to persons of other faiths, Douglas put together again a case for mutual irradiation, which "would try to provide the most congenial setting possible for releasing the deepest witness that the Buddhist or Hindu or Muslim might make to his Christian companion, and that the Christian might in turn share with his non-Christian friend."[42] The relationship between Christians illustrates how these four approaches would work. In a true ecumenism the suffering of another becomes **my** suffering, the joy of another **my** joy. We do not say, "There but for the grace of God go I," but "There go I."[43] Even coexistence can only be a transitional state to this true ecumenism.

Quakers, Douglas admitted, had hesitated before the ecumenical movement, though there had been some serious Quaker ecumenists. They have found themselves in foreign

193

territory in the search for a common creed or common structure. Within Quakerism there has also been a reluctance to trust ecclesiastical structures of any sort, which caused Quakers to view themselves as a movement rather than a church. At their best, they have touched "a spring of life that reaches beyond forms."[44] They have envisioned themselves as belonging to a "third stream," neither Protestant nor Catholic but mystical, "in which institutional and ceremonial and theological differences receded."[45] They found in this a desire to take part in anything which would heal brokenness and division but hesitant to practice full-scale participation.

The dramatic events of the last five years, however, had been drastic enough to compel Quakers to re-examine their negative outlook. John XXIII set in motion something they could not ignore,

> calling us to witness to the operative presence, here and now, of this fathomless love and concern that is at the heart of things: a presence which is already actively at work in the unconscious life of every part of the creation. By more contemplation, more piercing communication and sharing, more costly common undertakings of social concern, we might help to emerge above the threshold of the world's consciousness.[46]

The best way to implement all of this would be by a "functional ecumenism."

> A truly functional ecumenism wants to witness to the world how much God cares, and if this means stopping a war; or trying to learn how to share more equitably the world's material resources; or meeting an emergency human need, or joining the poor; or sending brotherly teachers and companions to live and share with those in another area; or teaching one another how to meditate, or how to pray, or how to kindle corporate adoration, or how to grow in the life

of devotion, or how to use the lives of past saints and heroes to re-kindle our commitment; or how great art, painting, sculpture and music can expand the soul; or how personal guidance and therapy may release the deeper life in us; or how the world of plants and animals and water and wind can temper our souls; a functional ecumenism will open us in these and in other areas to the witness of our fellows, whether Christian or the adherents of other world religions.[47]

Here Douglas cited the experiences of the colloquia between Buddhists and Christians in Japan and Hindus and Christians in India as evidence of what Christians might gain from mutual irradiation. Mutual irradiation "searches" Quakers, as Swiss Ambassador Jacques Cuttat urged, "to learn to listen to what the Holy Spirit has to say to us through the faith in Hinduism and Buddhism and Islam."[48] Not all can take part in such dialogues as these, but all can participate vicariously and thus learn from persons of other faiths.

Douglas thought that Quakers, in fact, "have a small and a peculiarly important role to play as catalysts" in an ecumenical hospitality between Christians and representatives of the world religions and also between Christians. Their distinctive contribution stems from the fact that they "are naturally oriented to start at the right end of this ecumenical endeavor—namely to begin from within and to draw the whole ecumenical process in this direction."[49] They will not be likely to contribute much to the intellectual debate, but beginning with the universal, limitless love of God enables them to approach the Buddhist or Hindu and to help create a climate of open and sincere seeking wherein "something happens in the course of understanding another's truth that irradiates and lights up one's own tradition and that on rare occasions may even give one a hint of a truth that embraces both, a hint of a hidden convergence."[50] The object is to confirm that which is deepest in the other and thus "lift for each other a further curtain into the ultimate truth."[51]

The Life of Prayer as the Ground of Unity

The ecumenism which Douglas Steere was projecting in "Mutual Irradiation" is an ecumenism rooted in a life of prayer. Looking backwards in 1970 at euphoric experiences of the past decade, he warned that these were not sufficient actually to turn Christians around.

> The new ecumenical drugs that we have taken have loosened us up, have improved the climate of our relations with each other, have even helped us with our chronic condition of the hardening of the categories, but apart from a few sporadic exceptions, we are still not able to produce a climate for turning around, for turning round inwardly, for turning round into the life and power of Christ, and for a deep inward passion to move along together and to listen and to speak and to act for the needs of all [persons].[52]

Like Dag Hammarskjold, Thomas Merton, and John Woolman, Douglas believed we must discover the radical medicine of prayer "with its steady drawing and its tendering, its lifting up and its putting down, its singling out and its bringing into focus the ever new decisions with which we are confronted, . . ."[53]

The question Douglas Steere put to ecumenists was whether or not the ecumenical movement had done anything to deepen the inner life, the life of prayer. Action clarifies prayer, but prayer cleanses action and restores its frame. Human beings possess a built-in need for prayer, and the ecumenical movement will have little future if it fails to help them find it. Yet in this no religious group has achieved adequacy. "Catholic, Protestant, Jew—in this matter of prayer we are all at the frontier."[54] We all need to pay attention to the deepest thing we know, to become collected, so our awareness may expand. To do this may not leave us comfortable, for God is the Iconoclast. Prayer may sweep away our boundaries and compel us to reassess all we have known until then. Even more deeply, it "may plunge us into the world's misery and make us expendable."[55]

In conclusion Douglas cited some hopeful experiments in prayer-grounded ecumenism: the Ecumenical Institute of Spirituality, the Gustave Weigel Society, the writings of Aelred Graham and Thomas Merton, the Zen Buddhist-Christian Colloquy in Japan. Catholics, Orthodox, Protestants, and persons of other faiths need each other, he said, need "this gentle nudging of each other within the fellowship of the ecumenical movement."[56] The question is whether religious groups will help to call out the natural human hunger for God.

Douglas Steere's significant contributions to ecumenism received due recognition in 1967 when The General Theological Seminary, America's oldest Episcopal seminary, awarded him with an honorary Doctor of Sacred Theology degree with nine other Christian leaders. The others included: Lakdasa de Mel, Anglican Bishop of Calcutta and Metropolitan of India, Pakistan, Burma and Ceylon; Archbishop Iakavos, Greek Orthodox Primate of North and South America; John Joseph Wright, Bishop of the Roman Catholic Diocese of Pittsburgh; Eugene Carson Blake, General Secretary of the World Council of Churches; Franklin Clark Fry, President of the Lutheran Church of America; Charles Moeller, Professor at the University of Louvain; Albert C. Outler, Professor at Perkins School of Theology, Southern Methodist University; Alexander Schmemann, Dean of St. Vladimir's Orthodox Theological Seminary; and Brother Roger Schutz, Prior and Founder of the Community of Taizé.[57s]

Notes

1. Douglas V. Steere, UNPUBLISHED JOURNAL, 31. Edward Morris Steere's negative feelings about the Free Methodist tradition of his father kept him away from church until Douglas was ten. His father's choices may have dampened Douglas' commitment to a single denomination.
2. Steere, JOURNAL, 70.
3. See Chapter 4, 39-40.
4. Steere, JOURNAL, 102.
5. Steere, JOURNAL, 102.
6. Steere, JOURNAL, 106.
7. Roman Catholic Modernists introduced critical historiography into Catholic biblical studies and into Church history. Pope Pius IX condemned them in two encyclicals, *Pascendi* and *Lamentabili*, in 1907. Von Hügel served as a sort of counselor to the Modernists. He was especially close to George Tyrrell, the English Modernist.
8. (London: Darton, Longman & Todd, 1964). On the object of this publication see also Steere, JOURNAL, 136.
9. See E. Glenn Hinson, "Ecumenical Spirituality" in *Spirituality in Ecumenical Perspective* (Louisville: Westminster/John Knox Press, 1993).
10. Steere, JOURNAL, 457-58 (1945); 482 (1948).
11. Accompanied by Johannes Schlüter-Hermkes, for example, he spent some time with Father Welty at the Dominican convent at Wallbersberg, near Cologne, during his sabbatical in 1947-48.
12. I have found the first comment on his possible attendance at the Council in Douglas' letter to Gilbert McMaster in Basel dated October 3, 1962. In it he noted that Friends at first showed little interest , but then decided to send someone. They asked Douglas, but he could not go because of his teaching responsibilities. Richard Ullmann was asked to attend Session One. In a *Letter to James W. Kennedy, Church of the Ascension, New York,* April 25, 1962, Douglas added a P.S.: "I do have an interest in the relationship between the Protestant and the Roman Catholic Church and should say that on that side I have a deep concern."
13. See Douglas V. Steere, *Letter to Richard K. Ullmann, Woodbrooke College, Birmingham, England,* February 19, 1963; Richard K. Ullmann, *Letter to Douglas V. Steere,* February 27, 1963.
14. Douglas V. Steere, *Journal from Rome,* Session 2 , I, 2.
15. Steere, *Journal from Rome,* Session 3, V, 5.
16. "Intervention by Douglas V. Steere on Chapter V, Schema XIII," 1. He objected to the qualification that "When God's law is not

evidently (*manifeste*) violated, the competent authority must be presumed to be right and its instructions must be obeyed."

17. Steere, *Intervention*, 2. His concern was another qualifying statement: "Nevertheless as long as international institutions give no adequate guarantee of peace, the possession of these armaments exclusively (*solum*) as a deterrent for an enemy equipped with the same weapons, cannot be said to be illegitimate."

18. Douglas V. Steere, *Journal from Rome*, Session 4, III, 14. On October 31 Monsignor Ramsallaer, a member of the commission working on Schema XIII, startled Douglas by telling him that his intervention "had been read out in the mixed Commission and thoroughly discussed there." Steere, *Journal from Rome*, Session 4, III, 7.

19. Steere, *Journal from Rome*, Session 2, I, 2.

20. Steere, *Journal from Rome*, Session 2, III, 2.

21. Steere, *Journal from Rome*, Session 2, III, 3.

22. Steere, *Journal from Rome*, Session 4, I, 11.

23. Douglas V. Steere, *Letter to the Council on the Ecumenical Schema*, November 17, 1963.

24. He cited the need for extending an invitation soon to give such representatives time to mull over the invitation, the importance of spelling out what would be expected of them to overcome suspicions and hesitations, and the value of such a secretariat consulting some of the dialogues and centers of dialogue now going on under non-Catholic auspices. He concluded with a rationale for his visit—that it was important not only to Quakers but to many other non-Catholics "that we dare not neglect our touch with our non-Christian brothers [and sisters] in the course of coming to a deeper understanding of our own common tasks within the Christian communion, . . ."

25. Douglas V. Steere, *Letter to Friends from Rome*, April 19, 1964.

26. Steere, *Journal from Rome*, Session 4, III, 6.

27. Steere, *Journal from Rome*, Session 4, III, 16.

28. Heschel phoned the Steeres from New York to check on the progress of this issue and pressed Douglas to stay with it.

29. Somehow the *New York Times* had obtained a copy and disclosed its content prematurely.

30. Steere, *Journal from Rome*, Session 2, III, 3.

31. Steere, *Journal from Rome*, Session 2, III, 5.

32. Steere, *Journal from Rome*, Session 2, IV, 5.

33. Steere, *Journal from Rome*, Session 4, I, 1. See also *Journal from Rome*, Session 2, II, 4, the earliest note.

34. In a letter to Douglas Steere, dated September 14, 1965, Merton made clear that his non-attendance was "not my choice, I assure you." He hoped to arrange for the Institute to meet at Gethsemani and plans were in the offing the year he died.

35. Steere, *Journal from Rome*, Session 4, I, 2.

36. A section of Chapter 15 is devoted to the continuing story of the Ecumenical Institute of Spirituality.

37. *Steere Travel Letter (1968): The Lambeth Conference in London*, 1.

38. *Steere Travel Letter, Lambeth*, 4.

39. *Steere Travel Letter, Lambeth*, 8.

40. Douglas V. Steere, *Mutual Irradiation: A Quaker View of Ecumenism*. Pendle Hill Pamphlet 175 (Wallingford, PA: Pendle Hill Publications, 1971), 6-7.

41. Steere, *Mutual Irradiation*, 7.

42. Steere, *Mutual Irradiation*, 8.

43. Steere, *Mutual Irradiation*, 10. Note the point his Lambeth experience made regarding the pain of Paul VI's encyclical *Humanae Vitae*.

44. Steere, *Mutual Irradiation*, 11.

45. Steere, *Mutual Irradiation*, 12.

46. Steere, *Mutual Irradiation*, 15.

47. Steere, *Mutual Irradiation*, 16.

48. Steere, *Mutual Irradiation*, 21.

49. Steere, *Mutual Irradiation*, 27.

50. Steere, *Mutual Irradiation*, 31.

51. Steere, *Mutual Irradiation*, 32.

52. Douglas V. Steere, "The Life of Prayer as the Ground of Unity," *Worship*, 45 (May 1971), 251.

53. Steere, "The Life of Prayer," 252.

54. Steere, "The Life of Prayer," 256.

55. Steere, "The Life of Prayer," 259.

56. Steere, "The Life of Prayer," 261.

57. Val Adams, "Seminary Honors Ten for Ecumenism," *New York Times*, November 9, 1967.

XIII

———◆·◆·◆———

Peacemaker Extraordinary

*N*early everything Douglas Steere did could be labeled peacemaking, the heartbeat of the Quaker tradition. Throughout his career he was a peace activist, "doing things that make for peace." Aiding striking miners in West Virginia, daring trips to Germany and the Scandinavian countries in 1937 and 1940, visiting work camps and civilian public service camps during World War II, training Relief and Reconstruction workers, organizing Quaker Relief for war-torn Finland, repeatedly touring Europe and Africa and Asia on behalf of the American Friends Service Committee or the Friends World Committee for Consultation, lobbying for a strong peace statement at Vatican II, arranging colloquies between representatives of the world's religions, and countless other activities were part and parcel of a ministry of reconciliation. For their work at the end of World War II, thanks in great part to Finnish Relief, the American and British service bodies of the Religious Society of Friends received the Nobel Peace Prize. To these must be added Douglas more direct peacemaking endeavors: service on national and international peacemaking commissions, participation in the American and International Fellowship of Reconciliation, organizing an East/West Colloquy at the height of the Cold War, and interceding with public officials in the United States to bring the war in Vietnam to a halt.

The gargantuan nature of the task viewed in macrocosm has sapped the soul of many a would-be peacemaker. "What difference will *my* little effort make? Will it be anything but a waste of time and energy?" Such thoughts crossed Douglas Steere's mind more than once as he and Dorothy sought to rally tiny, scattered bands of Friends and other activists around the globe to stay close to the Center and to let the motion of love direct them in their efforts, no matter how small. Here they followed in the footsteps of John Woolman. Woolman was model and mentor for Douglas and Dorothy Steere, and one will not easily understand how and why they did what they did without knowing something of this American Quaker saint's impact on their minds and hearts.

Woolman as Mentor and Model

Reading Woolman's *Journal* settled whatever doubts both Steeres may have had about joining the Religious Society of Friends. In her *Reminiscences and Reflections,* Dorothy observed:

> In that man we saw both the active and the contemplative sides so beautifully put together. He had an influence on us all during our early years in Quakerism, helping us to grasp the importance of the silent Meeting for the deepening of the inner life and, at the same time, the importance of implementing what came in the silence through the active life. He helped us see, too, how the testimonies were rooted in the value of every human being.[1]

Woolman's impact endured. As noted before, Douglas served as chairperson of the John Woolman Memorial in Mount Holly, New Jersey, from 1942 until 1954, reluctantly surrendering the office in order to chair the board of Pendle Hill. Woolman headed the list of those he labeled saints, and he regularly featured Woolman in classes in which he pointed students to preeminent models of the faithful life. He and Dorothy laced their lectures and writings with quotations from Woolman. More importantly, they found in Woolman the charter for all Quaker ministry, citing it in their volume on *Friends Work in Africa*.

> Love was the first motion, and thence arose a concern to spend some time with the Indians, that I might feel and understand their life and the spirit they live in, if happily I might receive some instruction from them, or they might be in any degree helped forward by my following the leadings of truth among them.[2]

For someone who knows both the Woolman and the Steere stories intimately it is not hard to see parallels. "Living in the spirit and dedication" of John Woolman in the peacemaking enterprise meant for Douglas Steere to keep so focused on the leading of Divine Love that he would not allow the magnitude of the problem to deter him from acting in a modest way to solve a problem, trusting God to use his small effort. From 1746 until his death in 1772, Woolman spent about one month out of every year traveling among the American colonies to lay upon Friends the burden of his heart concerning the keeping of slaves. He gave up a prosperous merchandising business and learned a tailor's trade that he might not be "so encumbered by the affairs of this life" he could not follow God's leading. He became what might be called a "quiet revolutionary," sensitive always to both slaves and slaveholders. He embodied his concern in little acted parables: pressing money into the hands of a slaveowner with whom he had stayed as a gift to help one slave purchase freedom; wearing undyed suits because the dye was produced by slave labor; traveling on foot after 1763 because slaves were not permitted to ride on horseback or in carriages; refusing to eat sugar, rum, and molasses imported from the West Indies because they were products of slave labor, all the while worrying lest too many follow his example and bring hurt to those he wanted to help. Woolman did not live to see the end of slavery. He died of smallpox in England in 1772 on a journey to bear witness at the center of the slaving industry. In the way of saints he trusted God to "work together for good" with one who loved God and humankind. By 1787, largely as a conscquence of John Woolman's witness, no American Quaker owned a slave!

Peacemaking Side Efforts

Before looking at activities more specifically aimed at peace-making, it will be useful for a fuller portrait to recall some side efforts connected with the Steeres' worldwide ministry of encouragement. In his characteristic way Douglas reached out from the beginning of his active career to establish ties with other peacemakers both within and outside the Religious Society of Friends. On his sabbatical in 1933, for instance, he furthered his acquaintance with Corder Catchpool, a British Quaker working in Berlin to effect reconciliation between Germany and Great Britain[3] and with Eberhard Arnold, founder of the Neuhof Bruderhof, a pacifist community near Fulda.[4] On the 1937 excursion through Germany he spent two days visiting the Hitler work camps[5] and touched base with various anti-Nazi groups. In Sweden he, Paul Braisted, and other Quakers spent another two days attending the an-nual meeting of the Swedish Fellowship of Reconciliation and peace leaders.[6] In Finland they spoke to a large peace meeting assembled in their honor at which they had to defend their pacifist views against those held by theological students.[7] On the hazardous 1940 trip to Germany, at the beginning of his shortened second sabbatical, he used the agency of Leonard Kenworthy in Berlin to obtain permission to visit British sol-diers captured at Dunkirk by citing Quaker care for German troops after World War I;[8] touched base with Quaker peace-makers such as Annemarie Cohen in Muenich, Greta Sumpf in Vienna, Rudolf Schlosser and Alfons Paquet in Frankfurt; and met others in Berlin who resisted Hitler. In Switzerland he furthered his acquaintance in Zürich with Schwester Anny Pflüger, a Quaker nurse helping Jewish refugees, and stopped in Lausanne to meet Helene Monastier, the Swiss Quaker peace champion, and Pierre Ceresole, founder of the International Voluntary Service Corps in Switzerland.

After the Second World War Quaker energies flowed naturally into relief and reconstruction efforts, for which various Quaker organizations had made preparation during the war years. In Germany during the first half of his third sabbatical (1947-48) Douglas strengthened peacemaking bonds effected on earlier trips. At the invitation of Ruth Oechslin, a Quaker jurist, Douglas spoke to Nazis interned near Bad Boll awaiting trial who wanted to know why they were being imprisoned for faithfulness to an idea. In his response he summarized the Quaker peace message:

> We must do away with war and we must re-assert the dignity and integrity of the divine image in man. It had been the purpose of the Quakers from the very beginning to re-assert this divine quality of human beings by their concern for them, even in small symbolic gestures. Nothing in our world is more important than this re-exaltation of the personal, the importance of individual men and women.[9]

On this same journey the Steeres encouraged Swedish Friends to continue the plan of Per Sundberg to bring twenty Germans to Viggbyholm School near Stockholm for a week of rest and refreshment. Douglas labeled it "a Swedish Quaker experiment in reconciliation." The Steeres participated in the meeting the week before Easter, March 23-30, 1948.[10] In a late spring trip down the western corridor of Germany through Switzerland, France, and England with his daughter Helen, Douglas made a point of stopping at Le Chambon to see André Trocmé's Protestant Lycée, which trained people in non-violence.[11] At Cambridge he urged Canon Charles Raven, a pacifist who believed reconciliation the most important thing in the world, and Herbert Farmer to write a pacifist Christian theology.[12] On his return to Copenhagen Douglas gave a lecture on "Quakers, Peace and War"[13] and visited a conscientious objectors' camp for young Danes. In Finland he arranged for the pacifist Minister of Defense, Kallinen, to meet Horace Alexander, a Quaker who had known Gandhi personally, to hear about Gandhi.[14]

Return journeys to Europe gave Douglas Steere ample opportunities to maintain the peace testimony which vibrated under the surface of all the remarkable work in which he and Dorothy engaged. Of particular concern in the early fifties were American pressures to rearm Germany, an issue Douglas addressed in an article published in *The Christian Century*, and to which he gave much attention in his travel letters.

In the meantime, the African journeys, especially to South Africa, challenged the peace witness in other ways. Given a slim Quaker presence in all except Kenya, Douglas made a point of establishing connections with persons and groups who shared the Quaker concern for racial harmony and justice. In Northern Rhodesia (later Zambia) he had a long conversation about Gandhi with Kenneth Kaunda, then a young African who was just released from prison.[15] Ten years later, he met Kaunda, then Prime Minister of Zambia, at an AFSC meeting in Philadelphia. In Kenya the Steeres spent some days in 1957 with British Quakers working to re-establish the Mau Mau prisoners and helping to set up centers in Nairobi and its environs to lessen overpopulation.[16]

Occasionally Douglas had opportunities to speak more directly about the darkening cloud of conflict in southern Africa. In 1957 in Johannesburg he delivered the inaugural lecture of a new series called the "Emily Hobhouse Memorial Lectureship," jointly sponsored by the IFOR and the Society of Friends, on "The Personal Factor in the Resolution of Conflict." Some years later, he managed to publish his own thoughts about the way to peace in Southern Rhodesia and the rest of southern Africa in his biography of the Anglican missionary "poet, saint and Christian presence" Arthur Shearly Cripps.[17]

On visits to Japan and India in 1954-55, 1959-60,1966-67, and 1970-71 Douglas challenged Christians to engagement with persons of Buddhist and Hindu faiths so that together they might address problems of conflict throughout the world. Gandhi and his teachings about non-violent social change took center stage in all the trips to India. In an article published in *The Christian Century* against the backdrop of the first trip, Douglas pointed out the contradiction Muslims, Hindus, and Buddhists see in missionaries' emphasis on the love of Jesus when Christians have employed crusades to exterminate them.[18] In early October 1955 he addressed the Quaker Five Year Meeting at Richmond, Indiana, on the roots of Quaker witness against participation in war. He elucidated three roots: their saying Yes to the burning love of God, their saying No to war that would kill those they are drawn to in love, and their determination to find alternative ways to effect peace.

Steere visits to the Middle East, undertaken with some hesitation, carried a more direct interest in reconciliation than the others by virtue of the degree of Jewish/Arab tension. Douglas saw in the pessimism of his friend Martin Buber about reconciliation a searching challenge for Quakers.[19] In a letter to Margarethe Lachmund in 1970, reporting on a second Middle East visit, he said he had not given up hope of reconciliation. As the stronger party, the Jews needed to be "more tractable and not have things completely on their own terms, of course, or this will never take place."[20]

A Quandry in Peacemaking

An invitation to Quakers to participate in the Communist-sponsored Seventh International Youth Festival in Vienna occasioned sharp debate as to how broadly Quakers should spread their cooperation in peacemaking. Douglas, present to speak to a monthly meeting of the diplomat circle of the Danish Quaker International Affairs Representative, entered the dispute on the side of participation despite the controlled propaganda. He argued that people need to hear another side, and that it is important to know the Communists themselves to operate in the same world. "If peace is not the mere absence of armed conflict but is vital interaction," he insisted, "then occasions of meeting are attempts to see whether this is possible today or whether the barriers are too great." [21] He arranged some conversations at the Quaker Center, inviting different guests. Some did their best to disrupt the Festival anyway, but Douglas defended Quaker participation. "We as Quakers believe in personal relations and in the possibility of answering to that of God in every [person]." [22] Though sessions were more controlled than he expected, the students had a way of breaking out.

Nevertheless, he found the event very foreign to the Quaker way. The Festival spared no expense to present costly cultural events.

> It was clear to me that this kind of mass occasion, which is engineered and obviously must be, with stadia, and loud speakers hysterically screaming "Peace and Friendship" and trying to get the group to chant it; with more things going on continually than people can even keep track of; with street meetings around a singer like Paul Robeson, is really so basically foreign to our way of working, that we as Quakers are baffled by it and hardly know where to take hold. When we have a seminar for young people it goes on for three weeks and with a group who number about thirty or forty. They live quietly together and in talk and play and dining and working together they reach across into each others' minds and hearts. When we set up a work camp it is rarely as large as that, and lasts twice as

long. *We believe in the small and the individual way of doing things* and therefore we are especially troubled by our ineptness in such gigantic affairs.[23]

An Enlarging Sphere

The serious efforts which Quakers and Douglas Steere put into peacemaking enterprises made him a natural choice to serve on some of the ad hoc peacemaking committees which World War II and the advent of the nuclear age spawned. Most notable were his service on a small commission on The Relation of the Church to War in the Light of Christian Faith (1944-45) sponsored by the Federal [later National] Council of Churches and led by Robert Calhoun and H. Richard Niebuhr; a national Commission on Atomic Warfare in the Light of Christian Faith (1945-46); and a Commission of the World Council of Churches on Christianity and the Prevention of War in an Atomic Age (1956-58). Work with the last group tested the consistency of his commitment to the pacifism of the historic peace churches.

Meeting twice in Switzerland and once in Great Britain in order to prepare a report to the Central Committee of the WCC, the Commission's international and interdisciplinary character posed challenges he had not found in Quaker meetings or the International Fellowship of Reconciliation. The majority in the group of just over a dozen opposed adoption of a radical position against nuclear armaments as a key to national defense, but agreed to devote a future session to the full pacifist position which renounced war itself. Before the latter could take place, however, the Central Committee called for an immediate report. The elaborate report, though cautious, ultimately accepted nuclear armaments as a legitimate form of defense. Douglas joined three others in drafting a minority statement rejecting this position. At that point the Commission was disbanded and the full pacifist viewpoint did not get its hearing. Looking backwards after the Second Vatican Council, Douglas found it "interesting" that the conservative Roman Catholic Church "all but acknowledged that no nuclear war could ever meet the conditions that the long cherished doctrine of the *Just War* had laid down as requirements for the Church's approval of war."[24] Ironically, Douglas' final year as President of the Friends World Committee for Consultation included attendance in January 1971 at the Central Committee Meeting of the World Council of Churches in Addis Ababa, Ethiopia, as a Quaker "Adviser." The meeting revolved chiefly around peacemaking-related issues—how to combat racism, dialogue with persons of other faiths, and non-violence in social change. He found "more than a little double-mindedness still present in this body on the tough issues that they faced from the outset."[25]

International Fellowship of Reconciliation

Peace concerns of the Religious Society of Friends and of IFOR run so closely parallel to one another that it is not surprising to discover that Douglas Steere played a major role in the latter from the time he joined it in the early thirties. At the request of IFOR he wrote in 1936 a widely used pamphlet which could help local groups organize for effective peace action in their own local communities. Entitled *The Peace Team*,[26] it updated ideas of the Third Order Franciscans.[27] During his European travels, he kept in close touch with European representatives of the Fellowship, particularly André Trocmé, the European secretary, and attended meetings on several occasions. Sometime in 1950 he was invited to become the national secretary of the Fellowship of Reconciliation. Although he declined that offer, he indicated that he would like to become a member of the International Fellowship. Early in 1951 he was nominated as chairperson of the North and South American sections of the IFOR, a position in which he worked closely with Nevin Sayre, grandson of Woodrow Wilson, as

210

secretary of the American section and with John C. Heidbrink as secretary for Church relations. Both Sayre[28] and Heidbrink[29] leaned heavily on his counsel during their terms as secretary. Douglas held this post until he was elected chairman of the Friends World Committee for Consultation in 1964.

Douglas Steere played a weighty role in IFOR. At the request of John Heidbrink he and Dorothy went to the Abbey of Gethsemani to encourage Thomas Merton in his peace initiatives.[30] When in the early sixties some members questioned the Christian-only make up of the organization, Douglas came down decisively on the side of tradition. In a letter mailed to the membership February 8, 1963, he thanked God that Heidbrink had not abandoned the organized churches, despite his impatience with them, but had tried to get witnesses in all the seminaries and to give aid and comfort to people like Thomas Merton. Devoting most of the letter to comments about the IFOR becoming "pharisaical" by being too Christian, Douglas argued that, in his own work of bridging the gulf with persons of other faiths, experience had shown that "this can only be sincerely done by those who stand deeply and firmly rooted in their own traditions that have plumbed them deeply enough to be driven out in profound respect and affection to come to know the brothers [and sisters] in the other faith." He favored exclusion of syncretists, Bahais, and "nervous universalists." He believed there were real differences between Christianity and other religions. Although there was no reason why some federation of Buddhist, Hindu, Muslim, and Christian could not be formed, IFOR is Christian and should not be apologetic about that. It must not alter its requirements in order to be all inclusive. "What we would seem to need, in the IFOR at least, is not to lower the qualifications, but to raise the performance." To drop Christian ties would be to repulse major figures such as Phillip Lasserre, Hildegard and Jean Goss-Mayr, Philip Eastman, André Trocmé, Arthur Blaxall, and many others. "Certainly we want no creedalism and we are concerned for the *latent* as well as the *patent* church, but the witness and example of Jesus Christ are and must remain central for us."

Douglas proceeded in this important position paper to lay out his vision for IFOR. He agreed with Nevin Sayre that IFOR's role is "the selection and servicing and keeping in circulation of a few revolutionary prophetic spirits." The successes of the past need not force change.

> The creation of literature, the development of training centers for youth, the preparation of teams to explore the radical experiments needed to implement the way of love in the midst of physical poverty of the developing countries: all of these have their natural place in our focus as an IFOR—a missionary arm of the few strong national groups of the FOR who are in a position to encourage this work and to support it.

Steere spoke of K.K. Chandy's ashram and his desire to travel as a peace emissary. Finally, he would rely on the judgment of others as to whether this was the time to found a Federation of Peace Societies of the World. He did not think IFOR should invest heavily in such a venture. He agreed with Gerald Bailey that small groups of committed persons in various places still have the greatest impact. He did not share the sense of doom some pacifists manifested. With P.T. Sorokin and Olive Shreiner he could see the dawn coming.[31]

East-West Colloquy

Given the Steere schedule of activities from 1960 to 1962, it stretches the imagination to think that Douglas would play a leading role in organizing a dialogue in Prague between Christian church representatives of eastern and western blocs to see if something could be done to promote East-West understanding in a period of heightening Cold War. The initiative for such a meeting originated in a conference Douglas, A.J. Muste, a staff member of IFOR, and others had in Paris with representatives of the Church Peace Mission, a group of clergy from the Marxist bloc.[32] Responding to an inquiry from Muste, Douglas expressed "a keen desire to answer the loneliness and hunger to advance the cause of Christian Peace on the part of some of these able Eastern Churchmen by helping to promote the kind of gathering that we are exploring," but he warned Muste not to kindle too high hopes for Prague as the place. Better just to promise a meeting.[33]

Plans for the colloquy moved forward rapidly despite early skepticism and changes of date and participants.[34] Originally scheduled for December 1961, it finally took place in Karolovy Vary (Carlsbad), about thirty kilometers from Prague, January 25-27, 1962,[35] during Douglas' year at Union Theological Seminary in New York. Although Muste, as Secretary, carried much of the administrative load, Douglas personally corresponded with potential western participants, whose numbers changed up to the last week, secured financial assistance,[36] and looked after details such as visas.[37] Despite a considerable number of those who had to express regrets, the list of western churchmen who attended was a notable one,[38] indicative of the high esteem in which Douglas Steere was held.[39] Western Europeans included Etienne Trocmé, André Benoit, Martin Niemoeller, Gordon Rupp, and Richard Ullmann.[40] Eastern participants were: Archbishop Nikodim of Moscow; Archbishop Kiivitt, Head of the Lutheran Church of Estonia; Professor Vitali Borgowoi (Borovoi), a professor in the Theological Academy in Leningrad; one Baptist representative from Moscow; Bishop Wantula, Lutheran Church in Warsaw; Professor D. Schmauch, University of Greifswald, German Democratic Republic; Bishop Bartha, Reformed Church of Hungary; Professor Palffy, Hungary; Pastor Karoly Toth, Budapest; and from Czechoslovakia, Professor Hromadka, Pastor Ondra, Professors Soucek, Lochman, Smolik, and Ziak of the Comenius Faculty in Prague; Professor Michalko, Lutheran Theological Faculty in Modra; and Bishop Varga of the Reformed Church.[41]

Douglas, employing suggestions of Richard K. Ullmann, also proposed the basic design for the program. John Bennett would open with some explanation of "the theological situation in America and the West and the bearing this might have on our social, economic, and political situation." Joseph Hromadka would take up the issue from the other side.[42] From there, the discussion would evolve in a personal way.

Glowing assessments came from both sides after the conference, but it had some uncomfortable moments. Heinz Kloppenburg, the east German facilitator, grew overzealous in his criticisms of West Germany, provoking a rejoinder from one of the westerners.[43] Following a thank you letter by Douglas which invited him to express his feelings freely, he wrote Douglas to apologize, wondering if he should come to America. "I never left a meeting so utterly depressed about my contribution as I did then," he explained. "But I hope that on the other hand and in spite of it some of the Americans will have felt the depth of despair in which we find ourselves at this particular situation in our country."[44] He thought it made sense to try to build bridges between Christians in the East and in America, but he doubted whether a German should do so. "We Germans are in between and do not know if we have the spiritual power to help in these matters." In his reply Douglas Steere revealed once again his remarkable gift for reconciling and lifting another to a higher level. If he came, Heinz would have a message for Americans. "But it must be in terms of Germany's full potential for good and for evil." He could help Americans see the agonizing choices Germany must make and how much they cost inwardly. Then, in a reflection which pierced the heart of the whole peacemaking enterprise and Douglas' own personalistic philosophy, Douglas added:

> Most of all, your own life will witness and you will find that at this point the way you live and the way you carry on day by day with those you meet, the way

you listen, the way you care—these are the continual witness that will ultimately matter. None of us has the final political wisdom but we are responsible to do what we can and then to live each day as in the presence of the One who alone can support those who believe that there is no situation that cannot be open to reconciliation.[45]

Judging by the responses of the participants, Kloppenburg's honest outburst did not cast a pall on the meeting. Most came away ecstatic, crediting Douglas Steere for an extraordinary experience in reconciliation. In a letter of appreciation to Joseph Hromadka immediately after returning to the United States Douglas himself summed up his own and others' assessment:

It was a profound experience for all of the men, and many of them have told me how much it meant to them. I think it will have long-lasting results in the way of personal relations and has done much to lead to a deeper understanding of the Christian witness as it must be given in both East and West.[46]

Hromadka replied a week later with his thanks and evaluation of the Colloquy:

It was for all of us a great experiment and experience and I may assure you of our admiration for you and other American friends primarily for their willingness to travel such a long distance only for a relatively short meeting. This fact in itself manifested your openmindedness and a real desire to come as closely as possible to us personally and to try as adequately as possible to understand both our problems and our mind. I hope it was just a beginning of our efforts for mutual understanding of our churches and our peoples. We all were deeply impressed by the collective climate of our brotherliness and responsibility.[47]

American participants uniformly credited Douglas. Dean Sayre thanked him for his "wonderful leadership and careful preparation" for an experience which had "enormously enriched" him.[48] John Coburn expressed "how eternally grateful" he was Douglas had made it possible for him "to attend that extraordinary conference," which preaching in a Czech Brethren church on Sunday crowned with a feeling of being "in the presence of the holy in an extraordinary way."[49] Harold Bender found the actuality "beyond all my expectation" and felt confident the Colloquy would "bear much fruit." He gave Douglas full credit: "Without you nothing would have come of our original hope and plan."[50]

As encouraging as the experience of the Colloquy may have been for those who attended, Douglas Steere did not let it trail off with the euphoria of the moment. Through the International Fellowship of Reconciliation he sought to arrange invitations to Jan Lochman and Josef Smolik, distinguished members of the Comenius Faculty at Charles University in Prague, to lecture in the United States.[51] Lochman, who later succeeded Karl Barth at Heidelberg, had agreed to come either November 1-December 15, 1962 or February 1-March 15, 1963.[52] Smolik also came and conferred with Thomas Merton at the Abbey of Gethsemani about peace issues.[53]

Although small groups of church leaders could not have expected to defuse political tensions between East and West, the Colloquy opened some lines of communication between them. In November 1962 Joseph Hromadka, as President of the Christian Peace Conference, shared his concern about the Cuban Missile Crisis. His somewhat one-sided statement evoked a caution from Douglas, which reveals what made him so remarkably effective as a peacemaker. He wrote frankly, yet lovingly. The Christian Peace Conference's statement, he observed, would be more effective if the committee which drew it up had some representative western members who could place the incident in a perspective which did not lay all the blame on one side.

This lack of perspective, even in such a loving statement as the one you sent, tends to discredit the objectivity of our deep common concern and makes those of us who love the same Lord and are trying in our best way to reach our governments toward creative peace, somewhat embarassed to have a statement made in the name of the Peace Council which does not reflect the full frame in which the criticisms are to be made.[54]

Looked at from the vantage point of thirty-five years of world history, the East-West Colloquy was only a blip on the screen. Yet it was an event of real significance, for it courageously set an example for the peace friendship tours to eastern Europe which eventually broke down barriers in East-West relations and helped to challenge totalitarian systems.

American Agony

Although Douglas Steere's years as Chairman of the Friends World Committee for Consultation (1964-70) and heavy investment of time in other activities precluded continuance as Chairman of the North and South American Section of IFOR, he and the Religious Society of Friends could not escape the American agony over the war in Vietnam as it dragged on and on. If Douglas had not paid much attention to the war himself while he chaired the FWCC, he got many reminders from Charles Schwieso of Menlo Park, California, whom Douglas labeled his "gadfly."[55] Nixon's presidency especially troubled Charles. He wanted the press to stop abusing Quakers by mentioning Nixon's membership in the Society of Friends.[57] All responsible church people should gather and read "Tricky Dick" out of the Christian fellowship and its care and consign his soul to hell. Billy Graham, too, if he wants to go with him. Douglas should excommunicate Nixon![57] Writing notes to him will not get him to stop the war. Douglas should call a meeting of Quakers in Philadelphia to excommunicate him![58]

Douglas and Dorothy, of course, did not need reminders. They agonized with many friends they were meeting all over the world. They received anguished letters from Quakers in service roles around the world. In a letter to Thomas Merton in April, 1968 Douglas lamented American inability to bring the war in Vietnam to a close.

> What a period we are in with Martin Luther King's assassination and the Johnson regime seeming to do everything to hinder taking up the wonderful initiative that was proposed to us a fortnight ago. How can we talk about peace in one breath and call up another 25,000 reserves with the other? No one can trust our sincerity any longer after exhibitions of this kind. [59]

The Steeres got very close to "this orgy of destruction" on their trip to the far east in 1970-71.[60] They saw close friends jailed for protesting involvement in Vietnam.[61] They counseled CO's. They interjected their personal pleas to President Johnson: "Your stature is on test. If you negotiate peace now, the world will acclaim you," they wrote.[62] However, the stand that Douglas could take and the role that he could play as Chairman of the FWCC were not as clear and unambiguous as his "gadfly" assumed. With the eyes of many Friends looking to him for guidance in such a turbulent time, he needed to give a Woolman-like response in which the principles of non-violence and love would govern action. He and Dorothy were beacons directing others through the storm.

One letter of Douglas Steere reveals that some pacifists were flirting with gnostic and anarchistic ideas as the solution to Vietnam. Citing a statement of John Woolman about possessions as the root of war, they were prepared to overturn the whole order of society. Douglas was not prepared to put a stamp of approval on such a radical solution. The cure would be far worse than the disease.

218

If the alternative to this is to have no possessions, then there are a whole nest of alternative problems that rise as to the way the insecurities of life are to be met without involving the individual in some massive mechanism that will supply these needs without at the same time committing us to an apparatus that will be out of control and as subject as individuals are to the evils of a great national ME or a great racial ME or a great BIG Brother ME of some other species. The man who has no theory of the state but burbles revolution as the answer to all—and so many pacifists today do this, thinking that if they can topple the existing evil entities that somehow, somewhere, without yielding their hatred of violence and mass coercion, some Rousseauian substitute will spring up out of the hearts of men—it is not likely to get far as a substitute for war.

So, Douglas went on to point out, one must give some thought to a viable alternative.

There can, you know, be a specious short circuit, a flight to the inner dimensions of consciousness that never gets deeply enough into the living center that Jesus got to and that his life in us still makes available, to compel the person to leave space and to reenter the earth's atmosphere and carry this inward discovery into the sinews of structures that can channel [the human] ME into more sensitive and efficacious ways of meeting the needs that possessions and the institution of property generally were devised to care for.[63]

One can see in Douglas' effort to sift everything carefully through the sieve of Christian tradition why so many looked to him with such confidence. Some were able at times to articulate that trust. A close personal friend, Elizabeth Chalmers, identified what others treasured in the Steeres' leadership. "The quality of your lives, the steadfast adherence to the standards we all long for, the humor, the tender concern, the serenity in spite of Nixon, Black Power, Vietnam, the shoddy relationships all over the place, etc. came through to us as strongly as ever and moved us deeply and helped us."[65]

As Chairman of the FWCC, Douglas took more formal measures to make the most of the Quaker peace witness. He arranged for U Thant, Secretary-General of the United Nations, whom he had met years earlier in Burma, to address the Friends World Conference meeting at Guilford College, Greensboro, North Carolina, on July 30, 1967. U Thant delivered a message which aroused "a strong desire in [those who attended] to carry to Washington the most urgent pressure to end the Vietnam war."[65] Douglas responded with remarks on the nature and ground of Quaker peacemaking. Subsequently, he wrote U Thant asking for a personal meeting on behalf of the Executive Committee of the FWCC "in order to express personally to you our deep thanks for your untiring efforts to secure an early settlement of the Viet Nam war and to offer you the assistance, modest as it may be, of the Religious Society of Friends in any area you think we may be of use."[66]

In his address following U Thant's, Douglas laid bare not only his own but the Quaker heart. The UN Secretary-General had not asked Quakers to help to kindle the desire for peace in the abstract, but "to help in relevant ways to quicken the so-largely-absent desire for the costly and often highly painful 'things that lead to true peace'."[67] To do this, Douglas went on to say, they must begin from within, where in the chambers of their own hearts "they may meet a Love so overwhelming that their earthly hearts are broken down and tendered, . . ."[68] Refusal to participate in wars, search for ways to identify with those who suffer wrong, and overturn those wrongs without violence will assuredly spring from and be renewed by this inward tendering. In Quaker peace endeavors Woolman's word is still adequate: "Love was the first motion." Closely linked to this, peacemakers must have faith "that we never work alone, and that when we are brought into this tendering, the holy seeds of concern are sowed in our hearts and often for very specific situations,"[69] whether locally or to the ends of the earth. In an era when the world is experiencing a shrinkage of compassion, of people willing "to pluck at the sleeve of the world and call attention to human needs,"[70] the inward tendering will increase faith in the processes of compassion, understanding, and reconciliation. All peacemaking energies are aimed at bringing back into focus the active presence and human faces of those the nations have shunned in order to justify their military or diplomatic operations against them. In what may seem bleak times, peacemakers will hold ever to two complementary essentials—sufficient grounding in the inward Christ that they will persevere in their peacemaking even when they cannot see results, and the ray of hope that humankind is "nearer to a break-through on the abandonment of massive war as an instrument for settling international conflicts than ever before in the history of [humanity]."[71]Dawn is coming.

Notes

1. Dorothy M. Steere, Unpublished *Reminiscences and Reflections,* 1992, 12-13.
2. Dorothy and Douglas Steere, *Friends Work in Africa* (London: Friends World Committee for Consultation, ca. 1954), quoting *The Journal of John Woolman and a Plea for the Poor,* edited by John Greenleaf Whittier, 192.
3. Douglas V. Steere, UNPUBLISHED JOURNAL, 168.
4. Steere, JOURNAL, 172.
5. Steere, JOURNAL, 212.
6. Steere, JOURNAL, 218.
7. Steere, JOURNAL, 225.
8. Steere, JOURNAL, 253.

9. Steere, JOURNAL, 461. This statement does not appear in *News from Douglas Steere,* British Zone, Germany, December 15, 1947, 2-3, which summarized the same incident.

10. Douglas V. Steere, *A Swedish Quaker Experiment in Reconciliation,* summarized the proceedings and listed participants.

11. Steere, JOURNAL, 485.

12. Steere, JOURNAL, 497.

13. Steere, JOURNAL, 499.

14. Douglas V. Steere, *A Visit to Finland,* Rouvaniemi, Finland, July 1, 1948, 4-5.

15. Steere, JOURNAL, 710.

16. Steere, JOURNAL, 750.

17. Douglas V. Steere, *God's Irregular: Arthur Shearly Cripps, a Rhodesian Epic* (London: S.P.C.K., 1973). See also Steere, JOURNAL, 761.

18. Douglas V. Steere, "The Quaker Message," *Christian Century,* 72 (August 3, 1955), 893-5.

19. Douglas V. Steere, *Travel Letter,* #5, Tokyo, Japan, January 24, 1960, 15.

20. Douglas V. Steere, *Letter to Margarethe Lachmund, Berlin,* February 28, 1970.

21. Douglas V. Steere, *Travel Letter,* #2, Cologne, September 30, 1959, 4.

22. Steere, *Travel Letter,* #2, 6.

23. Steere, *Travel Letter,* #2, 7. Italics mine.

24. Steere, JOURNAL, 735.

25. *Travel Journal of Douglas and Dorothy Steere, 1970-1971 Series,* #4, 13. Cf. also "A Quaker at the Central Committee Meeting of the World Council," *Religion in Life,* XIX (Winter 1949-50), 3-15.

26. He used the title *Cells for Peace,* but *The Peace Team* (New York: Fellowship of Reconciliation, n.d.) is the title under which it was published.

27. Steere, JOURNAL, 200.

28. See especially Douglas V. Steere, *Letter to John Nevin Sayre,* February 2, 1962; April 2, 1963; January 19, 1967.

29. See especially John C. Heidbrink, *Letter to Douglas V. Steere,* September 14, 1961; January 9, 1963.

30. Douglas V. Steere, "Report of Meeting with Thomas Merton," February 6, 1962.

31. *Letter of Douglas V. Steere to IFOR Members,* February 8, 1963.

32. Unpublished and undated "Memo on a Possible Meeting in 1961 of Western and Eastern Churchmen."

33. Douglas V. Steere, *Letter to A.J. Muste,* August 25, 1960; responding to letter of Muste dated August 19.

34. Two minutes record meetings February 4, 1961, at Dean John C. Bennett's apartment at Union Theological Seminary, New York, and

October 6, 1961, in Room 209, UTS. A.J. Muste also sent a letter reporting "New Development in Proposed Unpublicized Theological Discussion of East-West Churchmen" on September 20, 1961.

35. A.J. Muste, *Letter to Participants of East-West Colloquy,* October 18, 1961; *Letter to J.L. Hromadka,* October 20, confirming date, arrival time, preaching on January 28, financial support of eastern participants, list of western participants, and agenda.

36. The Irwin Sweeney-Miller Foundation supplied $3,500, of which Douglas returned $1,371. Undated letter of Douglas Steere to Irwin Miller and George Miller.

37. Douglas V. Steere, *Letter to Consul General of Czechoslovakia, Washington, DC,* December 22, 1961, gave names of persons applying for visas; *Letter to Joseph Hromadka,* December 22.

38. Heinz Kloppenburg, organizer in western Europe, in a *Letter to Douglas V. Steere,* December 29, 1961, remarked: "I think the group of Americans you have brought together is just an *outstanding* one."

39. Americans included: Methodist Bishops James K. Mathews and Kenneth Copeland; Harold DeWolf, a professor at Boston University School of Theology; Francis Sayre, Jr., Dean of the National (Episcopal) Cathedral, Washington, DC; John B. Coburn, Dean of Episcopal Theological Seminary; John Bennett, Dean of Union Theological Seminary in New York; Roger Shinn, a professor at Union; Hampton Adams, a minister of the Disciples of Christ; George Forell, a professor at Iowa State University; Harold Bender, Dean of (Mennonite) Goshen College Biblical Seminary; V. Carney Hargrove, Pastor of Second Baptist Church, Germantown, PA, and Vice-President of the Baptist World Alliance; Eugene Carson Blake, President of the United Presbyterian Church and later Secretary of the WCC; James I. McCord, President of Princeton Theological Seminary; and belatedly Dale Aukerman, theologian of the Church of the Brethren; as well as Douglas Steere and A.J. Muste. The list was compiled from a letter of Douglas Steere to Joseph Hromadka, December 6, 1961 with subsequent confirmation of Dale Aukerman in a letter dated December 21.

40. Douglas V. Steere, *Letter to Participants in the East-West Colloquy,* January 18, 1962.

41. Heinz Kloppenburg, *Letter to Douglas V. Steere,* January 11, 1962.

42. Douglas V. Steere, *Letter to American Participants in the East-West Colloquy,* January 9, 1961.

43. Douglas V. Steere, *Letter to John Nevin Sayre, IFOR, Nyack, NY,* February 2, 1962, observed that Kloppenburg did a wonderful job making arrangements but would have to be watched if he came to the United States.

44. Heinz Kloppenburg, *Letter to Douglas V. Steere,* February 16, 1962.

45. Douglas V. Steere, *Letter to Heinz Kloppenburg,* February 24, 1962.

46. Douglas V. Steere, *Letter to Joseph Hromadka,* February 2, 1962.

47. J.L. Hromadka, *Letter to Douglas V. Steere,* February 9, 1962.

48. Francis B. Sayre, Jr., *Letter to Douglas V. Steere,* February 6, 1962.

49. John B. Coburn, *Letter to Douglas V. Steere,* February 6, 1962.

50. Harold S. Bender, *Letter to Douglas V. Steere,* February 7, 1962.

51. Douglas V. Steere, *Letter to John Heidbrink,* February 1, 1962; *Letter to John Nevin Sayre,* February 2, 1962.

52. Steere, *Letter to John Nevin Sayre,* February 2, 1962.

53. Thomas Merton, *Turning toward the World.* The Journals of Thomas Merton, vol. 4, ed. Victor A. Kramer (San Francisco: HarperCollins Co., 1996).

54. Douglas V. Steere, *Letter to Joseph L. Hromadka,* November 21, 1962.

55. Charles Schwieso, *Letter to Douglas and Dorothy Steere,* September 22, 1967, with appended note by Douglas.

56. Charles M. Schwieso, *Letter to Douglas and Dorothy Steere,* January 27, 1968.

57. Copy of a Schwieso *Letter to Bronson [Clark?],* May 1, 1972; *Letter to Douglas and Dorothy Steere,* July 14, 1972, wanting to know why Douglas had not answered his earlier letter.

58. Charles M. Schwieso, *Letter to Douglas and Dorothy Steere,* January 3, 1973.

59. Douglas V. Steere, *Letter to Thomas Merton,* April 22, 1968.

60. *Travel Journal of Douglas and Dorothy Steere, 1970-71 Series,* #3-4, 5.

61. Lydia Stokes, *Letter to Douglas V. Steere,,* July 6, 1972.

62. Dorothy and Douglas Steere, Undated *Letter to Lyndon Johnson, White House.*

63. Douglas V. Steere, *Letter to Dear Friend,* March 5, 1973.

64. Elizabeth Chalmers, *Letter to Dorothy and Douglas Steere,* January 9, 1969.

65. Douglas V. Steere, "Some FWCC Reminiscences," *Friends World News* (1987), 5.

66. Douglas V. Steere, *Letter to U Thant,* January 28, 1968. The Secretary-General replied with thanks on April 2, 1968.

67. Douglas V. Steere, "Response to Address by Secretary General U Thant," 2.

68. Steere, "Response to U Thant," 7.

69. Steere, "Response to U Thant," 9.

70. Steere, "Response to U Thant," 11.

71. Steere, "Response to U Thant," 18.

XIV

Quaker Visionary and Guide

*I*n a "Memorial Minute" in March 1995, Radnor Monthly
Meeting perceptively observed that Douglas Steere
"represented the best of Quaker traditions" even as he
"strengthened an attitude of catholicity and abiding respect
for different religious views of Truth and paths to wholeness."
It ranked him among "Quakerism's other twentieth-century
departed spiritual leaders: Howard Brinton, Henry Cadbury,
Thomas Kelly, and Rufus Jones, among others."[1] Douglas
Steere was someone to whom Quakers around the world
looked for vision and guidance in an age which tried people's
souls by its potential both for awful evil and awesome good.
For them he was what one might call a "horizonal" person,
a person not simply shaped in the mold of this age but
transformed by his attentiveness to the Light Within so that
he could see what God is trying to bring into being beyond
the horizon.

A glance at his bibliography reveals that Douglas Steere directed some of his most creative thoughts and energies toward
interpreting and helping others to understand and appreciate
the Quaker tradition. The essence of Quakerism, as he understood it, with John Woolman as its premier representative, penetrated virtually everything he and Dorothy did and wrote. In
his interpretation he extended the work of his predecessor and

mentor at Haverford, Rufus Jones, but, laboring in a rapidly and radically changing Christian world environment, he added some dimensions not accessible to Rufus.

A glance at endowed lectureships which Douglas gave during a half century of active leadership attests Friends' recognition of his leadership: the William Penn Lecture at Arch Street Meeting House in 1937;[2] the Quaker Lecture at the Western Yearly Meeting of Friends in 1946; the Swarthmore Lecture at the London Yearly Meeting in 1955;[3] the Isaac T. and Lida K. Johnson Lecture at the Five Years Meeting of Friends, Richmond, Indiana, in 1960;[4] the James Backhouse Lecture at the Australia Yearly Meeting, Hobart, Tasmania, in 1967;[5] the Richard L. Cary Lecture at Bad Pyrmont, Germany Yearly Meeting in 1968;[6] the West Coast Quaker Lecture at Whittier College in 1968.[7] To these one might add a long list of addresses to various Quaker bodies on special occasions and an incalculable number of letters replying to Friends seeking his guidance vis-à-vis their own faith and the Quaker tradition.

Essentials of Quakerism

It may be useful to today's "seekers" to summarize Douglas' understanding of the Quaker way as reflected especially in an unpublished address he gave in the Quaker Theological Discussion Group Conference at Barnesville, Ohio, in 1959 on "Five Essentials of Quaker Faith Today" and amplify them with observations made in other writings. He was convinced that these five aspects were "central" and "peculiarly relevant to certain needs in our time." If Quakers "could live in this field of power and witness to it, we would not only kindle each other afresh but would have a hand outreached to the people waiting to be gathered out of whom our own Society has regirded itself in every generation."[8]

In his interpretation of Quaker origins Douglas Steere placed himself in the lineage of his colleague and mentor at

Haverford, Rufus Jones.[9] He located the movement in the mystical or contemplative tradition which had roots running back to the "seekers" of the seventeenth century whom George Fox drew together. Fox accentuated an InwardLight that dwells in the heart of ordinary people.

> In Quakerism as I know it, not mystical geniuses but ordinary men and women have experienced at first-hand the transforming power of the redeeming love of God in Christ and the cherishing of the growth of this consciousness. They have known the business of bringing their lives and conduct under its instant guidance. If this is not mystical, then we are quarreling over a definition.[10]

First, the heart of the Quaker tradition is *immediacy,* "a witness to the immediate presence, the inwardness, the accessibility, the utter simplicity of the relation of the living God to the soul of an ordinary [person]." Without the mediation of clergy or institution or sacrament, the God of the universe "can and does, here and now, make [Godself] known in the human heart, softening, tempering, quickening, goading and guiding that heart into a recognition of [God's] matchless love and caring; . . ." This intimate revelation takes place now, and God never lifts the siege at the ground of the soul.[11]

A second aspect, inseparably linked to the first, concerns *Jesus Christ.* "As we become more and more deeply aware of this siege of God within our souls, there is disclosed to us what God would reveal to us, what [God] is really like, how much [God] cares. And there in our very souls we find present the image of the Elder Brother, the type man, the redemptive act of God: Jesus Christ, our guide, our captain, and our teacher in the school of redemptive love."[12] Douglas was not prepared to agree with those within the Society who have lamented inadequate attention to the historical Jesus and the scriptural presentation of him and called for a creed. Historical knowledge through reading the scriptures has helped prepare people for this experience, "and Friends who skimp the Bible may beware." Jesus' earthly existence "is indeed a decisive revelation, and the crucifixion and resurrection were cosmic acts." But the Quaker concern is whether these are only outward beliefs or whether they become inward knowledge. "Have you inwardly known this? Has your life come under the guiding power of the living God as revealed in the Elder Brother? Is the living Christ being formed in you? Have you experienced the ordination of the pierced hands? Is he drawing you into the redemptive order of those living and dead who are joined to God for the reconciliation and healing of the world?"[13] Such questions cannot be answered like factual questions, and the replies will not be identical or the experience of a single kind. Early Friends did not find it hard to acknowledge the Jesus of history, for they met him "in a moment that took them beyond history, . . ." and trusted avidly in his promise that where two or three gathered, he would be in their midst.[14] Quakers have tied their view of Christ inseparably to their view of the redemptive community.

A third has to do with *the Quaker view of human nature.* Quakers reject the idea of utter depravity and damnation. There is always in humankind something "not of earth or of dust or of flesh or of time, but of God" that yearns for the living Christ and active membership in the redemptive community. Events of the twentieth century have heightened human consciousness of sin, but they did not surpass the savagery of the century in which the Religious Society of Friends came into existence. "Yet in spite of all this, in friend and in foe, at home and abroad, Quakers discerned behind the mask of all the contrary evidence, a view of a reachable center in [humankind] that hungered for the ministration and promise contained in the redeeming love of the living Christ and in God's immediate operativeness in this situation."[15] Quaker emphasis on "Christ *in* us" marks it off from the pessimism inherent in Protestant accent on "Christ *for* us." This is not to belittle the transformation wrought by "the burst of fresh power that

228

may stream through a life that comes from the Root."[16] But in the Quaker view God's concern for humankind did not begin at Calvary but at creation, so that there is always a capability of responding or of denying.

A fourth aspect, connected with their anthropology, is *the Quaker approach to nature and science.* Quakers regard nature "as open-ended, as neither automatically containing nor as utterly alien to a new order of redeeming love," a view which gives rise to a cosmic optimism, like Julian of Norwich's "And all shall be well. And all shall be well. And every manner of thing shall be well." Fox rejected the Fifth Monarchy Men's invitation to join them to see nature destroyed, to be replaced by an alien and heavenly order. The new order is already here, and we must live it. Nature is not closed to the new order. Rather, humankind is placed on earth to be a link in the chain between the creator-redeemer God, the living Christ, and the organic and inorganic world. Awareness of participation in this great chain of being makes Quakers feel at home in scientific investigation and spiritual healing. As it did with John Woolman, tenderness toward creation and minority groups caused Friends to refuse to support war. It has also restrained Quakers from withdrawal from the world to dwell in monastic-like communitarian structures. "With few exceptions, Quakers have stubbornly remained within the world, willing to be tempted in all things as all men [and women] are, willing to acknowledge the gravity-like pull of the world, yet seeking to answer the unquenchable longing for this redemptive order in the place and generation in which they lived."[17]

The fifth has to do with *the Quaker attitude toward its own vehicles of worship and corporate organization.* The structures of waiting in silence and of the manner of conducting business, fashioned by what Henry Cadbury called "the robust statesmanship" of George Fox, "were designed to channel the witness to the immediate revelation of God and to the indwelling of each [person] by the redemptive love of Jesus Christ."[18] What was revolutionary was that ordinary lay persons under the guidance of the Spirit were trusted to form a corporate instrument for the worship of God and the guidance of their practical affairs. Nevertheless, valued as the structures are, Quakers have not been willing to form them into a creed. In different periods they have devised all kinds of auxiliary types of meetings. Although he recognized their weaknesses, for example, in missionary work in Christian countries, where substantial portions of Quakers have adopted a pastoral system, Douglas was ready to dispense with the silent meeting or the business meeting "only with the greatest reluctance." For him, "this waiting type of worship is still a way of direct access to God" and "a means of respecting and encouraging this access in every person gathered."[19]

A Call to Holy Obedience

In the William Penn Lecture on "The Open Life" in 1937 Douglas sounded a challenge to Quakers which echoed throughout his life. Quakers, he said, no longer know much about the radical commitment of early Quakers. Now they act with caution. The prayer on their lips is: "Oh God, teach us to do thy will—*to a certain extent.*" What is needed is commitment to "the open life."

The conditions which he found in people of the open life were "a sense of vocation, a living in the decision, a yielding to the *principle,* a coming under holy obedience or into devotion, a life of practice *in* the presence of God."[20] The early Friends did not confuse sense of vocation with withdrawal from the world, a special form of ministry, or a special form of work; the real human vocation is yielding, being open to God. But it is from the principle that everything else springs—fellowship with the mystical body of Christ, social concern, reverence for life, courage to persist when others do what is wrong. The one condition where saint, mystic, and simple believer are all one is holy obedience or devotion.

230

Prayer brings us to holy obedience. The real query about prayer is: "Did thee yield?" "The apparatus is wholly secondary. But the recovery of the root, the being brought low, the being baptized into the condition of those in need, the yielding to the principle, the becoming subject to the root, coming to holy obedience, into devotion: that is the heart of prayer."[21] We can take failures in stride in holy obedience, relying on the grace of God. To complete all of these in the open life we must practice the presence of God.

FWCC Ambassadors

With the election of Douglas as clerk of the Friends World Committee for Consultation in 1964 the Steere ministry in the Religious Society of Friends came under the sponsorship of that body. The Steeres continued their globe trotting. The travels had much the same appearance as those sponsored by the American Friends Service Committee, focusing on the personal in encouraging Friends around the globe and enlarging the circle of friends farther and farther outwards. The shift in sponsorship and the widening of their reach prompt a brief account of trips taken in 1966-67 and in 1970-71 on behalf of the FWCC.

In 1966 the Steeres had three weeks of intensive work launching a fund drive for Pendle Hill, attending the Pendle Hill Board meeting, participating for three days in the Friends World Committee Interim Committee meeting at Pendle Hill and the Friends World Conference Committee at Greensboro, North Carolina, and lecturing at the Piedmont College Center. Then, they departed for Geneva on October 27 to confer with Victor Hayward, Director of the WCC Centers for the Study of the World Religions, about the colloquies to be held in Japan and India. Going from there to Rome, they visited the Secretariat for Promoting Christian Unity to report on the Ecumenical Institute of Spirituality meeting at Pendle Hill in 1966 and to plan for the upcoming colloquies and to finalize arrangements for two Roman Catholic observers to participate in the Friends World Conference at Guilford in July and August, 1967.

November 3 the Steeres flew from Rome to Cairo to visit friends at the Coptic Institute—two they had made in Rome and a Muslim professor Douglas had come to know in 1959. Departing from Cairo, they flew to Nairobi in a plane carrying military hardware for Uganda in the first class section! After attending Sunday Meeting, they went to the East Africa Yearly Meeting at the Ofafa Social Settlement, where Douglas spoke through an interpreter. In the afternoon they discussed with African Quakers the advisability of pressing for a Quaker Junior College, perhaps at Kaimosi. As Douglas suggested, the Africans decided to do some "market research" first to determine the need before launching such an institution. Douglas also spoke at the Anglican Cathedral hall on the Second Vatican Council.

From Kenya the Steeres visited Zambia, where they lunched with the American Ambassador, Robert Good, and his wife Nancy. From Zambia they flew to Salisbury. There they were met by Lady Tredgold and Lady Acton, whose husband headed the Red Cross in Rhodesia. They again stayed with Sir Robert and Lady Tredgold, close friends with whom they had lived two and a half years earlier while Douglas worked on the biography of A.S. Cripps. Douglas spent a day at the University of Salisbury talking with various persons he knew. He and Dorothy visited with Roman Catholic Archbishop Markall and dined with Anglican Bishop Alderson of Mashonaland and Dean Wood of the Salisbury Cathedral and his wife. After worshipping with Salisbury Friends on Sunday, Douglas spoke to the group. The Steeres spent five days in Bulawayo, staying with Roy and Irene Henson, the American Friends Service Committee representatives in that area. Douglas was impressed with the community use of the Meetinghouse built there. Both Steeres spoke at the General Meeting in Bulawayo.

From Salisbury the Steeres flew to Johannesburg, where they met with numerous friends. They spent two weeks in Capetown, including two days at the farm of Afrikaner novelist William De Klerk, and sought out those trying to do something about apartheid. In Durban they met Roman Catholic Archbishop Hurley, who served as President of the Race Relations Institute of South Africa and vigorously opposed the Bantu Education Act. They visited two hours with Alan Paton, with whom Douglas had been corresponding since their first meeting. They discussed Paton's biography of Jan Hofmyer, the Rhodesian situation, and Reinhold Niebuhr's *Moral Man and Immoral Society*. In Pietermaritzburg they stopped to see Edgar Brookes, another of the prominent South African reformers whom Douglas hoped to bring to Pendle Hill. They reviewed Quaker efforts by Bunty Biggs, Phyllis and Scarnell Lean, Jennifer Kinghorn, and Olive Gibson to overcome inequities in South Africa. In a travel letter Douglas concluded: "Once again we had drunk in South Africa's almost inimitable beauty and charm, and yet felt how braced she was against a policy that would give the non-whites a real sense of having a future of dignity and hope in this great country." He then proceeded to ask: "Will some unforeseen turn of history set in motion forces that will bring another racial policy?" He ended on a hopeful note: "Certainly on our visit we found undespairing men and women of every race who refuse to give up hope, but who admit that the hope comes more from within than from evidences in the present situation."[22]

Due to an airline strike in December, the Steeres had to fly directly to Perth, Australia, an exhausting twenty-three hours on a DC-7 with only refueling stops. In Perth they were hosted by Lawrence and Nancy Wilkinson. Lawrence, recently elected a senator in the Australian Federal Parliament in Canberra as a Labour candidate, was both a Quaker and the President of the Perth Fellowship of Reconciliation; he pushed the AFSC position on the war in Vietnam. Douglas found Australian Quaker concern for aborigines impressive. The Steeres, spending only two days in Adelaide, talked with the Meeting and held an evening discussion of Douglas' essay, "No Time but This Present," on the Quaker-Roman Catholic encounter. From Melbourne they flew to Hobart to take part in the Australian Yearly Meeting, one of the three chief links in a vast country among Australian Friends. The others were the bi-monthly magazine *The Australian Friend* and a Quaker school in Hobart. Just before the Yearly Meeting, the Steeres visited and spoke to a Quaker young people's camp, led a retreat attended by twenty-five Friends over the New Year, and took part in a two-day Summer School. At the opening of the Meeting Douglas gave the James Backhouse Lecture on the theme "On Being Present Where You Are." He was impressed at the Meeting by the commissioning of Patricia Hewitt, a Hobart Young Friend, for service in the Friends Rural Centre in Rasulia, India, as a fine representation of "the real character of the call and the answer in a genuine Quaker concern for service." [23] From Hobart the Steeres flew to Canberra the day after the Yearly Meeting. Douglas spoke to a packed Quaker Meeting on the aftermath of Vatican II, met the press, and was interviewed on radio and television. From Canberra they proceeded to Sydney to spend the weekend with Rudolf and Hanna Lemberg. A gifted scientist, Rudolf was Jewish by birth but Quaker by conviction.

From Sydney the Steeres flew to Christchurch, New Zealand, where they spent a well-deserved three weeks on holiday. They envisioned a twofold purpose in their visits among Friends: an FWCC visit to Friends themselves, and publicizing of Quaker presence through press interviews, radio broadcasts, lectures, and conferences. The New Zealand Council of Churches had arranged several conferences. At Dunedin the Steeres held a public meeting in the University Museum and several meetings at the Meetinghouse. Staying at Christchurch for five days with Muriel and John Morrison, they had an excellent visit with Roman Catholic Bishop Ashby and met the clergy of Christchurch for most of a morning. Roman Catholics invited Douglas to lecture at their St. Patrick's Hall. Douglas met some members of the philosophy department of the university and got interviews in the public press about the tragedy of New Zealand having yielded to the American demand that they send troops to Vietnam. At Wellington Douglas spoke to Roman Catholics and Protestants on "Creative Encounter of the World Religions." The Steeres also had a few intimate meetings with Friends, including Young Friends. At Otaki Douglas visited Ormund Burton, the famous New Zealand pacifist. At Wanganui the Steeres visited the Quaker School and Douglas addressed a meeting convened by the city's Council of Churches. Making their final stop in Auckland, where they stayed in a new Quaker hostel next to the Meetinghouse, they participated in a public meeting and another open meeting at the Friends' Meetinghouse, where Douglas spoke. The Catholic Archbishop attended. They also met Anglican Bishop Gowing.

Back in Sydney on Sunday Douglas led discussion of the work of the FWCC and listened to concerns. He made four fourteen-minute tapes and three shorter ones for the Australian Broadcasting Corporation, gave a twenty minute address to a Sunday Evening Club, and lectured at a Quaker dinner party for clergy of the Australian Council of Churches. From Sydney they flew to Brisbane, where Douglas spoke to a post-luncheon meeting of 150 students, nuns, and clergy at the University. From there they headed to Manila to spend a long weekend with faculty and staff of the new Union Theological Seminary.

Enroute to the colloquies in Japan and India, described in detail earlier, the Steeres touched down again in Hong Kong and Korea. From India they flew back to Rome. After a few days visiting Swiss Friends, five days in Finland, and six in Sweden, they crossed the channel to London to share some of their experiences with English Friends at William Penn House and with the Friends Service Council staff and to spend two days at the FWCC at Woodbrooke near Birmingham. Douglas also gave the Woodbrooke Lecture. The Steeres returned to the United States on May 24 to rest and ready themselves for the Friends World Conference in July and August.

In 1970-71 Douglas and Dorothy carried out one more worldwide tour on behalf of the FWCC—Hawaii, Japan, Taiwan, Hong Kong, Singapore, Indonesia, Thailand, Nepal, India, Kenya, the Central Committee Meeting of the WCC in Addis Ababa, Rome, Germany, and England. On this journey we see once again the remarkable gift of the Steeres for uplifting and encouraging others, helping Friends understand the challenges of their world, raising questions about the work of Friends in different areas, sharing insights drawn from now vast experience, assisting bodies like the AFSC and FWCC to make decisions, putting before the world the best face of Friends, projecting a vision and a hope. Of special interest to the FWCC on this trip was Douglas' careful discussion of a possible African Section of the FWCC with two Kenyan Quaker leaders, Filomene Indire and Nathan Luvai. As he presented it to them, such a section might furnish an information bank on all the Quaker projects going on in Africa, including Southern Africa, West Africa, Burundi, East Africa, Zambia, and Madagascar. The section could also arrange small seminars in connection with meetings bringing Friends together in Africa; handle the suggestion of African candidates for fellowships and African personnel desired for Quaker appointments; arrange for African participation in programs and research and writing projects being undertaken by the FWCC; keep the Quaker world aware of the opinions of the different sectors of the Quaker world in Africa; help to deepen the spiritual life of the Society of Friends; and facilitate the process of Quaker intervisitation.[24]

Clerk of the FWCC

Douglas Steere was in Europe in the summer of 1937 when 1,500 British and American Friends gathered at both

Swarthmore and Haverford Colleges to examine the witness and responsibility of the Religious Society of Friends and to give birth to what became the Friends World Committee for Consultation. From the beginning it offered in its triennial meetings and fifteenth-year world conferences a forum where small groups of Friends sprinkled all over the world might come together to share their concerns and insights. Douglas' first serious engagement with the FWCC occurred in 1956 when he was attending the Philadelphia Yearly Meeting of Friends. FWCC officers asked participants in this meeting to tell them what they wanted the FWCC to do that it was not doing. Douglas took this seriously and suggested that, if the FWCCwanted to become "more than an interim committee for staging World Conferences or for encouraging Quakers in intervisitation, they must help the Religious Society of Friends to lessen its confusion and make up its mind to be more decisive about several great issues upon which the future religious life of our generation may well depend." He listed four issues: (1) Sharing the heart of the Quaker message beyond their own ranks. (2) "facing the various attitudes of the Society of Friends toward missionary activity in other parts of the world." (3) opening themselves to the ecumenical movement. (4) "examining the Quaker attitude and responsibility for contact with the world religions like Islam, Hinduism and Buddhism and exploring a creative relationship between them and the Christian presence in our time." [25] Douglas went on to propose a series of working parties of the ablest people in the Religious Society of Friends to meet in London, Philadelphia, and Richmond to explore these issues and publish the results. The FWCC adopted his proposal, preparing four topics for the FWCC gathering at Bad Pyrmont in Germany in 1958 and publishing a small volume edited by Edwin Bronner.

As Douglas and Dorothy completed their work with the AFSC in 1961, the FWCC tapped him to give the opening address for the Triennial meeting in Kaimosi, Kenya, to the

Steeres already a familiar place. He spoke on a topic very near the heart of his own reflection on the nature and mission of the Religious Society of Friends. In a foundational address entitled "Beyond Diversities to a Common Experience of God" he pointed to three types of Quaker diversities: (1) within the Quaker group, (2) between Quakerism and other Christian groups, and (3) between the internalized witness of Quakers and that of the great world religions such as Islam, Buddhism, and Hinduism. Changes in Africa, he noted, posed a major challenge for Quakers. The question is: "*Has the Society of Friends, for all of its diversity, a common experience of God that can meet the longings and aspirations of the African heart and that can fearlessly face the best reaches of the African mind?*" Douglas answered with a hearty yes. One facet of this common experience is that Christ is found in different ways—by Thomas Kelly in an experience of failure, by Gurdial Malik in guidance found in crises of life, by Elizabeth Vining in the healing of her bereavement, by Douglas Steere in an experience of the surety of God's love in a dream,[26] by others through service. A second is that

> as [Quakers] have come to know the Inward Teacher, they have found that Jesus Christ exposes the nature of God just as the fires of a volcano expose the molten nature of the earth's center, and that, being brought into an inward feeling-sense of this love, they have become aware that they have been placed in a world of men and animals and plants and earth as a living and indispensible link in a great redemptive chain of being. In this awareness has come the realization that they can love God back only by responsibly loving [God] in [God's] creatures and in [God's] creation.[27]

A third facet is "the experience of the guiding hand of God in the ordinary affairs of life."[28] Knowing the guidance of God in small things changes the conduct of life and makes us view other persons differently. "When Quakers have been in a flood of life, they have been at home in their own souls, and have been attentive enough to hear, and obedient enough to attempt to follow, the drawing that came to them." [29] So many "nudges" come—to write a letter, to make a visit, to prepare for a certain service, to be available for a certain call. But we must be attentive to the Inward Guide if we would catch the signals. "Beyond all diversities, Friends' common experience of God, both corporately and personally, is marked by our being called to an ever-deeper attentiveness to the guiding hand of God in specific undertakings."[30]

One practical suggestion which Douglas wove into this address, the establishment of a Quaker Centre for Communication with Persons of Non-Christian Faiths, caught the eye of Herbert M. Hadley, American Secretary of the FWCC. In February, 1962, he informed Douglas that the FWCC was willing to "explore the possible existence of a concerned Friend who might be available for such service, and the readiness of an appropriate Quaker body to sponsor such a project." Of course, FWCC would want first to learn what the World Council of Churches, International Missionary Council, or other denominations might be doing in this area.[31]

During the six years between the conference at Kaimosi and the World Conference of the FWCC in Guilford, North Carolina, Douglas found his life "drawn very close to the FWCC." At Kaimosi he had mentioned that John XXIII planned to hold a Vatican Council II in Rome in 1962 and it was rumored that he intended to invite Observers representing each of the Christian churches to attend. When the Society of Friends was eventually invited to send one Observer, the FWCC, to whom Quakers turned to make the selection, asked Douglas to represent them.[32] He could not attend the first session and Richard Ullmann filled in for him, but he did participate in the other three sessions, Dorothy in two. The FWCC mailed the Steeres' *Journal from Rome* to about three hundred Friends and other persons.

Delaying until October 26, 1964 his arrival in Rome to attend the third session of the Second Vatican Council, Douglas was elected Clerk of the FWCC at the Ninth Triennial in Waterford, Ireland. Already experienced at clerking through service as clerk of the John Woolman Memorial and the Pendle Hill Board as well as the North and South American Section of the International Fellowship of Reconciliation, he brought to the clerk's role qualities which generated confidence among other Committee members, staff, and the larger network of persons who supported the FWCC. these qualities included love for the Religous Society of Friends; commitment to the work of the FWCC, AFSC, and other Quaker bodies at all levels; firsthand acquaintance with Quaker efforts on a worldwide scale; personal sensitivity, humor, `intelligence, and good sense; ability to deal with detail; and pastoral concern.

A loosely structured world body composed of very diverse and individualistic people trying to do gargantuan tasks challenged the leadership even of a person as richly gifted as Douglas Steere. As Clerk, among routine matters, he had to attend frequent meetings of the Advisory Committee or Interim Committee, secure financial support for the FWCC's projects,[33] seek closer coordination of FWCC work with that of other Quaker bodies,[34] encourage and assist staff,[35] help in planning triennial gatherings,[36] and look after the employment of new personnel. On the retirement of Blanche Shaffer from her position as Associate Secretary in 1969 Douglas guided the process of recruiting William Barton[37] and Tayeko Yamanouchi,[38] a Japanese friend, as associate secretaries of the FWCC. Although these six years flowed smoothly most of the time, there were sensitive occasions. An Interim Committee member from Paris took offense when Douglas directed her to go through "channels" about a matter of concern and wanted to know, "Since when does a Friend not speak truth directly to all other Friends and everybody else, for that matter?"[39] Later, she addressed a sharp letter to Blanche

Shaffer bitterly criticizing the decision of the FWCC not to send Filomene Indire of the East Africa Yearly Meeting to the NGO Human Rights Conference at UNESCO House in September.[40] Christopher Taylor, another Committee member, wrote Douglas to suggest that he could help in two ways to deal with the attack, which had left Blanche Shaffer "badly shaken."[41] He could reassure Blanche and kindly accept the resignation of this member from the FWCC.

Douglas dealt with the matter with characteristic tact and sensitivity. He wrote the member on behalf of the Advisory Committee affirming confidence in Blanche Shaffer and accepting the member's resignation. The Committee were troubled over her charges, he said, for Blanche had fulfilled her responsibility. They were sorry funds could not be found to bring Indire to the Quaker UN Project. In the future, that might be possible, but Blanche did the best she could with the budget. Her own trips had been planned and budgeted and could not be forgone in favor of Filomene's coming, as this member suggested. Douglas then proceeded to reflect on the whole issue of personal relationships within the FWCC.

> There must be room in our ranks for different points of view and for those who feel passionately the spiritual imperialism of the white in his [or her] relations with those of other colors. But there must also be some minimum of faith and confidence in each other's integrity if they are to accomplish anything together. We are sorry that you feel that this no longer exists in your relationship with the FWCC but in view of your letter, the members of the Advisory Committee gathered yesterday and accepted what we take to be your resignation. We are not likely soon again to have one who is so closely connected with UNESCO or who could give us such intimate touch with its workings and the groups asked me to thank you for the help that you have given us in the years that you have served.[42]

The Nominating Committee for the Friends World Committee for Consultation subsequently nominated Filomene Indire to succeed Douglas as Clerk of the FWCC, but he declined to accept it.[43]

Douglas Steere's correspondence with staff and other persons involved in the work of the FWCC reveals others' awareness of the Steeres' deep pastoral sensitivity joined to careful attention to detail.[44] During his tenure as Clerk, Douglas, in his own gentle and sensitive style, did nudge the FWCC forward in important mission initiatives. One of these was sponsorship of the interfaith dialogues at Oiso and Ootacamund. At the annual gathering of the FWCC Section of the Americas in 1965 he laid out his proposal for colloquies between Zen Buddhists and Christians in Japan and Hindus and Christians in India, and received its encouragement to present his proposal to the FWCC's Interim Committee when he returned via London from an exploratory visit to Japan and India in the late spring of 1966.[45] The FWCC gave enthusiastic support.

A second proposal was a Middle East peace initiative in 1969.[46] The FWCC agreed to associate itself with an AFSC report on the Middle East drafted by Landrum Bolling, President of Earlham College, if Douglas and Herbert Hadley, Associate Secretary of the FWCC, agreed. Douglas offered six pages of suggestions, most of which were incorporated, but felt still uneasy about the last part as too long and too assured on issues.[47] The proposed Middle East Mission began January 25, 1970, and lasted three weeks.[48]

A third initiative concerned enhancement of the work of Quaker residents in Africa and Asia as personal centers of outreach for both the service and the message of the Religious Society of Friends. Through personal contact in the Steeres' travels with many persons who could do this, Douglas became "convinced that with some central staff service and at small cost, the Friends World Committee could maintain communication with them and stimulate them to an increased level of usefulness." Believing that there was "a thin network of self-supporting Friends spread over the globe, a vast potential for the spiritual and social outreach of the Quaker message and of Quaker service," he suggested beginning in Africa, Asia, South America, or some other part of the world and seeking "through close personal touch with such Friends by means of correspondence, literature, and perhaps even occasional visitation, to learn of their insights into the situations where they reside, and to encourage their initiative and to help them to draw upon the Society's resources to assist them in any possible way."[49] The proposal sounds amazingly like what the Steeres were doing themselves! Douglas convened a group of ten in his home at Haverford to explore the proposal further.[50]

A fourth suggestion involved promotion of World Resources -One Per Cent Funds, an idea for distributing the earth's resources more equitably that emerged from the Friends World Conference at Guilford. Individual Friends were urged to set aside one percent of their income for this fund. Douglas worked closely with William Barton to get Yearly Meetings to establish One Per Cent Funds and One Per Cent Fund Committees. The Funds were to be used to allocate money to Third World projects and to influence public opinion about world resources at the local , national, and international level. The FWCC intended to cooperate with other bodies in this field, whether Quaker, other churches, or secular groups.[51]

Guilford

The high point of Douglas' creative leadership as Clerk of the FWCC was reached at the Friends World Conference held at Guilford College near Greensboro, North Carolina, in July and August 1967. That the Conference took place at Guilford College at all points up something of the peacemaking genius of both the Quaker way and Douglas Steere. When the FWCC held its Triennial meeting at Kaimosi in 1961, it had already been decided that the Friends World Conference would take place in 1967 in some part of the United States, and North Carolina Friends had made a strong case for Guilford College. Before the Clerk put the issue to the delegates, however, Sigrid Lund, a respected Norwegian Quaker, rose and explained that she could not attend if the Conference were held in a school that would not admit black persons as students. After a time of silence one person after another rose to say they agreed with her. In discussion which followed, some pointed out that the Conference could be held at the University of North Carolina Greensboro, which did admit black students. Douglas spoke to the President of Guilford College as they walked to lunch after this session and learned that the problem lay with the Board of the College; faculty, staff, and students wanted to change the policy. In mid-October he received a telegram from Floyd Moore, a former student now on the faculty at Guilford, saying that the Board had lifted the bar to admission of blacks.

The Friends World Conference at Guilford College crowned not only a term as Clerk of the FWCC but a life of selfless service on behalf of the Religious Society of Friends and world Christianity. Twelve hundred attended. They came from thirty-five countries and represented fifty-one of the fifty-four existing Yearly Meetings. There were nine observers: five from Christian groups—Roman Catholic, Greek Orthodox, Mennonite, and Brethren, as well as a representative of the National Council of Churches, two Jewish rabbis, and one Muslim. Looking at the Conference from the perspective of twenty years, Douglas summed up what it meant to Quakers: "We felt the power of this large body to draw, often for the first time, Friends from widely different accents in their form of Quakerism, and to give them the privilege of sensing the deep underpinning that holds our witness together."[52] Small "Worship-Sharing Groups," a revival of the small group meetings which had revitalized Christianity on many occasions before, helped to draw people together. The addresses of U Thant and Douglas Steere himself on the theme of peace reaffirmed and reinvigorated the Quaker mission and purpose.

Sigtuna

In August, 1970 Douglas brought his close association with the FWCC almost to its conclusion at the Eleventh Triennial Friends World Conference at Sigtuna, Sweden, another site which held pleasant memories for him and Dorothy by virtue of the semester they had spent there in 1948.[53] "The Future of Quakerism" seemed like a suitable theme for a people numbered in the hundreds in most of Europe.[54] Gunnar Myrdal opened with a reflection, which he did not want to call an address, on "The Human Factor in Development."[55] William Barton spoke on "Working Together in the World Family of Friends" and Pierre Lacout, a Carmelite converted to the Quaker tradition, on "George Fox: Prophet of the Future."[56] Douglas concluded with a challenging address entitled "Emerging Horizons."

In his address he pressed Friends to ask "What thou wouldst be?" personally, as a Religious Society of Friends and as a Friends World Committee, if they were "to witness to the deepest that we know."[57] Quakers must be willing to ask whether they are redundant, remembering that God has a way of dismissing redundant persons and groups and "replacing them with those who have listened and responded to the needs of the deprived ones and are in the real current of [God's] life-giving power."[58] The urgent question "What wouldst thou be?" comes from "disenchanted young people, sore and bruised by the continuance of the war in Indo-China and by decisions they face about their own response to compulsory military service" or the use of nuclear weapons or the worth of their educational system. What do such youth want? Coming as seekers, they want "an opportunity to have expanded in them what they have, on rare occasions, experienced in music, in art, in drama, or in intimate touches of another human being" and to experience, "at least in miniature, a community of released people."[59] They appreciate "personal, affectionate, caring experiences of draft counselling, of costly personal hospitality, . . . and the open reception they have been given in some of the action projects of the Quaker agencies, . . ." But they want more. "When they come to our Meetings they need to feel that they are entering a community that is itself in a stream of trans-forming power, of a power that is not directed at changing the visitors to make them like the regular attenders, but where all present are being lured into a continuing inward revolu-tion by One who gathers the Meeting."[60] They want to experience the joy of "jubilant community," knowing that Isaac Penington had not exaggerated in saying, "There is that near you which will guide you. O wait for it and be faithful unto it."

Another challenge comes from Roman Catholic friends, the laity and clergy as well as members and leaders of religious orders, drawn into involvement in racial, political, and social projects. Racial and social injustice and "the corrosive effect of budgetary and human commitments to the military throughout the West" have confronted them with two problems in which Quakers have a vital stake: (1) What is the Christian attitude toward violence in both military and police structures and in differing forms of guerilla activity? (2) What inward transformations and liberating power are required for a genuinely non-violent witness as found in Jesus, Tolstoy, Gandhi, Martin Luther King, Jr., and Cesar Chavez? Friends must now face the horizon of the "Just Revolution," for some have been lured into it. Catholics have little to learn "from Quakers with guerilla dreams."[61] To the contrary, Quakers have much to learn from César Chavez and his fasts and vigils before the Crucified Christ. By Roman Catholics, too, Quakers are challenged to attend to the unfinished business of the nature and order of a non-violent state, up to now almost completely neglected. Roman Catholics also force Friends to ask how, without traditional disciplines—daily reading of the breviary, required times of prayer and fasting, unworldly costumes, strict discipline under a superior, living in a cloister—one can stay involved and yet remain an instrument of Christ's peace.

A challenge comes, too, from a "functional ecumenism" in which we seek insights about our common problems from Hindus, Buddhists, Sufis, and Hasidists and liberate "that man from Galilee who was perhaps more fully alive than anyone who ever walked this earth" from his "Western envelope." Quakers will not play a role in this liberation by "succumbing to all the diseases of over-activism," to which they are so prone today, but only by keeping their involvement in the world in intimate touch with their inward involvement. They cannot separate their contemplation from their work nor their work from their contemplation. What will lift the Society is the *quality* of its life. The Friends World Committee has assisted in this by bringing "worship-sharing groups" to Friends' attention. It can also lift the inward life of the Society by making "a more vigorous and sustained effort to find the prophetic voices and free them for periods of service in ministry."[62] The FWCC has taken steps to promote this functional ecumenism in hosting colloquies between Christians and Buddhists or Hindus and can go further to take an active part in broader ventures. It is and must also go on encouraging more interpretation of Quakerism through non-Anglo-Saxon eyes, more equitable sharing of the earth's resources, and pilgrimages to different regions of the world, something which justifies what some count excessive expense to attend Triennial meetings.[63]

Shortly after Sigtuna, Christopher Taylor expressed what most other FWCC leaders felt about Douglas' leadership and correctly pointed to the Friends World Conference at Guilford as an epochal moment. "We all owe you a great debt for your leadership as Chairman and I wanted to add my thanks for the contribution you have made and in particular for steering and encouraging the Committee in the great new tasks laid upon it by the 1967 Guilford Conference."[64]

<hr>

Notes

1. Radnor Monthly Meeting, "Memorial Minute for Douglas V. Steere (1902-1995)," March, 1995.
2. Published as *The Open Life,* William Penn Lecture 1937(Philadelphia: Book Committee of the Religious Society of Friends, 1937).
3. Published as *On Listening to Another* (New York: Harper Brothers, 1955).
4. Published as *Rain on the Mountain* (Richmond, Indiana: Five Years Meeting of Friends, 1960).
5. Published as *On Being Present Where You Are.* Pendle Hill Pamphlet #151 (Wallingford, PA: Pendle Hill Publications, 1967).
6. Published as *Mutual Irradiation: A Quaker View of Ecumenism.* Pendle Hill Pamphlet #175 (Wallingford, PA: Pendle Hill Publications, 1971).
7. Published as *The Hardest Journey.* Pendle Hill Pamphlet #163 (Wallingford, PA: Pendle Hill Publications, 1969).
8. Douglas V. Steere, "Five Essentials of Quaker Faith Today," Unpublished Address Delivered to the Quaker Theological Discussion Group Conference, Barnesville, Ohio, June 27-July 1, 1959, 4.
9. In a lengthy footnote to his address on "Five Essentials of Quaker Faith Today," 13-15, he defended Jones against the charge that he led the Society of Friends astray by interpreting it as a philosophical or mystical movement and diverting it from its true prophetic Bible-centered base with Jesus Christ adequately placed at the center. This charge fails to take into account (1) what Jones was trying to deliver Quakerism from, namely, "the dead stereotype of evangelical and revivalistic religion that was increasingly taking over Quakerism in America at the close of the last century"; and (2) "how profoundly he did seize upon an unpurgably central element in the Quaker witness in his emphasis upon the mystical character of its treatment of the relation of man to God and to

Christ." Douglas thought Jones relied too much on certain elements of idealistic philosophy, had too much faith in psychological processes for self-improvement, and did not emphasize enough being drawn into a redemptive community. But he found in Jones's *Later Periods of Quakerism*, xvi-xvii, a testimony about Christ he thought even John Wilhelm Rowntree would have found acceptable.

10. Steere, "Five Essentials," 14. Douglas' selections for his Classics of Western Spirituality volume on *Quaker Spirituality* (New York: Paulist Press, 1984), confirm his location of Quakers in the mystical stream. They included the *Journal and Epistles* of George Fox, the *Letters* of Isaac Penington, the *Journal* of John Woolman, *Quaker Strongholds* by Caroline Stephen, selections from Rufus Jones and Thomas Kelly.

11. Steere, "Five Essentials," 4-5. His thought here is in harmony with Baron von Hügel's and Bernard of Clairvaux's. In his travels Douglas constantly sought out persons such as Romano Guardini and Reinhold Schneider from whom he could learn about the experience of God.

12. "Five Essentials," #5.

13. "Five Essentials," #6.

14. "Five Essentials," #6

15. "Five Essentials," #8.

16. "Five Essentials," #8.

17. "Five Essentials," #10.

18. "Five Essentials," #11.

19. "Five Essentials," #12. Douglas *On Speaking Out of the Silence*. Pendle Hill Pamphlet 182 (Wallingford, PA: Pendle Hill Publications, 1972) explains and makes a strong case for the silent meeting. Quakers come and sit in silence because they sense that "something is going on all the time, something that we have only partially grasped the meaning of, and we long to be brought more deeply into it" (6).

20. Steere, *The Open Life*, 4.

21. Steere, *The Open Life*, 24.

22. *Dorothy and Douglas Steere Travel Letters 1966/67, Number III: South Africa*, 10.

23. *Steeres' Travel Letters, Number IV: Australia and New Zealand*, 6.

24. *Travel Journal of Douglas and Dorothy Steere, 1970/71 Series, #3-4*, 11.

25. Douglas V. Steere, "Some FWCC Reminiscences," *Friends World News*, No. 129 (1987/2),3.

26. Douglas dreamed he had killed a man, but he experienced an overwhelming sense of God's forgiveness and love. He recounted this experience in the Stone Lectures at Princeton in 1957 and here.

27. Douglas V. Steere, "Beyond Diversity to a Common Experience of God," *Quaker Religious Thought,* V (1962), 10.
28. Steere, "Beyond Diversity," 12.
29. Steere, "Beyond Diversity," 13.
30. Steere, "Beyond Diversity," 17.
31. Herbert M. Hadley, *Letter to Douglas V. Steere,* February 14, 1962.
32. In a *Letter to Douglas and Dorothy Steere* dated February 10, 1967, the FWCC remembered how prophetic Douglas was regarding the need to send an Observer to Vatican II and "have good cause now to be thankful for it and for the growth of understanding that has followed."
33. See Douglas V. Steere, *Letter to Blanche Shaffer,* December 15, 1967, noting a cut of $600,000 in the budget of the Quaker UN Program; Blanche Shaffer, *Letter to Douglas V. Steere,* March 29, 1968, regarding fund raising in Great Britain; Lewis Waddilove, *Letter to Douglas V. Steere,* March 12, 1969, regarding plans of the London Yearly Meeting to increase contributions to FWCC.
34. Colin W. Bell, AFSC, *Letter to Douglas V. Steere,* January 16, 1968, offered several suggestions, citing the FWCC as the only body capable of heading up a permanent "world Quaker service." Douglas V. Steere, *Letter to Gilbert F. White et al.,* November 29, 1968, wrote to Interim Committee members concerning the desire of the FWCC to have increased consultation and coordination— interagency and transnational, for the planning and operation of Quaker mission and service.
35. Blanche Shaffer in Birmingham, England and Herbert Hadley in Philadelphia kept up a flow of information. Douglas wrote numerous letters to Shaffer related to her mother's illness and her own approaching retirement.
36. See Blanche Shaffer, *Letter to Douglas V. Steere,* March 7, 1969, regarding the Friends World Conference in 1970.
37. See Blanche Shaffer, *Letter to Douglas V. Steere,* June 21, 1968; Douglas V. Steere, *Letter to Gilbert F. White,* July 17, 1968; Christopher Taylor, *Letter to Douglas V. Steere,* July 19, 1968; Douglas V. Steere, *Letter to Blanche Shaffer,* December 31, 1968. In the last Douglas wanted Barton to assume the position by March, 1969.
38. See Tayeko Yamanouchi, *Letter to Douglas V. Steere,* February 26, 1970, regarding her decision to accept the invitation; Douglas V. Steere, *Letter to Tayeko Yamanouchi,* April 14, 1970, regarding clearance of her appointment by the Personnel and Advisory Committees and completion at the Triennial Meeting. Blanche Shaffer, *Letter to Douglas V. Steere,* March 6, 1970, confirmed his

recommendation of Yamanouchi. In the *Travel Journal of Douglas and Dorothy Steere, 1970/71 Series*, #1, 5, Douglas and Dorothy noted the pride of Japanese Quakers that one of their own would help to guide the future of the FWCC.

39. Kie K.S. Fullerton, *Letter to Douglas V. Steere*, February 1, 1968.
40. Kie K.S. Fullerton, *Letter to Blanche Shaffer*, July 11, 1968.
41. Christopher Taylor, *Letter to Douglas V. Steere*, July 19, 1968.
42. Douglas V. Steere, *Letter to Kie Fullerton*, July 23, 1969.
43. Copy of a *Memorandum of the* FWCC *Nominating Committee*, July 1, 1970.
44. See Blanche Shaffer, *Letter to Douglas and Dorothy Steere*, November, 1965.
45. Douglas made this quick visit to make arrangements in April and May. He arrived in London in early June.
46. The AFSC had sponsored work in the Middle East from 1948 on. The first service was a Gaza Strip Refugee Program. Subsequent programs included a Refugee Program in Western Galilee between 1948 and 1950 and a Work Camp Program in Israel between 1951 and 1957. See "Quaker Service in the Middle East," unpublished report.
47. Douglas V. Steere, *Letter to Blanche Shaffer*, undated but evidently May 1969.
48. William E. Barton, *Letter to Douglas V. Steere et al.*, December 23, 1969; March 2, 1970.
49. Formal Minute of the FWCC, cited by Douglas V. Steere, *Letter to Duncan McBryde, National Council of Churches of Christ*, October 5, 1967. David Leonard, *Letter to Douglas V. Steere*, October 30, 1967, responded with some suggestions for implementation.
50. Douglas V. Steere, *Letter to Lewis Waddilove*, December 15, 1967; Herbert M. Hadley, *Letter to Colin Bell*, January 5, 1968, containing a short summary of the December 9 meeting; Colin Bell, AFSC, *Letter to Douglas V. Steere*, January 16, 1968, making suggestions for strengthening the FWCC.
51. William E. Barton, *Letter to Clerks of Yearly Meetings*, May 7, 1970.
52. Douglas V. Steere, "Some FWCC Reminiscences," op. cit., 5.
53. Douglas V. Steere, *Letter to Gilbert White*, February 28, 1970, remarked that he would retire from the chair at the end of the year and did not expect to be very active thereafter. He and Dorothy, however, did include one last journey, as noted above.
54. According to an entry for *World Book* which Douglas wrote in 1969, the Religious Society of Friends numbered 200,000 worldwide. Of these 120,000 were in the United States, 21,000 in Great Britain, and 32,000 in Kenya.

55. Gunnar Myrdal, *Letter to Blanche Shaffer*, noted he would simply introduce discussion, and recommended his book on *The Challenge of World Poverty*.
56. Blanche Shaffer, *Letter to Douglas V. Steere*, March 26, 1970; Douglas V. Steere, *Letter to an (Unnamed) Editor*, October 10, 1970, reporting Lacout's conversion.
57. Cited in typescript here, p. 1; but "Emerging Horizons" was published in *The Friends Quarterly*, 17 (April 1971), 50-63.
58. Steere, "Emerging Horizons," #5.
59. Steere, "Emerging Horizons," #5.
60. Steere, "Emerging Horizons," #6.
61. Steere, "Emerging Horizons," #11.
62. Steere, "Emerging Horizons," #19.
63. In the last comment Douglas was picking up on a complaint voiced by many about the Eleventh Triennial Conference at Sigtuna. Sweden would probably have been one of the most costly places to visit. See his *Letter to French Friends*, August 3, 1970. He hoped they would attend the next Triennial.
64. Christopher Taylor, Birmingham, England, *Letter to Douglas V. Steere*, August 20, 1970.

XV

Contemplative Scholar

*D*ouglas Steere sensed early on that he had a calling to exercise his academic gifts in the field of devotion or spirituality, an area in which he made outstanding contributions. Most of his addresses and writings focus on some aspect of the life of the spirit in today's world. His first book, published in the Hazen Series, was *Prayer and Worship* (1938). This volume sold well over 200,000 copies, was translated into several other languages, and is still in print.[1] His second was his translation of Søren Kierkegaard's *Purity of Heart* (1938)[2] and the third, the William Belden Noble and Ingersoll Lectures at Harvard, *On Beginning from Within* (1943), a call for saints as the greatest religious need of the time. If a fuller sign was needed, he gave a further indication of the direction in which his scholarly work was headed in his address as President of the American Theological Society on "An Ascetical Theology for Our Time." In this paper he underscored the importance of prayer and other spiritual disciplines. Several things doubtless nudged him in this direction.

First and most basic were his own intense hunger and thirst to know God. Another element of this calling was the need of others, deep crying to deep. When he as "seeker" joined the company of "seekers" which goes under the name of "The Religious Society of Friends," he discovered others engaged in the same quest pressing and urging him to help them to know not just *about* God but rather to know God. As he led retreats and gave lectures and wrote, the circle of persons who looked to him spiraled ever outwards and, as it did, forced him to drill his well deeper and deeper to assure a steady flow from an authentic and inexhaustible source.

A third factor lay in those painfully searching times and circumstances in which Douglas came to clarity about his life's vocation—the Great Depression, World War II, the Holocaust, the Atom Bomb, the Cold War, Future Shock. Perhaps it was a case of Douglas Steere's deep joy meeting the world's deep need, Frederick Buechner's definition of calling. As Douglas himself observed in lectures given in the midst of the Second World War,

> what the religious life of the world needs most of all is not a new theology, not a vast new crop of brilliant students as candidates for ministry, not a union of all sects into one religious body, not a renewed missionary movement, not a revised program of evangelism. What it needs first and foremost is apostles or saints, men and women prepared to live in the full dispensation of Christian freedom.[3]

He spent his life calling out and equipping and challenging saints, for he heard in that need a summons to him. Of course, as Douglas his calling, he had doubts about it, and needed reassurance from noted scholars that it was fitting for a scholar to invest his or her life in something conventional academicians would not consider scholarly.

Ultimately, this calling to be a contemplative scholar had its source in Douglas Steere's attentiveness to the Inward Guide. If one may judge by the number of times the statement appears in his addresses or writings, the key to minding one's call is Isaac Penington's: "There is that near you which can guide you. Oh wait for it, and be sure ye keep to it."

254

Companions on the Contemplative Path

Douglas' writings overflow with wisdom drawn from men and women of special insight both past and present. The classics of Christian devotion suffuse the whole corpus. But it was especially from living saints that Douglas sought to draw wisdom. Gifted in personal encounter, from the beginning of his career, he made a point of reaching outward at every opportunity to glean insights from others. Almost without exception, the philosophers, theologians, and other people of insight he found himself most comfortable with were those who shared his philosophy of existential realism and left room for the mystical or contemplative element in religion.

At the head of the list would stand Baron Friedrich von Hügel and Rufus Jones. Neither of them, however, surpassed in significance for him a group formed by Henry P. Van Dusen in 1933, who called themselves the Younger Christian Thinkers. The group included some of the most eminent names in American religious life: besides Van Dusen, Reinhold and Richard Niebuhr, Robert Calhoun, Roland Bainton, John Mackay, John Bennett, Paul Tillich, Edwin Aubrey, Wilhelm Pauck, Francis Miller, Alexander Zabriskie, Joseph Hromadka, John Knox, George Thomas, and later on Theodore Wedel and Angus Dun, Episcopal Bishop of Washington.

The Younger Christian Thinkers met twice a year, first at Yale Divinity School and later at the College of Preachers in the back of the National (Episcopal) Cathedral in Washington, DC, for a weekend extending from Friday evening until Sunday afternoon. With their comradeship and heady discussion the group influenced Douglas in a major way. "No other association that I have ever belonged to had such an influence on me as being part of this group," he remarked years later, "and I think nearly all of the men in the group would say the same."[4] Papers started the sessions off and informal, open discussion followed. These, however, were not as significant for Douglas as the larger dynamic, and it was that which he tried to incorporate into groups such as the Ecumenical Institute of Spirituality to which he helped give birth. "The close personal friendships that grew up in this informal atmosphere, the sharing of books, of experiences, of new currents of thought, and the sharpening of our spiritual commitment in the little devotional services that we shared in leading, was all a part of it."[5]

Douglas' debt to Maria Laach, Damasus Winzen, Søren Kierkegaard, Nicholai Hartmann, Fritz Kunkel, and Romano Guardini was noted in Chapter 4. For the development of his understanding of prayer one other person, Reinhold Schneider, deserves mention. Douglas described Schneider after their initial meeting as "historian, poet and saint." Of the many persons he met during the months spent in Germany in 1947, Schneider "made the deepest impression" on him. Although very ill, "his spirit shines as you come in the room and you feel a real sense of the presence when you are with him." On his second visit they talked of the life of prayer, and Schneider said "that there is nothing more important today, nothing."[6] For him intercessory prayer "has become almost the whole of prayer." Prayer recreates the atmosphere around the world which humans need to survive. It impressed Douglas that Schneider got up at 3:00 a.m. to spend an hour on his knees in prayer for all. Sounding much like Douglas himself, as so many have known him, Schneider told of "his own inner struggle to try to give people hope, to call them up from the underworld of despair and deceit, into the open air of truth and courage and faith."[7] He appealed to Douglas and the Friends to help Germany ward off utter despondency, the great danger just after the war. Douglas looked in on Schneider repeatedly, corresponded, and sent books. He questioned Schneider especially about his experience of intercessory prayer.[8] Appreciation was mutual. In July 1949 Schneider thanked Douglas for the books and added, "I always think about you and I am convinced that the spirit of prayer and the powerful sense of Christian responsibility in which you live and work is the greatest blessing of all."[9] After a visit in 1950 Douglas described Schneider as "one of the real spiritual prophets of our time."[10]

A Life of Prayer

Douglas Steere embodied his learning about prayer in his own practice. From those stressful times at Harvard when he first discovered the power and meaning of prayer, he counted on persistent attentiveness to God to carry him. The Quaker silent meeting was essential. He put in writing what the meeting meant to him:

> The meeting for worship has sent tears down my eyes and cheeks. It has given me specific things to be done and the strength to undertake them. It has, on a few occasions, laid on my heart rimless concerns whose precise structure and whose outcome I could not foresee and kept them before me until they came to some degree of clarity. It has called me into the intercessory chain gang to pray for other people and for situations where the need was urgent. It has changed my mind when I did not mean to change it. It has firmed me up when I might have yielded. It has rested me. It has upset my sluggish rest. It has helped prepare me to live. It has fortified me in knowing that my ashes will eventually lie in the earth only a couple of hundred feet from where I am sitting at Radnor Meeting and has helped me to feel the Presence of the One who can bear me now and bear me then. It has scarified me and broken down the hull of my life and shown me how I might live. It has warned me that I am too cowardly to live that way, but reminded me for good measure that it is not what I give that makes me suffer, but what I hold back. It has comforted me and quieted me when I was torn and hurt and it has dug up the

garden of my soul when I thought that the present produce was all I could manage. In it I have physically slept and again I have been terribly awake. In it my mind has wandered like a hummingbird on holiday and yet in it I have felt moments of intensity and of concentration and awareness that have shown me what life could be.[11]

From early years Douglas also practiced a disciplined life of prayer in private. Every morning he spent thirty minutes or more in silent meditation, like Henry Hodgkin, the first director of Pendle Hill, "leaning on the window sill of heaven." Although Quakers have debated for most of their existence how to bring scriptures into their religious life, Douglas did not have any question about their importance in livening and deepening the inner life. When a Swedish Friend, Sven Ryberg, wanted to know the place of Jesus in Quaker devotional practice, Douglas cited his and Dorothy's custom of meditating on a passage of scriptures every morning.

For me the Society of Friends is and must remain in the Christian stream. This means that the Bible and especially the Gospels must be read continuously by Friends and crossed with their own inward experiences. Dorothy and I try to read them together every morning and it is a good deal as the African said to his missionary guide, "Sir, it is not I who am reading the Bible. It is the Bible that is reading me!" To face the accounts given there of Jesus Christ and of his unerring caring and his pointing to the Father and "his love that will not let us go" is to feel indeed that "in Jesus Christ, God came all the way downstairs" to [humankind] and invites [humankind] to come all the way upstairs into [God's] presence.[12]

This should not cut one off from the Hindu, Muslim, or Buddhist, for there is also the universal Christ "and this

258

for me must always be held together with the historical appearance of Jesus."

Traveling In

Douglas Steere engaged his mind and devoted his energies so extensively to the understanding and practice of prayer, illustrated them so richly, and carried them to such great depth it is probably presumptuous to attempt to put together a summary of his thought on the subject, but some attempt at that is needed to appreciate fully his contribution. Fortunately, he has made the task easier by distilling his rich brew in two thin volumes—*Prayer and Worship,* his first published book (1938), and *Dimensions of Prayer* (1962)—and numerous pamphlets and addresses. The subject, however, pervades virtually everything he wrote.

Readers of Douglas Steere's writings will not find expressions of doubt about the reality, significance, and power of prayer such as Douglas heard from Karl Barth in 1933. Growth in the inner life mandates prayer. "Prayer is for the religious life what original research is for science," he asserted in *Dimensions of Prayer.*[13] Neither was Douglas hobbled, as many Protestants have been, by fear that prayer would diminish the role of faith in Christian life. "Without practice, without discipline, without continuous devotion, without failure, correction, re-dedication, re-orientation," we cannot expect to grow.[14] "The religion of Jesus Christ is not a holding operation."[15] And prayer is the heart of that religion.

What is prayer? With Bernard of Clairvaux and a whole row of saints, Douglas Steere insisted that it is, first of all, *response* to God's initiative, to "the besieging love of God," one of his characteristic phrases. He liked to cite Bernard of Clairvaux's chiding words to monks who hurried early to the sanctuary to see if they could get there before God got up. "Do you awake?" Bernard asked. "Well, [God] too is awake. If you rise in the nighttime, if you anticipate to your

259

utmost your earliest awaking, you will already find [God] waking—you will never anticipate [God's] own awakeness. In such an intercourse you will always be rash if you attribute any priority and predominant share to yourself; for [God] loves both more than you, and before you love at all."[16] In an address given in his late years Douglas added to Bernard's word what he had learned from his own experience:

> It is hard for me to underline sufficiently what a difference it makes to enter prayer with a deep consciousness of this divine initiative. To be conscious that long before I make my response in prayer at all, something immensely costly and penetrating has been going on. That it continues during my prayer and that it continues to undergird my very life when I have turned from conscious acts of prayer to my other tasks of the day. This and nothing short of this gives my prayer its true setting. Prayer is a response to God's "is-ness." My prayer did not begin this encompassing love. That love has been like a poultice laid over me and laid over the world for its healing long before I came on the scene. When I pray I simply enter into this ongoing stream, and my act of prayer, precious and important as it truly is, is swept up into something infinitely vaster and is cleansed for use.[17]

Prayer takes hold of us and moves us to action. It is, therefore, even more than "the soul's sincere desire." It is "the process of intentionally turning the focus of the soul's sincere desire upon the active nature of the Divine Love and by every device within its power holding it there until it becomes engaged."[18] Many define prayer as "*speech* with God." Douglas, however, interpreted it as "more nearly *work* with God."[19] Although it may seem like something passive, it is really "the most intense activity."[20] Prayer is not Quietism. Sometimes we realize that we are not only *praying* but *being prayed in.*[21]

260

How do you pray? Douglas was not a "methods" person. He knew, as did many another contemplative, that simple is better. And he gave a few simple counsels. First, he advised, *find solitude.* Free yourself from "the hail of irrelevant stimuli" and "the pressure and temporarily satisfying narcotic of intense busyness in outward occupations" and let yourself become "collected." In a sermon "On the Collected and Uncollected Man" Douglas described the "uncollected" person as one who is pressed for time; has no time for private prayer or for leisurely reading, reflecting, or setting down thoughts; is impatient and thus crowds decisions, presses and maneuvers people; is likely to talk and not listen; operates only according to his or her own plan; and is divided. The "collected" person, by contrast, is "glad to have time to spare for God" and for others; is really present to others and not pining to be some other place; has time to look at the stars; is capable of being patient; is not afraid to sleep because he or she is grounded "in One whose triumph is already established"; is not utterly planless but has "a certain sense of seeing the things that happen to him over against eternity and, therefore, to catch something of the vast humor in their curiously crooked incongruity against that setting." Although the collected person is also divided, that person knows its source and the way to heal it, viz., through prayer.[22] You need to recognize that "solitude is the stronghold of the strong" and find a place for it in your life. It is not really an issue of "finding time" but of "the depth of the sense of need and of the desire."[23]

Second, *be there.* Be really present to God. As Douglas understood it, prayer is, above all, simple attentiveness. A regular time, a certain posture, preparation by reading the Bible or a devotional classic may help to put one in the proper frame. But these should not take the place of attention to God. The most important thing is to be *"present where you are."*[24]

Although Douglas recognized the importance and perhaps the necessity of *spoken* prayer for most, especially in beginning stages, he accentuated *silent prayer.* In modern culture we have become too inclined to talk and not to listen. *Listening* is more than hearing. Douglas liked to quote Indian chieftain Papunehang's words after hearing John Woolman pray, "I love to feel where words come from." Prayer goes beyond words. As another of Douglas' mentors, Isaac Penington, exhorted, "O! wait more and more to know how to keep *that* silence, which is of the power; that in every one of you, what the power would have silent may be silent . . ."[25] The body needs quieting, and "one day even the Christian religion will again have to attend to this training of the body."[26]

All who pray will have to cope with inevitable distractions. Don't be alarmed, Douglas counseled. Rather than trying to wrench yourself back to attention, "pray the distraction directly into the prayer."[27] When conflicting desires, demands, problems, suggestions, and plans intrude into the silence, just remember *whose* presence you entered in the silence. Use images drawn from scriptures or nature to center, and move beyond these to come into the presence of the silent one. "Silent prayer simplifies the confused, complex, conflicting heap of life's experiences. It makes us one again. It restores us to the creative matrix."[28]

What should we expect prayer to do? Few would doubt that it affects the person who prays. "To come near to God is to change" was an ancient Christian adage with which Douglas agreed, and, he added, to pray is to come near to God. Prayer awakens us to the love of God which encompasses us and leaves no alternative. When that love reveals to us our condition as no amount of introspection can do, we know both what must be put right and find the strength to do it. In prayer, God opens our locked room of personal hates and fear, self-pity and self-justification, or sin and changes us. Real prayer is more than *confessional;* it is *renewal.* It is this call to change which often leads us to stop our prayers.

No discussion of what prayer does should leave out *forgiveness.* Forgiveness opens the way for restoration of a broken relationship. "The whole witness of Jesus' life and death is to the unfathomable depths of God's forgiveness."[29] The one condition for being forgiven is to accept it.

Douglas Steere went further than many other scholars dared to go when he spoke about the *effects* of prayer. He was not among those who labeled prayer of petition "infantile" Christmas wishing, noting that God already knows what we need before we ask. He did not find the difficulties posed by sophisticated skeptics "so real as they sound."[30] "I have a strong suspicion that God is far less fastidious in this matter than are these sophisticated expositors of Christian prayer," he remarked.[31] We all must begin where we are and stay with it until we work through the trifling matters. If we are persistent, we will find our prayer changing. It is not a question of adding to God's knowledge or changing God's mind. A petition is our desire, longing, or aspiration which will remain part of us whether we bring it to God or not. If we live as friends of God in response to God's discerning love, how can we not lay our desires and longings before God for review and plead our case for them? The key question is not whether we get what we ask for but "Were you faithful? Did you yield?"[32]

In *Dimensions of Prayer* Douglas faced head on the question "Does prayer change things?" and siding with those who answered in the affirmative. He agreed with P.T. Forsyth's and William Temple's judgments that while God's ultimate purpose does not change, God's strategy "may vary infinitely."[33] "Can we not believe," he asked, "that many are secretly drawn by [God] to assume the burdens of those in need, to volunteer their services, or to appear in the place and at the time that they are needed?" He answered, "The Christian annals are full of accounts of those who answered such calls."[34]

Douglas did not back away from putting the question in its most extreme form, viz., whether we should pray for rain? Once again, he was not prepared to place a deep ditch between the physical and the psychological. As early as 1938, he noted changes in the attitude of medical science. Some physicians were beginning to admit that the faith of a patient would affect chances for recovery. Mind and body are not enemies; they function as a whole. And physical laws are not as inexorable as some suggest. We can neither prove nor disprove what effect prayer for rain or for healing may have. Prayer is a matter of cooperation between us and "our creative stem." Thence, we cannot place any absolute limit on petition. "The only limit is [human] need."[35]

Intercession, Douglas believed, touches the inner springs of prayer in a vital way. It is "the most intensely social act that the human being is capable of."[36]

> For when we hold up the life of another before God, when we expose it to God's love, when we pray for its release from drowsiness, for the quickening of its inner health, for the power to throw off a destructive habit, for the restoration of its free and vital relationship with its fellows, for its strength to resist a temptation, for its courage to continue against sharp opposition—only then do we sense what it means to share in God's work, in [God's] concern; only then do the walls that separate us from others go down and we sense that we are at bottom all knit together in a great and intimate family. There is no greater intimacy with another than that which is built up through holding him [or her] up in prayer.[37]

This is not a matter of changing God's mind or casting a spell over someone's life. God is already at work in that person's life. What we are doing is cooperating with God's active love as it lays siege to someone. No one can say what our prayer may contribute, but Douglas agreed with William Temple that "When I pray, coincidences happen, and when I do not, they don't," adding, "and that is perhaps all that there is to say."[38] As in all prayer, of course, we must prepare to yield. So our intercession may prove costly. We may find ourselves called on to set something right in our own lives or come to a clear

264

insight regarding things to be done. In prayer we come under holy obedience—to resist a social wrong, to write a letter, to visit a friend, to undertake a journey, to provide food for the hungry, to offer nursing care or fellowship, to forgive a wrong, to drop a grudge, or to undertake other tasks. Yet more is required than hints. We also need the strength to do what comes in "holy nudges." "There is nothing greater than this constant fidelity."[39]

In the activist sixties Douglas underscored still more strongly the integral interconnection of prayer and action. He warned his fellow Quakers of "the heresy of sheer activism" into which so many lapsed during that time.[40] Had they found a way in all their years of experience to hold the inner and the outer life together? He found the key in the journey inwards, "the hardest journey" and, in Dag Hammarskjold's phrase, also "the longest journey."

When we pray, we are enlisted in "the labor force of the kingdom of God." Prayer does not put us in a coma or religious reverie. As it quickens our inward life, we sense new directions and our inner resources are gathered to act. All of us, of course, can find excuses as we experience "holy nudges," but prayer plants seeds of concern or, as Quakers say, puts a "stop" in the mind, and we should not refuse the first small act God demands of us. The power of prayer still dwells within us when we move from intention to action. To be sure, we must scrutinize rationally the inner promptings which come in prayer, recognizing that we may and often do err. "Yet, if we are willing to have it questioned and are able to keep our faith in the living network into which our life has been drawn, then, if we take the wrong fork at any point, and its wrongness becomes clear, perhaps painfully clear to us, there is always the next fork of the road where we may be drawn back into the right direction."[41] Prayer may effect major mutations in our plans. It may call us back to our original commitment. It may intensify ethical concern. "Christian prayer brings a relentless clarity, but underneath its fierce realism and its costly baptism of personal responsibility, there is an equally steadying sense that in whatever we are called to do, we do not work alone, and that in spite of the lump of sin that is all too apparent, there is a great legacy of goodness to be drawn upon in humankind."[42]

Can we, as Brother Lawrence, Thomas Kelly, Frank Laubach, and others insist, "pray without ceasing" (1 Thess. 5:17) in our busy, activity-filled lives today? Douglas was convinced that we can if we love God and let that love move to the surface and give its glow to what we do. "In perpetual prayer, there is something that frames all that we do, something that goes on day and night beneath the stream of our consciousness: a gratitude, an adoration, an acknowledgement of creatureliness—of dependence upon God, that we are [God's] and [God] made us—a sense of encompassment."[43]

All who take prayer seriously will encounter "dry times," just as all the saints have confessed. Should we interpret that as a sign to stop and take a vacation until the desire returns? Like many another experienced pray-er, Douglas responded with an unequivocal no. We have entered into this life of prayer for the long haul, and we need prayer more rather than less during these "night shifts." Our faithfulness will tell who it is we mean to serve.

Although private prayer was the axis around which Douglas Steere's own life turned, as we have seen already, he also valued corporate worship as an essential ingredient in a healthy spiritual life. He did not sympathize with the considerable group who have contended that they could get along with private prayer or perhaps small groups and did not need corporate worship. He discerned in this attitude "a certain puffed-up spirit of loftiness, of pride, of superiority which goes badly with the fellowship in Christ into which the one who prays is called."[44] Its faults and frailties notwithstanding, the institutional church lifts us out of our private world into a public one, and draws us into an encompassing fellowship on a world scale. In its corporate worship it reminds us of

God's gift and demand. Church attendance may be a habit, but it is a good habit for human beings who, as Pascal reminds, are "as much automatic as intellectual."[45]

A complete prayer life must return constantly to its source in the besieging love of God, adoration, loving God back. All true prayer—whether contrition, petition, or intercession—is shot through with adoration. "In adoration we enjoy God. We ask nothing except to be near [God]. We want nothing except that we would like to give [God] all."[46]

Appreciation from the Academy

Douglas' peers in the academy appreciated the leadership he provided in this field of study. He was a gifted scholar, respected and sought after around the country. Enumeration of a few of his lectureships in colleges and universities gives convincing evidence of the esteem academic peers accorded him: the Reinicker Lectures at Episcopal Theological Seminary in Virginia (1939), the Ingersoll Lecture (1942) and the William Belden Noble Lectures (1943) at Harvard,[47] the Carew Lectures at Hartford Theological Seminary (1945), the Hoyt Lectures at Union Theological Seminary in New York (1947),[48] the Rauschenbusch Lectures at Colgate Rochester Divinity School (1952),[49] the Stone Lectures at Princeton Theological Seminary (1957),[50] the Shaffer Lectures at Northwestern University (1976).

In addition to these he gave lectures at several other colleges, universities, and seminaries virtually every year he was not abroad. In 1935-36, for instance, he spoke at Smith, Mt. Holyoke, Amherst, Fiske, and Howard University. In 1939-40 he spoke at the University of North Carolina, Emory, Spellman, Agnes Scott, Howard University, Smith, Cornell, Dartmouth, Moravian, and Connecticut College for Women. In 1948-49, he was heard at Cornell, Princeton, Antioch, Denison, Hampton Institute, Connecticut, Macalester, St. Thomas, Berea, Talladega, Lehigh, and Wells colleges or

DOUGLAS STEERE RECEIVING HONORARY DEGREE
FROM HAVERFORD COLLEGE

universities; at Yale, Union in New York, Episcopal in Virginia, Union in Richmond, Andover-Newton, and Drew theological seminaries. In 1949-50 he spoke at Washington University in St. Louis, Earlham, and Wilmington. In 1951-52 at Austin (TX) Presbyterian Theological Seminary, Talladega College (Alabama), Yale Divinity School, Rutgers University, the Chapel of the University of Chicago, Manchester College (Indiana), the University of Toronto, St. Paul's Church at Columbia University, Cornell, Vassar, and Wellesley. In 1952-53 Douglas gave lectures at Cornell, Wells, Mt. Holyoke, Vassar, Wellesley, Dartmouth, and Harvard Divinity School. He taught at Union Theological Seminary in the summer of 1947 and 1951 and as the Harry Emerson Fosdick Visiting Professor in 1961-62.

In 1949 Douglas' alma mater, then Michigan State College, awarded him its Distinguished Alumnus award. Lawrence

College, Appleton, Wisconsin, whose president was Nathan Pusey, later president of Harvard, honored him with a D.D. in 1950. Earlham gave him an honorary degree in 1953, Oberlin in 1954, and, as noted earlier, General Theological Seminary in New York in 1967. Haverford College conferred an honorary doctorate on him at its Commencement in 1970. He had fulfilled his calling well, and others recognized it.

Notes

1. Douglas V. Steere, *Prayer and Worship* (New York: Association Press, 1938), now published by Friends United Press, Richmond, Indiana.
2. Søren Kierkegaard, *Purity of Heart Is to Will One Thing: Spiritual Preparation for the Feast of Confession.* Translated by Douglas V. Steere (New York & London: Harper & Brothers, 1938).
3. Douglas V. Steere, *On Beginning from Within* (New York: Harper & Brothers, 1943), 33.
4. Douglas V. Steere, UNPUBLISHED JOURNAL, 182.
5. Steere, JOURNAL, 182.
6. *News from Douglas Steere,* British Zone, Germany, December 15, 1947, 1.
7. *News from Douglas Steere,* Geneva, Switzerland, November 9, 1947, 8.
8. See Douglas V. Steere, JOURNAL, 482, regarding the return visit of Douglas and Helen in the spring of 1948.
9. Reinhold Schneider, *Letter to Douglas V. Steere,* July 2, 1949.
10. *General Newsletter from Douglas Steere, #3,* Münich, 7-10 September, 1950, 15.
11. Douglas V. Steere, *Traveling In,* edited by E. Glenn Hinson. Pendle Hill Pamphlet 324 (Wallingford, PA: Pendle Hill Publications, 1995), 18-19.
12. Douglas V. Steere, *Letter to Sven Ryberg,* April 2, 1973.
13. Douglas V. Steere, *Dimensions of Prayer* (New York: Women's Division, Board of Global Ministries, The United Methodist Church, 1962), 2.
14. Douglas V. Steere, *Prayer and Worship* (New York: Association Press, 1938), 7.

15. Steere, *Dimensions of Prayer,* 4.
16. Bernard of Clairvaux, *Sermons on the Song of Songs,* cited in ibid., 10.
17. Douglas V. Steere, *Traveling In,* 17.
18. Steere, *Prayer and Worship,* 12.
19. Steere, *Prayer and Worship,* 13.
20. Steere, *Prayer and Worship,* 14.
21. Steere, *Prayer and Worship,* 14.
22. Douglas V. Steere, "On the Collected and Uncollected Man," unpublished sermon, First Presbyterian Church, Tallahassee, Florida, January 22, 1961.
23. Steere, *Prayer and Worship,* 17.
24. Steere, *Dimensions of Prayer,* 24.
25. Isaac Penington, *Letters,* cited in *Prayer and Worship,* 20.
26. Steere, *Dimensions of Prayer,* 20.
27. Steere, *Dimensions of Prayer,* 21.
28. Steere, *Dimensions of Prayer,* 26.
29. Steere, *Dimensions of Prayer,* 56.
30. Steere, *Prayer and Worship,* 28.
31. Steere, *Dimensions of Prayer,* 66.
32. Steere, *Prayer and Worship,* 29.
33. Steere, *Dimensions of Prayer,* 77.
34. Steere, *Dimensions of Prayer,* 78.
35. Steere, *Prayer and Worship,* 30.
36. Steere, *Dimensions of Prayer,* 80.
37. Steere, *Prayer and Worship,* 31.
38. Steere, *Dimensions of Prayer,* 83.
39. Steere, *Prayer and Worship,* 34.
40. Douglas V. Steere, *The Hardest Journey.* Pendle Hill Pamphlet 163 (Lebanon, PA: Sowers Printing Co., 1969), 13.
41. Steere, *Dimensions of Prayer,* 100-101.
42. Steere, *Dimensions of Prayer,* 107.
43. Steere, *Dimensions of Prayer,* 109.
44. Steere, *Dimensions of Prayer,* 112.
45. Blaise Pascal, *Pensées,* No. 140; in *Dimensions of Prayer,* 114.
46. Steere, *Prayer and Worship,* 35.
47. These first three were published together in revised form as *On Beginning from Within* (New York & London: Harper & Brothers, 1943).
48. The Carew and Hoyt Lectures emerged in a revised form as *Doors into Life through Five Devotional Classics* (New York: Harper & Row, 1948).
49. Published as *Work and Contemplation* (New York: Harper & Brothers, 1957).
50. Not published, but in them Douglas spelled out his basic philosophy.

XVI

Midwife of Saints

*T*hroughout his life Douglas Steere poured much energy into the fostering of sainthood. So many activities he engaged in beginning with his dissertation on Baron von Hügel had a bearing on that task—his teaching at Haverford; the resuscitation of Radnor Meeting; the founding of Pendle Hill; the worldwide visits and ministry of encouragement; lectures in colleges, seminaries, and churches; writings; retreats; the Ecumenical Institute of Spirituality. It would be hard to single out any time in his career when Douglas was not assisting in the birthing and nurturing of saints, of dedicated Christian lives.

Douglas chose this vocation consciously, or, perhaps it would be more accurate to say, the vocation chose him. Christianity in a minor key was not enough for him. He frequently quoted Leon Bloy's "There is only one sorrow, not to be a saint."[1] Like the founder of the Wesleyan movement, he searched tirelessly to raise the level of commitment to God, both his own and that of others. He made serious inquiry of every person of wisdom he met, and drilled deep into the Christian ascetic and contemplative tradition to learn how people become saints. The early forties seem to have been especially influential in the shaping and launching of his work as a midwife of saints.

Stages on the Way

I suspect that the perilous trip to Europe during the fall of 1940, the death of his colleague Thomas Kelly in January, 1941, and the editing of Kelly's writings for publication were "speaking to his condition." He and Kelly both suffered from drivenness. In *A Testament of Devotion*, which appeared in 1941, Kelly issued a powerful challenge to holy obedience of the kind that Douglas yearned for at this time.

> I have in mind something deeper than the simplification of our external programs, our absurdly crowded calendars of appointments through which so many pantingly and frantically gasp. These do become simplified in holy obedience, and the poise and peace we have been missing can really be found. But there is a deeper, an internal simplification of the whole of one's personality, stilled, tranquil, in childlike trust listening ever to Eternity's whisper, walking with a smile into the dark.[2]

Kelly and *A Testament of Devotion* came up in Douglas' conversation with Gerald Heard, to whom he turned for guidance.

In January 1942, fearing that the hectic pace of his life might turn him into a "religious stamp" of some kind, he decided, with Dorothy's blessing, to go west to visit Heard. Heard was an Anglican mystic and spiritual guide who was deeply engaged in the founding of Trabuco, a center for training in the spiritual life. In explanation Douglas wrote in his journal:

> Until this time in my life, I have been going places to which I have been invited and rationalizing this as being an answering of calls that were sent me. Now it gets clearer that I may have been going to places that paid my way and that I am becoming a kind of religious stamp that can be bought and stuck on but that

does not offer itself or take the initiative to go where *from within* it believes that it is right to go, and to decline invitations where I do not feel that I have something distinctive to contribute. The possibility of becoming the complete slave of outer stimuli is all too apparent from my experiences this past autumn.[3]

The two-and-a-half day visit with Heard at Laguna Beach was for Douglas a time to soak up all the practical insights about spirituality Heard could offer. He came each day for meditation and long visits with Heard to the cottage which Allan Hunter, Pastor of Mount Hollywood Congregational Church, and his wife Elizabeth had engaged. In his characteristic preference for wisdom in personal form, Douglas drew out of Heard something of the spiritual experience which had brought him to his present outlook and endeavor— notably his reaction against the highly judgmental views of an Irish grandmother who had reared him. She was "a fierce member of the Plymouth Brethren sect"[4] who had no qualms about God erasing even the memory of Heard's favorite Uncle Charlie because he was an alcoholic. Through psychical research Heard had returned, about 1927, to a concern for religion. Due to health problems, however, his interest had lagged until 1933 when his involvement in the pacifist movement in England nudged him into regular meditative exercises. "The further his meditation led him in towards the center the more clearly he saw that a wholesale reconstruction of life is required . . . ."[5] From 1936 on, this concern set his agenda.

Douglas and the Hunters questioned Heard about his personal regimen—two hours of meditation on arising in the morning, breakfast, two hours of writing followed by more meditation, lunch, writing until tea time, one hour of prayer, supper, reading until bedtime, prayer, and sometimes midnight watch. Douglas predictably took special interest in *why* Heard meditated immediately on arising, his belief that the dream level of consciousness can be guided and can help draw up the deepest level of the psyche to God, how he dealt with distractions, how important it is to open oneself to God utterly and completely, and his belief in purgatory here and now as well as beyond this life. Douglas and the Hunters explored with Heard his diminishment of the importance of Jesus as a companion and guide to God and his virtual abandonment of a personal God in his *Third Morality*. On the basis of Heard's acknowledgment that he would write the latter book in a different way than he had done originally and recognized that God drew people through different forms, Douglas commented, "I realized that neither he nor I were at the end of our pilgrimage."[6] Heard's real passion was "to encourage us to realize the utter necessity for complete abandonment in every detail of life in order for us to be ready for the visitation."[7]

Douglas and the Hunters also questioned Heard about his *Training for the Life of the Spirit,* which one Quaker had said sounded too much like "*straining* for the life of the spirit." They were not prepared to agree with Heard that the higher levels of prayer required the complete sublimation of the sex drive and that "sexual orgasm consumes and lowers the potential for the highest receptivity."[8] They also explored with him his critique of western society and the Second World War and his solution to the crisis of western civilization. The solution sounds remarkably similar to the one which Douglas unveiled in *On Beginning from Within:*

> some who are ready to risk all to provide society with a validity and a meaning and a future pattern and who keep their eyes on the real goals and are unshakable, unbuyable, and who bring a fresh integrity into society because they are not finally grounded in its secular values but are rooted and grounded in God and [God's] dream of a society of persons who deeply interpenetrate each other in responsible caring.[9]

Such can be accomplished only by those who "have a living center of prayer and meditation" and have faced the greed in themselves and the fears that lie behind the greed—fear of financial insecurity, ill health, being thought odd, or being no influence in one's time. "The revolution has to begin within us and God has the power to dislodge these levels of distortion in each of us."[10]

Before departing, the group visited Trabuco, in which they saw a glimmer of hope for western society,[11] and Douglas asked Gerald Heard to pray for him and Dorothy. In 1945 Heard became Douglas' spiritual director.[12] Trabuco, unfortunately, did not have a long life, something which Douglas ascribed in 1948 to a lack of commitment to the Christian tradition, gearing of the program so heavily to contemplation with few contemplatives by nature among residents, absence of strong social outreach, and absence of the combination of manual labor and prayer commended in the Benedictine tradition.[13] But Douglas continued to maintain contact with Heard up to the time of his death in 1972;[14] as late as 1962, in a meeting at Wainwright House in Rye, New York, Heard reported that he still persisted in his intercession for Douglas and Dorothy as he had promised twenty years before.

On Beginning from Within

Douglas signaled the direction in which his vocation was leading him in the Reinicker Lectures at the Episcopal Theological Seminary in Virginia in the fall of 1939, the Alden Tuthill Lectures at the Chicago Theological Seminary in 1942, and the William Belden Noble Lectures, which he gave at Harvard University in March and April, 1943.[15] The series of lectures, which was published in 1943 under the title *On Beginning from Within,* had as its subject "the intensification of the life of God in the individual hearts of men [and women]." In the first three lectures Douglas put forth a case for saints as the churches' most urgent need, examining the relation of the saint to society, the source of the authority that a saint exercises among fellow human beings, and the nurture of the inward life by a new set of devotional exercises. In two other lectures he veered slightly to one side to explore the debt of theology to devotion[16] and the prospect of death as an agency of individuation and as a power for awakening people to their dependence on God.[17]

In "The Saint and Society" he said that a saint can influence the *order* of society at its "vulnerable center" with a refocusing of its vision, dream, or purpose. Behind the facade of society at the vulnerable, fluid center always stands a person and a person's wants, and it is precisely there that the saint comes into play. What are saints? They are not first of all social reformers, but they do precisely that because in everything they are answerable to "a love at the heart of things." Saints are persons who begin with themselves and what they must do, not with denunciation of society and its wrongs. They *begin from within*. In everything, as Elizabeth Herman says, they refer "the smallest action to God."

Secondly, they are not professors who put to society a convincing set of arguments but persons who put before others "a life and an embarrassing invitation which they must decide to accept or reject."[18] Thirdly, they are persons with staying power, perseverance, possessing "a gristle" that will not give up short of total destruction. Fourthly, they are those who care personally and not abstractly for others. Fifthly, they regard all life as sacramental and deal with it in that way and know that group life is redeemable because they do not work alone.

Yet with it all, bound to their age just as their contemporaries are, they are not infallible. Only the unreflective would claim for them infallible wisdom.[19] How can such persons influence society? At two points—where their vision cuts through conventional wrappings to the issue itself and where their faithfulness in living a full life in response to the highest human calling impacts their generation.

276

It is a question of the dream, of the ideal, of the ulti-mate purpose of [humankind]. Establish that, and exemplify it in living specimens that can outlive, outlove, and outdie those whose lives are governed by a lesser end, specimens that can reveal not "bargains in brotherhood" but brotherhood as Francis revealed it in his comradeship of suffering with the poor, and the institution is attacked at its vulnerable core where it, too, must continually vindicate and renew itself or finally perish and be replaced.[20]

In "The Authority of the Saint" Douglas distinguished saints from geniuses. Saints are, above all, "men and women pre-pared to live in the full dispensation of Christian freedom."[21] They are persons who have completely abandoned themselves to God. The authority for such persons does not spring, as in the case of geniuses, from their native cleverness or intel-lectual brilliance or articulateness but from their yielding inwardly to the power and authority of God. Saints make a claim even upon geniuses, as they do on every person. This does not necessitate a plunge into blind anti-intellectualism. Geniuses, too, may become saints if they allow themselves to be drawn into "the noose of God." Not "*what* they brought" but "*where they are brought to*" is what matters.[22] The way God uses saints frequently differs from what either they or the world expects and certainly from the natural inclination of either. Witness Bernard of Clairvaux, Francis of Assisi, John Woolman, or the Curé d'Ars. Yet they live a fully human life. "It is because they embody the deepest and most exceptional longings in us all, because their commitment wounds and draws at these heroic longings which not even the heart of a genius can still, that the saints and apostles speak with such authority, strike at our lives, menace our lethargic torpor, and prepare us to let God work."[23]

In a third lecture Douglas laid out "A New Set of Devo-tional Exercises" for nurturing the life of saints, although he took seriously both liberal and more orthodox Protestant reservations about such practices. Liberals feared substituting them for life; the orthodox feared works-righteousness. He observed, however, that such practices "do not replace but encourage and quicken good works"[24] and that human beings do not "inevitably do what we know"[25] without training. Contrariwise, he invoked Pascal's assertion that "we are as much automatic as intellectual" to point out that we need devotional practices which will incline the whole person to respond to God. Exercises such as self-examination, meditation, mental prayer, swift ejaculation, confession, abstinence, simplicity, and spiritual reading have three aims: (1) to keep the external aspects of life from dampening or snuffing out "a deeper order"; (2) "to cut down the tree of self-aggrandizement that grows up in our souls and blots out the sight of other [persons] and of God"; and (3) to center our full powers—senses, habits, bodies, as well as minds—upon God and God's love.[26]

The "new" in the title of the chapter notwithstanding, Douglas chiefly commended well tried methods drawn from the past, notably Ignatius Loyola's *Spiritual Exercises,* to which he proposed some relevant modern alternations. He suggested replacing Loyola's military-style obedience with the creative obedience of friends working together in God's service and exchanging the grim ascetic practices of the past such as fasting, silence, and abstinence from marriage for a more joyous kind. He accentuated the continuing need for withdrawal, both daily and for longer periods annually, to be alone and enter into "islands" of silence. "There is no increasing of the pure seed of the spiritual life," he insisted, "that does not call for both initial and frequent returns to an island of silence."[27] With Loyola, he counseled meditation on the end and purpose of life and on sin, including social sin, and its consequences. Asceticism and meditation, however, only prepare the ground for prayer, the heart of which is to love God utterly and completely with a longing to bring every area of our lives, as well as other persons and institutions into creative obedience to God. In intercession we cooperate with God in the work of redemption. Above all, prayer is "attentive openness" to God and "working collectedly" in God's service.

Fostering sainthood persisted throughout Douglas Steere's active career. In 1946 he took the bold step as, President of the American Theological Society, of speaking on "An Ascetical Theology for Our Time." In his address he criticized the gross neglect of the field by competent Protestant theologians. The Neo-Orthodox dominated Society then had only one Catholic member, Jacques Maritain, and he had been recruited by Douglas' own effort. Although Douglase swam upstream, he received "an open hearing" and support from such distinguished friends as Edgar S. Brightman. Years later, he noted in his unpublished journal that nearly all his books "have been written in the same general stream with the focus on the nature and the significance of contemplation and its centrality in the spiritual stature of men and women."[28]

Retreat Master

Douglas envisioned retreats as one of the key means for intensifying the life of God in the individual hearts of men and women. He headed an avant garde of Protestants encouraging and developing retreats. Pendle Hill included a series of retreats in its annual cycle of activities, many conducted by Douglas and Dorothy from the thirties through the eighties. From an early date, Douglas was often called on to lead retreats in the Religious Society of Friends and in other denominations as well. In the early forties he began to experiment at St. Martin's House in Bernardsville, New Jersey, with a form of retreat adapted from the Benedictine model he had first experienced at Maria Laach. In 1941-42 he conducted retreats for the Layman's Movement of the Christian World, Yale Divinity School students, and clergy of the Episcopal diocese of St. Louis.[29] In the spring of 1946 he led a retreat for a large Student Christian Movement group in New England.[30] During the second half of his sabbatical at Sigtuna, Sweden, in the spring of 1948, he wrote *Time to Spare* "to introduce in Free Church circles the use of the weekend retreats which for the past years I had been carrying on regularly with those business and professional men from the New York area at St. Martin's House in Bernardsville, New Jersey."[31] In this book he set forth a case for retreats and explained in detail the method he employed.

As an antidote for people "slowly suffocating" and "panting for breath in the hysteria of haste, fear and self-saving that they are swept up in," he explained in the opening chapter, he envisioned retreats as a way to create "a fresh atmosphere, a fresh perspective, a fresh medium in which to confront our relationships to ourselves, to our fellows both inside and outside the organic associations of nation, race, class in which we stand, and first and last to that which bounds and upholds this swift life of ours."[32] Whenever crises have arisen in western civilization, some men and women, "haunted by the invisible drawing power of the figure of Jesus Christ and of His invisible presence," have stepped back to recover perspective—the desert monks, Basil of Caesarea, Benedict of Nursia, Augustine, Francis of Assisi, Bernard of Clairvaux. More recently, the same concern had come to life again in retreat centers such as the Iona Community, Kirkridge, Trabuco, Pendle Hill and Quaker retreat houses, the work camp movement, the Anglican retreat movement, Swedish "Bearers to Christ," post-war German evangelical academies, houses of prayer, French and Belgian "Jocists," the Catholic Worker Movement, and Alcoholics Anonymous. The overlap of these experiments does not herald a return to monasticism but points toward "a Benedict and a Francis who may draw men and women into as passionate a dedication to holy causes as the Middle Ages contained, . . ."[33] The retreat movement would focus on "the third order," those neither clergy or in religious orders. This would mean shaping:

these periodic occasions of withdrawal so that they will seek to develop a widely diffused stream of quickened and committed men and women who will plant themselves, thousands deep, at every strategic mode of contemporary life: in homes, in government, in churches, among sharecroppers and among the poorly clothed and fed and housed of the great cities, in factories and mines, in schools and colleges, in the quiet rooms where books are written or pictures painted, or in the noisy workshops of artisans and craftsmen.[34]

In brief, retreats could play a role in the transformation of individual lives and of society.

For his method, Douglas borrowed unabashedly from the Benedictine tradition, insisting on a similar combination of prayer, work, and study. He did not leave much to chance. In the main body of the book, "A Workbook on the Auspices for Withdrawal and Return," he described the setting, the preparation for, the conduct, and the follow up.

Regarding setting, he encouraged getting far enough away from one's normal habitat to prevent interruptions and to permit walking. Many places could provide adequate housing, but Douglas envisioned the ideal as including a quiet room for prayer and worship, a common room to conduct spiritual instruction and discussion, a library for devotional books, a dining room, single bedrooms well-insulated to preserve silence,[35] a kitchen large enough to permit several to work in it at one time, and an adequate workshop. Equipment such as chairs and beds should be comfortable but not too luxurious. More importantly, the retreat house should have a community who devote themselves to the cultivation of the devout life to serve it.

By way of preparation Douglas composed a carefully written letter to explain the character of the retreat and to encourage retreatants to be prepared to leave distractions such as newspapers, radios, letters, and telephones behind. He also asked them to do certain advance reading that could serve as common ground for all, e.g., certain passages of scriptures, *The Imitation of Christ,* or other devotional writings. Retreat leaders should organize even minor details such as room assignments in advance.

Among elements of retreats Douglas strongly emphasized *silence* as "perhaps the most important single factor in loosening the soul sufficiently from its encrusted attachment to the ocean bottom of the world's affairs and restoring in it the divine buoyancy that should lift it up again, . . ."[36] He made a case for silence in his opening retreat addresses. Although some retreat leaders debated whether to observe silence throughout, he favored maximum use of it to encourage attentiveness to God and to one another. Silence, however, is a preparation for the main element in the retreat, viz., *prayer.* Prayer is the reason for a *quiet room.* The intense self-scrutiny people undergo during a largely silent retreat necessitates some kind of escape valve which Douglas found in *manual labor,* another of the three mainstays in the Benedictine pattern. Three hours of manual work, he found, "relaxes the tension, restores the sense of objectivity as the retreatant confronts the resistances of the thing-world, and provides a time when he [or she] can silently hoe or scrub or saw or hammer in a truth that he [or she] has carried away from the time of spiritual instruction."[37] As the latter comment indicates, he thought the simpler forms of labor more helpful, but he emphasized also doing tasks which had obvious usefulness, e.g., repairing screens or assisting in the preparation and serving of food.[38]

Other elements of Douglas Steere retreats included: reading at meals, spiritual consultation with the director, devotional reading, corporate worship, discussion of spiritual concerns during common periods, and spiritual instruction. *Reading at meals,* another Benedictine custom, extended spiritual instruction. The availability of the retreat leader for *spiritual consultation* is necessitated by the group therapy going on in a retreat. Douglas and Dorothy Steere later sought to schedule consultations with each retreatant, if they could. Douglas often arranged walks. Retreat houses should select devotional books carefully as a way to supplement other things offered by the retreat. Douglas favored classics of devotion. For corporate worship he, understandably, was partial to silence, but he was increasingly comfortable with liturgical forms employed by different communities of faith. He made room for *discussion of spiritual concerns* on the second day to allow retreatants "to express what may be burning within them as a Christian task to be performed, or as an insight that has shaped itself up, or as inner and outer obstacles that must be faced, ..."[39] Spiritual instruction should not serve as a stage to exhibit the brilliance of the leader but to help people move forward in the spiritual life, to have their hearts restored, to become whole, to know what God is really like, to learn what is required of them, to discover what prayer and yielding to God can do to their lives, and, above all, to become saints, in Jacopone da Todi's definition, persons "in whom Christ is seen to live again."[40]

Douglas was concerned that the religious intensification people experienced in the brief time they spent together would carry beyond the retreat. How could retreatants follow up on what they began in the retreat? One way would be through participation in something like the Franciscan Third Order, living under a rule which combined prayer and a life of charity. For Protestants this could take the form of participation in the Iona Community Fellowship, the Kirkridge Fellowship, the Swedish Bearers to Christ, or similar groups. A second would be through membership in a cell group in a local church. A third would be to adopt a general rule such as "Advices for Fellowship of the Common Life." This Rule emphasized: (1) private prayer, (2) membership in a cell, (3) fellowship work (charity), (4) frugality and simplicity, (5) training of body and mind, (6) an annual retreat, and (7) skill in manual trades. Adoption of the General Rule, however, would not preclude following a private rule of life with some of the same commitments.

As outlined in *Time to Spare*, Douglas sought, in his cycle of spiritual instruction, times of corporate prayer and worship, readings at meal times, and silent leisure to enable participants to detach themselves from the distractions and stresses of their workaday world and to empower them for a return with richer and more responsible participation in that world. In the first spiritual instruction, he helped them to understand the importance of silence and how to make the most of it. In the first evening prayer, he reminded them of God's nearness and accessibility. For the first breakfast reading the next morning, introducing the work period, he read his pamphlet *Work and Contemplation*.[41] In the second spiritual instruction, he focused attention on "The Grace of God," underlining how prodigally God loves us. For the first luncheon reading, he read a selection from Elizabeth Herman's *Creative Prayer*.[42] In the third spiritual instruction, he challenged retreatants to respond to God's grace with complete abandonment as the only adequate response. In the second supper reading, he read selections from Claire Bishop's *France Alive*,[43] depicting the dedication and sacrifices of worker-priests in meeting human needs in France after World War II. For the second evening prayer, he used a prayer drawn from Charles Peguy's *Basic Verities* recording God's pleasure with sleep. In the second breakfast reading, he read another of his pamphlets, *A Quaker Meeting for Worship*,[44] with its accent on silence to introduce a silent meeting for worship of 45 minutes to an hour for Sunday morning. Following discussion of spiritual concerns, he read selections on prayer from Alexis Carrel's "Prayer Is Power" and Edward Leen's *Progress through Mental Prayer*.[45] In his final spiritual instruction, he issued "A Call to the Practice of Prayer."

The model he crafted must have worked for many people, for few persons have had more repeat invitations to lead retreats than Douglas Steere. No one can tally accurately the number of retreats he and Dorothy, despite the fullness of their normal schedules, led among Quakers and other Protestants and, after the Second Vatican Council, among Roman Catholics,[46] in addition to parachurch organizations such as the Disciplined Order of Christ[47] and retreat centers such as Kirkridge[48] and the Vineyard.[49] Although he hesitated to repeat retreats in the same location, many groups prevailed upon him to do so, either arguing that the participants would not be the same[50] or that it did not matter because people valued Douglas himself.[51] He was also called on to lead retreats nearly everywhere he went on his world travels.

Consultant in the Fostering of Sainthood

Douglas' success as a retreat leader, the depth and creativity of his writing, his wide firsthand acquaintance with experiments in cultivation of the inner life throughout the world, his penchant for gleaning wisdom from others, and his willingness to share his energies and ideas made him a much sought after consultant in the development of retreat ministries. We have already looked at the significant role he and Dorothy played in the founding and functioning of Pendle Hill and similar centers in other parts of the world and at St. Martin's House in Bernardsville, New Jersey, where he led retreats between 1940 and 1950.[52] He was, likewise, significant in the development, among other experiments, of Wainwright House by the Laymen's Movement for a Christian World; the Church of the Savior's Dayspring; and the Academy for Spiritual Formation of The Upper Room, the spiritual arm of the United Methodist Church.

When, in 1951, Fonrose Condict made Wainwright House available to the Laymen's Movement, Douglas was asked to serve as a trustee, a position he filled until the mid-eighties.[53] Retreats he conducted at Wainwright House about every other year from the early sixties on were among the most popular offered. In May 1963 Robert M. Cox, the director, informed Douglas that his retreat June 7-9 had filled up before notice of the retreat was sent out, disappointing many who wanted to attend.[54] In 1977 he helped plan the "Guild of Spiritual Guidance," a two-year program to explore and deepen the spiritual life which focused on a study of Jungian psychotherapy, the disciplined prayer life, and extended experience of spiritual friendship with a companion who also sought to deepen the interior life.[55] Beginning in February 1979, he did five weekends on the practice of meditation and various aspects of prayer for the Guild.[56]

Dayspring, founded in 1953 on a 175-acre tract in the hills of Maryland to facilitate the retreat needs of the Church of the Savior, also owed much to Douglas Steere. Dorothy Ham (Devers), active in its ministry from the start, attibuted to him a large part in shaping what it is "because of your wise counsel at the outset and your sustaining encouragement over the ensuing years."[57] Douglas led numerous retreats there too, evidently beginning in 1961,[58] and nurtured it, much as he did Wainwright House, by returning honoraria.[59]

In 1983 Danny Morris, an official of the Upper Room, invited Douglas and other consultants to Nashville to seek their counsel about the development of the Academy for Spiritual Formation, a two-year program "designed to offer lay and clergy persons an in-depth opportunity to intentionally resource their spiritual formation in a wholistic and ongoing manner."[60] The five-day sessions of the Academy, which began May 17, 1983, looked remarkably similar to Douglas' retreat model except for their somewhat more academic slant. Their core elements consisted of (1) small "Covenant Groups" sharing personal stories, (2) only two lectures a day by qualified faculty followed by an hour of silence and thirty minutes for discussion, and (3) corporate prayer three times daily. Douglas himself lectured during the second session of the first Academy October 25-30, 1983, on (1) Meditation, (2) Movements of Prayer, (3) Intercessory Prayer, (4) Mind Your Call, and (5) Spiritual Reading.[61]

Individuals, groups, and churches serious about deepening of the inner life turned often to Douglas to seek his guidance. They invited him to speak about retreats.[62] They entreated him to counsel them.[63] Behind this undoubtedly stood experience such as John King's. In a letter to Dorothy and Douglas he exulted: "That wonderful weekend with you went right down to where all the best things go in my life—to that deep area where intellect is unimportant and a hidden gathering takes place."[64] The Steeres brought more than information and insight to their retreats. They brought themselves and, in themselves, an authenticity and integrity of lives enriched and enlarged by prayer. After they led a retreat at the Carmelite Monastery in Baltimore, Constance Fitzgerald wrote to say that she was "always deeply touched by your gentleness and inner beauty and integrity—and by the depth of your love for each other." It meant much to her that they came to the monastery. "Your concern for me that last morning really touched my heart."[65] What Douglas recommended could also be tried and proven. In 1961 Mary Lyman wrote: "You have helped me so much! Your writings, together with the self that I have been permitted to know somewhat, these have had a major part in shaping of this self, . . ." She too had been asked to lead retreats. "And how deeply I feel the impact of your leadership as I try to help these folks."[66]

A Continuing Legacy

Douglas Steere's legacy continues in the Ecumenical Institute of Spirituality which he and Godfrey Diekmann envisioned at coffee breaks during the Second Vatican Council. However significant ecumenically, the Institute's accent rested from the beginning on the concern which fueled Douglas' life and work. In brief opening remarks during the initial meeting at St. John's Abbey in Collegeville, Minnesota, August 31- September 6, 1965, he sketched the vision he and Father Diekmann hoped the group would pursue. They would seek "a real engagement that will leave none of us as we are," "take a penetrating look at the nature and role of ascetic theology in our time" and "try to determine where fresh work needs to be undertaken," and "assess the inner and outer situations of our time into which our concern for a vital spiritual tradition must come." He pointed to "tools," such as depth psychology and spiritual practices of non-Christian religions, which might assist their endeavor. For more than four hundred years, he observed, Christians had undertaken their search "hermit-like . . . in their separate cells of tradition." Perhaps the time had come to rediscover what monks in the desert had learned about the value of a common approach.[67]

As one would expect, over three decades the Ecumenical Institute of Spirituality has changed its constituency. By 1966 only three charter members remained. The group has self-consciously retained its balance of Catholic and Protestant or Orthodox traditions to assure exposure to varied approaches to spirituality. The most noteworthy shift has been the inclusion of women beginning in 1967. In 1996 they made up half the membership.

Since its founding in 1965, the Institute has combined the sharing of personal experience and activities during the year with experiences of different contemplative communities and cutting-edge discussions of spirituality. They enlisted authorities in different areas as well as called on the wisdom of members. Meetings, held alternately in Catholic and Protestant or Orthodox centers to expose members firsthand to the variety of traditions in spirituality, have touched on many themes basic to the spiritual life. In recounting them one can mark the major trends of the current "Awakening" posited by some historians.[68] During the late **sixties**, the Institute focused on the journey outward, with such topics as openness to the world (Pendle Hill, 1966), holiness (Mount Savior Monastery, 1967), styles of spirituality (Kirkridge, 1968), and hope (St. Vladimir's Seminary, 1969).

During the **seventies**, interest shifted to the journey inward, giving attention to new forms of contemplation (Grailville, Ohio, 1971, and Dayspring, 1972); Christian Zen and transcendental meditation (Wainwright House, 1973); prayer and liberation (St. Joseph's Abbey, MA, 1974); piety, food, and energy (Washington, DC, 1975); spiritual direction and personality types (Princeton Theological Seminary, 1978); and loneliness and solitude (Sisters of Loretto, Nerinx, KY, 1979, and Kirkridge, 1980).

During the **eighties**, the accent fell more heavily on the outworking of spirituality in different traditions and in life with studies of: spirituality and retreats for the eighties (Marriottsville, MD, 1981); African-American Protestant and Roman Catholic spirituality (Highland Park, NJ, 1982); spirituality in contemporary Protestantism and in the Carmelite tradition (Holy Spirit Monastery, Conyers, GA, 1983); education for the devout life (Society of St. John the Evangelist, Cambridge, MA, 1984); women and spirituality (St. Joseph's Provincial House, Daughters of Charity, Emmitsburg, MD, 1985); health and spirituality (Cenacle Retreat House, Highland Park, NJ, 1986); home and pilgrimage imagery in spirituality (The Cenacle, Lantana, FL, 1987); the experience of God in Baptist and Orthodox traditions (The Southern Baptist Theological Seminary, Louisville, 1988); compassion in Thomas Merton and Martin Luther King, Jr. (Boynton Beach, FL, 1989); and creation spirituality (St. John's Abbey, Collegeville, MN, 1990).

In 1990 and 1991, recognizing that Douglas would not always be present to inspire and guide, members spent quite a bit of time trying to revision the Institute and committed themselves to its continuance. During this period of inner searching, themes did not manifest a clear pattern. They included: standing on holy ground (Scarritt-Bennett Center, Nashville, TN, 1991); spirituality in ecumenical perspective (Pendle Hill, 1992); the power of myth in Christianity (Pendle Hill, 1993); contemplation in Islam, Buddhism, Hinduism, and

Carmelite spirituality (St. Mary's Seminary and the Carmelite Monastery, Baltimore, 1994); the city as a context for biblical faith (Servant Leadership School, the Church of the Savior, Washington, DC, 1995); Thomas Merton (Abbey of Gethsemani, Trappist, KY, 1996); and spirituality and urban violence (Richmond Hill, Richmond, VA, 1997).

After taking part in a meeting of the Ecumenical Institute of Spirituality at Dayspring in 1972, Elizabeth O'Connor wrote to Douglas to say "how much it meant to [her] to have the New Year's weekend in that special company at Dayspring. Obviously you are the Prior of this group—its Spiritual Director, evoker of gifts."[69] Douglas might have winced a little at her choice of words, but she was right. Not only in the Ecumenical Institute of Spirituality but in all he had done to intensify the life of God in the individual hearts of men and women, he led the way in a most earnest search, and in doing so he helped Protestant Christians to rediscover the wisdom of the centuries and to feel passionately again about the homing instinct which leaves us restless until we find rest in God.

Notes

1. E.g., Douglas V. Steere, *On Beginning from Within* (New York and London: Harper & Brothers, 1943), 10.
2. Thomas R. Kelly, *A Testament of Devotion* (New York: Harper & Bros., Publishers, 1941), 74.
3. Douglas V. Steere, UNPUBLISHED JOURNAL, 279.
4. Steere, JOURNAL, 282.
5. Steere, JOURNAL, 283.
6. Steere, JOURNAL, 284.

7. Steere, JOURNAL, 284.
8. Steere, JOURNAL, 285.
9. Steere, JOURNAL, 286.
10. Steere, JOURNAL, 286.
11. Douglas described Trabuco in *Time to Spare* (New York: Harper & Brothers, Publishers, 1949), 18, as a place in which Heard, Aldous Huxley, Allan Hunter, Malcolm Dana, and others "have made prayer and meditation the core of their search."
12. Franklin ?, *Letter to Dorothy Steere,* February 1, 1945.
13. Steere, JOURNAL, 521f.
14. Heard invited Douglas to lead a retreat at Trabuco in 1944 (Gerald Heard, *Letter to Douglas Steere,* May 25, and September 4, 1944, expressed appreciation for the retreat.). In 1948 Douglas contacted Heard to find out why he had abandoned Trabuco. When Heard led a retreat at Wainwright House in the fall of 1954, Douglas invited him to speak at Haverford (Steere, JOURNAL, 571.). In 1957 Douglas visited Heard in California. He described it as "another of those stirring visits where Gerald Heard shared to the very core some of the fresh flood of insights that had come to him since our last visit at Wainwright House three years before." (Steere, JOURNAL, 743.) In a letter dated July 21, 1971, Allan Hunter reported to Douglas that Gerald Heard's health had broken down. January 15, 1972, Eugene Exman wrote to Douglas wanting him to ask Allan Hunter why Trabuco had failed. In a letter of September 4, 1972, Michael Barrie reported that the Heard Collection was being placed in the Research Library at UCLA and asked for copies of any letters he had received from Heard.
15. Steere, *On Beginning from Within,* vii.
16. He gave "Devotion and Theology" to a conference of about 800 Methodist clergy at Evanston, Illinois, in the winter of 1938-39.
17. This was the Ingersoll Lecture, given at Harvard in 1942.
18. Steere, *On Beginning from Within,* 17.
19. In an address given at Union Theological Seminary entitled "Spiritual Renewal in Our Time," *Union Seminary Quarterly Review,* 17 (November 1961), 33-56, he varied the characteristics slightly. The sixth quality was: Saints, above all, are prayerful.
20. Steere, *On Beginning from Within,* 31.
21. Steere, *On Beginning from Within,* 33.
22. Steere, *On Beginning from Within,* 44.
23. Steere, *On Beginning from Within,* 54.
24. Steere, *On Beginning from Within,* 58.
25. Steere, *On Beginning from Within,* 59.

26. Steere, *On Beginning from Within*, 60-61.
27. Steere, *On Beginning from Within*, 68f.
28. Steere, JOURNAL, 375.
29. Steere, JOURNAL, 287.
30. Steere, JOURNAL, 377.
31. Steere, JOURNAL, 479.
32. Steere, *Time to Spare*, 13, 14.
33. Steere, *Time to Spare*, 27.
34. Steere, *Time to Spare*, 28.
35. He was very insistent on the need for individual rooms.
36. Steere, *Time to Spare*, 49.
37. Steere, *Time to Spare*, 53.
38. The number of participants in Steere retreats created logistical problems for this element and led him to revise his plan. Most jobs were connected with assistance in preparing and serving food, washing dishes, cleaning up after the retreat, making beds, etc.
39. Steere, *Time to Spare*, 62.
40. Steere, *Time to Spare*, 66.
41. Douglas V. Steere, *Work and Contemplation* (Philadelphia: American Friends Service Committee, 1947).
42. Elizabeth Herman, *Creative Prayer* (New York: Harper & Brothers, 1940).
43. Claire H. Bishop, *France Alive* (New York: Declan X. McMullen Co., Inc., 1947).
44. Douglas V. Steere, *A Quaker Meeting for Worship* (Philadelphia: Committee of Ministry and Counsel, Philadelphia Year Meeting, 1937).
45. Alexis Carrel, "Prayer Is Power" in *Getting the Most Out of Life* (Pleasantville, NY: Reader's Digest, n.d.); Edward Leen, *Progress through Mental Prayer* (New York: Sheed and Ward, 1935).
46. E.g., St. Benedict Center, Madison, WI, March 14-15, 1970 (Sr. Mary David, OSB, *Letter to Douglas V. Steere*, January 12, 1970); Christian Brothers, Pittsburgh and Ontario, Canada, several times (Martin Helldorfer, *Letter to Douglas V. Steere*, May 29, 1972; July 3, 1972; December 15, 1972 regarding a retreat conducted December 11-13, 1972 in Pittsburgh; Martin Helldorfer, *Letter to Douglas V. Steere*, July 18, 1973; November 13, 1973, regarding a retreat conducted in Windsor, Ontario, December 12-14, 1973); Carmelite Monastery, Indianapolis, IN, 1974 (Sr. Elizabeth Melrich, OCD, *Letter to Douglas V. Steere*, June 7, 1973); Carmelite Monastery, Baltimore, MD (Connie Fitzgerald, *Letter to Douglas and Dorothy Steere*, July 15, 1973)

47. See Lois Owens, *Letter to Douglas V. Steere*, December 3, 1964, asking him to lead a retreat for the Disciplined Order of Christ, Midwest Region, on the theme "Christ Within You"; Douglas V. Steere, *Letter to Dorothy Steere*, April 27, 1965, reporting on this retreat held near Kansas City at Unity Village; Allan A. Hunter, *Letter to Douglas V. Steere*, December 4, 1964, asking him to lead a retreat for the Order, West Region, in 1966.

48. John Oliver Nelson, the founder, an intimate friend of Douglas, patterned Kirkridge after the Iona Community. He often called on Douglas to lead retreats.

49. The Vineyard was a church renewal retreat center founded by Findley B. Edge, Professor of Religious Education at The Southern Baptist Theological Seminary, Louisville, Kentucky. Douglas held his first retreat there May 6-8, 1971 (Findley B. Edge, *Letter to Douglas V. Steere,* January 30, March 10, 1970; February 8, May 11, 1971). He returned September 20-22, 1973 (Findley B. Edge, *Letter to Douglas V. Steere, July 7, August 7, 1972; September 27, 1973*).

50. See Martin Helldorfer, *Letter to Douglas V. Steere,* July 3, 1972, regarding retreat for Christian Brothers in Pittsburgh December 11-13, 1972.

51. See Findley B. Edge, *Letter to Douglas V. Steere,* September 20-22, 1972, assuring Douglas that he could do exactly the same thing.

52. Steere, JOURNAL, 544.

53. Steere, JOURNAL, 1983.

54. Robert M. Cox, *Letter to Douglas V. Steere,* May 6, 1963.

55. Steere, JOURNAL, 1977, 1.

56. Steere, JOURNAL, 1978. In 1984 he returned his honorarium to the Guild of Spiritual Guidance, accepting only reimbursement of train fare.

57. Dorothy Ham, *Letter to Douglas V. Steere,* Advent 1972.

58. William T. Ham, *Letter to Douglas V. Steere,* March 9, 1961, thanked him for an "unforgettable experience." On the history see Elizabeth O'Connor, *Journey Inward, Journey Outward* (New York: Harper & Row, Publishers, 1968), 91-100.

59. Carolyn ?, *Letter to Douglas V. Steere,* May 21, 1968, thanking him for the retreat and return of his honorarium.

60. Danny E. Morris, Unpublished paper entitled "Birthing of an Academy," 3.

61. Steere, JOURNAL, 1983.

62. E.g., Harold S. Ingalls, *Letter to Douglas V. Steere,* April 25, 1961, inviting him to speak about retreats at Deer Hill in Hughsonville, New York. Douglas replied May 31, 1961, reporting that he had done four

retreats at Pendle Hill this year and felt that silence is "the thing which is doing the work of touching people's lives and healing them." (Douglas V. Steere, *Letter to Harold B. Ingalls,* May 31, 1961.)

63. Brian Frost, Programme Director, Notting Hill Ecumenical Centre, London, *Letter to Douglas V. Steere,* May 18, 1972, noted that the secretaries would like to meet with him because of his book *Time to Spare.*
64. John King, *Letter to Dorothy and Douglas Steere,* May 15, 1972.
65. Constance Fitzgerald, *Letter to Douglas and Dorothy Steere,* July 15, 1973.
66. Mary Lyman, *Letter to Douglas V. Steere,* October 16, 1961.
67. Douglas V. Steere, "Common Frontiers in Catholic and Non-Catholic Spirituality" in *Protestants and Catholics on the Spiritual Life,* edited by Michael Marx (Collegeville, MN: Liturgical Press, 1965), 42-55.
68. E.g., William G. McLoughlin, *Revival, Awakening, and Reform* (Chicago: University of Chicago Press, 1965).
69. Elizabeth O'Connor, *Letter to Douglas V. Steere,* January 26, 1972.

XVII

Consummate Correspondent

No account of Douglas Steere's life would be complete without some attention to his consummate skill in correspondence. He expanded an already unbelievably expansive ministry of uplift through personal contacts with cards, notes, and letters. Already, in early correspondence with his parents, he manifested a gift for letter writing, but it grew and blossomed as he widened the range of correspondents. In the thousands and thousands of letters that filled sixty-two boxes with his correspondence one will find perfunctory letters attending to business, but most of Douglas Steere's letters have arms that reach out and embrace that correspondent with the same warm attentiveness and sense of presence one experienced in meeting him personally. He reached out to others through letters just as he did through personal meeting and had a way of being really present in his letters. The Steere "Travel Letters," published first in 1937, widened immensely Douglas' reach.

Douglas viewed letter writing, both private and public, as a crucial aspect of his ministry. Citing "heavy correspondence" with friends in England, Germany, and Scandinavia in the years following his European sabbatical in 1947-48, he labeled it "of primary importance." His commentary on the importance of correspondence contains a clue to the secret of its value to so many.

The web of friendship is not something that spins it-self, but it is fed both in holding others up in thoughts and caring and in reaching out to them in letters. It is a rich experience to hold another before you as you write and to make the letter reach out to the deepest thing you know in another. . . . Personal visits face to face cannot be equalled for a truly intimate relation, but close on its heels is the possibility of reaching out, and being reached out to, through letters.[1]

Echoed in these words is Martin Buber's statement in a meeting at Haverford College in December 1951, "The greatest thing a man [or woman] can do for another is to confirm the deepest thing in him [or her]." This had imprinted itself indelibly on Douglas Steere as a letter writer. In personal letters as in face to face meetings he affirmed and uplifted others.

Others noticed something special about both Douglas' and Dorothy's correspondence. After receiving one of their letters, Douglas' Aunt Bess Steere spoke for many others when she said: "You and Dorothy always write such loving, understanding and satisfying letters."[2] A. Burns Chalmers, a long- time friend from Oxford days, remarked, after Douglas visited him in the hospital: "Let me say, too, that your letters through the years, many of which I have kept, have been a great strength and 'upbuilding' to me always."[3] Tim Kinsolving, Rector of St. James' Church in New York City, underscored what lay behind such appreciation:

Though I may receive a number of letters I am rather certain that none could mean to me quite as much as yours. I look to you with the same admiration that I once did to Rufus Jones. It is you, of course, not I, who have been used by God to be prodigiously influential as a witness to the centrality of the Christian emphasis that must come first, the inner life and the dedication and involvement in the redemptive purpose.[4]

Ellen Douglas Leyburn, President of Agnes Scott College, wrote after Douglas had lectured there:

> I have just been re-reading your two kind greetings of the fall and the beautiful note of last Easter, all of which have meant more to me than you can know. Your taking time to make me feel the reality of your friendship in the midst of all the claims upon you is deeply heart-warming to me; and you seem always to know what to say to bolster my courage in the way that really helps, as indeed it helps me simply to think of you.[5]

When one considers the extent of Douglas Steere's ministry, the personal cast of his letters is nothing short of astonishing. Deborah Halfdan-Nielsen fingered what many others could say. "I admire, Douglas, that you, a person who must be writing a limitless number of business letters, can keep such a personal tone in your letters to me, and I will tell you, it gives me much pleasure."[6]

Letters to His Father and Mother

Douglas owed much of his skill and sensitivity as a correspondent to Baron von Hügel, but even before he became acquainted with the Baron's life and thought, he displayed a special tenderness and pastoral touch in letters to his parents. Douglas loved his parents, especially his father, dearly, and early on he paid attention to some "holy nudges." He took care to inform them about himself and his activities, but he went beyond that to offer spiritual care. After attending a father and son banquet during his second year at Harvard he wrote to Edward Steere:

> I thought of you often and realized how much more we have seemed to understand each other in the last three or four years. Just being around with you on that day last December made me appreciate it particularly.

These days as I work with young people whose folks are aeons away from them—who share no confidences with them—who are too busy to live any of their own lives into the boy's—I thank providence that I have had a Dad who first told me the secrets of life—who took me a berrying with him—who came out and played catch with me occasionally and to whom I didn't feel hesitant about taking anything that was on my chest to get his opinion on. These aren't idle bouquets, Dad—I mean them.[7]

Years later, he sent Edward birthday greetings with another tender note:

How I wish I could clasp your hand and look into your eyes and tell you this. Your fine, clear life that has been spent in giving us a start and then in helping Mother and now Inez [Edward's second wife] and so many neighbors and friends besides is one that we are all proud of and we thank God for such a good Dad as we have had.[8]

Douglas exhibited remarkable pastoral sensitivities. He often extended a filial embrace as he remembered his father and mother regarding seven-year-old Helen's death in 1913. On their fortieth wedding anniversary in 1939 he recalled "memorable" events including "scarlet fever and the awful wrench of Helen's going and the prolonged siege with Bruce."[9] On the anniversary of Helen's death, May 26, 1946, he opened to his father's gaze the unhealable wound in his own heart:

This day I cannot pass over without remembering the year 1913 and what it cost you and Mother, Dad. With precious children of our own, we come to realize afresh what such separations may mean. Helen and I were alone here tonight before the fire and when she came

298

down in her nightie to say goodnight, we had prayers together and remembered her namesake. Some time when you and Helen are together, I want you to tell her about the elder Helen—Your Mother whose name she bears too so that she will know that they are living in her.[10]

A short time later, he anticipated, too, pangs of grief his father might experience on Ruby Steere's seventieth birthday six years after her death and recalled:

Her hunger for beauty, her deep enjoyment of new things, her love of reading, her concern for us—even to whether our tie was properly adjusted or the hat turned down, or trousers pressed—her utter disregard of herself if something had to be done, her scorn of self-hoarding or saving, her longing to live as much into life as each day would hold— . . .[11]

A natural at spiritual guidance, Douglas took time to guide Edward in offering pastoral comfort to Charlie Whitcomb, a close friend who faced a crisis during the Great Depression. His advice is revealing of his unapologetic confession of faith in God, his insight into spiritual care, and his skill at practicing the art of caring for others, now showing the impact of Von Hügel on his life:

You will help him face what is before him Dad. It will test your faith and make you turn to a source beyond yourself to do it if I am not mistaken—but you will help him. You may not say a great deal to each other— you two. But there will be the pressure of your hand grips, the understanding looks, the long silences in your conversations when talk will not be necessary— that will help him. But in the last instance no one can help him—but him who lives among us all and it will be as your times together sense the presence of that third who lives and shares in your friendship that the greatest strength will come to Charlie. For in the real crises of life we all walk indian file—alone—then there is only one companion and even the veil of death will not separate us from him. Give Charlie my love. I shall be thinking of him often.[12]

Although Douglas did not correspond as frequently with his mother, during his retreat at Maria Laach in 1933 he felt prompted to write a letter which she cherished the remaining years of her life. A copy of the letter has not been located, but Douglas recorded in his journal the circumstances which prompted him to write it. In reading Nygren's *Agape and Eros* he was struck by the fact that God's love does not depend on our merits but only on God's "spilling this out on every creature without the slightest calculation." As he walked and pondered, "suddenly a whole new vision of my mother poured in on me and the walls of reticence and undemonstrative acceptance of each other broke down in me and I realized how much I loved her and more importantly how much she had loved me over all of these years without ever being free to express it in the obvious ways." He turned around, hastened back to the monastery, and immediately wrote a letter "pouring out all of this realization of her caring and asking her forgiveness for my not having sufficiently expressed it to her before." Ruby, overwhelmed, responded with a warm letter and, at the close of her life in 1940, let Douglas know how much this had meant to her.[13]

Letters to Dorothy

Almost from the time they first met in 1925, Dorothy became Douglas' chief correspondent. They exchanged searching and tender letters as they explored their relationship leading up to their marriage in 1929. Throughout their marriage they kept a steady stream of correspondence flowing back and forth in times when Douglas found it necessary to pursue a ministry on his own, which happened often when Helen and Anne were small and could not travel so easily, but also when Douglas undertook risky excursions. In these letters, often written daily, you can see how steadfastly he kept Dorothy in mind as a loving presence, sought to share experiences, and tried to anticipate and assuage anxieties in advance of her letters. The street ran both ways here, though, for Dorothy attuned herself to her much-traveled husband with the same skill he displayed. She, too, manifested remarkable gifts of spiritual care, not just for Douglas but for thousands of friends they made everywhere they traveled.

In Douglas' letters to Dorothy during his dangerous trip to Germany and the Scandinavian countries in 1940, he sought to speak to the ambivalence and anxiety she must have felt about the whole venture. Writing almost daily at the beginning, he explained the hazards involved, his method of getting credentials, and the nature of the task—visitation. Then, in one letter he added, "You will never know what it means to me to have you come completely with me in this venture."[14] Thereafter, he posted her on the progress of the trip—frustrating delay in Lisbon waiting for a visa to Germany, the breakthrough there and then in getting a French visa, various happenings. Here and there, he interjected his characteristic notes of hope. On securing the visa to France he remarked, "Things have opened up in a way that one can not fully understand unless there is a deeper hand in it than our own."[15] Sensing noticeable demoralization everywhere, he picked up some hopeful signs in Switzerland.

> In the face of this one hears of magnificent little groups of Christians purged of all illusions and ready for what may come, with preaching that reaches the life and springs out of the Bible, one hears of the longing for intervisitation and of the hunger for Christian fellowship in these times and sees the work of the days ahead emerging.[16]

Sometimes his letters took a more deeply personal turn. From Berlin in early October, he confessed the "gnawing" in his heart to see her and his thoughts about "the new obedience and the open life for our day—its ideal *is* the Holy Family, nothing less. And to have known and lived in such a relationship with so gallant a partner as you, dear one, is a gift beyond measuring."[17] In December he wrote from Viggbyholm, reporting on a two-hour visit with Per Sundberg, its founder. He then slipped into a far more intimate reflection on their life together in view of his unusual sense of calling.

> I dream of you each night and in the dreams I feel linked to you and mixed with you in a way that is for me an utterly new dimension of our life together. It is as though this were where we were meant to be together and that here we were destined to have come into a new love and a new common experience and purpose. These people are our people, darling, that is clearer to me each day and it seems as though you and the girls should be in this with me and that it is in some mysterious way that your spirits are sharing it with me. So it was tonight as I sat feeling the warm strong friendship of these two fine people who are living at Viggbyholm the kind of family life with their own children and their faculty and the children of others that God meant us all to live.[18]

Douglas' dream took a tangible form in 1947-48 when the Steere family lived in Sweden and Helen and Anne attended school at Viggbyholm.

Often separated from Dorothy for long periods when she could not accompany him on his travels, he never let much time lapse between letters, nor did she in responding. Douglas took care to keep Dorothy informed on his solo trip to Europe during the summer of 1945 to get the Finnish Relief effort underway. He wrote letters daily en route to Sweden and then as often as he could during stays in

302

Stockholm and on an exhausting trip to Finland to assess the needs of the Finns, especially in Lappland. When she was unable to attend the Third Session of the Second Vatican Council with him in the fall of 1964, he wrote nearly every day to report on the Council, meetings with friends, and personal matters.[19] Even though his "Letters from Rome" contained much the same information, the personal ones included much more colorful sidelights and comments on the happenings at the Council. Dorothy's responses reveal how deeply she too had entered into the spirit of the Council and into the joys and sorrows of friends who counted on her just as they did on Douglas.[20] Each tried to buoy the other, as one of Dorothy's reciprocal comments well illustrates. "You are a mighty sturdy ship yourself, dear D.V.S. I marvel at all you carry with such sweetness and apparent ease and freedom from strain."[21] Later, as Douglas continued on a speaking tour after the Council, she complimented him on his "wonderful lively and *funny* letters," which she shared partly with others.[22] A faint complaint crept into a subsequent letter, however, as Douglas continued the tour. She was not liking life without him.[23]

The Steeres exchanged letters, too, during shorter separations such as when Douglas was away to conduct retreats,[24] attend conferences,[25] make shorter trips abroad.[26] Dorothy seemed both to understand and to appreciate the absences, but she also worried about his health and safety. During Douglas' brief trip to Japan and India in the spring of 1966 to lay the groundwork for the dialogues between Buddhists and Christians and Hindus and Christians, she expressed in one letter how "glad and proud" she was "that barriers have come down and that you find yourself able to talk with these people *really*—not surfacely."[27] She stamped her approval on the trip. "It does seem as if doors had been opened in miraculous ways and that you had been led in what you have done." But she worried about his hectic schedule and health in the heat.[28]

Letters to Friends

Douglas Steere's mindboggling activities and accomplishments make it easy to understand why he built up a veritable mountain of letters during his long career. In an era when telephones had not yet achieved the level of convenience and sophistication they provide today, he *had* to turn out reams of letters to plan, organize, and arrange all of the projects, many of world scope, which he undertook. Nevertheless, a superactive life will only explain in part the *extent* and *character* of his correspondence. Although he had to write letters to discharge the many tasks he took upon himself, the letters he wrote show that what primed his pump was an urgent desire and gift, dwelling deep within him, to commune with others and to be irradiated by the light within them. A common endeavor often led to lifelong friendship and correspondence.

Douglas used letters to forge and maintain strong ties with hundreds of friends throughout his life. To name only a few of his early acquaintances, he corresponded repeatedly with Burns Chalmers and Don Stevenson, friends of Oxford days; Maria Schlüter-Hermkes, who guided him to Maria Laach in 1933 and arranged meetings with Roman Catholic scholars in the field of spirituality; Gerald Heard, his spiritual guide during the forties; Dorothy Day, founder of the Catholic Worker; Heikki Waris, Director of Suomen Huolto and co-worker in Finnish Relief; and thousands more persons both eminent and ordinary.

Characteristically, there shone out often in Douglas' letters the same rays of light and challenges to rise above our present circumstances which he brought in face-to-face encounters. He reached out to encourage other Friends in their work. Writing to David Richie, working in the Quaker Mission in Warsaw, Poland, just after World War II, he slipped in a reminder as to "how I thank God for your life and for what your spirit is meaning over there."[29] Noting the burden of Uniola Adams's work in Liberia as part of a transition to

304

African control, he cheered her with, "It is wonderful that you are there and with all the difficulties you are inwardly strong enough to carry them."[30] To Mildred Ringwalt, leader of a Quaker Meeting at Chapel Hill, he said, "You must feel the responsibility of being a mother to this Meeting and I know how much you are giving of yourself to it. What a joy it is to be God's instrument in setting some of these things in motion."[31] He counseled Lillian Hughes in Blackville, South Carolina, regarding her stated preference to teach in a Quaker school:

> In some ways you may be far more needed there than you would in a Friends School. The kinds of things that you open up in your social studies teaching are wonderful. I am sure there is no way of evaluating what you are doing, but our job in this world is to sow the seeds, not to try to be too concerned about the harvest, at least in tabulating it.[32]

To Richard Keithan in India, he sent a check and added, "We are so deeply thankful for the witness you bear, and we feel that you are speaking for all of us out there."[33]

He often plowed a deep furrow as he offered encouragement, disclosing himself at his masterful best. He rejoiced with Pat Hislop, a Friend from New Zealand, recovering from hepatitus and dysentery which had prevented her from discharging her ministry and proceeded to say:

> I am sure that the interval will only heighten the effectiveness of your work from this time on. "Man proposes and God disposes" as the old saying is and while I do not believe in so absolute a predestination as this implies on the surface, yet I do believe that God works on us in special ways upon the occasion of these abrupt shatterings of our proposals, and that if we yield, a new level of guidance often appears. You know those wonderful words of Isaac Penington, "There is that

near you which will guide you. O wait for it, and be faithful unto it." It is always near. But we are not always open. But when the shattering of our proposals comes, then it often makes us open and we begin to listen to that which is near us to guide us and has been and will be near, and a new level of holy obedience is drawn out of us to our infinite enrichment and to the blessing of the work in which we stand.[34]

Three years later, he gently counseled and encouraged Pat Hislop as she reached a decision to receive baptism, confirmation, and communion in the Roman Catholic Church and to enter a religious order.[35]

His encouragement traveled far beyond the Quaker orbit. He told Maria Schlüter-Hermkes, who was doubting her abilities to carry on just after the war as her husband's health failed, that he knew "few persons who are so plunged in the life of God at the center and that gives me a great sense of easiness and of assurance that you will be given strength to carry all these things."[36]

Douglas did not miss many opportunities to let wider friendships help him advance his concerns for peace or dialogue. George Appleton, Bishop of Perth, West Australia, whom he had come to know at the Second Vatican Council and who shared many of his peace concerns, was chosen Anglican Archbishop of Jerusalem. On this occasion, Douglas wrote:

> Your deep grasp of the principle of reconciliation and your concern for the mutual irradiation of the great world religions and your spiritual concern for the deeper discovery of what life in Christ and his message as the universal man [mean] will all serve in this situation with such power and strength.[37]

He added that Paul Minear, "a really great spiritual person" with whom Appleton would have much in common, would soon be at Tantur, the Ecumenical Institute for Advanced

Studies near Jerusalem. Shortly afterward, he wrote Charles Malik, formerly Lebanese Ambassador to the United Nations but now teaching at American University in Beirut, to let him know that he was thinking of him "during these last days when your country has been going through such turmoil" and noted the appointment of Appleton, "a man of vast humane sympathies, a great apostle of reconciliation, a man who is most open toward the interpenetration of the world religions, and a great human being."[38] In a later letter to Malik he reported that he had spent an hour with Abraham Heschel, "told him about your vision of a common cultural cluster in that tier of states," and wondered if Malik could plan his return to Lebanon in such a way as to permit "an unhurried visit with this great spirit."[39]

Sometimes Douglas found himself acting in the role of personal peace ambassador. He revealed the gift he had for reconciling, for instance, in the delicate way he tried to help Claire Huchet Bishop understand the critical comment of a French friend which had deeply offended her.

> I quite understand the feeling that you have and can see that the way in which my French friend put this may stir up this kind of reaction in a person who is deeply sensitive, as you are, to all of the dissidences and agonies in the world. I think that my friend had the deep sense that back of all of these dissidences is one who is sheer love and sheer caring and cherishing, who is luring the world to Him and it is this God that he speaks of when he speaks of enjoying God. If one is going to be blocked by the dissidences from breaking through to this deeper level where alone they can ever be brought together, then there is no hope and no Christian position. For that reason, I still feel that my friend is right theologically on the deepest level, but certainly there was no attempt in this essay to deal with the problem of evil and I would have to confess that I

think that there is no final resolution of this problem. It is a mystery, but it is a mystery beyond which there is something that, when it touches us, we dare to cling to it regardless of the unresolved character of those disorders that we must give our very lives themselves to trying to overcome.[40]

He reached out far and often when friends lost loved ones. On the death of Rejnar Halfdan-Nielsen, one of his earliest and most intimate Danish friends, he comforted Deborah: "I think of his humor and that sly smile of his when something struck his fancy. I also think of his love of life and of the deep pride he had in his family. He was also deeply proud of you, Deborah, and of all that the new school had accomplished."[41] To Curtis Watson, U.S. Educational Commissioner for France, at the time of his mother's death, he wrote:

> There is something about the passing on of both parents that leaves you on your own as you never quite were before. In spite of all we say, it does mean something to have someone who is so deeply interested in us and with whom we can share our little triumphs and know that when things go badly someone really deeply understands and cares. Now we have to stand in this relationship with others.[42]

Some letters reveal how deep ran the Steeres' acquaintance and friendship. On learning of the death of Lena Sundberg, wife of Per, founder of Viggbyholm School, Douglas wrote their son, Gunnar, to offer comfort:

> I think you know how much we loved both Lena and Per, and her passing brings a real sense of loss to us, as to you. She always had so much life and vigor and joy down in her and her skills with her hands were always so much in evidence and her way of holding your good-sized family together and caring in a special way for

308

each individual one of you was something that showed us the great woman that she was.[43]

Some exchanges delved deeply into matters which stood at the center of Douglas' being. He and Emelia Fogelklou Norlind, whose profound mystical faith awed him from his first encounter with her on the visit to Sweden in 1937,[44] typically focused on "the deep things of God." Just after returning from a month in Germany in 1939, she expressed appreciation for his kind and warm letter which helped her through the following months.[45] In 1948 she wrote to thank him for "these helpful brotherly lines" he had written and to express fear for her "so much less functional hearing." Then she added, "Much grace is given to you. May you always have that in mind when weariness and sorrow for the world's need will fill your heart."[46]

These two walked much the same path in their search. Emelia corresponded in preparation for the retreat they were to lead together June 6-8 about some of her reading:

> I love Sullivan, for instance: "The error of theologies is to give shape for all time to what was seen once in a moment that transcends time." or: "Creeds are cracked in what leads through the crack in religion. . . . Man's fundamental need is for ecstasy—and ecstasy is the canceling of isolation. . . It is togetherwithness. And such precisely is the central source of love.[47]

On returning from the funeral of Elin Wägner, another "mother" of Swedish Quakerism and a noted writer, she recalled their exchanges two days before Wägner died.

> Our talk—with silences in between—and our prayers then, showed how she was ready to go through whatever door she should be led, the door we call death, or the door of continued living here. She was surrounded by love and loving attentions, though in deep

quiet (although several relatives were in the house). All the village people felt her as theirs.[48]

Douglas and Emelia also exchanged advice about their scholarly and literary endeavors. In a letter to her in June 1954, Douglas offered comfort in the death of one of the leading members of the small band of Quakers in Sweden and then asked her opinion regarding some thoughts he entertained about doing a small book on Isaac Penington, a favorite of both.[49] He bolstered her in her writing and assisted in getting some of it translated into English by his former colleague, Howard Lutz.[50] Douglas uplifted others, but Emelia too, knew how to look at life in a positive way. Just after the Second Vatican Council, she wrote Douglas and Dorothy to say how thankful she was that he was the Quaker Observer at the Council and added, "I know how Vietnam-things must ache within your hearts. But in such a manifestation as this end of the Concilium, there is a great rainbow of hope for humanity."[51] In 1970, two years before her death at 94 on September 26, 1972, Douglas personally delivered a "Minute" of love and appreciation for Emelia Fogelklou Norlind on behalf of the Eleventh Triennial Conference of the Friends World Committee for Consultation.[52]

Douglas also found a soul friend in Alan Paton. A deep common concern for humanity bonded them immediately on the Steeres' first trip to South Africa in the spring of 1953, during which they visited Paton three times in Durban, where he was devoting himself to the building up of Botha's Hill, a community for Africans recuperating from tuberculosis.[53] Not long after these visits, Douglas wrote to Paton about the latter's second novel, which he had reviewed for *The Friend,* and to inquire about Paton's view of the application of United Nations pressure on South Africa through commissions to end apartheid.[54] Paton responded, in considerable detail to say that commissions appointed by the UN tended "to harden government opinion, antagonise middle opinion, encourage white Liberal opinion and all non-white opinion." He would "feel a loss if this ceased to be the case," but he did not find the manner in which it was done helpful. It would be best to find a way to make South Africans feel ashamed rather than hostile. He enumerated five conclusions:

> (1) Too many small countries seem to be represented in these Commissions. (2) If more white countries were represented, their opinions would carry more weight. (3) The closest care should be taken in the writing of the document. (4) You should, while disembowelling a man, give him the impression that you are merely fondling him. (5) What a pity that America could not take its place beside South Africa in the dock and leave the Court humbly penitent. What a shake-up that would be to us![55]

In reply, Douglas, always careful to take others with utmost seriousness and waiting until he could send a copy of his review, noted some changes in the UN Commission which he thought might be helpful. He proceeded to elaborate some further steps that could be taken, in essence embracing Paton's last point:

> What now needs to be done is some assembling of constructive material as to how situations of this kind have begun to be solved in other territories where they exist and trying to see how this world problem which South Africa shares in would be assisted there as in other territories. It is only on some such constructive general shouldering, both of the guilt and of the responsibility that I see any real hope of the UN action doing anything lastingly effective. I am not a particular admirer of Canon Collins and of his headline getting type of attack. I am afraid it is too easy.[56]

The Steeres returned to South Africa several times in the next two decades and sought the Patons out on each occasion.[57]

Douglas and Alan took a keen interest in the major writing projects the other engaged in during the sixties. Both focused on the African problem—the former was a biography of Arthur Shearly Cripps, saintly Anglican missionary to Rhodesia; the latter, a biography of Jan Hofmeyr, Jan Smuts' younger colleague and Paton's mentor in non-violent ending of apartheid.[58] Paton envisioned Hofmeyr's model for South Africa as the one most likely to overcome the deep divisions and lead to an inclusive society.

Douglas Steere's remarkable capacity for caring through letter writing got one of its severest tests in the case of his intimate friends Henry and Betty Van Dusen. In the Younger Christian Thinkers, who began meeting in 1933, he and Henry forged the strong spiritual and social ties that welded them together. As we have seen earlier, Henry arranged for Douglas to speak and teach at Union Theological Seminary repeatedly, including the Harry Emerson Fosdick Visiting Professorship in 1961-62. Douglas had reciprocated by involving Henry in such things as the East/West Churchmen's Colloquy in 1962. Following Van Dusen's retirement, he and Betty remained active, spending some time in South Africa. Henry also wrote a biography of Dag Hammarskjöld.[59] Henry, however, began to suffer from depression. In a letter to Douglas in 1964 he spoke of missing "responsibility for souls" during his retirement and a deepening of despair about three major areas—the ecumenical movement, especially the World Council of Churches; South Africa; and the Second Vatican Council and Pope Paul VI.[60] Except for a hiatus of two years as Van Dusen worked on the biography of Hammarskjöld,[61] he and Douglas kept up an active correspondence. In the early seventies his depression evidently deepened as his and Betty's health grew increasingly fragile. Late in January 1975 Elizabeth Stevens informed the Steeres that Henry and Betty had attempted suicide, but only Betty had succeeded. Their son, Hugh, sent the Steeres a statement his parents had prepared. Douglas, sensing how Henry must have felt with the way things turned out, immediately wrote him a letter "in which I poured out my love for him and my thankfulness for all that he had meant to me." Douglas then "begged him to follow out the searching wisdom of the old Abbé of Tourville to 'Go bankrupt! Let our Lord love you without justice! Say frankly, "He loves me because I do not deserve it; that is the wonderful thing about Him; and that is why I, in my turn, love Him as well as I can without worrying whether I deserve to be allowed to love Him. He loves me although I am not worthy; I love Him without being worthy of Love."' Douglas then went on to say, "I know no other way of loving God. Therefore burn your account book!"[62] He followed this with a second letter and sent both by Hugh. When questioned by others about his response to the suicides, Douglas replied, "My response is to give bottomless thanks to God for their lives and to trust them to the infinite merciful and redeeming love in the heart of God."[63]

So many other letters mirror the Steere mastery of the art of spiritual care through letter. One more will have to suffice, the Steeres' exchange of letters with Thomas Merton. What brought them together initially was a common concern for peacemaking. At the request of John C. Heidbrink, Secretary for Church Relations of the American Fellowship of Reconciliation, Douglas and Dorothy made a trip to the Abbey of Gethsemani on February 6, 1962. As one would expect, the hour and a half visit touched on other common interests—notably spirituality, encounter with persons of other faiths, and the possibility of starting an American branch of Una Sancta,[64]—and the bond grew through correspondence.[65]

The first of Douglas' letters came about a year later in response to Merton's sending a copy of *The Thomas Merton Reader*, and focused on Merton's ideas on spiritual direction as well as peacemaking.[66] There followed some exchanges about François Fénelon.[67] Thereafter, Douglas tried to keep Merton informed about the Second Vatican Council, penning personal notes from the first session he attended as the Quaker

313

Observer-Delegate[68] and sending copies of the Steere "Journal from Rome."

The happenings at the Council brought Merton's name to the surface immediately as Douglas and Godfrey Diekmann envisioned the idea of an ecumenical institute to explore spirituality.[69] When Father Abbot James Fox angered and disappointed Merton by refusing to let him attend the initial meeting at St. John's Abbey in Collegeville, Minnesota,[70] the Steeres did their best to offer personal care. Dorothy, receiving Merton's anguished letter[71] about the abbot's refusal while Douglas was away, candidly sized up the issue and outlined a strategy of personal care.

> The enclosed letter from Tom Merton speaks for itself. I think you sense how difficult it is for him to accept the discipline of his Abbot when he would so appreciate this kind of gathering. I should think it would be well worth writing to [Barnabas] Ahern [one of the persons attending] about him and his longing, if there is any chance that the Abbot's mind might be changed. What a human person he reveals himself to be in this letter, and how very warm and loving it is, as always! I feel so deeply thankful for his friendship, and I think we must be sure to go see him before too long. He sounds hungry for real friendship with people who share the same longings.[72]

Although the Abbot did not yield, Douglas did not give up his efforts to involve Merton in some way in the Institute, nor did Merton give up hope of taking part. Douglas sent a recap of the first meeting.[73] In March and April 1968 he explored with Merton whether the Abbey might not host the annual meeting of the Ecumenical Institute of Spirituality.[74] Sadly, the death of Merton on December 10 foreclosed on that possibility, but the Institute did visit the Abbey twice afterwards—January 1979 and 1996. Following Merton's death, moreover, it was Douglas Steere who was asked to write the Foreword to

Merton's *The Climate of Monastic Prayer,* published also as *Contemplative Prayer.*[75]

Travel Letters of Douglas and Dorothy Steere

The Steere travel letters, more than eighty in all, have supplied much of the material for this biography along with Douglas' journal and need not receive extended comment except to underline how important they were in Douglas' ministry. Looking back, he wrote that these were "perhaps one of the most effective vehicles of communication that I have ever discovered."[76] The American Friends Service Committee and the Friends World Committee for Consultation who sponsored and distributed them, as well as many individual recipients, concurred in that judgment. Like Minona Kashi, a Japanese Friend studying at Harvard, many found that the letters "have stirred my imagination and thinking very much."[77] Gerard Casey in Kenya found "so much in these excellent papers that is stimulating and thought-provoking."[78] Kenneth I. Brown, after reading the "superb" Lambeth report, urged Douglas to write "either an autobiography of the Spirit, or your own magna charta of spiritual freedom and maturity" and include and expand many of the deep spiritual insights from the travel letters.[79] On reading the *Travel Journal of Douglas and Dorothy Steere, 1970-71,* 3 and 4, Will Fox discerned what made the travel letters so illuminating and instructive for many:

> Long ago you must have realized that you have been given a most remarkable gift for finding your way rapidly to the real person of those you meet; not only have you accepted the responsibility of such a gift, but I am sure you have disciplined yourself to develop it and then use it to the glory of God. Again & again I marvel in these Jnals. at the way you can make such good use of brief encounters by having really meaningful times

while most of us waste them in superficialities. More and more I really do find I am accepting some new contact as a potentially "holy" occasion—because each one of us is a unique expression of [the One] who has created us.[80]

The Steere travel letters did much more than record their itineraries. They were an integral part of the worldwide ministry of Douglas and Dorothy Steere. Readers will discern some evolution over thirty-five years, but all of the letters retained the warm, engaging personal style and sense of presence which marked letters to individuals. They brimmed over with information bearing on the worldwide mission of the Religious Society of Friends,[81] but persons obviously mattered most to Douglas and Dorothy Steere. With their vivid personal style, they enabled Quakers and others all over the world to travel with them to places the readers could not visit personally, to become acquainted with the challenges with which a rapidly changing world confronted them, to see what individuals and groups such as the American Friends Service Committee or the Friends World Committee for Consultation were doing, to claim ownership for some part of a global mission, and to gain a vision for their own participation in it. In person and in their letters the Steeres put before others challenging lives and searching invitations.

Notes

1. Douglas V. Steere, UNPUBLISHED JOURNAL, 532.
2. Bess Steere, *Letter to Douglas and Dorothy Steere*, August 13, 1962.
3. A. Burns Chalmers, *Letter to Douglas V. Steere*, May 6, 1968.
4. Tim Kinsolving, *Letter to Douglas V. Steere*, January 21, 1969.
5. Ellen Douglas Leyburn, *Letter to Douglas V. Steere*, December 16, 1962.
6. Deborah Halfdan-Nielsen, *Letter to Douglas V. Steere*, July 24, 1968.
7. Douglas V. Steere, *Letter to Edward M. Steere*, February 27, 1925.
8. Douglas V. Steere, *Letter to Edward M. Steere*, June 9, 1946.
9. Douglas V. Steere, *Letter to Edward and Ruby Steere*, December 11, 1939.
10. Douglas V. Steere, *Letter to Edward and Ruby Steere*, postmarked May 30, 1946.
11. Douglas V. Steere, *Letter to Edward and Inez Steere*, July 14, 1946.
12. Douglas V. Steere, *Letter to Edward M. Steere*, June 8, 1936.
13. Steere, JOURNAL, 45.
14. Douglas V. Steere, *Letter to Dorothy M. Steere*, August 13, 1940.
15. Douglas V. Steere, *Letter to Dorothy M. Steere*, August 28, 1940.
16. Douglas V. Steere, *Letter to Dorothy M. Steere*, September 6, 1940.
17. Douglas V. Steere, *Letter to Dorothy M. Steere*, October 6, 1940.
18. Douglas V. Steere, *Letter to Dorothy M. Steere*, December 4, 1940.
19. He wrote immediately on his return to Rome October 27 and followed with letters on October 29 and 30.
20. See Dorothy M. Steere, *Letter to Douglas V. Steere*, November 1, 10, 1964. She was saddened that the peace statement had not gone well.
21. Dorothy M. Steere, *Letter to Douglas V. Steere*, undated.
22. Dorothy M. Steere, *Letter to Douglas V. Steere*, January 4, 1965.
23. Dorothy M. Steere, *Letter to Douglas V. Steere*, February 28, 1965.
24. E.g., Douglas V. Steere, *Letter to Dorothy M. Steere*, April 27, 1965, from the Disciplined Order retreat near Kansas City; Dorothy M. Steere, *Letter to Douglas V. Steere*, April 27, 1965, sending mail.
25. E.g., during the initial meeting of the Ecumenical Institute of Spirituality at Collegeville, Dorothy M. Steere, *Letter to Douglas V. Steere*, September 1, 1965.
26. Douglas V. Steere, *Letter to Dorothy M. Steere*, October 2, 4, 5, during a trip to England.
27. Dorothy M. Steere, *Letter to Douglas V. Steere*, New Delhi, India, May 18, 1966.
28. Dorothy M. Steere, *Letter to Douglas V. Steere*, Beirut, Lebanon, May 25, 1966.

29. Douglas V. Steere, *Letter to David Richie,* July 11, 1947.

30. Douglas V. Steere, *Letter to Uniola Adams,* May 2, 1961.

31. Douglas V. Steere, *Letter to Mildred Ringwalt,* May 25, 1961.

32. Douglas V. Steere, *Letter to Lillian Hughes,* November 30, 1961.

33. Douglas V. Steere, *Letter to Richard Keithan,* January 8, 1962.

34. Douglas V. Steere, *Letter to Pat Hislop,* undated but found in November 1969 correspondence.

35. Pat Hislop, *Letter to Douglas V. Steere,* June 18, 1973, thanked him for his "wonderful" letter and explained her decision. In a letter dated December 17 she reported loving care by Friends at her baptism and clarity about her decision.

36. Douglas V. Steere, *Letter to Maria Schlüter-Hermkes,* October 8, 1948.

37. Douglas V. Steere, *Letter to the Rt. Rev. George Appleton,* January 20, 1969.

38. Douglas V. Steere, *Letter to Charles Malik,* undated but obviously around the time of Appleton's installation.

39. Douglas V. Steere, *Letter to Charles Malik,* June 10, 1969. Malik replied on June 25, promising to do his best to get in touch with Heschel the next time he was in New York. October 16, 1969, Malik wrote to apologize that he had been unable to meet with Heschel due to his hospitalization and commended Quaker peace efforts in the Middle East.

40. Douglas V. Steere, *Letter to Claire Huchet Bishop,* October 8, 1969.

41. Douglas V. Steere, *Letter to Deborah Halfden-Nielsen,* May 3, 1961.

42. Douglas V. Steere, *Letter to Curtis Watson,* May 24, 1961.

43. Douglas V. Steere, *Letter to Gunnar Sundberg,* January 23, 1973.

44. In his JOURNAL, 218, he commented that she and Elin Wägner, one of Sweden's leading women writers who had joined the Religious Society of Friends the year before, "are really the stuff of those great mystical women of the 13th and 14th centuries." In a *Letter to Dorothy M. Steere,* June 20, 1939, he gave notable attention to a lecture on Birgitta of Sweden by Emelia Fogelklou Norlind. He corresponded also with Wägner, e.g. December 25, 1944, to comment on his fear lest Quaker work in Finland be a "meditation circle for the leisured class."

45. Emelia Fogelklou Norlind, *Letter to Douglas V. Steere,* May 12, 1939.

46. Emelia Fogelklou Norlind, *Letter to Douglas V. Steere,* April 8, 1948.

47. Emelia Fogelklou Norlind, *Letter to Douglas V. Steere,* May 12, 1948.

48. Emelia Fogelklou Norlind, *Letter to Douglas V. Steere,* January 19, 1949.

49. Douglas V. Steere, *Letter to Emelia Fogelklou Norlind,* June 7, 1954.

50. See Emelia Fogelklou Norlind, *Letter to Douglas V. Steere,,* July 4, 1959; Howard Lutz, *Letter to Douglas V. Steere,* November 27, 1972; June 30, 1973.

51. Emelia Fogelklou Norlind, *Letter to Douglas and Dorothy Steere*, February 3, 1966.

52. Douglas V. Steere, *Letter to Emelia Fogelklou Norlind*, August 3, 1970; *Letter to Dorothy M. Steere*, August 6, 1970.

53. Steere, JOURNAL, 605-7.

54. Douglas V. Steere, *Letter to Alan Paton*, October 27, 1953.

55. Alan Paton, *Letter to Douglas V. Steere*, November 6, 1953.

56. Douglas V. Steere, *Letter to Alan Paton*, December 12, 1953.

57. See Douglas V. Steere, *Letter to Alan Paton*, January 16, 1961, regarding hopes for a luncheon meeting and visit during a July 31-August 1 stopover. The last visit occurred in 1975.

58. Alan Paton, *Letter to Douglas V. Steere*, July 21, 1964, noted that Oxford University Press would publish his biography of Hofmeyr October 1 and that he was looking forward to Douglas' biography of Cripps. Douglas V. Steere, *Letter to Alan Paton*, March 23, 1965, thanked him for a copy of the Hofmeyr biography and gave a fairly detailed review. He promised a brief review for *Friends Journal* and a longer one when Scribners' published the book in the United States. Douglas' biography of Cripps, of course, did not appear until 1973. Paton wrote a review of it [Alan Paton, *Letter to Douglas V. Steere*, September 24, 1973].

59. Henry P. Van Dusen, *Dag Hammarskjöld: The Statesman and His Faith* (New York: Harper and Brothers, Publishers, 1967).

60. Henry P. Van Dusen, *Letter to Douglas V. Steere*, September 13, 1964.

61. See his letter February 16, 1967, apologizing that he had not written for two years due to his work on the biography.

62. Douglas V. Steere, *Letter to Henry P. Van Dusen*, cited in JOURNAL, 1975, 3.

63. Steere, JOURNAL, 4.

64. Douglas V. Steere, Unpublished "Notes on Conf. with Thos. Merton," Feb. 6, 1962. Heidbrink and Merton began corresponding in October 1961. *The Hidden Ground of Love*, edited by William Shannon (New York: Farrar, Straus, Giroux, 1985), 401-430, contains Merton's letters to Heidbrink.

65. The correspondence which is extant has been published in *The Merton Annual: Studies in Culture, Spirituality, and Social Concerns* (Collegeville, MN: Liturgical Press, 1994), 23-53.

66. Douglas V. Steere, *Letter to Thomas Merton*, March 7, 1963.

67. Merton wrote to Douglas on April 9 and Douglas responded on April 23. Merton wrote again on May 16 and Douglas replied on June 13, just after the death of Pope John XXIII. Douglas V. Steere, *Letter to Thomas Merton*, April 23, June 13, 1963.

68. Douglas V. Steere, *Letter to Thomas Merton,* September 30, 1963.

69. Douglas V. Steere, *Letter to Thomas Merton,* April 19, 1964.

70. In a journal entry for February 14, 1965, Thomas Merton, *A Vow of Conversation: Journals 1964-1965* (New York: Farrar, Straus, Giroux, 1988), 147f., found it hard to put his anger behind him.

71. Thomas Merton, *Letter to Douglas V. Steere,* February 20, 1965.

72. Dorothy M. Steere, *Letter to Douglas V. Steere,* February 23, 1965.

73. Thomas Merton, *Letter to Douglas V. Steere,* September 14, 1965.

74. Douglas V. Steere, *Letter to Thomas Merton,* March 25, April 22, 1968.

75. Thomas Merton, *The Climate of Monastic Prayer* (Kalamazoo, MI: Cistercian Publications, 1969); *Contemplative Prayer* (Garden City, NY: Doubleday, 1971), 9-14.

76. Steere, JOURNAL, 200.

77. Minona Kashi, *Letter to Douglas V. Steere,* August 26, 1967.

78. Gerard Casey, *Letter to Douglas V. Steere,* October 18, 1967.

79. Kenneth I. Brown, *Letter to Dorothy and Douglas Steere,* October 2, 1968.

80. F. Will Fox, *Letter to Douglas V. Steere,* May 14, 1971.

81. Florence Blaxall, *Letter to Douglas and Dorothy Steere,* June 4, 1971, marveled at "your abilities to take in so much."

XVIII

Existential Realist

$\mathcal{F}$or Douglas Steere, philosophy served as a handmaiden
in his urgent quest to know God. What met this need
most effectively was a philosophy which he designated
Existential Realism. The phrase is instructive, for it located
Douglas' personal stance vis-a-vis some of his chief philosophical mentors—Pascal, Kierkegaard, and Friedrich von Hügel.
He found in von Hügel's "Critical Realism" support for the
conviction which had already been taking shape in his own
experience, viz., the grounding of religious experience in the
Other. To fill in some deficiencies in von Hügel's thought, however, he drew on the Existentialism of Pascal and Kierkegaard.
In some reflections on the Stone Lectures which he gave at
Princeton Theological Seminary in 1957, he summarized his
philosophical perspectives and indicated their linkages.

> The final two messages searched my own philosophi-
> cal frame and, outside of my class seminars, reached
> as near as I have ever come to expounding my own
> philosophical position as an Existential Realist. They
> reflected my debt to Baron Friedrich von Hügel's re-
> alism: the givenness, the overagainstness, the thereness
> of the ultimate reality. The lectures equally highlighted
> Pascal's and Kierkegaard's Existentialism where the

accent is put so fiercely on the costly role of the subject: the response, the yielding, the vulnerable openness, the abandonment to the abyss of love that is the condition of receptivity that is required in order to be pierced by the ever-present Other.

Somewhat surprisingly perhaps, though logically, in light of his avowed debt to von Hügel and Blaise Pascal, Douglas proceeded further to identify his position in relation to the Roman Catholic existentialist Gabriel Marcel.

> In my own generation I have found that Gabriel Marcel has come as close as anyone to this position of Existential Realism. I must confess that I have always found Gabriel Marcel exasperating for only starting strains of thought and then for failing to carry them through. Certainly my own published writings while far from Marcel's brilliance of expression may well have suffered from much the same disease![1]

If we keep in mind that Douglas constantly drew wisdom from an endless number of other sources, piped it through his own fertile mind and sensitive heart, and poured it into his philosophical tank, we can use this statement as a guide to how he thought and how his philosophy took shape.

Knowing God

Knowing God was the issue which occupied Douglas Steere throughout most of his life. Not surprisingly in light of his long interest in prayer, he focused the question of "Apprehending and Being Apprehended," the title of his Stone Lectures, on the experience of adoration and corresponding thankfulness. Behind adoration and thanksgiving is a givenness, a transcendence, but they require on our part "a receptivity, an openness, a teachableness, a Mary-like sitting" in the presence of the Other.

In the realism of Baron von Hügel Douglas found the grounding he sought for prayer of adoration and thanksgiving. The Baron emphasized in an almost exaggerated way the mystery of communication which takes place between the apprehender and what is apprehended. Behind this mystery lies a profound gap between the two. In realism what is apprehended does not owe its existence to the act of being known by the mind. Yet neither does it deny that the apprehender and what is apprehended "really interpenetrate" one another. We can know and be known despite the mystery of the Other, but we must always make such claims with reticence. As in science there is "a mysterious surd" at the core of things which always escapes the scientists' observation, so too in the spiritual realm. The haunting sense of the unknown and unfinished lures the person of faith just as it does the creative person in any field, like Jan van Eyck inscribing in the corner of his paintings, *"Als Ich kan."* Douglas interpreted this to mean, 'This is not what I had hoped for, but it is the best I can manage.'"

Douglas raised the question as to whether in adoration we *want* to apprehend God. Humanly we do, but "the saints care nothing for the business of *knowing* God." They want only to *love God back* as God has loved them from all eternity.[2] Love transforms the will. Yet in the act of adoration there is evidence of apprehension, like Isaac Penington's, "I have met with my God. I have met with my Savior, and he hath not been present unto me without his salvation, but I have felt the healing drop upon my soul from within my soul under his wings."[3] Contrary to the view of Martin Buber and Abraham Heschel that this claim would It-ify God, Douglas argued that this need not be so. Buber himself observed that we can affirm what is deepest in another person without it-ifying the other. Jesus and the mystics called on others to open themselves to divine love. "In faith I face myself in a longing for the presence, and by grace my longing is met and fulfilled."[4]

Douglas thought that the existentialists', especially Pascal's and Kierkegaard's, contribution lay in identifying things that get in the way of communion with God or, as he phrased it, "cut us off from the living flame."[5] Realism invites us to communicate with the Given. Existentialism, on the other hand, forces us to look closely at the personal involvement required for knowing God. Pascal and Kierkegaard emphasized "the radical discontinuities" between God and our human intellect and would thus "prevent any easy escalator view of the intellect that would enable us to discover some ontological identity and pass smoothly and painlessly from one of these existent spheres to another."[6] Though not denying that an individual person may pass from one level to another—from the intellectual to that of love or from the ethical to the spiritual—they insist that such a person cannot go with a crowd but must go single file and at the price of suffering. What existentialism does is not new; it is essentially what ascetic theology has done for many centuries.

Existentialism, however, must always view itself as an auxiliary; it cannot function as an independent philosophical system. When it tries to do so, it runs the risk of lapsing into a "demonic nihilism," just as has happened in one of its modern wings. Combined with realism, it can carry out its fruitful function. Together, the two, each preserving its own integrity, can produce "a climate where prayer, worship, and inner transformation that can prepare men and women to speak to any age, can take place."[7]

Why don't human beings learn in this life how to pray, to be attentive to God, "to move with an awareness of God's presence"? That was the most serious of all questions for Douglas Steere, one who out of life experience found profoundly true T.S. Eliot's conviction that life is just a chance to learn how to pray. The answer he received from both existentialists and ascetics was that exposure to "the living flame" threatens our continuing as we are and we fear its cleansing power. As Kierkegaard put it, God would do away with something in every person. Existentialism digs down into the human subconscious resistances which destroy attention and block obedience. It exposes the deep insecurities and unconquered fears which prevent sustained attention. Like ascetic theology, it tries to reveal how much of our conscious and unconscious life must be done away with before we can arrive at a state of fearlessness. It does not try to make choices for us; rather, it is content to awaken us from our apathy, which the world thinks is normal, and to individuate us, singling us out of the crowd and compelling us to face the consequences of our choices. So thought Pascal and Kierkegaard and Miguel de Unamuno, the Spanish existentialist. Above all, choices force us to confront our own mortality to remind us of our crisis. In the extentialist approach lies implicit an answer to why we do not pray: to do so would produce a crisis in us that would transform, change, and strip us of our contrived security in our own little worlds. For them as for the ascetics, all sin is flight from attentiveness, dispersion, apathy, numbness. They do their best to expose this sin so that we may come to ourselves. Where a physician would say, "I bind the wound; God heals it," existential realists say, ""I unbind, I expose the wound; God heals it."[8]

Douglas Steere on "The Mystical Experience"

In a paper on "The Mystical Experience" delivered at a symposium on mysticism in 1966, Douglas left clear evidence of his lifelong passion to know God, as well as the continuing impact of Baron von Hügel. In this address he sought "to assess the legitimacy and the significance for religion, for ethics, for philosophy, and for culture of the substantial body of human experience down through the ages which has been called 'mystical' and which has claimed to have had direct and immediate touch with what is regarded as ultimate reality."[9] Asking whether the mystical experience was a regression to an infranoetic (within the mind only) condition,

325

he cited von Hügel, E.I. Watkin, and William Ernest Hocking against George Santayana. Santayana believed mysticism contributed nothing positive to culture but represented a reversion to an infranoetic condition or animallike sensualism which betrays whatever is significant in human culture. Von Hügel, Watkin, and Hocking, on the contrary, thought mystics gave direct confirmation of the highest human hopes: In *religion* mysticism witnesses directly "both to the unutterable holiness of the ground of being and to the well of infinite tenderness and love present there." This well is "directly accessible" to humankind and moves humanity in its depths. In *ethics* it restores the "inner bond" between persons. In *philosophy* it undergirds humanity's hope that it can bridge the "all-too-visible cleft" between its knowledge and what is ultimately real. The mystics have already crossed the cleft, so that although each branch of knowledge always remains provisional, it has some ultimate meaning.[10]

In response to whether the negative theology of the mystic is anti-intellectual, Douglas called on the witness of Teresa of Avilà, Meister Eckhart, Jan van Ruysbroeck, and John of the Cross to the contrary. In his own conclusions he clearly echoed Baron von Hügel. He believed that mystics, first of all, are concerned to witness to "the immeasurable plenitude" of what they have encountered. This is "a qualitative Other" which is "so majestically transcendent," "given," "over-against" that it could not possibly be a projection of themselves, their own goodness, or their own beauty. Second, the Other is "so full and so rich" that, in its presence, it silences all of their "cosmic compliments." Third, it "overfloods" the mystics' mental faculties and absorbs them into "the all-encompassing fullness of its ground" to such a degree that it causes distinctions between subject and object to disappear. At least for a moment the only appropriate response is the Vedic adoration, "Wonderful! Wonderful! Wonderful!" The whole history of mysticism negates the view that mystics are reduced to permanent silence, that their ethical insights "have remained forever after in the dazzling darkness," or that their mental powers have been "permanently anesthetized." There is no doubt at all, Douglas believed, that the mystics have something important to say about the ultimate nature of things, ethical values, and culture.[11] Besides, the negative theology holds together the two ends of the spectrum of mystical experience, that is, while God is ultimately unknowable in the fullness of the divine Being, still God is not so transcendent as to be inaccessible to human beings.

Despite the denial of mystics that experience of God can be fathomed, they have given oblique evidences of its reality: (1) in the counsel that mystics give those who want to prepare themselves for such experiences; (2) in reports of what the experience has done to their own lives; and (3) in tests used to distinguish false from authentic mystical experiences. Citing James B. Pratt and von Hügel, Douglas distinguished the mystical experience from what was once called "hysteria." The mystics evince strength of will and determination to serve the divine will.

Against those who would consider mystics enemies to ethics, religion, and culture, therefore, Douglas cast his lot with those who saw in them a source for the invigoration and revitalization of all three. In religion as in ethics and culture, mystics hold up their "secure experience of the fathomless ground of love" against the absoluteness of any one form or shape of the institution or of the dogmas that may have gotten out of line with the Divine Love that they have experienced.[12] The mystics may not supply a map, as William James has suggested, but they "point" to new territory. If there is a natural mysticism in all persons, more vivid mystical experiences articulate and fulfill these intimations. Mystics play a dual role—in their affirmation and fearlessness toward science and philosophy and in their witness to the fullness of what is ultimately real.

Douglas concluded this paper by positioning mystical experience vis-à-vis four well-known philosophical postures—

the Idealism of Hegel and Schelling, the Existentialism of Pascal, the Neo-Thomist Realism of Jacques Maritain, and the Critical Realism of Baron Friedrich von Hügel. Although he considered Hegelian idealism "a possible philosophical setting," he thought it "dubious" to equate idealism with mysticism. His high regard for Pascal and Kierkegaard notwithstanding, moreover, he found it difficult "ever to consider existentialism as more than an auxiliary or preparative philosophy, because of its readiness to ignore nature, to pour contempt on all ontology, and to lay its entire focus upon the willed choices of the subject."[13] Maritain made the final level of mystical revelation the capstone of his *Degrees of Knowing*, but, without any revision of its philosophy of nature or categories of sense or abstraction, his Thomism has not received the attention it deserves outside Roman Catholic circles.

Predictably, then, Douglas cast his lot with the critical realism of Baron von Hügel in a slightly revised form. Although von Hügel completed his work before existentialism swept the present generation, he stated a strong case for some form of *critical* realism as the most congenial and adequate philosophy to explain mystical phenomena. He, of course, framed his case against all forms of idealism as "inadequate to account for the givenness, the otherness, the sheer transcendent aspect of the mystical encounter."[14] Contrariwise, he believed realism "adequate not only to describe the inflooding of the mystical experience but the fact that, with the very miracle of communication, there was also an experience of a plenitude that transcended any vessels that the mind had to contain it."[15] Douglas proposed revision of von Hügel's position by adding "an existentialist dimension to deal with the many-dimensioned involvement of the self in any such mystical encounter." He thought the form of existential realism which would do justice to the phenomena of mysticism had been put forward "in fragmentary form" by Gabriel Marcel. But Marcel needed to give greater consideration to nature and to the aesthetical and ethical realms "to which it is the task of any adequate philosophy to respond."[16]

He closed with an apology for "betrayal" of the mystics. Mystical experience doesn't really require justification to science and philosophy. Yet the effort may be worthwhile if they can illuminate one another.

Douglas Steere and Baron von Hügel

The extent of von Hügel's influence on Douglas' existential realism merits closer examination, particularly to see where they diverged from one another. It would be difficult to determine who contributed most to the shaping of Douglas' thought—Rufus Jones or Friedrich von Hügel. Rufus Jones personally and the writings of both of them came into his life at a critical stage in his quest to know God and in the formation of his philosophy. The fact that Douglas wrote his dissertation on von Hügel's "attempt to interpret and evaluate mystical experience from the epistemological position of a 'critical realist'," however, assured a depth of attention to detail which even collegiality with Rufus Jones could not have guaranteed. Von Hügel's realism helped to reassure Douglas as his philosophy took shape that he would not end up empty-handed in his search for God. He found in von Hügel one who, *on most carefully reasoned and researched grounds,* had unshakeable confidence in God's "Is-ness."[17]

> The constantly recurring thesis in Friedrich von Hügel is the "givenness" of God. All men [and women] have a dim, somewhat implicit, but not the less direct experience of trans-subjective reality. When the content of this experience is most deeply explored it will be found to reveal the operative presence of a spiritual order.[18]

Von Hügel pointed Douglas down the path toward an adequate epistemology, and Douglas found few places where he disagreed. The Baron, according to Douglas' interpretation, based his "*critical* realism" on two principles: (1) that God exists independently of the perceiving mind and is not altered by the mind's apprehension and (2) that the presence of interpretative elements and possible error in human knowledge of God does not negate the relevance of such knowledge entirely.[19]

Focusing on the transcendent element in human apprehension of God, von Hügel asked not *whether* but *how* this apprehension is possible. He concluded that mystical experience can only be accounted for by an objective order—an Other. At home in the sciences and drawing from them abundant illustrations of the realistic approach to the religious realm, he insisted that even the most elemental knowledge is aroused by the impact of the Other, which "must be independent and distinctive enough to give the shock necessary to arousal."[20] The human mind is made to contemplate objects other than itself, just as the telescope is. To confirm his point, von Hügel probed into sense experience, experience of time, and experience of creative activity to discover the source of "a normative, independent, spiritual reality."[21] He was convinced that a spiritual order, a transcendent reality, penetrated nature at every point and could thus be discerned by human senses. Similarly, he argued that a sense of contingency, change, and finitude in human experience of time revealed "the operative presence of an infinite *Other* that serves to give worth and meaning to the successiveness of events."[22] Like Rufus Jones, he conceived of humans as "amphibians" who can experience spiritual reality in events of time. He found evidence of experience of the Other in human feeling that they have never quite learned all there is to know in any field. All true scientists, artists, philosophers, and moral strivers, at their best and deepest moments, sense that "some abiding trans-subjective other-than-human or even more-than-human reality or force, or law, is manifesting itself" in their experiences. They also know that their inter-

330

pretations of such reality "give but a very incomplete, ever imperfect, conception" of such realities.[23] Crossing paths with another whom Douglas would make a target of his subsequent research, von Hügel found in Kierkegaard "a monumental witness for the transcendent, objective nature of the religious object."[24]

Von Hügel did not stop at giving only the transcendent side, for that would lead to agnosticism. He went on to emphasize that the transcendent character of the Other implied "some degree of the operativeness of the Other upon the mind as its very condition."[25] The question he and other Realists struggled with was the *degree* of independence. Von Hügel did not give precise allegiance to any one position, but he generally subscribed to the *critical* realist view. As summarized by Douglas Steere, critical realism emphasized three points: (1) The Other is not *contained in* the mind, but it *is* apprehended there. (2) It is apprehended by the mind, "if not exhaustively at least with varying degrees of comprehension." (3) Although it possesses and retains its own integrity of content, it is sufficiently accessible for the mind to gain its outlines and grasp its general laws.[26] Sometimes, Douglas thought, von Hügel rose so high in his focus on transcendence that he did not make room for the mind to "transcend" the transcendence of its object, so as to "know of the nature of its object" to a significant degree.[27] So concerned was he to root out agnosticism that he made no attempt to justify the operativeness of the religious Object on the mind. He believed that scepticism posed as much danger to science as to religion.

It was, however, Douglas believed, as evidence for "the degree of relevance" of our knowledge of God that von Hügel made his real contribution. He divided evidences into two classes: (1) not only evidence for the existence of God but clues to the nature of God also in common experiences of objects in space, events in time, and acts of will, and (2) vivid religious experiences which bring "a penetrating note of clear insight" which could help us interpret less direct and less vivid evidence.[28] Von Hügel accentuated the contrast between human and divine, but he left room for human experience of God: "God is beyond even our noblest and deepest conceptions, yet [God] is beyond them in their direction, [God] is definitely nobler and deeper than them all."[29] He did not, therefore, go as far as Otto in emphasizing otherness nor certainly as far as Karl Barth, for whom God was totally Other.

In the mystics von Hügel, and Douglas after him, discerned "an even more telling witness to human capacity" to experience God.[30] Mystical experience enables one to apprehend not only the *that* but to some extent the *what* of the Transcendent. Von Hügel, however, did not accept the experience of mystics uncritically. He used the most rigorous tests. Yet Douglas thought he did not pay sufficient attention to the mystics who emphasized God's unknowability. "By knowing *what* God is not, then, the mystic has indeed expressed a considerable degree of knowledge in which he has done more than communicate *that* God is but has begun as well to apprehend *what* God is."[31]

Although von Hügel replied to Feuerbach rather than to modern psychologists, Douglas was convinced that he had responded adequately to psychologists' charging the mystics with *illusionism*. Von Hügel admitted excesses in the mystical element which led to such charges but divided criticisms into three groups. He saw grounds for the charge of illusion in one group, namely, Quietism and a tendency to ignore Evil. He admitted, too, that certain personalities, such as Catherine of Genoa, are particularly subject to auto-suggestion and mon-ideism. Whether an experience is caused by the Other can neither be proved nor disproved by ascribing it to these. He also conceded that symptoms of mystical experience are similar to those experienced by deranged persons, but he distinguished Catherine's from experiences of hysteria on the grounds that she maintained a synthesis of different elements in her personality—notably in administering the Pammatone Hospital—which distinguished her experiences from the hysterical. Von Hügel focused not on the *presence* but on the *use* of such experiences. He found additional evidence needed to verify the experience of the mystics

> not by surface sensations, visions or ecstacies, but rather by its underlying fruitfulness in illuminating other experience, in restoring a freshness and resiliency to the life of the experiences, in energizing the will to a new and higher level of integrated activity, of so unifying and concentrating all of the cognitive, volitional and imaginative powers as to greatly heighten their selective capacity resulting frequently in fresh, creative moral and spiritual insights.[32]

Catherine moved from egocentric to integrated theocentric. Nonetheless, von Hügel did not ask special consideration of critics of mysticism but put his case alongside theirs. Even the mystics recognized the danger of illusion, anthropomorphism, and naive realism and did not think their experiences infallible. Mathematical certainty, which would reduce the subjective element almost to nothing, is virtually unattainable. Subject and Object cannot be separated so neatly in religious experience, and the interpretative element must play a greater role in this field.

Douglas spotted "a most glaring defect" in von Hügel's failure to make a systematic inquiry into the nature of the process through which the mystical experience occurred. The latter emphasized the *volitional* and only hinted at the *imaginative* or *interpretative*. He stressed the intense stimulation and energization of the deep levels of "imagination" and will as one of the chief marks of mystical apprehension. He did not give much attention to the systematic use of traditional mystical stages—purgation, meditation, contemplation, and union, but Douglas believed he made some "exceptionally valuable, and as far as I know, original suggestions" regarding ascetic disciplines which free the mystic from "the clamorous physical and psychical whims of the undisciplined self," which make it hard to keep the mind focused on God.[33] He emphasized the importance of religious institutions to preserve and transmit tradition.

Douglas found another deficiency here in the fact that von Hügel had not answered Kant's contention that no knowledge arises except by sense perception, and had not shown how mystical perception may transcend the senses. "He has not shown how mystical apprehension may take the interpretative function of the mind which normally operates upon sense materials, and transform it for its purposes into a direct organ of apprehension."[34] Nevertheless, von Hügel mitigated this grave omission by his *critical* realism. He thought that mystics recognize the inadequacy and yet at the same time are convinced that they can really know God. This sense of inadequacy is called on to witness to the very Objectivity and Transcendence of God. Von Hügel readily admitted that no human knowledge escapes the shadow of error but insisted that, if one applies all the tests, the likelihood of illusion is reduced.

In a concluding critique of von Hügel's critical realism, Douglas, although strongly appreciative, raised three questions: (1) In his analysis of mystical apprehension, von Hügel failed to relate sense perception to the type of apprehension involved, as his approach seemed to require. Mystics had learned to prepare for the invasion by God "by pulling in the drawbridges to the outer world of physical activity, by the slow process of learning to still them . . ." How, then, could von Hügel "regard *mystical apprehension* as in a continuous succession with the processes operative in ordinary sense perception?"[35] He needed to do more with imagination. Had he carried his study further, he probably would not have done that; instead, he would have pressed deeper into study of volition rather than imagination. (2) Is "critical realism" the best way to describe the mystics' way of knowing? Or is it "an alien system of interpretation imported from the realm of sense perception?"[36] (3) Has von Hügel himself sought in his mature years "to provide an intellectual corrective for the mystical enthusiasm of his earlier years?"[37] Such questions notwithstanding, Douglas sustained the Baron's realism against the idealism of his colleague Rufus Jones. In the final analysis, von Hügel's treatment of the problem of mysticism and its realistic interpretation was "almost invariably *practical* rather than *theoretical,*"[38] showing that he "at bottom remained ever a voluntarist."[39]

Douglas Steere and the Existentialists

How to know God drew Douglas Steere toward the realism of Baron von Hügel. Why more people do not hunger for such knowledge pulled him toward the existentialism of Pascal, Kierkegaard, Unamuno, and Heidegger. It is not hard to discern what attracted Douglas Steere toward Blaise Pascal and Søren Kierkegaard, whom he labeled "the Danish Pascal."[40] Both had deep insight into human nature. Although Douglas could criticize Kierkegaard because of an excessive emphasis on the *solitary* and inadequate social perspective, he shared Kierkegaard's intense concern for *the individual*[41] and opposition to Hegelian Idealism which made the individual "a mere passing-point, a moment, in the cosmic process."[42] "Central in the thought of Søren Kierkegaard is his master category *the individual,*" Douglas noted in his "Translator's Introduction" to *Purity of Heart*. "All of his thought ultimately had to pass through the needle's eye of whether or not it compelled men [and women] to face their sovereign responsibility as individuals."[43] Just as Kierkegaard posited whatever hope there was of rescuing the Danish church from its absorption into the mass or the prevailing culture in the individual, so Douglas placed his confidence "in the intensification of the life of God in the individual hearts of men [and women]."[44] Against the background of two world wars, a massive depression, and the resurrection of extreme nationalism Kierkegaard made far better sense than a liberal Idealism which regarded modern science, philosophy, and ethics as manifestations of the will of God.[45]

Martin Heidegger's thought was not integrated into Douglas' to the same extent as Pascal's and Kierkegaard's, but he put to his contemporaries some of the same critical questions Pascal and Kierkegaard raised for theirs. Douglas considered Heidegger "Germany's greatest philosopher" and, by comparison with Karl Jaspers and Nicholai Hartmann, "out of all proportion the more original and the one whose contribution will be likely to last."[46] Heidegger emphasized the "givenness" (*Dasein*) of human existence and the importance of the human search for meaning. These ideas were making a major impact on German theology, e.g., on the systematic theology of Paul Tillich and the New Testament interpretation of Rudolph Bultmann. Douglas went out of his way to visit Heidegger during his trips to Germany, beginning in 1947. Heidegger's Nazi leanings had resulted in his removal from a teaching post after World War II and exile in Todtnauberg, a small village near Freiburg. But that did not deter Douglas from making calls and interpreting Heiddeger's thought sympathetically. He stoutly defended him against charges of atheism.[47] Heidegger received Douglas warmly and obviously appreciated the Steere visits. When Douglas came on August 14, 1950, Heidegger met his bus, a half hour's climb to his hut, and showed much interest in the model of Pendle Hill as an alternative to the university. He, too, took pleasure in the search for what lies at the heart of things.

DOROTHY AND DOUGLAS AT VICTORIA FALLS
1955

DOUGLAS STEERE WITH HIS FATHER, EDWARD
1952

FRIENDS CENTER IN TOKYO
1970

YUKI BRINTON, DOROTHY AND DOUGLAS STEERE
WITH FRIENDS AT PENDLE HILL

AFSC INTERNATIONAL WORK CAMP GROUP FOR
RELIEF AND RECONSTRUCTION IN FINLAND

1976

RELAXING
AT MACKINAW

DOROTHY'S 75TH BIRTHDAY
1982

GRAND OPENING OF THE NEW FIRBANK CRAFT STUDIO
AT PENDLE HILL

Douglas Fishing at
Helen's Farm
1970s

Douglas
July 26, 1984

DOROTHY AND DOUGLAS
DIABLO, WASHINGTON
1985

Douglas V. Steere
ON THE OCCASION OF BEING AWARDED
THE Decoration OF
Knight First Class of the White Rose of Finland
"IN RECOGNITION OF HIS SERVICES ON BEHALF OF FINLAND."
1987

Notes

1. Douglas V. Steere, UNPUBLISHED JOURNAL, 745.
2. Douglas V. Steere, "Apprehending and Being Apprehended," 3, 13f. Underline mine.
3. Cited in Steere, "Apprehending," 3, 14.
4. Steere, "Apprehending," 3, 16.
5. Steere, "Apprehending," 4, 1. Douglas assigned to this lecture the theme of "Apprehension and the Living Flame."
6. Steere, "Apprehending," 4, 5.
7. Steere, "Apprehending," 4, 7.
8. Steere, "Apprehending," 4, 15.
9. Douglas V. Steere, "The Mystical Experience," in *Together in Solitude* (New York: Crossroad, 1982), 129.
10. Steere, "The Mystical Experience,"140-41.
11. Steere, "The Mystical Experience,"145.
12. Steere, "The Mystical Experience,"149.
13. Steere, "The Mystical Experience,"155.
14. Steere, "The Mystical Experience,"154.
15. Steere, "The Mystical Experience,"155.
16. Steere, "The Mystical Experience,"155.
17. One cannot overestimate how crucial the discovery of von Hügel was to Douglas. His study at Harvard (1923-1925) had plunged him into near despair for a time (cf. Chapter 3, p. 5). Although he regained his equilibrium, he was just beginning to make some headway in his search when he went to Oxford as a Rhodes Scholar (1925-28). Von Hügel died in 1925 and must have come to Douglas' attention as he began his studies. Reading some of the Baron's writings would have quickly shown him how much von Hügel could "speak to his condition." The very formulation of Douglas' dissertation topic shows that he expected the Baron to help him resolve the burning issue of his life—how can we know God.
18. Douglas V. Steere, "Critical Realism in the Religious Philosophy of Baron Friedrich von Hügel," Unpublished Ph.D. Dissertation, Harvard University, 1931, 5.
19. Steere, "Critical Realism," 13.
20. Steere, "Critical Realism," 61.
21. Steere, "Critical Realism," 64.
22. Steere, "Critical Realism," 72.
23. Friedrich von Hügel, *Essays and Addresses in the Philosophy of Religion*, 63-64; cited in Steere, "Critical Realism," 98.
24. Steere, "Critical Realism," 107.

25. Steere, "Critical Realism," 125.
26. Steere, "Critical Realism," 127-8.
27. Steere, "Critical Realism," 128.
28. Steere, "Critical Realism," 134.
29. Von Hügel, *Essays and Addresses,* 2nd series, 181. Cited in Steere, "Critical Realism," 139.
30. Steere, "Critical Realism," 146.
31. Steere, "Critical Realism," 164.
32. Steere, "Critical Realism," 194.
33. Steere, "Critical Realism," 230f.
34. Steere, "Critical Realism," 267.
35. Steere, "Critical Realism," 291.
36. Steere, "Critical Realism," 295.
37. Steere, "Critical Realism," 296.
38. Steere, "Critical Realism," 306.
39. Steere, "Critical Realism," 308.
40. Douglas V. Steere, "Translator's Introduction," to Søren Kierkegaard's *Purity of Heart Is to Will One Thing* (New York: Harper & Row, Publishers, 1938), 9.
41. He dedicated the work to "That Solitary Individual."
42. Steere, trans., *Purity of Heart,* 17.
43. Steere, trans., *Purity of Heart,* 14.
44. See Chapter 15, 287.
45. Note Douglas' differentiation of his views from those of Rufus Jones on this point in Chapter 13, n. 51.
46. *News from Douglas Steere,* British Zone 4, Germany, December 15, 1947, 2.
47. In JOURNAL, 1976, 4, Douglas wrote: "Knowing him, I had never accepted the widespread myth of his atheism."

XIX

---◆---

"Life Lent to Be Spent"

"*L*ife was lent to be spent" was a Douglas Steere axiom, and he kept spending his generously until the late eighties when Alzheimer's disease began to take its toll. After wrapping up his second term as clerk of the Friends World Committee for Consultation with one last swing through Africa, Asia, and Europe in 1971, he and Dorothy scarcely changed pace or activities. Many people, not just Friends, still looked to them as models and guides, and they kept giving of themselves without stint.

A Busy and Useful Retirement

The *extent* of Steere activities in this busy and useful retirement boggles the mind almost as much as the earlier part of the story. Although Douglas retired from it in 1963, the Steeres continued a close association with Haverford College. They lived in the Rufus Jones House on the campus, and Douglas had an office in the Quaker Library until they moved to Quadrangle, a full-care retirement complex, in late 1989.[1] In 1973 the Provost asked him to serve for a year on the T. Wistar Brown selection committee. The College invited him to deliver the commencement address for 1978, giving him an opportunity to reminisce about persons who had made his career very special—Henry Gillett, Rendel Harris, Rufus

Jones, Albert Schweitzer, Martin Buber, Pope John XXIII.[2] In 1984 Douglas took part in the Gest Committee of Haverford College, a group deliberating on lecturers for the school's cross-cultural study of religions.

Douglas continued to publish. His biography of Arthur Shearly Cripps[3] finally appeared in the fall of 1973. His first book, *Prayer and Worship,* was republished in 1978. At the same time he agreed to edit a volume on *Quaker Spirituality*[4] for the Classics of Western Spirituality series published by the Paulist Press. In 1982 he collected several previously published essays for *Together in Solitude*[5] and in 1987 another collection for *Gleanings,* to which he added a brief spiritual auto-biography, "Mind Your Call."[6] He also published pamphlets,[7] journal articles,[8] and forewords or articles for books written or edited by others.[9]

The Steeres continued their visitations. Although prostate surgery in July, 1975 prevented Douglas' return to Japan to participate in the ninth annual Buddhist/Christian collo-quium as he had hoped,[10] he managed to follow up on a "con-cern" to make a third trip to southern Africa, October 6 to November 20, 1975. Once again, he offered encouragement to groups of Friends throughout southern Rhodesia and South Africa. Coming shortly after the appearance of *God's Irregular: Arthur Shearly Cripps,* the Rhodesian portion of his journey raised poignant memories. The Bishop of Mashona-land told Douglas that he had been so touched by the account of Cripps walking or running thirty-two miles between the mission stations in Mashonaland that he was visiting throughout his entire diocese of 460 miles in 1975. In South Africa Douglas again spent time with such long-term anti-apartheid activists as Alan Paton, Edgar Brookes, Bishop Zulu, and Fred Van Wyck, the Secretary General of the South Afri-can Race Relations Institute, and made new acquaintances such as Beyers Naude, founder and secretary of the Christian Institute, vigorous opponent of apartheid, and advocate of the full economic, social and political rights of each person.[11]

More strikingly, the Steeres visited Europe almost every year from 1974, until a fall hospitalized Dorothy in 1984. Even after that, Douglas scheduled a brief visit from April 29 until May 24, 1985. Commissioned in part by the Friends World Committee for Consultation, the visits gave Douglas and Dorothy an opportunity to do an inventory of long-standing concerns. Many familiar names, places, and interests dating back to their earliest visits to Europe turned up in reports on these journeys.

Throughout their journeys they focused on ministry to Friends, holding retreats, speaking, and otherwise providing encouragement; they included numerous other concerns as well. One was *ecumenism*. In 1974, 1976, and 1979, for instance, they again visited the Commission for Promoting Christian Unity and the Secretariat for the Non-Christian Religions in Rome. "My agenda was to get from each of them their estimate of the effectiveness of the new Secretariat of the Non-Christian Religions which in my eyes was one of the most important potential steps that Vatican II had taken," Douglas remarked concerning the 1974 visit.[12] Changes in leadership and improved relations between the Secretariat and the Committee on the World Religions of the World Council of Churches encouraged him. In 1974 the Steeres also visited in Geneva with John Taylor, director of the Committee on World Religions of the wcc. A second concern was *peacemaking*. They contacted peacemakers in various places: in 1974 Hans Schuppli, a Swiss Quaker who had spent four months locked up in an old castle for protesting the required military service, in Lützelfluh; Magda Trocmé, recently widowed by the death of André, in Geneva; and Vivi Paquet-Woeller near Coblenz; in 1976 Jan Brugelman, son of Asta, a very active leader in the German FOR, and Vivi Paquet-Woeller in Coblenz; Carl Friedrich von Weizsäcker in Münich; Annemarie Cohen in Konstanz; Anny Pflüger in Zürich; in 1979 IFOR Secretary Jim Forest at Alkmaar, Holland, the center for European IFOR; Vivi Paquet-Woeller near Coblenz and Margarete Lachmund[13] in Cologne; Hildegard Goss-Meyer in Vienna; and Hans Schuppli in Lützelfluh.

A third was *Quaker work in Scandinavia*. They checked on the progress of various projects they had helped to implement years before: in 1974 Gunnar Sundberg's Folk High School in Stockholm and Sven Ryberg's experimental farm opened to others besides Quakers in the area; Esko Saari at Viittakivi and Heikki and Emmy Waris in Finland; in 1976 friends involved in the Finnish Relief project and in Viittakivi.

The Steeres continued an already vital spiritual ministry. Their nearly annual retreats at Pendle Hill were noted earlier. Other retreats among Quaker and various Protestant groups were too numerous to give a specific list. What especially distinguished this phase of their ministry was its expansion to include an increasing number of Roman Catholic groups. Douglas spoke several times at Rosemont College near Philadelphia between 1973 and 1984. He did a number of retreats for various religious orders in the seventies and eighties. He lectured at the Abbey of Gethsemani. He led a retreat for Christian Brothers in Sante Fe, New Mexico. He gave lectures to the Christian Brothers in Windsor, Ontario. He addressed the annual gathering of the Sisters of Loretto in Nerinx, Kentucky, and spoke to the community during a meeting of the Ecumenical Institute of Spirituality .

The Steeres continued vital participation in the Ecumenical Institute of Spirituality and other organizations devoted to the promotion of spirituality. Douglas served as a trustee on numerous boards. Besides Pendle Hill, these included the boards of the Earlham School of Religion (1975-84), the Lewis M. Stevens Trust, Wainwright House, and *Religion in Life*. Numerous other organizations sought the Steeres' counsel on spirituality. Douglas' service to the Upper Room in Nashville was noted in an earlier chapter. In 1973 the Steeres led a Lilly Endowment conference on the spiritual life in Marriotsville, Maryland. During the summer of 1976, they participated in a three-day discussion organized by the Lilly

Foundation on "the most effective ways, in our dispersed lives, to deepen the interior life of prayer."[14] In 1977 Tilden Edwards called on Douglas to take part in an evaluation of Shalem, an institute for spiritual formation and direction in Washington, DC, with a group of scholars, teachers, and clergy.

Douglas remained a well-known speaker on spirituality during these years. In 1974 he addressed the Women's National Day of Prayer at Riverside Church in New York. In February 1975 at Washington University in St. Louis, he took part in the celebration of the 100th anniversary of Albert Schweitzer's birth, giving a testimony as to what Schweitzer meant to him and a University lecture on the topic, "By Whose Clock Do We Run?"[15] Shortly after this, he spoke to several classes, lectured to the faculty on the Quaker way of reaching decisions, and gave a founder's day address at Guilford College in North Carolina. In 1976 he spent the month of May in residence and gave the annual Shaffer Lectures at Northwestern University in Evanston, Illinois, on "Four Explorers of the Inner Life" and "The Conspiracy against the Interior Life."[16]

In 1978 Douglas spoke at Princeton Theological Seminary, shared a panel at General Theological Seminary in New York with Peter Berger and Robert Thurman of Amherst College, and chaired a panel at Columbia University commemorating the tenth anniversary of the death of Thomas Merton. In 1979 Douglas spoke in Sage Chapel at Cornell University and in the Upper Room in Nashville, which honored him with its national award. Douglas contributed significantly to the design of the Academy for Spiritual Formation and lectured to the first Academy in October 1983, and continued do so regularly up to 1990.[17] He also gave a public lecture recounting his own spiritual pilgrimage at Wake Forest University in 1983.[18] He continued to lecture or give retreats at Wainwright House as late as December of 1987.[19]

In 1978 Leslie and Nellie Blasius honored him by establishing the Douglas Steere Lectures at Bay View, Michigan, requesting that Douglas himself do the honors the first two years. Modestly, Douglas remarked, "It proves again that the Lord has a sly sense of humor."[20] Predictably, he focused, as he did on numerous other occasions, on persons from whom he had learned much about the spiritual life: Meister Eckhart, John Woolman, Søren Kierkegaard, Evelyn Underhill, Thomas Kelly, Bernanos, Simone Weil, Friedrich von Hügel, Arthur Shearly Cripps, and Charles Williams. Douglas recommended other lecturers to Bay View up to 1987.[21]

The Steeres continued, too, their ministry by letter. In his *Journal, 1983-1984* Douglas mentioned somewhat poignantly letters of encouragement written to so many and noted the illnesses of many, many friends. Time had taken its toll, but both Douglas and Dorothy persisted in embracing others in their trials with the same warm attentiveness they had shown throughout their lives. They shared experiences in the spiritual life. They consoled friends when spouses died, when they were ill, when they needed encouragement. Others reciprocated when those who had ministered to them had to be ministered to. February 3, 1984 Dorothy slipped on ice and fell on the Haverford campus, where she had gone to hear Angela Davis. She broke her hip. On February 5, she underwent surgery. Douglas had to cancel their tickets for a trip to Europe they had scheduled for May and to write dozens of letters to people they had planned to visit. Flowers, letters, and cards poured in, and women at Radnor Meeting organized a "look after Douglas" movement.

God's Irregular: Arthur Shearly Cripps, a Rhodesian Epic

Douglas invested so much time and energy in writing a biography of Arthur Shearly Cripps that, among the activities of his mature years, it merits special consideration. It might seem a little strange to those who did not know Douglas Steere that an American Quaker would write a biography of a high church Anglican missionary to Rhodesia. The idea originated

344

during the Steeres' journey to Salisbury (now Harare in Zimbabwe) either in 1953 or 1955 and grew firmer in Douglas' mind in the fall of 1957. Before leaving Salisbury, Douglas took another look at the old trunk in the public archive in which Cripps' papers were held. "I came away with an even stronger resolution that when I retired at Haverford I wanted to write a biography of the life of this amazing poet, saint and Christian presence," he reported in his Journal years later, "one of my dreams that some seven years later I was able to undertake, although it was not until 1973 that it was actually published."[22] Between the third and fourth sessions of the Second Vatican Council (January to October, 1964), he and Dorothy spent some time in Salisbury working on the biography.[23] His busy schedule, however, prevented his completing it until 1971. He then had to watch as the publishers whittled away half of the original 330 pages. He had to secure strong endorsements in order to get it published. When the work did appear, Douglas' long-time friend Nette Bossert astutely observed that "one can feel that your whole heart is in it."[24] Why did he undertake such a costly work?

The chief reason surely was because he saw in Cripps' life and work a non-violent model for dealing with the challenge all of southern Africa faced—ending apartheid and transferring power to the majority of the people. As Douglas depicted him, Cripps followed in the footsteps of Francis of Assisi and came remarkably close to the self-denying model of John Woolman.[25] Douglas thought Cripps came closest to personal self-disclosure in his long poem on "The Death of St Francis," composed before he went to Rhodesia as a missionary. After quoting a portion on Francis's experience of the stigmata as signs of "The worm-like weakness of my wasted life" and of "My service worthless to win back his world" and "To feel as mine the starving of his poor," Douglas commented: "It is hard to believe that this poem, coming as it does with Cripps turned thirty, at the height of his powers as a poet, and at a major fork of decision in the road of his religious commitment, is not to

345

be taken as a clue to the struggle that was going on behind the façade of this well-established Essex parish priest."[26]

Cripps modeled as best he could the voluntary poverty of Francis to the point that his family thought him "quite mad." He put "his life and his salary and his personal income and all that he could beg from his friends" at the disposal of the Mashonas.[27] He identified as completely as he could with the people he served, and they recognized him as their Francis of Assisi. But there were also analogies to Woolman, the Steeres' foremost model. His requesting 3rd class booking to return to England in 1909 invoked for Douglas the memory of John Woolman booking passage to London in steerage because he believed this better suited his work for the oppressed. Others volunteered to pay cabin fare for him, but he did not relent. He remarked concerning the offer that "friends, having expressed their desire that I might have a more convenient place than steerage, did not urge it but appeared to leave me to the Lord."[28] Cripps, too, resisted the pressure as a matter of principle, saying, "believe me I am not merely prejudiced but acting on principle in refusing your kind offer of a second class fare. . . . Please book the class and cabin I have asked for."[29] Douglas did not mention this directly, but Cripps' walking and jogging and refusal to take advantage of modern transportation to identify with the Mashonas are reminiscent of Woolman's decision in 1763 to stop riding horseback or in carriages because slaves could not use either. "Though travelling on foot was wearisome to my body," he wrote in his *Journal,* "yet thus travelling was agreeable to the state of my mind."[30]

In light of the reception it received when published, it is strange that *God's Irregular* required staunch backing from persons who knew the Rhodesian situation well to persuade its British publisher to take a risk on it. Especially helpful was the support of Martin Jarrett-Kerr, a priest of the Community of the Resurrection in Leeds, England. In 1972 Jarrett-Kerr remarked that he had written his first review (of the manuscript for publication) four years before and now found it (in a shortened form) still more relevant, in view of what was happening in Rhodesia. He called it "a deeply moving biography, a unique record of a man whose life has never been written" and "an important historical document for the understanding of what was Southern Rhodesia" from 1900 to 1952. Douglas "has performed a remarkable feat of 'empathy' in writing this life. For he is a Quaker, and Cripps was a high-church Anglican in the tradition of Gore, and—though he became more and more independent in his thought—never lost his profound sacramentalism." He went on to add:

> Unless this book is published, not only may the memory of a remarkable man disappear, but much essential documentation of repressive legislation against the black people (especially attempts to drive Rhodesian Africans off the land by taxation, and to deprive them of their own soil by land-appropriation) may fade from memory. The book throws valuable light on a process which found its logical culmination in U.D.I. and in the apartheid legislation that has resulted from it.[31]

Almost entirely favorable responses greeted *God's Irregular* when it finally appeared in 1973,[32] surely confirming Douglas in pursuing his dream. It not only opened minds, it touched hearts. Leonard Mamvura, a Mashona and close friend of Cripps, said, "It is the book I shall read for the rest of my life."[33] Noel Brettall, another Rhodesian, on receiving the galleys, wrote to say, "Your story does quite splendidly what it sets out to do, to give a credible shape to Cripps' noble and fiercely austere, but often perplexing character."[34] Richenda Scott wrote from Banbury, England:

> It is a long time since I have read a book which gave me so much pleasure. I really did hate coming to the end of it. You have done a magnificent job in making

this attractive figure come alive—and all your readers must be grateful to you for sharing your own interest and perspective of him so fully with us.[35]

Many close scholarly friends—George Thomas,[36] John MacMurray,[37] Raymundo Panikkar[38]—added similar accolades. The breakdown of the awful system of apartheid and the achievement of majority rule through costly, non-violent means in southern Africa, most recently in South Africa, may add a note of confirmation as well. When in the future historians consider all the factors, they will doubtless have to admit that Nelson Mandela's twenty-seven years in prison counted as much as all the threats of violence in effecting a peaceful shift of power from the white minority to the overwhelming majority in South Africa.

Life's Vulnerabilities

We must turn now to the final part of our story wherein life's vulnerabilities caught up with Douglas Steere. Douglas learned early on about life's vulnerabilities—his seven-year-old sister's death, his scrape with death by drowning at age thirteen, his brother Bruce's death at age forty-three, his mother's death at age sixty-five. Not long after his mother's passing, reflecting his existentialist leanings, he devoted the Ingersoll Lecture at Harvard to "Death's Illumination of Life." Western society tries to conceal death, but those willing to lay aside this fashion of the time may find that facing up to one's own death may illuminate "the nature and meaning of life with a clarity that no other consideration could approach."[39] It can do four things. (1) The threat of death strips the *Me* and makes it realize that it alone must face the transformation to dust and ashes. (2) It individuates, forcing one to be that solitary individual. (3) Practicing dying in the little deaths all humans face may heighten our awareness both of our own limitedness and of our longing to respond to the Source that

348

confronts the *Me*. In an obvious reference here to his mother's death, Douglas commented:

> An adult who loses a mother in death not only discovers that he must now live from a deeper root of self-responsibility after this change, but he is usually swept by a feeling of caring for her that makes him in one swift glance both thankful for what she has done and meant to him in a way that he has never been before, and at the same instant conscious that he is searched to the very core of him for his own failures to make a full response to that love.[40]

(4) Finally, persons whose lives are sorted out by approaching death learn that "Life is lent to be spent" in service of others. Douglas closed with a word from Miguel de Unamuno, the Spanish existentialist, "Sow yourselves, sow the living part of yourselves, in the furrows of life."[41]

Douglas also knew the vulnerability of human beings to suffering. He made vulnerability one of the four qualities essential in listening to another. He observed how much better the lepers on the island of Molokai in Hawaii heard Father Damien the morning that he began his sermon, "Brothers, *we* lepers." And how much better he heard them![42] But human beings resist and avoid suffering. In an article "On Being Vulnerable," Douglas applauded the honesty of an unnamed French writer, "I want to love, but I do not want to suffer." Then he went on to query whether anything could be more absurd than "to love redemptively and to place limits on our involvement."[43] He cited the example of Matilda Wrede, the Finnish woman who literally spent her life, from teen years on, caring for prisoners. Despite their cheating, deceiving, outwitting, and failing her, she went on trusting and showing them that nothing they did could shake her faith in their reformability. As Abbé Huvelin reminded Friedrich von Hügel, Jesus did not redeem people by preaching but by suffering.[44]

The amount of attention Douglas gave to our common human vulnerability notwithstanding, he did not dwell at length on his own vulnerabilities. Part of the reason for that must be that he enjoyed rather good health most of his life. Serious challenges to his health occurred infrequently— scarlet fever at age twelve, a toe infection which held on for a while during the Steeres' first trip to the Second Vatican Council, a hernia operation, a broken ankle, and prostate surgery in 1975. The last may have worried him the most because his friend George Thomas had died from cancer spreading from prostate just before Douglas discovered that he would undergo surgery.[45] Another factor was his involvement in some kind of ministry to the extent that he did not have time to dwell on his own frailties. He was other-directed, focused on caring for others. On January 15, 1984, he shared with Radnor Meeting a von Hügel statement around which his own views revolved: "Caring is the best thing in the world; caring is all that matters; Christianity taught us to care."[46]

Dorothy's extended recovery from her fall in 1984 may have raised to a more personal level the issue of vulnerability. Just after that, he got word that Christopher Taylor, one of the leading British Friends, had died. He remarked in his Journal, "It was a dark night with Dorothy suffering and Christopher gone." Although Douglas could report good progress in Dorothy's healing, he had to wait a full month for her to return home on March 3 because she had to go to a rehabilitation center first. When she did get back, he was concerned about her "cruel set of exercises." "I conclude that the doctor and physiotherapist who concocted these exercises are inspired by a principle that only what hurts— heals!"[47]

For Douglas himself, however, the vulnerability to which he had responded in so many others, through his friendship, retreats, writing, and other ministries, came in the form of Alzheimer's, that awful disease which hardens brain cells, scrambles thinking, wipes out both long and short-term memory, and hastens death. At one time people simply dismissed it as an affliction natural to aging. Medical researchers today indicate that it is much worse than the wearing out of some parts; it is a disease.

Dorothy noticed the first signs of Alzheimer's disease in the late eighties even as Douglas continued at a slower pace his schedule of speaking, writing, retreat-leading, and corresponding. Correspondence between Douglas and members of his family indicates a schedule in the process of diminishment. Up to 1988, he was still writing his characteristically informative, clear, and loving letters including exact information about stocks and bonds, speaking engagements, the Horn's cat, lectures he had heard or books he had read, etc.. By 1991 the letters had grown shorter and had taken on a different character. Douglas repeated himself at times. Sometimes he addressed both Helen and Anne as if they were strangers who had come to visit or to help. Occasionally what he was saying was incoherent. There were sometimes more lucid moments, but Alzheimer's was winning.

Such diminishments of the mind notwithstanding, Douglas' last letters, just like his presence, were full of love. He ended them with "hugs" and his "affectionately, DVS" (the favorite family address for him). He wrote of sending Helen "a lovable cat who is 'the *winner of the week*'" and hoped she would "love him just as I do."[49] He looked forward to Christmas in 1991 when the Steeres would have "our family lovingly together."[50] He observed in virtually every one of his late letters how much people at Quadrangle loved Dorothy and (he could have added) Douglas. In what may be his very last letter to Helen, perhaps in 1992, he was urging "a long and personal visit" with the Horns. He spoke of his love for Radnor Meeting and Quadrangle and of Dorothy being much loved in both places. Then, as if a dark cloud had parted to let a ray or two of sunshine through, he concluded: "It is such a joy to make this little visit and know how much we will enjoy having you here. Dorothy's spirit

351

is a precious gift to us all. We send a loving visit with ever so much pleasure. A hug to each of you. Affectionately, DVS."[51]

Close friends of the Steeres will know the loving and effective way in which Dorothy cared for Douglas during those painful last years until his death on February 6, 1995. As long as he drove (until 1991), on "bad days" she had to give simple directions. She had to arrange for his baths. She had to see that a friend, David Eynon, accompanied him on his walks. She had to humor him. She had to tend to the most elemental needs. Sometimes she was dealing with a child, at other times with a caged tiger. Helen Horn graphically expressed the vulnerability of these last years and what Dorothy coped with day by day:

> The last night you sat by my fire, before you went to the nursing center, you were ninety-two. No longer in the Big Time. Physically vulnerable. Muddled by Alzheimer's Disease. Tiring easily, so that we had left Mother with friends at the Revels matinee to give you a nap before supper. You wouldn't stretch out on my bed, however, although you agreed to a blanket around your knees at first. You seemed charmed for a while by the flickering logs. As I remember, I sang you "The Capecod Boys," a sea chanty you taught us back in the 40s as we tramped the windy deck on shipboard, bound for your sabbatical year in Sweden. You still responded warmly to music and beat your hand on the arm of the chair, chiming in on the "Heave-a-ho, heave-a-way's."
>
> You were bewildered, though, about where you were and what I was doing at Pendle Hill, when you grasped that this was that place. I explained once again how I was a visiting teacher and consultant with students there. Almost competitively, you spoke up for yourself, saying you too had done a number of things there that people seemed to appreciate. (You had only helped to found the place, lectured there, written pamphlets,

contributed money and chaired the Board for 16 years!) You felt the strangeness of being out of your apartment and without Mother. Dark had fallen. You were used to an early dinner. You became restless, suggesting that we head for home. I assured you Mother would be along soon and then we could go. I offered you tea, but that wasn't what you needed. You stood up and began to pace. The Alzheimer's Disease had your brain stiffened into routines that I was flouting. Mother had become your anchor in a sea of confusion. Where was Dorothy? It was time for bed. Where was your bed? You found your long heavy coat and put it on. You clapped on your hat. Your will was still like iron. You growled that it was way past time to go.

I felt as though I were in a cage with a great bear raging to escape. You strode to the door and swung it open, then bolted off down the hall. I scribbled Mother a note, grabbed my coat and car keys and ran after you, praying you wouldn't fall down the stairs. It relieved you somewhat to get into the car. I drove you round and round the campus. Mother finally appeared. You were visibly relieved. God knows I was too. We drove quickly home. The outing had stretched your limits. It was the last time you went anywhere but Radnor Meeting for Worship. I came back worn thin from dealing with the dementia Mother faced in you day after day.

To those who believe as Douglas did in a "love at the heart of things," this story does not and cannot end here. The indwelling of the living Christ and the enabling power of which that assures us should make us aware that "this life is undergirded by and swept up into a greater life that is at work here and that will carry us on into it as we pass from this life."[52] Douglas Steere's life as a whole has kindled anew that "greater life" at work here and now.

Notes

1. Douglas V. Steere, *Letter to Helen Horn,* December 15, 1989, noted that he was glad for the "Center." In another letter to Helen, February 18, 1990, he observed that the Steeres were "chugging along here at Quadrangle."
2. Douglas V. Steere, *Reflections* (Philadelphia: The Wider Quaker Fellowship, 1978). In his UNPUBLISHED JOURNAL 1975, 2-7, Douglas noted that, on receiving the invitation, he planned to echo what he had said at Kirkridge in an address honoring John Oliver and Jane Nelson, May 3, 1975. That address on "The Role of the Sojourner in the Kirkridge to Come" cited the model schools offered by the Brothers of the Common Life.
3. Douglas V. Steere, *God's Irregular: Arthur Shearly Cripps, a Rhodesian Epic* (London: S.P.C.K., 1973).
4. *Quaker Spirituality,* edited by Douglas V. Steere. The Classics of Western Spirituality (Ramsey, NJ: Paulist Press, 1984). The Philadelphia Yearly Meeting of the Religious Society of Friends republished the *Introduction from Quaker Spirituality* in 1988.
5. Douglas V. Steere, *Together in Solitude* (New York: Crossroad Publishing Co., 1982).
6. Douglas V. Steere, *Gleanings, a Random Harvest* (Nashville, TN: The Upper Room, 1987).
7. Douglas V. Steere, *On Speaking Out of the Silence.* Pendle Hill Pamphlet 182 (Wallingford, PA: Pendle Hill Publications, 1972); *On Confirming the Deepest Thing in Another* (Winona, MN: St. Mary's College Press, c. 1975).
8. Douglas V. Steere, "A Quaker at the Central Committee Meeting of the World Council," *Religion in Life,* 40 (Summer 1971), 267-72; "Contemplation and Leisure," *Humanitas,* 8 (November 1972), 287-306, later published as a pamphlet; "Sanctity and a Man's Eyebrows," *Friends Journal,* 19 (July 1/15, 1973), 363; "Swiss Island of Healing in a Bruising World," *Friends Journal,* 19 (March 1, 1973), 142; "Don't Forget Those Leather Gloves," *Friends Journal,* 21 (February 1, 1975), 72-75; "A Lively Picture of Rendel Harris," *The Friend,* 136 (December 15, 1978), 1557-59 "Some Dimensions of the Quaker Decision-making Process," *Friends Journal,* 28 (May 15, 1982), 5-9.
9. Douglas V. Steere, "Enomiya-Lassalle zum Achtzigsten Geburtstag," in *Munen Muso: Ungegenstandliche Meditation,* edited by G. Stachel

354

(Mainz: Matthias Grünewald-Verlag, 1978), 29-33; Foreword to *Beyond Majority Rule: Voteless Decisions in the Religious Society of Friends* by Michael John Sheeran (Philadelphia: Philadelphia Yearly Meeting, 1983), vii-xi; Foreword to *Dialogue, the Key to Understanding Other Religions* by Don K. Swearer (Philadelphia: Westminster Press, c. 1977), 13-17; Foreword to *Feeding Fire* by John Coburn (Wilton: CN: Morehouse-Barlow Co., 1980), 11-12; Foreword to *Letters to Scattered Pilgrims* by Elizabeth O'Connor (San Francisco: Harper & Row, c. 1979); Foreword to *Pendle Hill: A Quaker Experiment in Education and Community* by Eleanor Price Mather (Wallingford, PA: Pendle Hill Publications, c. 1980), v-vi; Foreword to *Prayer and Liberation,* edited by M. Basil Pennington (Canfield, OH: Alba House, 1976), xi-xix; Foreword to *Reality and Radiance* by Howard T. Lutz (Richmond, IN: Friends United Press, 1985), 9-13; "Gegenseitige Erweckung," in *Aktiver Friends: Gedenkschrift für Friedrich Siegmund-Schultze (1885-1969),* edited by Hermann Delfs (Soest, Netherlands: Mocker und Jahn, 1972), 153-56; "The Quaker Meeting for Business," in *Quakerism a Way of Life: In Homage to Sigrid Helliesen Lund* (Skoleveien, Norway: Norwegian Quaker Press, 1982), 115-23; "The Ultimate Underpinning," in *To God Be the Glory. Sermons in Honor of George Arthur Buttrick,* edited by Theodore A. Gill (Nashville: Abingdon Press, 1973), 65-73.
10. Steere, JOURNAL 1975, 8, recorded that the surgery took place July 2, 1975. The growth, fortunately, was not cancerous.
11. Douglas V. Steere, *A Report on a Quaker Journey to Southern Africa (October 6-November 20, 1975).*
12. Steere, JOURNAL 1974, 4. See also JOURNAL 1976, 10.
13. Douglas was instrumental in Haverford College's awarding of an honorary doctorate to Margarete Lachmund, a German Quaker leader who strongly resisted the Third Reich. She accepted it on behalf of German Quakers.
14. Steere, JOURNAL, 1974, 5.
15. Steere, JOURNAL, 1975, 6-10.
16. Steere, JOURNAL, 1976, 4.
17. Douglas V. Steere, *Letter to Helen Horn,* February 18, 1990, noted his participation in an Academy for Spiritual Formation at Madison, Wisconsin. Other letters indicate that he served on an Academy faculty at Camp Sumatonga in 1986 and 1988.
18. Published as "A Quaker's View of Transcendent Experience" in *Civil Religion and Transcendent Experience,* edited by Ralph C. Wood and John E. Collins (Macon, GA: Mercer University Press, 1988), 137-53.

19. Douglas V. Steere, *Letter to Helen Horn*, December 2, 1987, reported a trip schedule for the next day.
20. Steere, JOURNAL, 1979, 9.
21. Douglas V. Steere, *Letter to Helen Horn*, July 16, 1987, reported the lecturer for August 1987 would be the Methodist Bishop of Iowa.
22. Steere, JOURNAL, 761.
23. Seven years later would have been 1964. In *Douglas and Dorothy Steere Travel Letters 1966/67. No II: Rhodesia*, he reported that he and Dorothy had stayed with Sir Robert and Lady Tredgold two and a half years before while he worked on the Cripps biography. Since the account was written in late 1966, the Steeres must have been in Salisbury during the spring of 1964. Alan Paton, *Letter to Douglas V. Steere*, July 21, 1964, indicates that Douglas had informed Paton about his work on the biography.
24. Nette Bossert, *Letter to Douglas and Dorothy Steere*, July 7, 1973.
25. Interestingly, John R. H. Moorman, Bishop of Ripon, England, and one of the leading biographers of Francis of Assisi, *Letter to Douglas V. Steere*, August 6, 1973, found Cripps much like Brother Douglas, another of those Douglas Steere greatly admired. Moorman intended to publish a biography of Brother Douglas.
26. Steere, *God's Irregular*, 13-14.
27. Steere, *God's Irregular*, 71.
28. *The Journal of John Woolman*, edited by Phillips Moulton (New York: Oxford University Press, 1971), 165; in Steere, *God's Irregular*, 72.
29. Citing Letters in Diocesan Strong Room in Salisbury, Rhodesia; in Steere, *God's Irregular*, 73.
30. *The Journal of John Woolman*, edited by Phillips P. Moulton, 150.
31. Martin Jarrett-Kerr, *Letter to Emory Bucke*, Editor of *Religion in Life*, February 1, 1972.
32. According to Emory Bucke, Editor, *Religion in Life* published two reviews by different John Oliver Nelsons because one was very critical. (Emory Bucke, *Letter to John Oliver Nelson*, June 26, 1973.) Phyllis Lean, a South African, gave it a mixed review for the Johannesburg *Sunday Times*. She found it "in some ways" "great—in others 'patchy'." She wrote Douglas on June 26, 1973, to say: "I get the impression that you were too hurried or had not enough research backing—but it is a great South African story worthy of taking its place in the school of writing established by Olive Schreiner."
33. Leonard Mamvura, *Letter to Douglas and Dorothy Steere*, January 12, 1973. The Steeres probably reminded him of Cripps, for they had helped his son, John, with college tuition and checked repeatedly on his progress. See Leonard Mamvura, *Letter to Douglas and*

Dorothy Steere, February 25, 1972, thanking them for financial help to educate his children; Mary Petty, *Letter to Douglas and Dorothy Steere,* May 7, 1972, thanking them for a check for John Mamvura; Leonard Mamvura, *Letter to Douglas and Dorothy Steere,* April 23, 1973, reporting full loan granted John by the University of Rhodesia.

34. Noel Brettall, *Letter to Douglas V. Steere,* November 12, 1972.
35. Richenda Scott, *Letter to Douglas V. Steere,* May 24, 1973.
36. George Thomas, *Letter to Douglas V. Steere,* May 15, 1973.
37. John MacMurray, *Letter to Douglas V. Steere,* June 5, 1973.
38. Raymundo Panikkar, *Letter to Douglas V. Steere,* June 23, 1973, said that he had to stop reading for a while because it was "becoming too 'personal.'"
39. Douglas V. Steere, *On Beginning from Within* (New York and London: Harper & Brothers, Publishers, 1943), 123.
40. Steere, *On Beginning,* 140-141.
41. Steere, *On Beginning,* 149.
42. Douglas V. Steere, *On Listening to Another* (New York: Harper Bros., Publishers, 1955).
43. Douglas V. Steere, "On Being Vulnerable," *Friends Intelligencer,* 197 (August 26, 1950), 499.
44. Steere, "On Being Vulnerable,"500.
45. Steere, JOURNAL 1975, 8.
46. Steere, JOURNAL 1984, 3.
47. Steere, JOURNAL 1984, 15.
48. Douglas V. Steere, *Letter to Helen Horn and Anne Nash,* September 1, 1991.
49. Douglas V. Steere, *Letter to Helen Horn,* September 13, 1991.
50. Douglas V. Steere, *Letter to Helen Horn,* November 23, 1991.
51. Douglas V. Steere, *Letter to Helen Horn,* undated and not mailed but found by Dorothy. Helen guessed 1992.
52. Douglas V. Steere, *Letter to Joe and Edith Platt,* undated but probably September 1972, in response to an article from the *Christian Century* based on a Bultmannian interpretation of the resurrection.

Bibliography

Based on a Bibliography Compiled by Eva Walker Myer

BOOKS

Dimensions of Prayer. Nashville, TN: Women's Division of Christian Service, Board of Missions, The Methodist Church; New York: Harper & Row; London: Darton, Longman & Todd, 1962.

Dimensions of Prayer. rev. ed. Nashville: The Upper Room, 1997.

Doors into Life through Five Devotional Classics. New York: Harper & Row, 1948.

Friends Work in Africa. With Dorothy Steere. London: Friends World Committee for Consultation, 1955. Supplement to *Friends Work in Africa.* Birmingham, England: FWCC, 1960.

Gebet und Andacht von Douglas V. Steere. Translation of *Prayer and Worship* by Therese Herzog. Bad Pyrmont: Leonhard Friedrich, 1948.

Gegenseitige Erleuchtung. Berlin: Religiose Gesellschaft der Freunde (Quaker) in Deutschland, 1968.

Gleanings, A Random Harvest : Selected Writings of Douglas V. Steere. Nashville, TN: The Upper Room, 1987.

God's Irregular: Arthur Shearly Cripps, A Rhodesian Epic. London: S.P.C.K., Holy Trinity Church, 1973; and Northumberland Press, Ltd., n.d.

The Imitation of Christ. Arranged and edited by Douglas Van Steere. Living Selections of the Great Devotional Classics, No. 6. Nashville, TN: The Upper Room, 1950.

Introduction from Quaker Spirituality. Philadelphia: Philadelphia Yearly Meeting of the Religious Society of Friends, 1988.

On Beginning from Within. New York and London: Harper & Brothers, 1943.

On Beginning from Within. and *On Listening to Another.* New Introductory Essay by Douglas Van Steere. New York: Harpers, 1963.

On Listening to Another. New York: Harper, 1955. Published in England as *Where Words Come From.*

The Practice of the Presence of God by Brother Lawrence [Nicolas Herman]. Edited and arranged by Douglas Van Steere. Nashville, TN: The Upper Room, ca. 1950.

Prayer and Worship. Hazen Books on Religion. New York: Association Press, 1938; Richmond, IN: Friends United Press, 1978.

Prayer and Worship [Chinese]. Shanghai: The Association Press of China, 1947.

Purity of Heart Is to Will One Thing: Spiritual Preparation for the Feast of Confession, by Soren Kierkegaard. Translated with introduction by Douglas Van Steere. New York and London: Harper & Brothers, 1938.

Quaker Spirituality. Edited with introductory essay by Douglas Van Steere. Ramsey, NJ: Paulist Press, 1984.

Spiritual Counsel and Letters of Friedrich von Hugel. Edited with introduction by Douglas Van Steere. London: Darton Longman & Todd, 1964.

Time to Spare. New York: Harper, 1949.

Together in Solitude. New York: Crossroad Publishing Co., 1982.

The Very Thought of Thee. From three great mystics: Bernard of Clairvaux, Jeremy Taylor and Evelyn Undershill. Edited by Douglas Van Steere and J. Minton Batten. Nashville, TN: The Upper Room, 1953.

Where Words Come From: An Interpretation of the Ground and Practice of Quaker Worship and Ministry. London: George Allen & Unwin, Ltd.; Friends Service Committee, 1955. Published in the U.S. as *On Listening to Another.*

Work and Contemplation. Five Rauschenbusch Lectures, Colgate-Rochester Divinity School. New York: Harper & Brothers, 1957.

PAMPHLETS

Att Leva Oppet (The Open Life). Utgivare, Sweden: Vanneras Samfund i Sverige (Kvakarna); Stockholm: Oskarsklunde Boktryckeri, 1938.

Bethlehem Revisited. Pendle Hill Pamphlet #144. Wallingford, PA: Pendle Hill Publications, 1965.

Community and Worship. Pendle Hill Pamphlet #10. Wallingford, PA: Pendle Hill Publications, 1940.

Contemplation and Leisure. Pendle Hill Pamphlet #199. Wallingford, PA: Pendle Hill Publications, ca. 1975.

Douglas Steere Speaks. Brooklyn, NY: Leonard Kenworthy, n.d.

Eine Quakerandact. Bad Pyrmont: Leonhard Friedrich, [1947].

Expectations of Wainwright House. Rye, NY: Wainwright House, 1953.

Friends and Silence. Philadelphia: Friends General Conference, n.d.

The Hardest Journey. Pendle Hill Pamphlet #163. Wallingford, PA: Pendle Hill Publications, 1969.

Inward Preparation for the Life of Peace. New York: Episcopal Pacifist Fellowship, 1956.

Kvakarandakt. Radioforedrag. Translation of *Quaker Meeting for Worship.* Helsingfors, 1946.

A Manual on the Need, the Organization, and the Discipline of Cells for Peace. New York: Fellowship of Reconciliation, 1947.

Meditations for a Quiet Day. Cincinnati, OH: Women's Division of Christian Service, Board of Missions and Church Extension, The Methodist Church, 1945.

Mutual Irradiation: A Quaker View of Ecumenism. Pendle Hill Pamphlet #175. Wallingford, PA: Pendle Hill Publications, 1971.

On Being Present Where You Are. Pendle Hill Pamphlet #151. Wallingford, PA: Pendle Hill Publications, 1967.

On Confirming the Deepest Thing in Another. Winona, MN: St. Mary's College Press, ca. 1975; Philadelphia: Wider Quaker Fellowship, 1983.

On Speaking out of the Silence. Pendle Hill Pamphlet #182. Wallingford, PA: Pendle Hill Publications, 1972.

The Peace Team. New York: The Fellowship of Reconciliation, n.d.

Prayer in the Contemporary World. Pendle Hill Pamphlet #??? New York: National Council of Churches in the U.S.A., for Church Women United; Wallingford, PA: Pendle Hill Publications,1966.

A Quaker Meeting for Worship. Philadelphia: Committee of Ministry and Counsel, The Philadelphia Yearly Meeting, 1937.

A Quaker Meeting for Worship [Hindi]. Translated by Maya Paramhars, ca. 1970.

A Quaker Meeting for Worship, by Douglas Van Steere, and *Expression of the Spirit in Service,* by Clarence E. Pickett. Transcript of Radio Address, April 23, 1944. Philadelphia: Society of Friends, Fellowship Council, 1944.

Quakers and the Inward Journey. Richmond, IN: Indiana Yearly Meeting, 1965.

Reflections. Philadelphia: Wider Quaker Fellowship, 1978.

Selections from the Writings of Bernard of Clairvaux.. Arranged and edited by Douglas Van Steere. Nashville, TN: The Upper Room, 1961.

Selections from the Writings of Evelyn Underhill. Arranged and edited by Douglas Van Steere. Nashville, TN: The Upper Room, 1961.

The Soil of Peace, the Human Factor in Reconciliation. Washington, DC, and Chicago: Human Events, Inc., 1946.

Toward the Practice of Prayer. Philadelphia: Friends Book Store, 1932.

ARTICLES IN JOURNALS

"And the Cock Crew." *The Friend* (London), 115 (July 5, 1957) 589.

"At Kaimosi and Nairobi, Kenya." With Dorothy Steere. *Friends Journal,* 1 (August 6, 1955) 87-88.

"'At My Best in a Classroom'." *Quaker Life,* Series IV, No. 1 (January 1963) 18-19.

"At the German Yearly Meeting in 1940." *The Friend* (Philadelphia), 114 (December 12, 1940) 218-19.

"Beyond Diversity to a Common Experience of God." *Quaker Religious Thought,* V (Autumn 1963) 1-17.

"Blanche Shaffer." *The Friend* (London), 132 (June 28, 1974) 748.

"Caring Is All That Matters." *Monastic Studies,* 8 (September 1972) 14-17.

"Catholics and Non-Catholics Confer." *The Friend* (London), 123 (October 22, 1965) 1273-74.

"A Challenge to Quaker Reticence." *The Friend* (Philadelphia), 108 (November 8, 1934) 150-51.

"A Challenge to Quaker Social Thinking." *The Friend* (Philadelphia), 47 (May 5, 1933) 555-56.

"A Chapter in Protestant-Catholic Encounter, 1918-1962." *Religion in Life*, 32 (Autumn 1963) 497-507.

"Christian and Zen Buddhist Scholars Meet." *The Friend* (London), 125 (April 14, 1967), 440-43.

"A Christian Approach to the World Religions—Part I." *Friends Journal*, 2 (August 4, 1956) 492-94.

"A Christian Approach to the World Religions—Part II." *Friends Journal*, 2 (August 11, 1956) 509-11.

"Christian-Zen Colloquium." *Friends Journal*, 13 (May 15, 1967) 270-71.

"Comment on 'The Quaker Interpretation of the Significance of Christ,' by Maurice Creasey." *Quaker Religious Thought*, 1 (Autumn 1959) 22-27.

"Common Frontiers in Catholic and Non-Catholic Spirituality." *Worship*, 39 (December 1968) 605-18.

"Contemplation and Leisure." *Humanitas*, 8 (November 1972) 287-306.

"Crashing the Thought Barrier of Our Time." *Friends Journal*, 4 (May 3, 1958) 278, 285.

"A Critique of Social Theory." *The Friend* (London), 117 (September 18, 1959) 1063-64.

"Discussion on Dialogue with Men of Other Faiths." *Ching Feng*, 13 (1970).

"Dr. Schweitzer of Lambarene." *The Friend* (Philadelphia), 126 (July 24, 1952) 22-25.

"Don't Forget Those Leather Gloves." *Friends Journal*, 21 (February 1, 1975) 72-73.

"Douglas Steere's Plan for 'Mutual Irradiation'." *The Friend* (London), 126 (December 6, 1968) 1529-31.

"Ecumenism, the Jews, Religious Liberty." *The Friend* (London), 122 (January 3, 1964) 22-26.

"Education for Worship Based on Silence." *The Friend* (London), 123 (July 16, 1965) 849-50.

"Emerging Horizons." *The Friends' Quarterly*, 17 (April 1971) 50-63.

"The Evangelical Academies in Germany." *Friends Quarterly*, 5 n.s. (April 1951) 79-86.

"Evangelism and Christian Fellowship." *Religion in Life*, 8 (Winter 1939) 3-13.

363

"Extracts from a Roman Journal." *Friends Journal*, 11 (January 1, 1965) 13.

"Extracts from a Roman Journal." *Friends Journal*, 11 (November 1, 1965) 531-33.

"Extracts from a Roman Journal." *Friends Journal*, 11 (December 1, 1965) 585-86.

"A Final Report from the Vatican Council." *The Friend* (London), 123 (January 1, 1965) 17-20.

"Finland's George Fox." *The Friend* (London), 136 (September 15, 1978) 1153-54.

"A First Dispatch from the Vatican Council." Part I. *The Friend* (London), 121 (October 25-1963) 1232-33.

"A First Report of the Vatican Council." Part II. *The Friend* (London), 123 (October 22, 1965) 1264-68.

"For God So Loved the World." *The Friend* (London), 126 (December 13, 1968) 1565-68.

"Foreword to An Anatomy of Worship." *Pastoral Psychology*, 11 (March 1960) 10-15.

"A Fresh Look at Retreats." *Religion in Life*, 36 (Spring 1967) 100-107.

"Friends and Finland." *Friends' Quarterly Examiner*, 78 (July 1944) 174-76.

"Friends' Contribution." *The Friend* (London), 126 (December 27, 1968) 1628-31.

"Friends World Committee Meets in Sweden." *Friends Journal*, 16 (October 1, 1970) 531.

"Further Comments on the Vatican Council." Part III. *The Friend* (London), 121 (December 27, 1963) 1531-32.

"Geneva in War-Time." *The Friend* (Philadelphia), 114 (October 17, 1940) 136-37.

"Has Ghana Gone Totalitarian?" *Friends Journal*, 4 (February 15, 1958), 102-3.

"Have Christians an Answer? Mutual Irradiation." *Religion in Life*, 28 (Summer 1959) 395-405.

"Hope of Glory and This Present Life." *Theology Today*, 10 (October 1953) 367-74.

"Implementing Our Religion." *The Friend* (Philadelphia), 108 (March 14, 1935) 298-99.

"In the Backwash of War." *The Friend* (Philadelphia), 114 (October 31, 1940) 151-54.

"In the Morning Sow Your Seed." *Friends World News*, No. 98 (Winter 1972) 470.

"The Inner Bidding—Norway, 1963." *Friends Journal*, 9 (November 1, 1963) 462-63.

"Is the Social Gospel Adequate to Become the Religion of the Next Generation?" *The Crozer Quarterly*, 12 (April 1935) 128-41.

"Jericho Road Again." *The Friend* (Philadelphia), 121 (January 29, 1948) 251-52.

"Jesus Christ in the Quaker Meeting." *The Friend* (London), 123 (July 9, 1965) 813-14.

"Journal from Rome (I)." *Friends Journal*, 9 (December 15, 1963) 536-38.

"Journal from Rome (II)." *Friends Journal*, 10 (January 1, 1964) 10-12.

"Journal from Rome (III)." *Friends Journal*, 10 (January 15, 1964) 34-36.

"Journal from Rome (IV)." *Friends Journal*, 10 (February 1, 1964) 56-58.

"Journal from Rome (V)." *Friends Journal*, 10 (February 15, 1964) 82-84.

"Kenya's Friends." *Friends Journal*, 13 (January 15, 1967) 34-35.

"A Lambeth Conference." *Friends Journal*, 14 (November 1, 1968) 550-51.

"The Lambeth Conference." *Friends Journal*, 14 (December 1, 1968) 614.

"The Lambeth Conference 1968." *Religion in Life*, 37 (Winter 1968) 612-15.

"A Leak in the Roof." *The Friend* (London), 112 (November 15, 1954) 1097.

"Letter from Down Under." *Friends Journal*, 13 (May 1, 1967) 246-47.

"Letter from Europe." *Friends Journal*, 16 (January 1, 1970) 20.

"Letter from Europe." With Dorothy Steere. *Friends Journal*, 16 (March 1, 1970) 145-46.

"Letter from Europe." With Dorothy Steere. *Friends Journal*, 16 (March 15, 1970) 177.

"Letter from Lebanon." With Dorothy Steere. *Friends Journal*, 16 (May 1, 1970) 273.

"The Life of Prayer as the Ground of Unity." *Worship*, 45 (May 1971) 250-61.

"A Lively Picture of Rendel Harris." *The Friend* (London), 136 (December 15, 1978) 1557-59.

"A Makere College in East Africa." With Dorothy Steere. *Friends Journal*, 3 (August 31, 1957) 569.

"The Meaning of Mysticism within Christianity." *Religion in Life*, 22 (Autumn 1953) 515-26.

"Meetings with Hindus and Zen Buddhists." *The Friend* (London), 126 (December 20, 1968) 1597-1600.

"Multiracial University: A Genuine Instrument of Partnership." *Friends Journal*, 4 (February 1, 1958) 72-73.

"Mutual Irradiation." *Religion in Life*, 28 (Summer 1959) 395-405.

"The Mystical Experience." *Review and Expositor*, 71 (Summer 1974) 323-44.

"'Now and Zen' for Quakers." *Friends World News*, No. 82 (August 1967) 210-12.

"O Blessed Cock." *Friends Journal*, 3 (January19, 1957) 38-39.

"Ole Olden, Indomitable Norseman." *Friends Journal*, 9 (March 15, 1963) 132-33.

"On Beginning Where We Are." *The Friend* (London), 116 (January 24, 1958) 105-6.

"On Being Vulnerable." *The Friend* (London), 108 (August 18, 1960) 611-12.

"On Creative Reading." *The Friend* (Philadelphia), 106 (May 12, 1932) 254.

"On Dove's Feet." *Christianity and Crisis*, No. 9 (1951) 66-68.

"On Emptying the Water Butts." *The Friend* (London), 113 (September 30, 1955) 931-32.

"Open Letters on Books." *The Friend* (Philadelphia), 112 (November 17, 1938) 167-68.

"The Open Life." *The Friend* (London), 95 (August 20, 1937) 765-67.

"An Open Moment Approaching." *The Friend* (London), 128 (January 23, 1970) 79-81.

"Opening Address." *Worship*, 39 (December 1965) 581-82.

"The Oxford Group and Quakerism." *The Friend* (Philadelphia), 106 (February 5, 1933) 375-76, 389-90.

"Peace, War and Conscientious Objection, Vatican Council Deliberations." *Friends World News*, No. 78 (April 1966) 10-12.

"Postscripts to a Roman Journal." *Friends Journal*, 12 (February 1, 1966) 58-59.

"Prayer and Action." *Friends Journal*, 16 (August 1/15, 1970) 420.

"Prayer and Ecumenism." *Friends Journal*, 16 (October 1, 1970) 515-16.

"Prayer and the Modern Man." *Friends Journal*, 15 (January 15, 1969) 37-38.

"Protestant Piety Today." *Religion in Life*, 19 (Winter 1949-50) 3-15.

"A Quaker at the Central Committee Meeting of the World Council." *Religion in Life*, 40 (Summer 1971) 267-72.

"Quaker Experiments in the Conquest of Interior Space." *Friends World News*, No. 89 (Winter 1969) 326-27.

"Quaker Grey among the Anglican Purple." *Friends World News*, No. 86 (Winter 1968) 284-85.

"A Quaker International Institute for West Africa?" *Friends Journal*, 4 (April 19, 1958) 249.

"A Quaker Looks at the Vatican Council." *Friends World News*, No. 72 (April 1964) 56-59.

"A Quaker Looks at the Vatican Council." *Religion in Life*, 33 (Autumn 1964) 569-76.

"A Quaker Meeting for Worship." *The Friend* (Philadelphia), 111 (December 16, 1937) 229-30.

"A Quaker Meeting for Worship." *The Friend* (London), 95 (June 18, 1937) 579-81.

"The Quaker Message." *The Christian Century*, 72 (August 3, 1955) 893-95.

"The Quaker Message: Unique or Universal?" *The Friends' Quarterly*, 9 (April 1955) 1-7.

"A Quaker Observer Looks at the Lambeth Conference." *The Friend* (London), 126 (August 30, 1968) 1081-83.

367

"A Quaker View of Ecumenism." *The Friend* (London), 126 (December 6, 1968) 1529-31.

"A Quaker Visitor in Present-Day France." *The Friend* (London), 98 (November 29, 1940), 659.

"Quakerism in the Service of the State." *The Friend* (Philadelphia), 107 (March 29, 1934) 319-20.

"Quakers of the World Conference." *The Christian Century*, 84 (September 6, 1967) 1140-42.

"Reconstruction Training at Haverford." *The Haverford Review*, 3 (1944) 12-14, 31.

"Remembering Schweitzer." *The Friend* (London), 133 (August 15, 1975) 931-32.

"Rufus M. Jones as Scholar and Teacher." *Haverford Horizons*, 4 (December 1962) 3-4.

"Rufus Jones as Teacher." *The Friend* (London), 121 (February 8, 1963) 155-56.

"Sanctity and a Man's Eyebrows." *Friends Journal*, 19 (July 1/15, 1973) 363.

"The Scholarship of Rufus Jones." *The Friend* (London), 121 (February 15, 1963) 188-89.

"A Second Dispatch from the Vatican Council." Part II. *The Friend* (London), 121 (December 13, 1963), 1472-74.

"A Second Report of the Vatican Council." *The Friend* (London), 123 (November 26, 1965) 1433-35.

"Solitude and Prayer." *Worship*, 55 (1981) 120-36.

"Some Dimensions of the Quaker Decision-making Process." *Friends Journal*, 28 (May 15, 1982) 5-9.

"Some Distinctly Quaker Aspects of Our Recent Asian-African Journey." *Friends World News*, No.46 (September 1955) 3-6.

"Some Reflections on Religious Education." *The Friend* (Philadelphia), 105 (October 5, 1931), 195-96.

"Some Reflections on Religious Education." *The Friend* (Philadelphia), 105 (October 5, 1931) 207-8.

"A Spiritual Document." *The Friend* (Philadelphia), 107 (October 26, 1933) 135-36.

"A Spiritual Document from Denmark." *The Friend* (London), 92 (June 29, 1934) 595-97.

"Spiritual Power—Whence It Comes." *The Friend* (Philadelphia), 115 (December 16, 1941) 134.

"Spiritual Renewal in Our Time." *Union Seminary Quarterly Review*, 17 (November 1961) 33-56.

"The Spiritual Task of Teachers Today." *Sisters*, 45 (1975) 5-13.

"The Spirituality of Friedrich von Hugel." *Worship*, 47 (November 1973) 540-46.

"The Swarthmore Lecture: A Brief Digest." *The Friend* (London), 113 (June 3, 1955) 560-61, 605-7.

"A Swedish Quaker Experiment in Reconciliation." *The Friend* (Philadelphia), 121 (April 22, 1948) 345-47.

"A Swiss Island of Healing in a Bruising World." *Friends Journal*, 19 (March 1, 1973) 142.

"The Swiss Yearly Meeting." *The Friend* (Philadelphia), 114 (November 14, 1940) 172-73.

"The Hospital in Kenya." *Friends Journal*, 3 (November 16, 1957) 741-42.

"The Task Ahead for the Friends World Committee for Consultation." *Friends World News*, No. 74 (December 1964) 83-86.

"The Things that Lead to Peace." *Friends Journal*, 14 (February 1, 1968) 53-54.

"Three Areas of Concern." *Friends Journal*, 11 (June 15, 1965) 309-11.

"'Thy Will Be Done'—The Spiritual Basis of Our Christian Service." *Friends Journal*, 7 (August 1, 1961) 313-14.

"To Help in South Africa." With Dorothy Steere. *The Friend* (Philadelphia), 127 (March 18, 1954) 315-17.

"Travel Letter from Rhodesia." *Friends Journal*, 13 (February 1, 1967) 62.

"A Visit to Sweden." *The Friend* (Philadelphia), 111 (October 7, 1937) 138-39.

"Walter Fales, 1896-1953)." *The Friend* (Philadelphia), 128 (August 19, 1954) 50-51.

"What Then Must We Do?" *Friends World News*, No. 92 (Winter 1970) 380-81.

"William Wistar Comfort." *The Friend* (London), 114 (February 10, 1956) 114-15.

"A Word from Scandinavia." *The Friend* (Philadelphia), 126 (August 7, 1952) 37-38.

ARTICLES IN BOOKS

"Biographical Memoir" in *A Testament of Devotion* by Thomas R. Kelly. New York and London: Harper & Brothers, 1941, 1-26.

"Biographische Erinnerungen" in *Heiliger Gehorsam* by Thomas R. Kelly. Translated by Alice Brugger and Gertrud Meylan. Bad Pyrmont: Leonhard Friedrich, 1946.

"Break the New Ground" in *Break the New Ground*. Edited by Charles W. Cooper. Birmingham, England: Friends World Committee for Consultation, 1969, 3-14.

"Common Frontiers in Catholic and Non-Catholic Spirituality" in *Protestants and Catholics on the Spiritual Life*. Edited by Michael Marx. Collegeville, MN: Liturgical Press, 1965, 42-55.

Contribution to *More than Conquerors* by Dorothy Webb. London: Friends Home Service, 1970, 5, 11.

"Development for What?" in *Development for What?* Edited by John H. Hallowell. Published for Lilly Endowment Research Program in Christianity and Politics. Durham, NC: Duke University Press, 1964, 213-34.

"The Devotional Literature of Christianity" in *The Vitality of the Christian Tradition*. Edited by George F. Thomas. New York and London: Harper & Brothers, 1945, 185-203.

"Enomiya-Lassalle zum Achtzigsten Geburtstag" in *Munen Muso: Ungegenstandliche Meditation*. Edited by G. Stachel. Mainz: Matthias Gruenewald-Verlag, 1978, 29-33.

Foreword to *Beyond Majority Rule: Voteless Decisions in the Religious Society of Friends* by Michael John Sheeran. Philadelphia: Philadelphia Yearly Meeting, 1983, vii-xi.

Foreword to *Contemplative Prayer* by Thomas Merton. London: Darton, Longman and Todd, ca. 1969, 7-14.

Foreword to *Dialogue, the Key to Understanding Other Religions* by Don K. Swearer. Philadelphia: Westminster Press, ca. 1977, 13-17.

Foreword to *Feeding Fire* by John Coburn. Wilton, CN: Morehouse-Barlow Co., 1980, 11-12.

Foreword to *Letters to Scattered Pilgrims* by Elizabeth O'Connor. San Francisco: Harper & Row, ca. 1979, ix-xi.

Foreword to *Pendle Hill: A Quaker Experiment in Education and Community* by Eleanor Price Mather. Wallingford, PA: Pendle Hill Publications, ca. 1980, v-vi.

Foreword to *Prayer and Liberation: Papers Presented to the Tenth Annual Ecumenical Institute of Spirituality*. Edited by M. Basil Pennington. Canfield, OH: Alba House, 1976, xi-xix.

Foreword to *Reality and Radiance: Selected Autobiographical Works of Emilia Fogelklou*. Translated by Howard T. Lutz. Richmond, IN: Friends United Press, 1985, 9-13.

Foreword to *The Climate of Monastic Prayer* by Thomas Merton. Cistercian Studies Series, No. 1. Spencer, MA: Cistercian Publications, 1969; Shannon, Ireland: Irish University Press, 13-27.

"Friedrich von Hugel as Spiritual Director" in *Search for Meaning*. Rye, NY: Wainwright House, 1960, 45-88.

"Gegenseitige Erweckung" in *Aktiver Freunde: Gedenkschrift fur Friedrich Siegmund-Schultze (1885-1969)*. Auflagende bei Hermann Delfs. Soest, Netherlands: Mocker und Jahn, 1972, 153-56.

"The Golden Rule" in *Great Expressions of Human Rights*. Edited by R.M. MacIver. Religion and Civilization Series. New York: The Institute for Religion and Social Studies, Jewish Theological Seminary of America, 1950, 51-59.

"Introduction" to *Beyond Dilemmas*. Edited by Seeva Bright Laughlin. New York, Philadelphia and London: J.B. Lippincott Co., 1937, 11-28.

"Introduction" to *Introduction to the Devout Life* by Francois de Sales. Translated and edited by John K. Ryan. New York: Harper, 1952, vii-xviii.

"Introduction" to *Kicked by God* by Sok Hon Ham. Translated by David E. Ross. Baltimore: Wider Quaker Fellowship, 1969, 3.

"Introduction" to *Responsibility and Illness* by William N. Chambers. Berwyn, PA: n.p., 1961.

"Introduction" to *Three Letters from Africa* by Edgar H. Brookes. Pendle Hill Pamphlet #139. Wallingford, PA: Pendle Hill Publications, 1965, 5-7.

"Introduction" to *Works of Love* by Soren Kierkegaard. Translated by David F. Swenson and Lillian Marvin Swenson. Princeton, NJ: Princeton University Press, 1946, vii-xiv.

"A New Set of Devotional Exercises" (from *On Beginning from Within*) in *Fellowship of the Saints*. Edited by Thomas Samuel Kepler. New York: Abingdon-Cokesbury, 1948, 765-75.

"No Final Formula for Retreats" in *Call to Adventure*. Edited by Raymond J. Magee. Nashville: Abingdon Press, 1967, 39-50.

"Notice Biographique" in *La Presence Ineffable* by Thomas R. Kelly. Translated by Marie Butts. Geneve: Labor et fides, 194?, 9-42.

"On the Power of Sustained Attention" in *Then and Now: Quaker Essays in Honor of Henry J. Cadbury*. Edited by Anna Cox Brinton. Philadelphia: University of Pennsylvania Press, 1960, 284-302.

"Opening Address" in *Protestants and Catholics on the Spiritual Life*. Edited by Michael Marx. Collegeville, MN: Liturgical Press, 1965, 1-2.

"Prayer and Worship" in *The Religious Life*. Edited by Georgia Harkness. New York: Association Press, 1953, Section II, 1-68.

"The Quaker Meeting for Business" in *Quakerism a Way of Life: In Homage to Sigrid Helliesen Lund*. Skoleveien, Norway: Norwegian Quaker Press, 1982, 115-23.

Quotations in *More Than Conquerors: Anthology of Relevant Quotations from Fox, Eckhart, Fenelon, Underhill, Jones, and Steere*. London: Friends Home Service Committee, 1974.

"Religious Encounter" in *Buddhism and Culture: Dedicated to Daisetz Teitaro Suzuki in Commemoration of His Ninetieth Birthday*. Edited by Susumu Yamaguchi. Kyoto, Japan: Nakano Press, 1960, 170-80.

"A Religious Minority in Action: The Society of Friends" in *Group Relations and Group Antagonisms*. Religion and Civilization Series. New York: Institute for Religious and Social Studies, Jewish Theological Seminary of America, 1944, 97-117.

"The Task Ahead for the Friends World Committee for Consultation" in *The Creative Centre of Quakerism*. Birmingham, England and Philadelphia: Friends World Committee for Consultation, 1965, 68-86.

"A Theology of Practical Mysticism" in *Men Who Shape Belief*. Philadelphia: Westminster Press, 1955, 30-41.

"The Ultimate Underpinning" in *To God Be the Glory: Sermons in Honor of George Arthur Buttrick*. Edited by Theodore A. Gill. Nashville, TN: Abingdon Press, 1973, 65-73.

TRAVEL LETTERS OF DOUGLAS AND DOROTHY STEERE

I. Germany and Scandinavia, Summer 1937

1. *Travel Letter from Douglas Steere*
   Aboard train to Munich, July 24, 1937

2. *Travel Letter from Douglas Steere*
   Aboard train from Breslau to Guben with Henry Gillett, July 17, 1937

3. *Travel Letter from Douglas Steere*
   Sweden, August 15, 1937

4. *Travel Letter from Douglas Steere*
   Stockholm, Sweden, August 25-27, 1937

5. *Travel Letter from Douglas Steere*
   Finland, September 1, 1937

6. *Extracts of Letter from Douglas Steere*
   Bulken, Norway, September 6, 1937

II. Germany and Scandinavia, September-December 1940

7. *Some Glimpses of the European Scene from within Germany September-December 1940*
   Lisbon, Portugal, January 15, 1941

III. Poland, 1945

8. *Report on Quaker Visit to Poland Sept. 30-Oct. 10, 1945*

IV. Germany and Scandinavia, 1947-48

9. *Excerpts of Letters from Douglas V. Steere*
   Stockholm, Sweden, Sept. 2, 1947 (No. 1)

10. *News from Douglas Steere*
    Berlin, Germany, Sept. 26, 1947 (No. 2)

11. *News from Dorothy Steere*
    Frankfurt/Main, Germany, Nov. 17, 1947 (No. 3)

12. *News from Douglas Steere*
    Frankfurt/Main, Germany, Dec. 8, 1947 (No. 4)

13. *News from Douglas Steere*
    Cologne, Germany, Dec. 9, 1947 (No. 5)

14. *News from Douglas Steere*
    Bad Pyrmont Revisited, Dec. 12, 1947 (No. 6)

15. *News from Douglas Steere*
    British Zone, Germany, Dec. 15, 1947 (No. 7)

16. *News from Dorothy Steere*
    Ore, Sweden, Dec. 29, 1947 (No. 8)

17. *News from Douglas Steere*
    Viggbyholm, Sweden, Dec. 30, 1947 (No. 9)

18. *News from Douglas Steere*
    Received in Philadelphia Jan. 2, 1948 (No. 10)

19. *News from Douglas Steere*
    Sigtuna, Sweden, Jan. 20, 1948 (No. 11)

20. *A Swedish Quaker Experiment in Reconciliation: Report on the Viggbyholm Conference*
    Viggbyholm, Sweden, Mar. 23-30, 1948 (No. 12)

21. *News from Douglas Steere*
    London, England, May 13, 1948 (No. 13)

V. Africa, Spring and Summer 1953

36. *Newsletter #1 from Dorothy and Douglas Steere*
    Rome, Italy/Kano, Nigeria, Feb. 22-23, 1953

37. *Newsletter #2 from Dorothy and Douglas Steere*
    Lambarene, French Equatorial Africa, Mar. 9, 1953

38. *Newsletter #3 from Dorothy and Douglas Steere*
    Cape Town, S. Africa, April 6, 1953

39. *Newsletter #4 from Dorothy and Douglas Steere*
    Durban, S. Africa, May 26, 1953

40. *Newsletter #5 from Dorothy and Douglas Steere*
    Salisbury, Southern Rhodesia, June 12, 1953

41. *Newsletter #6 from Dorothy and Douglas Steere*
    Nairobi, Kenya, June 20, 1953

42. *Newsletter #7 from Dorothy and Douglas Steere*
    Bad Pyrmont, Germany, July 1953

43. *Newsletter #8 from Dorothy and Douglas Steere*
    Mackinaw City, Michigan, Aug. 15, 1953

VI. Asia and Africa, 1954-55

44. *Douglas and Dorothy Steere's Travel Letter #1*
    Hong Kong, Nov. 30, 1954

45. *Douglas and Dorothy Steere's Travel Letter #2*
    Delhi, India, Dec. 28, 1954

46. *Douglas and Dorothy Steere's Travel Letter #3*
    Delhi, India, Jan. 26, 1955

47. *Douglas and Dorothy Steere's Travel Letter #4*
    Salisbury, Southern Rhodesia, Mar. 22, 1955

48. *Douglas and Dorothy Steere's Travel Letter #5*
    Johannesburg, South Africa, Mar. 31, 1955

49. *Douglas and Dorothy Steere's Travel Letter #6*
    Accra, Gold Coast, Apr. 27, 1955

50. *Douglas and Dorothy Steere's Travel Letter #7*
    Galway, Ireland and Mackinaw City, Michigan, June 15, 1955

X. Vatican II, Session 2, Rome, Fall 1963

63. *Journal from Rome (I)*
Rome, Sept. 27, 1963

64. *Journal from Rome (II)*
Rome, Oct. 7, 1963

65. *Journal from Rome (III)*
Rome, Oct. 19, 1963

66. *Journal from Rome (IV)*
Rome, Nov. 4, 1963

67. *Journal from Rome (V)*
Rome, Nov. 18, 1963

XI. Vatican II, Session 3, Rome, Fall 1964

68. *Journal from Rome (IV and V)*
Rome, Oct. 26, 1964 (Burns Chalmers was an accredited Observer-Delegate during Session 3 and wrote *Journal from Rome (I-III)* before Douglas arrived. Douglas attended an FWCC meeting in Ireland at which he was elected Chair of the FWCC.)

XII. Vatican II, Session 4, Rome, Fall 1965

69. *Journal from Rome (I)*
Rome, Sept. 13, 1965

70. *Journal from Rome (II)*
Rome, Sept. 25-26, 1965

71. *Journal from Rome (III)*
Rome, Oct. 15, 1965

73. *Journal from Rome (IV)*
Rome, Nov. 1965

74. *Journal from Rome (V)*
Rome, Dec. 1965

Index

A

Abbé of Tourville 313
Abe, Masao 171
Abernathy, Ralph 59
Academy for Spiritual Formation
 4, 285, 343
Acton, Lady 232
Adam, Karl 46, 101
Adams, Uniola 304-5
Addams, Jane 84, 149
AFSC (American Friends Service
 Committee) 3, 58, 59, 61, 62,
 65, 85, 100, 101, 102, 105, 106,
 107, 108, 119, 121, 129-146, 151,
 152, 154, 157-178, 201, 232, 236,
 315, 316
Ahern, Barnabas 190, 314
Alderson, Bishop 232
Alexander, Horace 206
Alexander Macomb Club 19, 21
Alfrink, Cardinal 18, 185
Alter, Karl, Archbishop of
 Cincinnati 184
American Philosophical Associa-
 tion 2
American Theological Society 2,
 90, 253, 279
Andrewes, Lancelot 191
Andrews, C.F. 163
Andrews, James 153
Appleton, George 192, 306-7
Arch Street Meeting 3, 113
Ariga, Tetsutaro 171
Arnold, Eberhard 101, 204
Ashby, Bishop of Christchurch,
 N.Z. 234
!ubrey, Edwin 255
Augustine 280

B

Bailey, Gerald 212
Bainton, Roland 255
Barclay, Mary 149
Barth, Karl 46, 101, 216, 259, 332
Bartlett, Percy 104
Barton, William 240, 245
Basil of Caesarea 280
Bea, Augustin 183, 186, 187, 188
Bender, Harold 216
Benedict of Nursia 185, 189, 280,
 281
Bennett, John 214, 255
Benoit, André 213
Benz, Ernst 103
Bergson, Hewíi 96
Bernadotte, Count 150
Bernanos 344
Bernard of Clairvaux 189, 259, 277
Bernhardt, Joseph 103
Bhave, Vinoba 161, 166
Biggs, Bunty 233
Birlingham, Sybil, Aunt 36
Bishop, Claire Huchet 284, 307
Bjorkquist, Manfred 133
Blake, Eugene Carson 197
Blake, William xiv
Blasius, Leslie and Nellie 343
Blaxall, Arthur 139, 144, 191, 211
Blaxall, Florence 139
Bloy, Leon 271
Bolling, Landrum 242
Bonhoeffer, Dietrich 91
Bossert, Nette 345
Boston University School of
 Theology 25
Braisted, Paul 120, 130, 131, 132,
 160, 204

B

Braunmueller, Willfred 103
Brayshaw, Neave 40
Brent, Charles 191
Brettall, Noel 347
Bridget of Sweden 185
Brightman, Edgar S. 279
Brinton, Anna 58, 120, 122
Brinton, Howard 120, 225
Bromell, Anna Petit 116
Bronner, Edwin 237
Brookes, Edgar 140, 233, 240
Brown, Kenneth I. 37, 315
Brügelman, Asta 104
Brügelman, Jan 341
Buber, Martin 24, 49, 97, 98, 165, 207, 296, 323, 340
Buchanan, Douglas 139
Buchanan, Scott 25
Buchinger, Otto 135
Buechner, Frederick 254
Bultmann, Rudolf 32, 336
Burton, Ormund 235.
Butler, Cuthbert, Bishop 185
Butterfield, Kenyon 42
Buttrick, George

C

Cadbury, Emma 101, 130
Cadbury, Henry 104, 115, 116, 225, 229
Calhoun, Robert 209, 255
Campbell, Helen 123, 126
Campenhausen, Hans von 102
Carrel, Alexis 284
Cary, Mary 45, 101
Cary, Richard 45, 101, 130
Casey, Gerard 315
Catchpool, Corder 131, 204
Catherine of Genoa 332, 333

Catherine of Siena 185
Caulfield, John 190
Cedegren, Elsa 132, 150, 152
Cedegren, Hugo 132
Ceresole, Pierre 136, 205
Chalmers, A. Burns 32, 96, 136, 137, 296, 304
Chalmers, Elizabeth 219
Chandy, K.K. 161, 163, 166, 212
Chavez, Cesar 246
Chetsingh, Doris 173
Chetsingh, Ranjit 173
Clark, G.N. 29-30
Coburn, John 189, 216
Cohen, Annemarie 134, 135, 204, 341
Colloquia in Japan and India 169-174, 197, 242, 303
   (Participants 176-77, n. 34)
Comfort, William 31, 99
Commissions of Peacemaking, DVS Service on 209-10
Condict, Fonrose 285
Conscientious Objection 184-85
Copeland, Charles Townsend 26
Cosby, Gordon 190
Cox, Robert M. 285
Cragg, Glenn 9
Cragg, Kenneth 137, 191
Crandall, Reuben 9
Cripps, Arthur Shearly 191, 207, 232, 312, 340, 344-48
Curé d'Ars 277
Curtis, Francis 19, 21
Cuttat, Jacques 168, 195

D

D'Arms, Chet 27
Damien, Father 349
Danforth, William H. 99, 154
Daniélou, Jean 187

Davies, Horton 190
Day, Dorothy 98, 184, 304
Dayspring 286, 289, 290
De Klerk, William 233
Demos, Raphael 25
Desjardins, Paul 109
Dessauer, Philip 102
Diekmann, Godfrey 2, 189, 287, 314
Dirks, Walter 103
Dodd, C.H. 32
Dodds, William 131
Donne, John 191
Douglas, James 184
Dubois, Bishop 185
Dumoulin, Heinrich, S.J. 171
Dun, Angus 255
Dunant, Henri 149
Dupré, Louis 169

E

East/West Colloquy (1967) 201,
 212-17, 312
 (Eastern participants 213;
 American participants 223,
 n. 39)
Eastman, Philip 211
Eaton, Ralph 25
Eckhart, Meister 43, 95, 326, 344
Ecumenical Institute of Spirituality
 xiii, 64, 189-91, 197, 231, 256,
 271, 287-90, 314-15, 342
Edwards, Tilden 343
Ehlen, Nicholas 105
Eliot, T.S. 191, 324
Episcopal Theological Seminary,
 Cambridge, MA 38, 180, 189
Essentials of Quakerism 226-30
Exman, Eugene 101, 137
Eyck, Jan van 323
Eynon, David 352

F

Farmer, Herbert 106, 116, 206
Fenélon, François 313
Feuerbach, Ludwig 332
"Finnish Concern, The" 147-56,
 201
Fitzgerald, Constance 287
Fogelberg, Miss 133
Forchammer, Henni 46, 101
Forest, Jim 341
Forsyth, P.T. 263
Fox, George 46, 114, 117, 227, 229
Francis of Assisi 149, 159, 185,
 277, 280, 345-46
Freiday, Dean 168
French, W.H. 27
Frick, Hanna 105
Frick, Otto 105
Friends Service Committee (See
 AFSC)
Friends World Conference,
 Guilford, NC, 1967 174, 220-
 21, 239, 243-45, 247
Friends World Conference,
 Sigtuna, Sweden, 1970 245-48
Friends World Committee for
 Consultation (FWCC) 3, 62,
 108, 122, 143, 166, 182, 191,
 201, 210, 217, 231, 235, 236-43,
 315, 316, 339, 341
Fry, Elizabeth 133
Fry, Franklin Clark 197
Fuchs, Emil 102, 135
Fulbright, James 27

G

Gandhi, Mahatma 139, 161, 166,
 206, 207, 246
Gandhi, Manilil 139, 140, 144
Garrett, Alfred 130

G

Gävernitz, Schultze von 131, 135
Geddes, Charles 164
Geismar, Eduard 46
George, S.K. 161
Gerard Groote 185
Gibson, Olive 233
Gillett, Henry T. 30, 40, 90, 130, 131, 132, 180, 339
Good, Nancy 232
Good, Robert 232
Görres, Ida 105
Goss-Meyer, Hildegard 184, 211, 342
Goss-Meyer, Jean 184, 211
Gowing, Bishop 235
Graham, Aelred 197
Graham, Billy 217
Grenfell, Wilfred 25
Griffiths, Bede 166
Guardini, Romano 47-48, 101, 102, 131, 182, 256
Guild of Spiritual Guidance 286

H

Hadley, Herbert M. 239, 242
Halfdan-Nielsen, Deborah 101, 132, 297, 308
Halfdan-Nielsen, Rejnar 101, 132, 308
Ham (Devers), Dorothy 286
Ham Sok Han 170
Hammarskjöld, Dag 196, 265, 312
Harden, George 59
Häring, Bernard 184, 189, 190
Harris, Rendel 32, 339
Hartmann, Nicholai 47, 101, 256, 336
Harvard University 2, 4, 42, 43, 44, 48, 53, 78, 84, 89-112. 117, 121, 155, 182, 226, 271

Harvey, Thomas 153
Haverford College 2, 4, 42, 43, 44, 48, 53, 78, 84, 89-112, 117, 121, 155, 182, 226, 271, 339, 340
Hayward, Victor 169, 231
Heard, Gerald 272-75, 304
Hegel, G.W.F. 328
Heidbrink, John C. 211, 313
Heidegger, Martin 32, 49, 104, 335, 336
Heiler, Frederick 32, 103
Heim, Karl 46, 101, 102
Hemming, Douglas 21
Henson, Irene 232
Henson, Roy 232
Herbert, George 191
Herman, Elizabeth 276, 284
Hermann, Carl 103, 135
Hermann, Eva 103, 135
Herwegen, Dom Ildefons 45
Herzog, Theresa 139
Heschel, Abraham Joshua 164, 188, 307, 323
Hewitt, Patricia 234
Hildegard of Bingen 185
Hisamatsu 159, 167
Hislop, Pat 305-6
Hitchcock, Douglas 6, 8
Hocking, William Ernest 25, 26, 98, 109, 326
Hodgkin, Henry T. 43-44, 115, 116, 258
Hodgkin, Joy 44, 114
Hoffding, Harold 32
Hofmyer, Jan 233, 312
Hohhammer, Manfred 103
Holborn, Professor 103
Hon, Ham Sok 170, *171*
Hoover, Herbert 153
Hoover, John 141
Hoover, Virginia 141
Hopko, Thomas 190

Horn, Becky 86
Horn, David 83, 86
Horn, Helen (See Steere, Helen)
Hough, Lynn Harold 42
Hromadka, Joseph 213, 214, 215, 216, 255
Huddleston, Trevor 139
Hügel, Baron Friedrich von xi, 2, 30, 32, 37, 43, 54, 91, 97, 181, 255, 271, 297, 299, 321, 322, 323, 325, 326, 327, 328, 329-35, 349, 350
Hughes, Lillian 305
Humbert-Claude, Father 186
Hunter, Allan 273, 274
Hunter, Elizabeth 273, 274
Hurley, Archbishop of Durban 233
Huvelin, Abbé 349
Hyma, Albert 54

I

Iakavos 197
Imitation of Christ, The 43, 52, 54, 282
Indire, Filomene 236, 241, 242
Inge, W.R. 40, 180, 191
International Fellowship of Reconciliation (IFOR) 3, 109, 201, 206, 210-12, 217, 240
Iona Community 280, 283

J

Jacks, L.P. 40
Jacopone da Todi 283
Jaenicke, Joachim 103
James, William 97, 327
Jarrett-Kerr, Martin 346-47
Jaspers, Karl 102, 336
Jesus and the Quaker Tradition 227-28, 246, 258

Jewish People 188
John of the Cross 326
John Woolman Memorial 3, 108, 109, 121, 202, 240
John XXIII, Pope 110, 194, 239, 340
Johnson, Lyndon 218
Johnston, W.W. 24, 27, 37
Jones, Elizabeth 90, 137
Jones, Mary Hoxie 90, 121, 122
Jones, Rufus 2, 26, 31, 32, 33, 40, 42, 43, 89, 90-94, 95, 96, 98, 108, 115, 116, 117, 137, 225, 226, 227, 255, 329, 330, 335, 339-40
Jones, Thomas 137
Jones, Betty 122
Jones, Tom 122
Joyce, Bishop 184
Julian of Norwich 229
Jungblatt, Kamel 165

K

Kahn, Zafrilla 98
Kant, Immanuel 29, 47, 95, 96, 334
Kashi, Minona 315
Kaunda, Kenneth 206
Keithan, Richard 305
Kelly, Thomas R. xiii, 96, 102, 107, 158, 225, 238, 266, 272, 344
Kelsey, Arthur C. 94, 190
Kent, Charles Foster 26
Kenworthy, Leonard 134, 135, 204
Kierkegaard, Søren 32, 101, 253, 256, 321, 324, 325, 328, 331, 335-36, 344
Kilduff, Thomas 190
Kilpi, Elvo 152
King, Coretta Scott 59
King, John 297
King, Martin Luther, Jr. 59, 246, 289

385

K

Kinghorn, Jennifer 233
Kinsolving, Tim 296
Kirkridge 280, 283, 285, 288
Kjekstad, Erling 133, 152
Klein, Norbert 171
Kloppenburg, Heinz 214-15
Knox, John 255
Knox, Ronald 40, 180
Koenig, Joseph Cardinal 184, 186, 187
Kraus, Herta 148
Krukenberg-Gonze, Elizabeth 131
Kruse, Cornelius 136
Kunkel, Elizabeth 47, 131, 134
Kunkel, Fritz 29, 47, 57, 101, 123, 131, 134, 256

L

Lachmund, Margarethe 104, 135, 207, 342
Lacout, Pierre 245
Lagerlof, Selma 133
Laity Role in the Church 185-86
Lakdasa de Mel 197
Lake, Kirsopp 25
Lambeth Quadrilateral (1968) 4, 191, 315
Lasserre, Phillip 211
Lassila, Antti 155
Laubach, Frank 266
Law, William 191
Lawrence, Brother (Nicholas Hermann) 266
Lean, Phyllis 233
Lean, Scarnell 233
Lechner, Robert 190
Leclercq, Jean 189, 190
Leen, Edward 284
Legatis, Fritz 134, 135

Legatis, Martha and 134, 135
Lemberg, Hanna 234
Lemberg, Rudolf 234
Lester, John 54
Lewis, C.S. 191
Lewis, Clarence I. 25, 26, 27
Lewis, Lloyd 124
Lewis M. Stevens Trust 342
Leyburn, Ellen Douglas 297
Lilje, Hans 104
Lindsay, A.D. 29
Linton, Albert O. 132, 133
Lochman, Jan 213, 216
Loescher, Frank 143
Loescher, Mildred 144
Loyola, Ignatius 278
Lubac, Henri de 187
Luecke, Richard 190
Lull, Raymond 159
Lund, Sigrid 244
Luthuli, Albert 139, 140, 144
Lutz, Howard 322
Luvai, Nathan 236
Lyman, Mary 287

M

MacEachron, Dorothy (See Steere, Dorothy)
MacEachron, Grandfather 54, 58, 74, 75
MacEachron, Jennie 58
MacIntosh, Archibald 100
MacKay, John 44, 255
Macleod, George 106
Macmurray, John 29, 348
Makary, Father 165
Malik, Charles 98, 163, 164, 307
Malik, Gurdial 161, 238
Mamvura, Leonard 347
Mandela, Nelson 139, 348

please
check
" - also see
Crandall?

Love at the Heart of Things

was composed on a Power Macintosh 7600 computer using Adobe Pagemake 6.0 and typefaces from the Adobe Type Library: ITC New Baskerville for the text with Zapf Chancery and Adobe Wood Type Ornaments. Adobe Caslon was used for the front cover. 60# Gladfelter Recycled paper was used for this printing of 4,000 copies.

History of the Type Faces

British printer John Baskerville of Birmingham created the types that bear his name in about 1752. New Baskerville was designed by George Jones in 1930 and licensed by the International Typeface Corporation in 1982. This Baskerville design has a delicacy and grace that come from long, elegant serifs and the subtle transfer of stroke weight from thick to very thin.

Barbara Lind and Joy Redick designed Adobe Wood Type Ornaments in 1990-91. These ornaments are based on the unusual and intricate designs originally made in wood for use as eye-catching display work in the nineteenth-century.

Zapf Chancery, designed in 1979 by Hermann Zapf, is a contemporary script based on Italian chancery handwriting. The chancery hand was developed during the Italian Renaissance and originally used for formal and informal work by the scribes in the papal offices.

Based on seventeenth-century Dutch old style designs, William Caslon's typefaces appeared in 1722. Caslon's designs met instant success and became popular throughout Europe and the American Colonies. They were used for the first printings of the American Declaration of Independence and the Constitution. Adobe Caslon is based on specimen pages printed by William Caslon between 1734 and 1770.

Book Design by
Eva Fernandez Beehler and Rebecca Kratz Mays